David Rorer

A Treatise on the Law of Judicial and Execution Sales

David Rorer

A Treatise on the Law of Judicial and Execution Sales

ISBN/EAN: 9783744667173

Printed in Europe, USA, Canada, Australia, Japan

Cover: Foto ©Suzi / pixelio.de

More available books at **www.hansebooks.com**

ON THE LAW OF

JUDICIAL AND EXECUTION

SALES.

By DAVID RORER,

OF THE IOWA BAR.

CHICAGO:
CALLAGHAN AND COMPANY.
1873.

Dedication.

PREFACE.

Perhaps few branches of the law are of more interest to the public than those of Judicial, and of Execution, Sales; more especially of real property.

The policy of these States, unlike that of England, has everywhere encouraged the distribution of landed property, not only by rendering it liable to change of ownership *in fee*, by ordinary bargain and sale, but also by sales on writs of execution, and on decrees of the courts. Hence, much of the landed wealth of the country is held or claimed under titles and sales made by coercion of law.

It is with the hope that this first effort to bring these subjects into a system, may in some degree lighten the labors of his professional brethren, and aid them in that correct administration of justice which is the true object of all courts and lawyers, that this volume, which was originally begun for the author's own convenient use, is brought before the public.

A desire to compass the several subjects in as few words as practicable, and thereby save the labor of tedious research, has diminished the size of the work at the cost, in reality, of more care and labor than would have been otherwise required.

If it shall meet from courts and lawyers a favorable

reception, the labors of the author will thereby be more than repaid.

The author desires, in conclusion, to express his great obligation to the Editor, J. A. L. WHITTIER, Esq., of the Chicago Bar, for the careful and able manner in which he has revised it for and seen it through, the press.

DAVID ROHER.

BURLINGTON, IOWA, 1873.

CONTENTS.

PART FIRST.

THE NATURE OF JUDICIAL AND OF EXECUTION SALES.

CHAPTER I.

THE NATURE OF JUDICIAL SALES.

CHAPTER II.

THE NATURE OF EXECUTION SALES.

PART SECOND.

JUDICIAL SALES OF REAL PROPERTY.

CHAPTER III.

JURISDICTION OF THE COURT ORDERING THE SALE.

CHAPTER IV.

THE SALE.

CHAPTER V.

JUDICIAL SALES TO ENFORCE LIENS ON REAL PROPERTY.

CHAPTER VI.

SALE OF LANDS IN PROBATE FOR PAYMENT OF DEBTS.

CHAPTER VII.

GUARDIAN'S SALES AND SALES IN PROCEEDINGS FOR PARTITION.

CHAPTER VIII.

CHAPTER IX.

THE DEED.

CHAPTER X.

SETTING ASIDE SALE.

CHAPTER XI.

ESTOPPEL.— WARRANTY—CAVEAT EMPTOR.

CHAPTER XII.

COLLATERAL IMPEACHMENTS — VOID JUDICIAL SALES — RETURN OF PURCHASE MONEY.

PART THIRD.

JUDICIAL SALES OF PERSONAL PROPERTY — CORPORATE FRANCHISES — PROPERTY AND STOCKS.

CHAPTER XIII.

JUDICIAL SALES OF PERSONAL PROPERTY.

CHAPTER XIV.

JUDICIAL SALES OF CORPORATE FRANCHISES, PROPERTY AND STOCKS.

PART FOURTH.

EXECUTION SALES OF REAL PROPERTY.

CHAPTER XV.

WHAT INTEREST IN LANDS MAY BE SOLD, AND IN WHAT ORDER.

CHAPTER XVI.

THE WRIT — THE LEVY — AND NOTICE OF SALE.

CHAPTER XVII.

THE SALE.

CHAPTER XVIII.

THE DEED.

CHAPTER XIX.

SETTING SALE ASIDE.

CHAPTER XX.

REDEMPTION.

PART FIFTH.

EXECUTION SALES OF PERSONAL PROPERTY.

CHAPTER XXI.

THE WRIT.

CHAPTER XXII.

THE LEVY.

CHAPTER XXIII.

THE SALE.

CHAPTER XXIV.

EXECUTION SALES OF CORPORATE FRANCHISES, PROPERTY AND STOCKS.

PART SIXTH.

EXEMPTION FROM SALE—APPLICATION OF PROCEEDS.

CHAPTER XXV.

EXEMPTION FROM SALE.

CHAPTER XXVI.

INDEX TO CASES CITED.

JUDICIAL AND EXECUTION SALES.

JUDICIAL AND EXECUTION SALES.

PART FIRST.

NATURE OF JUDICIAL AND OF EXECUTION SALES.

CHAPTER I.

THE NATURE OF JUDICIAL SALES.

I. OF JUDICIAL SALES IN GENERAL.

§ 1.   As a judicial act is one "supposed to be done *pendente lite* of some sort or other,"[1] so a judicial sale, is, in contemplation of law, a sale made *pendente lite;* a sale in court, and the court is the vendor.

§ 2.   It matters not to the contrary, that it is made through the instrumentality of a master, commissioner, or other functionary, appointed thereto by the court; it is not valid or binding, and confers no right to the property sought to be sold, until confirmed by the court. By such confirmation, it is judicially made the act of the court, and is therefore a judicial sale. The master or commissioner, in conducting it, acts by authority of, and as the instrument or agent of the court.

§ 3.   In the language of the court, in *Bozza v. Rowe*— " the master is the mere instrument of the court, acts under

---

1 Medhurst *v.* Wait. 3 Burr. 1259.

its directions, and is subject to its control, * * * * and his acts, under the decree when regular, are considered those of the chancellor—and that the biddings are not binding and can not be enforced, until approved by the court." [1]

§ 4. In *Griffith v. Fowler*,[2] the case cited from 18 Vermont, the learned Judge (REDFIELD), speaking of sales in Admiralty, says—"But these cases bear but a slight analogy to sheriff's sales in this country or in England. Those sales are strictly judicial sales and are merely carrying into specific execution a decree of the court *in rem*, which by universal consent binds the whole world." And again, in the same case, it is said: "It is plain, then, that a sheriff's sale is not a judicial sale."

§ 5. If the sheriff be appointed by the court, instead of a master or commissioner, to conduct the sale, as in the *Minnesota R. R. Co. v. St. Paul*,[3] yet he sells by virtue of the decree, and not by virtue of his office of sheriff, and the sale is the sale of the court when confirmed.

§ 6. In *Williamson v. Berry*, the United States Supreme Court characterize a judicial sale as one " made under the process of a court having competent authority to order it, by an officer legally appointed and commissioned to sell."

But the court obviously refer here to the sale in a popular sense, or to that part of the transaction which consists of the doings of the master or person conducting the sale, and not to

---

[1] 30 Ill. 198; Andrews *v.* Scotten, 2 Bland, 629; Williamson *v.* Berry, 8 How. 547; Southern Bank *v.* Humphreys, 47 Ill. 227, 636; Harrison *v.* Harrison, 1 Md. Ch. Decs. 331; Mason *v.* Osgood, 64 N. C. 467; Hurst *v.* Stull, 4 Md. Ch. Decs. 391; Sewell *v.* Costigan, 1 Md. Ch. Decs. 208; Moore *v.* Shultz, 13 Penn. St. 102; Vandevere *v.* Baker, *ib.* 121,126; Wagner *v.* Cohen, 6 Gill. 97; Iglehart *v.* Armigo, 1 Bland, 527; Mullikin *v.* Mullikin, 1 Bland, 538; Thorn *v.* Ingram, 25 Ark. 52; Freeman *v.* Hunt, 3 Dana (Ky.), 621; Young *v.* Keogh, 11 Ill. 642; Ayres *v.* Baumgarten, 15 Ill. 444; Penn *v.* Heisey, 19 Ill. 297; Rawlings *v.* Bailey, 15 Ill. 178; Blossom *v.* R. R. Co. 3 Wall. 207; Minnesota R. R. Co. *v.* St. Paul, 2 Wall. 609, 640; Griffith *v.* Fowler, 18 Vt. 394. In Yerby *v.* Hill, 16 Texas, 377, 381, the court by WHEELER, Justice, say: "His purchase is not complete, and no title vests until the action of the court, confirming the sale;" Halleck *v.* Guy, 9 Cal. 181, 195.

[2] 18 Vt. 394.

[3] 2 Wall. 609, 640.

that final action of the court which alone confers validity, and which terminates the sale by the judicial act of confirmation. For in the same connection the court say "that such sales, until approved by the master and confirmed by the court, give no title to a purchaser of an estate which he may have bargained to buy." [1]

§ 7. In *Williamson v. Berry*,[2] the court hold that the approbation of the master or person conducting the sale does not complete a title in a purchaser; but that this is only "one step towards a purchaser's getting a title."

This language of the court fully bears us out in the assumpsion that in describing a judicial sale as one made under "the process of a court having competent authority to order it, by an officer *legally* appointed and commissioned to sell," they mean only that the proceedings up to the final confirmation are conducted by such officer until the bargain is agreed to, when the purchaser, "before he can get a title," (in the language of the court) "must get a report from the master (or person selling) that he approves the sale," and "that report then becomes the basis of a motion to the court, by the purchaser, that his purchase may be confirmed." [3]

It is equally clear, that by the term—"by an officer legally appointed and commissioned to sell," is meant an appointment and commission from the court, and not the ordinary ministerial officers of law courts, as sheriffs, or marshals, in mere virtue of their commission.

§ 8. True it is, that the powers of the chancellor is such that he may dispense with many of the formulas attendant usually on judicial sales in his court, but this power of dispensation is not an attribute of inferior courts, acting under a limited chancery power conferred by statute. As, for instance, courts of probate, or others exercising probate jurisdiction in proceedings for sale of a decedent's lands, or the lands of a ward. Such tribunals may not dispense with, but must carry out all such requirements as the statute demands as indispensa-

[1] 8 How. 546.
[2] Ibid.
[3] Ibid.

ble to validity, whatever they may be. But omission as to such as are directory only is merely error.[1]

§ 9. In *Mason v. Osgood Adm'r*,[2] the Supreme Court of North Carolina hold the following to be the law in relation to a sale of lands by an administrator: "He is a mere agent of the court to execute a naked power, and a purchaser acquires no right to the land until the sale is confirmed and title made, under an order of the court granting the power of sale," and that, "if the administrator fails to report the sale, the purchaser may apply to the court by a motion in the cause for a rule to compel such return, so that the court may confirm the sale if it sees proper. * * * In our case the sale was not confirmed, the plaintiff has no right to the land, and no claim to equitable relief."

The case cited from North Carolina was of a bill filed in chancery to coerce a deed from an administrator by one who had bid off the land at the sale, and who was refused a conveyance by the administrator. The chancellor held that the remedy was by motion in the same court that ordered the sale.[3]

§ 10. In the case of *Halleck v. Guy*,[4] the Supreme Court of California use the following language in reference to the nature of administrator's sales of lands in probate: "The mode of sale is pointed out by express statute. When sold, the report of the sale is made by the administrator to the court, and unless confirmed by order of the court there is no binding sale, and no title can pass to the purchaser. To be valid, the sale must first be ordered by the court, and afterwards confirmed by it. The order for the sale and the order of confirmation are both judicial acts; and these two concurring make the sale a judicial sale, and, therefore, not within the statute of frauds." And again the court say: "It is true that there is a difference in the *mode* of enforcing a sale ordered by a court of chancery and that of a sale by order of the probate court. But this difference in the mere mode does

[1] Williamson *v.* Berry, 8 How. 546.
[2] 64 N. C. 467, 468
[3] Ibid.
[4] 9 Cal. 181, 195.

not affect the character of the sale itself. When a sale is made under a decree in chancery the bidder may be committed for contempt if he refuses to comply with his bid." * * * *
"If we concede that the probate court can not commit the bidder for contempt when he fails to comply with his bid, this does not change the character of the sale." [1]

§ 11. In *Hurst v. Stull*,[2] the court say of a decree of sale for purchase money: "It was a proceeding *in rem*, and by the decree the land was condemned to pay the claim of the party who sold it, and in whom the legal title still remains. Although the court in the execution of this decree and others of a like nature employs a trustee, that officer is its agent, the court itself being the vendor, acting through the instrumentality of its agent. And in *Glenn v. Clapp*,[3] the same court characterize such sales as "transactions between the court and the purchaser."

In *Vandever v. Baker*,[4] the Supreme Court of Pennsylvania say of an administrator's sale of lands that it is a "judicial sale," and has been so ruled more than once.

§ 12. In a legal sense, the sale is made by the court itself in enforcement of its own orders and decrees, wherein is described the property to be sold. The person who conducts the same is merely the instrument, or means used by the court to bring about such executory agreement as the court closes, if satisfied therewith, by final act of confirmation, which makes the court the vendor.[5] Such sale is unlike a sheriff's sale on ordinary common law, or statutory execution, which is a *ministerial*, and not a *judicial* act; and in making which the law regards the officer, and not the court, as the vendor.[6]

---

[1] Halleck *v.* Guy, 9 Cal. 181, 196.

[2] Hurst *v.* Stull, 4 Md. Ch. 391, 393; Iglehart *v.* Armiger, 1 Bland, 527; Foreman *v.* Hunt, 3 Dana, 622; Campbell *v.* Johnson, 4 Dana, 186.

[3] 11 G. and J. 1, 8.

[4] 13 Penn. St. 126.

[5] Ib. and Foreman *v.* Hunt, 3 Dana, 622; Campbell *v.* Johnson, 4 Dana, 186; Armor *v.* Cochrane, 66 Penn. St. 308. In the latter case the court characterize the person conducting the sale as "the mere *organ* of the court, in making the sale." Bozza *v.* Rowe, 30 Ill. 198.

[6] Gowan *v.* Jones, 10 S. and M. 164; Griffith *v.* Fowler, 18 Vt. 394. "On

The decree for a sale, though so far final that an appeal will lie, is not final but interlocutory, in such other respects, as it does not reach, contemplated by the proceeding, which are only attained

considering the nature of sales under authority of the Court of Chancery, the first inquiry which suggests itself is, who are the real parties to the contract? This very idea of a contract implies that there is one party able and willing to contract and another to contract with. It implies a perfect capacity and free will, in each of the parties to the agreement. To a contract of sale, made under a decree of this court, neither of the litigating parties can be considered as the vendor; although they, with others, such as creditors, who may be allowed to come in afterwards, may be very materially interested in the sale. The plaintiff can not be considered as the vendor; because, oftener than otherwise, he has no title, always states his inability to sell, and prays the court to decree that a sale be made.

"The defendant can not be the vendor; because he always positively refuses to part with his property, unless forced, or sanctioned in doing so by the power of the court. If, then, neither of the litigating parties can be seperately deemed to be the vendor, it is clear that they can not both together be so considered.

"But such sales are always made by an agent; in England, by a master; in this State, by a trustee. Private contracts may be made and executed in person or by attorney; but the attorney is never considered as one of the contracting parties—he exercises no will or power of his own—he is merely the medium, or conduit, through which the will of the contracting party is expressed. The master or trustee is the mere attorney of the court, acting under a specially delegated authority. And, in no case, is a master or trustee authorized to do more than to accept an offer or proposal to contract, which is of no sort of validity unless it be accepted, ratified and confirmed by the court. *It is the court itself, for the benefit of all interested,* therefore, *who is the vendor* in such cases?

"But it may be said, if the court be the vendor in sales made by its trustee, would it not follow, for the same reasons, that a court of common law must be considered as the vendor in sales made under its writ of *fieri facias,* by the sheriff? The cases are essentially different. The writ of *fieri facias* is a general authority or command to the sheriff to make so much money by sale from the personal estate of the defendant. By this writ the executive officer of the court is commissioned to seize the whole, any part, or so much of the defendant's personal estate as may be necessary to raise the specified sum of money. No particular articles of property are ever designated. By statute, this power, given by the common law writ over personal estate, has been extended over real estate. And the same writ, and nearly the same principles of law, now apply to both species of property.

"The real or personal estate with which the Court of Chancery deals is, however, always in one form or other distinctly specified in the proceed-

by confirmation, thereby giving finality to the proceedings. The sale is not made by authority of the person in charge of it, but by authority and under control of the court, "which prescribes, or ought to prescribe the time, manner and conditions of the sale." [1]

§13. When an acceptable bidder is found, and an agreement as to terms is attained, then report thereof is made to the court, and the court confirms it or not, at discretion. [2]

Before such confirmation the purchase is so incomplete that a loss by fire falls on the vendor or owner, though it occur after acceptance of the bidding and after report of the sale. [3]

ings; and the sale is made only because the court is asked to have it made to accomplish the objects of the suit. In the proceedings at common law, from the commencement to the *fieri facias*, no property is designated. At common law, the terms and manner of sale are regulated by law; in chancery, they are regulated by the court. At common law if the sheriff, in seizing the property and making the sale, conforms to the established regulations applicable to all cases, (and he can sell in no other manner), the sale is final and valid as soon as it is made. But in chancery the sale is, in no case, binding and conclusive, until it has been expressly approved and ratified by the court. If it be made in a manner wholly different from that prescribed by the court, it may yet' be sanctioned; or, if it be made in all respects conformable to directions, it may still be rejected. And hence, it is obvious that in one case it is the Court of Chancery who is the real vendor, and in the other the sheriff, or executive officer of the court.

"In an English case, which arose on a sale under the authority of the Court of Chancery, decided in the year 1721, in which the question was, whether the purchaser should be compelled to complete his purchase or not, the matter is spoken of as one perfectly settled. 'Upon a contract betwixt party and party,' says the chancellor, 'the contractor would not be decreed to pay an unreasonable price for an estate; so neither ought the court to be partial to itself, and to do more upon a contract *made with itself*, or carry that farther, than it would a contract betwixt party and party. On the other hand, the court might be said to have rather a greater power over a contract made with *itself* than with any other.' And in other cases of recent date, when the subject has been brought into view, the court has, in like manner, been spoken of and considered as the vendor." Andrews v. Scotten, 2 Bland, 629.

[1] Moore v. Shultz, 13 Penn. St. 102; Coffee v. Coffee, 16 Ill. 141; Harlan v. Merrill, 3 Dana, 181; Sowards v. Pritchett, 37 Ill. 517.

[2] Williamson v. Berry. 8 How. 547; Harrison v. Harrison, 1 Md. Ch. 331; Moore v. Shultz, 13 Penn. St. 502; Taylor v. Gilpin, 3 Met. (Ky.) 544; Sowards v. Pritchett, 37 Ill. 517.

[3] Wagner v. Cohen, 6 Gill. 90, 102; *Exparte* Minor, 11 Ves. 559.

§ 14. In *Harrison v. Harrison*,[1] the court affirms the doctrine of *Andrews v. Scotten*, and say it is the well understood law, "that in sales made under authority of decrees in chancery, the court is the vendor, the trustee being the mere agent or attorney of the court, under a special, delegated authority, and the true character of such a sale is that it is a transaction between the court and the purchaser; and a private sale, as well as a public sale, may be made if the court deems it advantageous.

§ 15. In the case of *Harrison v. Harrison*,[2] the court further say: "The differences are so many and material," between sales by a trustee in chancery and sales on execution by a sheriff, "that it is impossible with safety to apply any one principle to them both. But the vital difference perhaps with reference to the question now under consideration is, that the sheriff's sale, if made conformably to law, is final and valid, and passes the title; whereas, chancery sales, the court being the vendor, are not binding and conclusive, until approved and ratified by the court."

And such, too, is the current of authorities. The court affirms the sale or not, at its discretion, and until affirmed, the supposed sale is no sale, and confers no rights.[3]

But if the purchaser take and keep possession it may become ratified and valid by lapse of time.[4]

It is not the sale of the officer or person charged with it, for apart from the court he has no power to sell. But when confirmed, it is the sale of the court.[5]

---

[1] 1 Md. Ch. Dec. 332, 333. "These sales are less expensive than when made on executions; more time is allowed to make them; the discretion of the court is exercised as to time, manner, and terms of sale; whereas, on sales by a sheriff, all is by compulsion, and no credit is allowed; he can not offer one entire piece of property for sale in parcels; the administrator can divide and sell as best subserves the interest of the heirs, and sell only so much as the emergency of the case requires." Grignon's Lessee v. Astor, 2 How. 343, 344.

[2] 1 Md. Ch. Dec. 335.

[3] Taylor v. Gilpin, 3 Met. (Ky.) 544; Williamson v. Berry, 8 How. 547; Mason v. Osgood, 64 N. C. 464; Thorn v. Ingram, 25 Ark. 52.

[4] Gowan v. Jones, 10 S. and M. 164.

[5] Ib. and preceeding cases cited.

§ 16. In *Sewell v. Costigan*,[1] the same doctrine is holden.
The court say: "In fact, the sale made by him (the trustee) is
the sale of the court, he being the mere instrument or agent.
by whose hands the court acts."—"It is the sale of the court,
and not his sale."

§ 17. In *Foreman v. Hunt*,[2] the Supreme Court of Kentucky draw the distinction between sheriff's sales at law and
judicial sales as follows: "Sales under execution are made by
an officer of the law, who is required by law, as well for the
benefit of plaintiffs and defendants as others who may be
injured by his official defalcations, to give bond and good
security for the faithful discharge of his duties," and remark
that "the law is the only guide of the sheriff," that his sales
are perfect and complete, and that the title passes to the purchasers without confirmation (ordinarily) of the court; but that
"a commissioner appointed by the chancellor to sell is the
mere *ministerial* servant and agent of the chancellor." That
he has no guide but his instructions in the decree; gives no
bond; must report to the court; and that a sale, that is, an
agreement to sell, made by him is not valid "until it is sanctioned by the chancellor." It is in operative until confirmed
by the court. In *Bussy v. Hardin*,[3] it is holden that "the
highest bidder at sales under decrees does not, like a bidder at
sheriff's sales under execution, acquire any independent right
to have the purchase completed; but is nothing more than a
preferred bidder, or proposer for the purchase, *subject* to confirmation by the chancellor."

§ 18. We may add that a judicial sale is made *pendente lite;*
whereas, an execution sale is made after litigation in the case
is ended; for, as we have before seen, a judicial act is some-
thing done during the pendency of a suit.[4] The suit does

[1] 1 Md. Ch. Dec. 208, 209.
[2] 3 Dana, 621.
[3] 2 B. Mon. 407.
[4] Midhurst *v.* Waite, 3 Burr. 1262. In Girard Life Ins. Co. *v.* Farmers'
and Mechanics' Bank, 57 Penn. St. 397, the court, in discriminating between
an order of sale and a writ of execution, uses the following language:
"The word execution has always been understood as meaning a *writ*, to

not end with the decree of sale; the proceeding still continues until final confirmation. So, the converse of the principle follows, that what is done *in pais* after litigation is ended, or after the cause is finally disposed of, if there were no adverse litigation, is not done judicially, and is not a judicial act, but is executive or else is ministerial.

§ 19. Another remarkable distinction may here be noticed betwixt judicial and executive sales. In some decrees for judicial sales the primary object of the order or decree is to sell the property, and in such cases the sale can not be prevented, except by judicial interference. But the writ of execution, on judgments at law, or when issued on money decrees or orders to pay money, commands the officer to levy the money of the property of the debtor, and though a sale is the consequence of such levy if the money be not paid, yet the primary object of the writ is to get the money, and therefore its payment to the officer holding the writ by the debtor prevents a sale.

§ 20. So likewise in some proceedings and decrees for judicial sales, as in mortgage foreclosures, decrees to enforce statutary liens, vendor's liens, and such other orders of sale as are merely designed to enforce payment of a sum of money; as the primary object of the proceedings is to make the money, the debtor may put an end to the proceedings and prevent the sale by paying the amount.

§ 21. In *Griffith v. Bogart,*[1] Justice GRIER speaks of an execution sale as a *judicial* sale. But by reference to that case it will be seen that it emanated from Missouri, where by the statute law execution sales at law are reportable to the court for confirmation. That the sale in question had been so reported and confirmed, as is shown by the learned justice; wherefore he says, "the deed was acknowledged in open court according to law. At this time, all parties interested could and would have been heard, to allege any irregularities in the proceedings that would justify the court in setting it aside.

give possession of a thing recovered by judgment or decree. It is clearly distinguishable from a mere order of sale."

[1] 18 How. 59, 164.

* * * * But when objections are waived by them, and the judicial sale founded on these proceedings is *confirmed* by the court, it would be injurious to the peace of the community and the security of titles to permit such objections to the title to be heard in a collateral action." Here it is the judicial act of confirmation that gives judicial character to the sale. Such, too, is the case in Pennsylvania, and some other States.

§ 22. Justice Story puts the distinction betwixt judicial and ministerial or execution sales, seemingly, upon the same ground. In *Arnold v. Smith*,[1] which arose in reference to an administrator's sale of lands in probate in Rhode Island, the learned justice considers the sale within the statute of frauds, for that it is not a judicial sale, in as much as such sales in Rhode Island are not required by law to be confirmed by the court.

§ 23. And we think we will be generally borne out in the suggestion that whenever execution sales are characterized as judicial, they either have to be confirmed by law, or else the expression has been casually made. The characterizing them as such very recently in head notes and indexes of books, of reports, is a mere matter of taste of the reporter, and of no authority.

§ 24. Though there be judicial acts from which no appeal will lie; yet, it is a general principle that appeals or error may be taken only from judicial acts and decisions. Tested by this general principle, sales under orders and decrees, by person designated by the court, are eminently judicial.

§ 25. Not only the decree or order of sale itself, but also the order of confirmation, which is the very essence of the sale, may be reviewed in an appellate court. The one conferring the power to sell; the other giving validity to the sale when agreed upon. For, though the order of confirmation is ordinarily a matter for the discretion of the court, yet it is such a reasonable and wholesome discretion that if abused or unwisely exercised the order may be appealed from. The New York Court of Appeals (SELDEN, Justice), in treating of the term

[1] 5 Mason C. C. 414, 420, 426.

judicial uses the following language: "The lines between the various departments are not and can not well be very precisely defined, and there are many duties which may be with equal propriety referred to either. Duties of this class, and they are very numerous, necessarily take their character from the departments to which they are respectively assigned. The same power which, when exercised by one class of officers not connected with the judiciary, would be regarded and treated as purely administrative, becomes at once judicial when exercised by a court of justice. This is shown by the definitions uniformly given of the word judicial. Webster defines it thus: 'Pertaining to courts of justice, as judicial power;' and again: 'Proceeding from a court of justice, as a judicial determination.' Referring then to Bouvier, the learned Justice gives his definition as, 'Belonging to or emanating from a judge as such, the authority vested in judges.' The court then add that 'Whatever emanates from a judge as such, or proceeds from a court of justice, is, according to these authorities, judicial." [1]

§ 26. But from the sheriff's sale, as such, made on execution, no appeal lies. He makes no judicial decision. It matters not to the contrary, that the writ of *fieri facias* is a judicial writ.[2] The sheriff who is to execute it is a ministerial, or executive, officer, and his acts in that respect are but ministerial. No appeal lies therefrom. Those acts and the sale growing out of the same, can only be questioned or assailed by some direct proceeding, except in those courts where the practice is to report the same for confirmation by the court, which are an exception to the general rule. In such cases, the sale is open to attack on the motion in court to confirm. And although when affirmed, they thereby partake of the character of judicial sales, notwithstanding their being made by the ministerial officer and on execution, yet these are exceptional cases and give no judicial character to ordinary sales on execution, which stand or fall on their own validity and in which no confirmation is required.

[1] Matter of Henry Hooper, 22 N. Y. 67, 82.
[2] 3 Bac. Abt. Title, Judicial writs which lie after judgment, 698.

Judicial sales occur in probate and in chancery proceedings for partition of real estate, where a division of the property cannot be made in kind.[1] In guardian and administration sales of land in probate.[2] In mortgage foreclosures by equitable proceedings; proceedings to enforce vendors' liens;[3] in statutory liens for street improvements made by municipal corporations;[4] and we may add, whenever a right or proceeding is enforced, by a sale made by a judicial order or decree, under direction of the court as contradistinguished from sales on execution.

When the statute or local practice do not dispense with confirmation of such sales, the officer, commissioner, or person conducting them, acts as the instrument merely of the court, without authority to bind creditors, debtors, or heirs, simply by his own act, who are bound only by the action of the court, in final confirmation, the court alone having power to represent and bind them.[5]

§ 27. In a certain classes of cases such sales, when perfected, are said to confer ownership on the purchaser, by a right paramount to that of the heir, as owner.[6] Thus in administration sales of real estate to pay debts of decedents, the court ordering them enforces a lien in law, acts in the exercise of a right paramount to that of the heirs. Without law there are no heirs. Heirship is not a natural right. It is created by law, is different in different States, and is changed

[1] Sacket v. Twining, 6 Harris, 202; Hilton v. Williams, 35 Ala. 503; Girard Life Ins. Co. v. The Farmers' & Mechanics' Bank, 57 Penn. St. 388; Williams v. Case, 3 Bland, 215; Allen v. Gault, 3 Casey, 473.

[2] Grignon's Lessee v. Astor, 2 How. 338; Moore v. Shultz, 13 Penn. St. 98.

[3] Kershaw v. Thompson, 4 Johns. Ch. 610.

[4] Ohio Life & Trust Co. v. Gordon, 10 Ohio (N. S,) 557, 565; Gould v. Garrison, 48 Ill. 258; Dillon, Municipal Corporations, Sec. 660; McInerry v. Read, 23 Iowa, 410.

[5] Moore v. Shultz, 13 Penn. St. 102. (The court have this power by law, subject to which rights of property are holden). Williamson v. Berry, 8 How. 547; Rawlings v. Bailey, 15 Ill. 178; Ayres v. Baumgarten, and Wright v. Phelps, 15 Ill. 444.

[6] Grignon's Lessee v. Astor, 2 How. 338; Bofils v. Fisher, 3 Rich. Eq. 1; Sheldon v. Newton, 3 Ohio (N. S.) 494, 501; McPherson v. Cundiff, 11 S. & R. 420.

or varied from time to time. The same law-making power
that creates it, vests the property in the heir subject first to
the prior right of creditors of the decedent, if there be not
other sufficient assets, to have it sold for the payment of their
debts, and also gives the court the paramount power of ascertaining the debts and selling the property to pay the same;
so, also, for purposes of making partition.

§ 28.   In *Myer v. McDougal*,[1] this paramount lien of
creditors upon the lands of a deceased debtor, or other his
estate, for payment of their debts, is fully recognized by
WALKER, Justice, in the following terms: "The devise of the
land to Elizabeth Hayden, by Robert Hayden, was subject to
the payment of his debts; and the devisee and her grantees
took and held the premises subject to such indebtedness, which
operated as a lien upon them, and the creditors may enforce
such lien by administration, from heirs or devisees."

The court here cite *McCoy v. Morrow*[2] as to the same
effect, and to the point that the lien must be enforced within
a reasonable time.

§ 29.   A decree of sale, to effect a partition of interests, or
to pay debts of a decedent, virtually takes possession of the
estate, and vests it in the court, for the purposes of distribution.[3]   In the language of the court in *William's Case* just
cited, "a decree for a sale to effect a partition, or to pay debts,
virtually takes possession of the estate, and vests it in the
court for the purposes of distribution."

§ 30.   Judicial sales properly speaking occur only in proceedings wholly or partly *in rem.*[4]   In this respect, they are
widely contradistinguished from execution sales, at law, where
the judgment is exclusively *in personam*, and wherein the
sale is that of the officer and not that of the court.

§ 31.   Some judicial sales are in proceedings purely *in rem.*

[1] Myers v. McDougal, 47 Ill. 278, 280; McCoy v. Morrow, 11 Ill. 519.

[2] McCoy v. Morrow, 18 Ill. 519.

[3] William's Case, 3 Bland. 215; Beauregard v. New Orleans, 18 How.
497, 503.

[4] Grignon's Lessee v. Astor, 2 How. 338; Beauregard v. New Orleans, 18
How. 497, 502, 503; Florintine v. Barton, 2 Wall. 210, 216.

Others are in proceedings partly *in rem* and partly *in personam*. In either case, the order, or decree of sale, is *in rem;* it is against the property itself.

II. JUDICIAL SALES IN PROCEEDINGS PURELY IN REM.

§ 32. Proceedings purely *in rem* are where the court in its plenary power of the law, based on legislative will and the authority of the government, lays hold of and acts directly on the property itself, and transfers its ownership to the purchaser, by a title paramount to that of the owner, and "without regard to the persons who may have an interest in it."[1] Such proceedings are not by virtue of any contract of the owner, express or implied, but "are analogous to proceedings in admiralty," and "all the world are parties."[2] "The estate passes to the purchaser by operation of law."[3]

§ 33. The purchaser, it is said, claims not their title, but one paramount.[4] The paramount right of the government to seize or lay hold of the property of decedents and distribute it in kind, or else, if that be impracticable by way of partition, then to sell the same and distribute the proceeds. Or by a still more stringent measure, if need be, to sell the same for payment of the ancestor's debts and distribute the proceeds to the extent of the debts among the creditors, to satisfy claims of a higher or paramount grade in law, than the claim of the heirs. In the case cited from Alabama, *Satcher v. Satcher*,[5] the Supreme Court of that State use the following language in reference to sales in probate: "It is the settled doctrine in the decisions of this court, that the proceeding before the

---

[1] Grignon's Lessee *v.* Astor, 2 How. 338; Bofil *v.* Fisher, 3 Rich. Eq. 1; Sheldon *v.* Newton, 3 Ohio (N. S.) 494; Beauregard *v.* New Orleans, 18 How. 497, 503; Satcher *v.* Satcher, 41 Ala. 26; Florintine *v.* Barton, 2 Wall. 216.

[2] Ibid.

[3] McPherson *v.* Cunliff, 11 S. & R. 428: Grignon's Lessee *v.* Astor, 2 How. 338; 3 Bouvier, 131, 132.

[4] Moore *v.* Shultz, 13 Penn. St. 102; Grignon's Lessee *v.* Astor, 2 How. 319; Beauregard *v.* New Orleans, 18 How. 502.

[5] 41 Ala. 26.

2

probate court, for the sale of lands of a decedent, is *in rem;* that the jurisdiction of the court attaches upon a petition setting forth a statutory ground of sale; and that the order of sale is not void, although the proceedings may abound in errors, if the petition contain the above stated jurisdictional allega- tions."

And in the same case, the doctrine is still more definitely asserted so as to expressly negative the necessity of notice or jurisdiction of the persons in interest, and say that "The proceedings in the probate court for the sale of decedent's lands is held, by a long chain of decisions not now to be questioned, to be *in rem;* and therefore the validity of the orders can never depend upon the fact that the court has acquired jurisdiction of the persons of the parties. The requisition of notice is just as plainly and as positively made in the act of 1822, as as under any subsequent law. Under the act of 1822 the order of sale was not void on account of want of notice. It was so settled by the decisions of this court. We cannot decide to the contrary unless we disregard the doctrine of *stare decisis* and overturn decisions which constitute a rule of property under which millions of dollars worth of land are probably held."[1]

And in *Wyman v. Campbell,*[2] a still earlier decision of the same court, it is holden that "the proceeding of the orphans' court is *in rem,* against the estate of the intestate, and not *in personam.* The order by that court for the sale of real estate, so far as the question of jurisdiction is concerned, may well be compared to the condemnation of goods by a court of exchequer, where jurisdiction attaches upon a seizure—it merely professes to divest the title of the ancestor without affecting the persons or other property of the heirs."

§ 34. The courts of Alabama thus very clearly recognize the paramount right of the government to act upon the title

[1] Satcher v. Satcher, 41 Ala. 26, 39; King v. Kent, 29 Ala. 542; Matheson v. Hearin, 29 Ala. 210; Field v. Goldsby, 28 Ala. 218; Wyman v. Campbell, 6 Porter, 219; McPherson v. Cunliff, 11 S. & R. 430; Lightfoot v. Lewis, 1 Ala. 479.
[2] 6 Porter, 219, 232; Lynch v. Baxter, 4 Texas, 431.

of the ancestor to the postponement of the heir. In such cases there are no adverse parties litigant. The rights of those previously interested in the property are transferred from the property to the fund produced by the sale.[1] This is by the same right and power that enables the government to regulate descents, make distribution of estates, make partition, and to sell such property as is not divisable in kind; or may not be so distributed if personal.

§ 35. Such is the power of the government and courts in this respect, that the judicial arm reaches every possible interest. The rights of "unborn remainder men" and of persons "who are not before" the court, "may be concluded;" the court "acts upon the property" and the rights of parties in interest, as before stated, are "transferred from the property to the fund." Such is the ruling and the language of the court in *Bofil v. Fisher* and kindred class of cases. In the case of Bofils the court say: "To say that the court could not under circumstances like these, convey away the fee, would be to assert a doctrine that would render conditional limitations and contingent remainders an intolerable evil to a growing and prosperous community."

§ 36. By such proceedings and sales, in probate, to pay a decedent's debts, where jurisdiction has attached, the purchaser, in some of the states, holds the lands freed from all liens and claims, save dower, in the resulting interest of decedent's heirs in the dower lands, and except such liens as are of such a character that the amount thereof cannot be rendered certain (as for instance, to suppose a case, a life annuity) so that the same may be paid off out of the proceeds of sale.[2]

§ 37. In probate sales to pay debts, this rule of paramount

Bofil v. Fisher, 3 Rich. Eq. 1; Miller's Exrs. v. Greenbaum, 11 Ohio St. 486; Moore v. Shultz, 13 Penn. St. 98; McPherson v. Cunliff, 11 S. & R. 130.

[2] Moore v. Shultz, 13 Penn. St. 102, 103; Grignon's Lessee v. Astor, 2 How. 338; West v. Townsend, 12 Ind. 434; Western Penn. R. R. Co. v. Johnson, 59 Penn. St. 290, 294. In this last case the court say: "It is a familiar principle that a judicial sale extinguishes liens, not estates or interests of third persons." Cadrus v. Jackson, 52 Penn. St. 295.

right in the court extends to creditors and heirs only, and not to adverse claimants of title otherwise than through the heirs.[1]

§ 38. Though this plenary power of the proper court, over the real estate of a deceased debtor, may seem unwarranted and anomalous at the first view, yet is not more so than is the power which the law gives the administrator or executor over the personal effects, which he may sell and dispose of, for the payment of debts without regard to the heirs, who are, nevertheless, in either case, entitled to the property if there be no debts or it be not sold in the course of administration.

We are not unmindful that the personality is said to vest in the executor or administrator. But not unconditionally; only for a purpose; and *quere* as to the administrator? For, if so, must it rest in abeyance until his appointment? His title is more in the nature of authority to collect, preserve, and if need be, or the law require it, to sell. All which is without any notice to the heirs and is by force of the same law and law-making authority that decides who shall be heirs.

The power to confer heirship implies power also to define the terms on which it shall be conferred.

§ 39. The doctrine laid down in Pennsylvania, that judicial sales discharge all liens susceptible of being ascertained to a certainty, is not to be understood as assuming to vacate or destroy, but rather to discharge the same out of the proceeds of sale according to priority so as to close the title to the purchaser.[2] And sales made in proceedings for partition being in their nature judicial sales, have the same effect.[3]

---

[1] Shields v. Ashley, 16 Mo. 471.

[2] Girard Life Ins. Co. v. Farmers' & Mechanics' Bank, 57 Penn. St. 388, 396, and see Miller's Exrs. v. Greenbaum, 11 Ohio St. 436.

[3] Girard Life Ins. Co. v. Farmers' & Mechanics' Bank, 57 Penn. St. 388, 396, 397. In this case the court say on this subject: "We come then to the more general question, whether a sale in partition by writ discharges the lien of a mortgage on the undivided interest of one of the parties. A sale in partition is always for the purpose of enabling division. It is authorized only when it has been determined that the land, which is its subject, cannot be divided according to the command of the writ 'without prejudice to, or spoiling the whole.' When that appears, the law directs a sale in order to convert that which is impartible into an equivalent that

Hence, the court held in the case of the Girard Life Ins. Co. that the sale in partition under the statute, though the statute makes no provision to such effect, discharged a prior mortgage lien upon the partitioned premises.[1]

is capable of distribution. Such a sale is eminently judicial—more strictly so than is a sale by a sheriff under an execution. It is made under an order of the court; its subject is in the hands of the court, and the proceeds are necessarily brought into court for distribution. The act of 1799 requires that the moneys or securities realized from the sale 'shall be brought into court,' to be distributed. The whole proceeding is more directly the act of the court than is any other sheriff's sale, where the officer acts under instructions of the attorney, and where he may and often does distribute the purchase money of the property sold, without any supervision or direction of the court. That Orphans' Court sales in partition are judicial sales, was decided in Sacket v. Twining, 6 Harris, 202, and recognized in Jacob's Appeal, 11 Harris, 477. I am not aware that it has been directly decided whether a sale in partition by writ in a common law court, is judicial or not, though Allen v. Gault, 3 Casey, 473, substantially rules that it is. But without any positive determination, it is impossible to doubt that it is to be so regarded. It certainly has everything which in other cases is regarded necessary to make a sale judicial, and it is even less under private control than almost any other which is confessedly such. Next it is to be observed that judicial sales in this state discharge all liens. This is a rule of almost universal application. There are, indeed, some exceptions to it, created by express statutory enactment, and others growing out of the peculiar character of the lien or encumbrance; but it has long been regarded as sound policy that property purchased at a judicial sale should pass into the hands of the purchaser clear of all mere liens. Exceptions to the rule are allowed only from necessity. If property be thus sold, the chances are greatly increased that it will bring its full value, thus benefiting alike the owners and lien creditors. Sales in partition have never been recognized as exceptional, and it is not easy to discover any reason why they should be. In them it is as much for the interest of the owners of the land and for holders of liens upon it, or parts of it, that purchasers shall not be compelled to look after incumbrances, as it is in any other judicial sale. And incumbrancers have the same notice that is given to them in ordinary cases of sales under a *renditioni exponas*. They have no reason to complain, therefore, if their liens be discharged from the land, and attached to its full equivalent the proceeds of the sale. Surely a sale in partition should not be taken out of the general rule which regulates judicial sales and their consequences without some controlling reason. Exceptions are not to be multiplied unnecessarily."

[1] Girard Life Ins. Co. v. Farmers' & Mechanics' Bank, 57 Penn. St. 388. The court, in this case, quoting the language in Williard v. Norris,

§ 40. In Illinois it is holden that a proceeding on *fieri facias* to foreclose a mortgage under the statute, is a proceeding *in rem* and not *in personam.*

In such case the practice is for the court to find the amount due against the defendant and order a sale of the mortgaged premises on special execution.[1] The sale, however, is none the less a judicial sale, for the judgment and writ name the property to be sold, and the condemnation of the property is by judgment *in rem,* although personal judgment is some times also given against the defendant.

III. Judicial Sales in Proceedings Partly In Rem, and Partly In Personam.

§ 41. Judicial sales, in proceedings partly *in rem* and partly *in personam,* are where the proceedings are of a mixed nature, being directly against the property and also, personal against the owner, as in proceedings to foreclose deeds of mortgage by judicial sale.[2] In such cases, there is procedure *in rem* against the property, and at the same time personal process against the mortgagor to bring him as defendant into court.

1 Rawle, 64, that "nothing could more clearly show how notorious is the rule that in every judicial sale in Pennsylvania the land goes to the purchaser clear of all judgments and mortgages, and that out of the purchase money the sheriff, at his own risk, is to pay off all these liens, according to their priority, in so much that, though the act of assembly about partitions makes no mention of liens, yet by analogy drawn from the notorious usage of the commonwealth, an allowance was adjudged to the sheriff for the fees paid for search as of judgments and mortgages, the owners of which might afterwards call upon him for the money." The court add: "For these reasons we hold that a sale made in partition by writ under act of 1799 does discharge the lien of judgments and mortgages upon the land sold, having the ordinary effect of other judicial sales." Girard Life Ins. Co. *v.* Farmers' & Mechanics' Bank, 57 Penn. St. 396, 397. But a different rule in regard to incumbrances seems to prevail in Illinois. In McConnel *v.* Smith, 39 Ill. 289, it is said that, "As a general rule, subject it may be to some exceptions, a purchaser, at an administrator's sale, acquires it (the property) with all the incumbrances to which it is liable."

  [1] Williams *v.* Ives, 49 Ill. 512.

  [2] Kershaw *v.* Thompson, 4 John. Ch. 609; Downing *v.* Palmeteer, 1 Mon. 64.

A decree in this class of cases and sale thereon only confers title as against the parties to the suit.[1]

§ 42. The decree of foreclosure and sale is partly *in rem*, being directly against the property;[2] whilst so much of it as bars the right of redemption is *in personam*, divesting the defendant, as it does, of the personal right to redeem. The proceeding is predicated upon the defendant's contract of indebtedness and mortgage, and not upon the plenary power of the court over the subject matter, irrespective of the parties in interest. Yet the sale is none the less a judicial sale, and the sale of the court. The deed, where the record of the mortgage is regular, relates back and confers title by relation to the date of the mortgage as against intervening claims.

§ 43. In some of these cases, for instance when the defendant is not found, but is brought in by publication, the proceedings assume very nearly the features of those which are purely *in rem*. But there is still a difference; for the debt and mortgage deed exist in contract and are no less the basis of the proceeding than they are when the defendant is brought personally into court.

§ 44. The judicial sale involved in the case of *Minnesota Co. v. St. Paul, post*, referred to was conducted by the United States marshal, but not by virtue of his powers of office under the law. It was no less judicial as made by him than it would have been if made under direction of a master. The court ordering the sale clothed him, in virtue of the order, with a master's powers in that particular. In considering the case of Minnesota Co. v. St. Paul, the United States Supreme Court, speaking of the marshal's appointment, say that he was "directed to make the sale instead of a master commissioner;" and that the sale so made "was confirmed by the order of the district court." Yet as more and other property was sold than was included in the decree, the court held the sale of that part which was not included in the decree invalid notwithstanding its confirmation. The Supreme Court attribute the con-

[1] Haines v. Beach, 3 John. Ch. 459.
[2] Kershaw v. Thompson, 4 John. Ch. 609.

firmation, as to the excess, to an oversight, and do not decide
positively as to the power of a court to confirm in such a sale,
with knowledge of the departure from the decree, but remark
that "cases in this (Supreme) court would seem to decide that
it cannot,[1] and they refer to *Shriver v. Lynn*[2] and *Gray v.
Brignardello.*[3]

§ 45. The sale then which was here brought in question
was clearly a judicial sale, though made by the same person
who exercised the office of marshal, or if preferred by the
marshal, for it were competent for the court to so designate
and appoint him. This sale is regarded by the Supreme Court
of the United States as judicial, wherein they liken it to a
"master's sale" in this, "that a purchaser or bidder at a master's sale" subjects himself "*quod hoc* to the jurisdiction of
the court," and that therefore the purchasers were estopped to
deny being within the jurisdiction of the court as parties in
litigation in the case.[4]

---

[1] Minnesota Co. v. St. Paul, 2 Wall. 640, 641. And in Gaines v. New
Orleans, 6 Wall. 714, the Supreme Court of the United States hold that a
probate court "could not by a subsequent order give validity to sales made
by executors which were null and void by the law of the state when they
were made."

[2] 2 How. 43.

[3] 1 Wall. 637.

[4] Minnesota Co. v. St. Paul, 2 Wall. 634.

CHAPTER II.

THE NATURE OF EXECUTION SALES

I. They are Ministerial Sales.

II. The Officer Selling is, in Law, the Attorney of the Execution Debtor.

III. There is No Warranty. The Rule *caveat emptor* Applies.

IV. They are Within the Statute of Frauds.

V. Effects of Subsequent Reversal of Judgments, or Quashing the Execution.

I.   They are Ministerial Sales.

§46.   In making ordinary execution sales, simply by virtue of his office, the sheriff or marshal acts as the ministerial officer of the law, not as the organ of the court.   He is not its instrument or agent, as in judicial sales, and the court is not the vendor.   His authority to sell rests on the law and on the writ, and does not, as in judicial sales, emanate from the court.   The functions of the court terminate at the rendition of the judgment, except where confirmation of the sale is the practice.   The court does not direct what shall be levied or sold, or how the sale shall be made.   The law is the officer's only guide.[1]

§47.   This very principle was distinctly avowed by the Supreme Court of the United States—Daniel, Justice—in *Griffin v. Thompson*,[2] in reference to which that court characterize the marshal's functions in enforcing an execution at law in the following terms: In reference to his powers and duties the court say that he is the "officer of the law, and is bound to fulfil the behests of the law; and this, too, without special

[1] Bac. Abt. Sheriff, M.; Foreman v. Hunt, 3 Dana, (Ky.) 614, 621; Gantley's Lessee v. Ewing, 3 How. 714; Todd v. Philhower, 4 Zabr. 796; McKnight v. Gordon, 13 Rich. Eq. (S. C.) 222; South v. Maryland, 18 How. 396, 402; Armis v. Smith, 16 Pet. 309, 313; Griffin v. Thompson, 2 How. 256, 257.

[2] 2 How. 256, 257.

instruction or admonition from any person." Unlike a master or commissioner, selling on decree in chancery, the law is his guide; whilst the master or commissioner are subject to the guidance and the order of the court. In the language of the learned Justice REDFIELD, "It is plain then that a sheriff's sale is not a judicial sale. If it were, no action could be brought against the sheriff for selling upon execution property not belonging to the debtor."[1]

§ 48. There are exceptions to this rule, some of which may be stated. When by the law the sale is required to be reported to the court for confirmation, and is only binding when confirmed by the court, in such cases sheriff's sales, on ordinary execution, partake of the nature of *judicial* sales; for the act of confirmation is a *judicial* act, and is spread upon the records. This distinction, to-wit: the necessity of confirmation, is the line drawn by Mr. Justices STORY and BALDWIN on the circuit, and GRIER delivering the opinion of the Supreme Court of the United States, as contra-distinguishing *judicial* from *execution* sales.[2]

§ 49. Another exception to the rule first above stated is, in mixed cases of law and equity; in which special executions issue under the statute, partly partaking of the nature of an execution at law and of an order of sale in chancery. Here the precise character of the sale depends upon the special features of each case. It may be *judicial*, and it may be *ministerial*, as either feature predominates; and it may partake of the qualities of each in some respects.

§ 50. In ordinary execution sales, the court neither order the execution nor the sale. There are, however, special instances when ordinary writs of execution are ordered by the court, as when there is satisfaction wrongfully entered of a judgment, or returned of an execution, satisfaction will be set aside and an alias writ of execution will be ordered; but when issued, it is none the less, a mere ordinary execution, and on it the sheriff sells under the power of the law.

---

[1] Griffith v. Fowler, 18 Vt. 394.

[2] Thompson v. Philips, 1 Bald. C. C. 264; Arnold v. Smith, 5 Mason, C. C. 414, 420, 421; Griffith v. Bogart, 18 How. 158.

§ 51. The exercise of this power, however, is invoked by the writ of execution. The act of selling is ministerial.[1] The officer selling is for that purpose constituted by law the agent and attorney of the execution defendant;[2] and is not, as in judicial sales, the agent or instrument of the court.[3]

§ 52. The title under sheriff sale passes to the purchasers, as a general rule, without the express sanction or confirmation of the court,[4] which possesses only the negative power of setting aside the sale for cause. To this, however, there are exceptions in several of the States, where, by law, confirmation is required.[5]

§ 53. In the latter class of cases the sale, by the judicial act of confirmation, becomes in some respects a judicial sale, and as such is characterized by Justice BALDWIN, in *Thompson v. Philips*, a case which arose under the laws of Pennsylvania, and where by the courts in other Pennsylvania cases the practice is to confirm in open court at the time of the acknowledgment of the deed. In that case the court say: "In this State the reception of an acknowledgment of a sheriff's deed is a judicial act, in the nature of a judgement of confirmation of all the acts preceding the sale, curing all defects in the process or its execution, which the court has power to act upon."[6] When the acknowledgment is thus taken and the deed or sale confirmed, then, in contemplation of law, everything which has been done is considered as done by the order or under the sanction of the court.[7]

---

[1] Bac. Abt. title Sheriff, M. 689, 691; Todd *v.* Philhower, 4 Zabr. (N. J.) 796.

[2] Cooper's Lessee *v.* Galbraith, 3 Wash. C. C. 546, 550; Swortwell *v.* Martin, 16 Iowa, 519.

[3] Foreman *v.* Hunt, 3 Dana, 622; McKnight *v.* Gordon, 13 Rich. Eq. (S. C.) 222.

[4] Foreman *v.* Hunt, 3 Dana, 614, 621, 622.

[5] Curtis *v.* Norton, 1 Ham. 278; Thompson *v.* Philips, 1 Bald. C. C. 246, 272; McBain *v.* McBain, 15 Ohio St. 337.

[6] Thompson *v.* Philips, 1 Bald. C. C. 272; Smith *v.* Simpson, 60 Penn. St. 169; McBain *v.* McBain, 15 Ohio St. 337.

[7] Thompson *v.* Philips, 1 Bald. C. C. 272; Voorhees *v.* The U. S. Bank, 10 Pet. 472, 476; McBain *v.* McBain, 15 Ohio St. 337; Woods *v.* Lane, 2 S. and Rawle, 54, 55.

II. The Officer Selling is, in Law, the Attorney of the Execution Debtor.

§ 54 The sheriff or other officer making the sale is empowered by law to convey by deed to the purchaser, under an execution, all the right, title, interest and estate of the defendant, as fully (but not to warrant) as the defendant himself, or an attorney empowered for that purpose by him, could do. The officer, in fact, acts as such attorney or agent, appointed for that purpose by law.

§ 55. The purchase money is applied to the use of the defendant in the discharge of his debt; between him and the purchaser the law raises a contract, in like manner as if the conveyance (without warranty) had been made by himself.[1] We have chosen in most of the above to appropriate the very language of that great Jurist, Justice Washington.

§ 56. In *Cooper's Lessee v. Galbraith*,[2] Justice Washington says: "The sheriff is empowered by law to convey by deed to the purchaser, under execution, all the right, title, interest and estate of the defendant, as fully as the defendant himself, or an attorney empowered for that purpose by him could have done. The officer, in fact, acts as such attorney, appointed for that purpose by law."

And the same doctrine is held in South Carolina. In *Massey v. Thompson*,[3] Justice Colcock said: "The defendant ought not to be permitted to oppose the title of a purchaser. The sheriff's deed is his. He has received the consideration. It has been applied to the payment of his debts. He should be estopped." The doctrine is again reasserted by Justice Inglis, in *McKnight v. Gordon*.[4]

[1] Cooper's Lessee v. Galbraith, 3 Wash. C. C. 546, 550; Swortzell v. Martin, 16 Iowa, 519; Conway v. Nolte, 11 Mo. 74; McKnight v. Gordon, 13 Rich. Eq. (S. C.) 222; Kilgore v. Peden, 1 Strob. Eq. 19

[2] 3 Wash. C. C. 550.

[3] 2 N. & McCord. 105.

[4] 13 Rich. Eq. 222, 239.

III. There is No Implied Warranty. The Rule of *Caveat Emptor* Applies.

§ 57. In making a sale under execution the sheriff or other public officer professes to sell only the interest or estate of the judgment debtor in the premises.

He is not bound to convey with a warranty; neither does the law imply one: The rule of *caveat emptor* applies. Let the buyer beware of the title for which he bids.[1]

§ 58. The purchaser acquires only the title of the execution defendant as it existed at the date of the judgment, if such judgment is a lien upon the premises sold;[2] and if not a lien, then from the date of the levy of the execution;[3] but if suit is by attachment, then the purchaser takes title from the date of the levy, or as in attachments, delivery of writ,[4] or as in some of the states from the test, and in others from the delivery of the writ.[5]

If the officer convey with warranty, he binds himself thereby, personally, and no one else.[6]

§ 59. Purchasers at execution sales cannot, when there is no fraud, excuse themselves from paying the amount of the purchase money, nor avoid their bid by showing that the judgment debtor had no title to the property sold, or that his title thereto was defective.

The maxim *caveat emptor* applies in all its strictness. There is no warranty. The officer sells only the title of the debtor.[7]

---

[1] Hammersmith v. Espy, 19 Iowa, 444, 446; Dean v. Morris, 4 G. Green, 312; Ritter v. Henshaw, 7 Iowa, 97, 100; Avant v. Reed, 2 Stew. 488; Philips v. Johnson, 14 B. Mon. (Ky.) 172; Harth v. Gibbes, 3 Rich. 316; Reed's Appeal, 13 Penn. St. (1 Harris, 476); Rockwell v. Allen, 3 McLean, 357; Creps v. Baird, 3 Ohio St. 277; Lang v. Waring, 25 Ala. 625; Coyne v. Souther, 61 Penn. St. 457.

[2] Smith v. Allen, 1 Blackf. 22; Bac. Abt. title Execution, 725; Miller v. Finn, 1 Neb. 255.

[3] Boyd v. Longworth, 11 Ohio, 235.

[4] Shirk v. Wilson, 13 Ind. 129.

[5] McLain v. Upchurch, 2 Murph. 353; Lewis v. Smith, 2 S. & R. 157.

[6] Rockwell v. Allen, 3 McLean, 357; The Monte Allegre, 9 Wheat, 616.

[7] Camden v. Logan, 8 Iowa, 434; Dean v. Morris, 4 G. Greene, 312; Dean v. Frazier, 8 Blackf. 432; Rogers v. Smith, 2 Carter (Ind.) 526; Engleman v. Clark, 4 Scam. 486.

§ 60. Such sales are none the less sheriff's sales if the officer, at the instance of the plaintiff and defendant in execution, sells on a credit; and therefore the collection of a note given for such purchase money cannot be evaded by reason of failure of title.[1]

IV. THEY ARE WITHIN THE STATUTE OF FRAUDS.

§ 61. Execution sales, in the absence of any memorandum of the officer selling, are considered within the statute of frauds.[2] The case here cited arose in Maryland, where no formal deed is made by the sheriff, but the return of the sheriff constitutes the purchaser's muniment of title. The same rule, however, prevails in reference to the statute of frauds where deeds are executed by the sheriff.

§ 62. Such sales by the sheriff are made under the law and not under direction of the court, and not being sales of the court as are judicial sales strictly such, they are within the statute. But the judicial sale, being a sale in court, the buyer becomes a party to the case and is in court, and the court will not allow its own proceedings to be repudiated under the statute.

V. EFFECT OF REVERSAL OF JUDGMENT.

§ 63. Sales made under process issued, or irregular or erroneous judgments, are not affected by the subsequent reversal of such judgments for mere error or irregularity.[3] But the contrary is the settled doctrine, where the reversal is for want of jurisdiction to render judgment. Sales in the latter

---

[1] Killgore v. Pedan, 1 Strobt. 18.

[2] 4 Kent, Com. 434; Remington v. Linthicum, 14 Pet. 84; Hart v. Rector, 13 Mo. 497; Chapman v. Harwood, 8 Blackf. 82; Hadden v. Johnson, 7 Ind. 394; Barney v. Patterson, 6 Har. & J. 182.

[3] Williams v. Cummins, 4 J. J. Marsh. 637; Barney v. Patterson, 6 Har. & J. 182; Reardon v. Searcey, 2 Bibb. 202; Coleman v. Trabine, 2 Bibb. 518; Sneed v. Reardon, 1 A. K. Marsh, 217; Estes v. Booth, 20 Ark. 583; Bank of U. S. v. Bank of Washington, 6 Pet. 8; Ponder v. Moseley, 2 Fla. 211; McLogan v. Brown, 11 Ill. 519; Herrick v. Graves, 16 Wis. 157; Stinson v. Ross, 51 Maine, 556; Cox v. Nelson, 1 Mon. 94,

class of cases are void *ab initio*. There can be no valid sale without a valid writ, and no writ is valid as an execution that is based on a void judgment.[1]

§ 64. Against mere irregularities, it is the policy of the law to sustain execution sales, as against the judgment debtor.

§ 65. In Indiana, when the execution plaintiff is purchaser at an execution sale, and the judgment is thereafter reversed, the sale is void under the statute;[2] and so likewise if the judgment be reversed only in part; as for costs, when the sale is made for both debt and costs.[3]

§ 66. In Ohio, under the appraisement law of 1841, sales at law on execution are required to be confirmed by the court. It is there holden that when the execution plaintiff is purchaser and has not conveyed the property away to a *bona fide* purchaser by the reversal of the order of confirmation, the sale becomes a "nullity" and the title is "divested" out of such execution purchaser.[4]

§ 67. It is further held by the Iowa court, in *Twogood v. Franklin*,[5] that the effect of the reversal is to avoid the sale and defeat the title in the hands of such execution purchaser, so buying with notice of appeal, and also the title of his grantee, who takes by purchase, under him, with knowledge, after the reversal of the judgment.

The latter result follows as a matter of course, as a grantor can confer on one having like notice with himself no better title than he himself has.

§ 68. In Iowa, it is provided by statute that *bona fide* execution purchasers of property, under a judgment that is subsequently reversed, shall not be affected in their title by such reversal.[6]

The courts of that state hold, however, that where an appeal is taken from a judgment, although there be no supersedeas

---

[1] Abbe *v.* Wood, 8 Mass. 79.

[2] Hutchens *v.* Doe, 3 Ind. 528; Doe *v.* Crocker, 2 Carter, 575.

[3] Hutchens *v.* Doe, 3 Ind. 528.

[4] McBain *v.* McBain, 16 Ohio S. 337, 349.

[5] 27 Iowa, 239.

[6] Revision of 1860, Sec. 3541.

bond given, and the plaintiff takes execution and purchases thereon pending the appeal, that such execution purchaser is not, in reference to such a transaction, a *bona fide* purchaser; that he is not within the provisions of said section 3541 of the Revision, and that his grantee buying after reversal is in a like condition.[1]

[1] Twogood *v.* Franklin, 27 Iowa, 239.

PART SECOND.

JUDICIAL SALES OF REAL PROPERTY.

CHAPTER III

JURISDICTION OF THE COURT ORDERING THE SALE.

I. THE JURISDICTION IS LOCAL.
II. JURISDICTION IS POWER TO HEAR AND DETERMINE.
III. THERE MUST BE JURISDICTION OF THE SUBJECT MATTER AND OF THE PARTICULAR CASE.
IV. TITLE PASSES BY OPERATION OF LAW.

I. THE JURISDICTION IS LOCAL.

§ 69.   Jurisdiction of real property can only be obtained by the tribunal of the country wherein the property is situated. Lands lying in one state cannot be reached or sold under an order, license, or decree, of a court of another and different state. The jurisdiction is local. The *lex loci rei sitæ* governs.[1]

II. IT IS POWER TO HEAR AND DETERMINE A CAUSE.

§ 70.   Jurisdiction in the court is power to "hear and determine" the particular cause involved.[2]   If this power to

---

[1] Watts *v.* Waddle, 6 Pet. 400; Story, Conflict of Laws, Secs. 19, 20, 538, 543; Nowler *v.* Coit, 1 Ham. 519; Brown *v.* Edson, 23 Vt. 435; *Ex parte* Read, 2 Sneed (Tenn.) 375; Rogers *v.* McLain, 31 Barb. 304; Tardy *v.* Morgan, 3 McLean, 358; McCormack *v.* Sullivan, 10 Wheat. 192; Wilkinson *v.* Leland, 2 Pet. 627, 655; Price *v.* Johnson, 10 Ohio, St. 390; Blake *v.* Davis, 20 Ohio, 231; Lattinger *v.* R. R. Co. 43 Mo. 105.

[2] United States *v.* Arredondo, 6 Pet. 709; Grignon's Lessee *v.* Astor, 2 How. 338; Beauregard *v.* New Orleans, 18 How. 502, 503; Wilder *v.* City of Chicago, 26 Ill. 179, 182; Shelden *v.* Newton, 3 Ohio St. 494; Smiley *v.* Sampson, 1 Neb. 56, 70. In Grignon's Lessee *v.* Astor, the United States

hear and determine the particular case does not exist in the court in point of law, then there can be no jurisdiction of the case.

If it does exist, then to confer actual jurisdiction of the particular case, or subject matter thereof, the jurisdictional power of the court must be invoked or brought into action, by such measures and in such manner as is required by the local law of the tribunal. When this is done, it is then *coram judicis*. If this be not done, there is, at least, error, if not want of validity in the proceedings.

§ 71.   The manner of conferring actual jurisdiction of the particular case is variously modified and regulated by the

Supreme Court say: "The power to hear and determine a cause is jurisdiction; if the petitioner presents such a case in his petition, that on a demurrer the court would render a judgment in his favor, it is an undoubted case of jurisdiction; whether on an answer denying and putting in issue the allegations of the petition, the petitioner makes out his case, is the exercise of jurisdiction conferred by the filing a petition containing all the requisites, and in the manner required by law. 6 Pet. 709. Any movement by a court is necessarily the exercise of jurisdiction. So to exercise any judicial power over the subject matter and the parties, the question is, whether, on the case before the court, their action is judicial or extra judicial, with or without the authority of law, to render a judgment or decree upon the rights of the litigant parties. If the law confers the power to render a judgment or decree, then the court has jurisdiction what shall be adjudged or decreed between the parties, and with which is the right of the case, is judicial action by hearing and determining it. 12 Pet. 718; 3 Pet. 205. It is a case of judicial cognizance and the proceedings are judicial. 12 Pet. 623. This is the line which denotes jurisdiction and its exercise. In cases *in personam*, where there are adverse parties, the court must have power over the subject matter and the parties; but on a proceeding to sell the real estate of an indebted intestate there are no adversary parties, the proceeding is *in rem*, the administrator represents the land, 11 S. & R. 432; they are analogous to proceedings in the admiralty, where the only question of jurisdiction is the power of the court over the thing, the subject matter before them, without regard to the persons who may have an interest in it; all the world are parties. In the orphans' court and all courts who have power to sell the estates of intestates, their action operates on the estate, not on the heirs of the intestate; a purchaser claims not their title, but one paramount. 11 S. & R 426. The estate passes to him by operation of law. 11 S. & R. 428. The sale is a proceeding *in rem*, to which all claiming under the intestate are parties, 11 S. & R. 429, which directs the title of the deceased. 11 S. & R. 430."

enactments of the different states in regard to notice and matters of practice, and which should severally be conformed to as necessary to give validity to the proceedings. To effect this the petition or plaint must be such as is sustainable on demurrer.[1]

§ 72. But although such conformity, as to notice and other matters of practice, may not appear to have existed from the record itself, yet if jurisdiction of the particular cause fully attached by such petition as is sustainable on demurrer, then the existence of notice and other incidental requirements will be inferred after judgment or decree; and the question in regard to the same will not be open to collateral inquiry. The record, including the presumptions in law, so arising therefrom, will be received, on collateral inquiry, as verity.[2]

---

[1] Morse v. Goold, 11 N. Y. 281; Jackson v. Babcock, 16 N. Y. 246; Gibson v. Roll, 30 Ill. 172; Johnson v. Johnson, 30 Ill. 215; United States v. Arredondo, 6 Pet. 709; Reddick v. The Bank, 27 Ill. 147; Alabama Conference v. Price's Exrs. 42 Ala. 49; Grignon's Lessee v. Astor, 2 How. 338; Goudy v. Hall, 30 Ill. 109; Whiting v. Porter, 23 Ill. 445; Mason v. Messenger, 17 Iowa, 268; Smily v. Sampson, 1 Neb. 56, 70.

[2] Morrow v. Weed, 4 Iowa, 77; Grignon's Lessee v. Astor, 2 How. 219; Reeves v. Townsend, 2 Zab. 396; Paul v. Hussey, 35 Maine, 97, 100; Fox v. Hoit, 12 Conn. 491; Wilson v. Wilson, 18 Ala. 176; Sheldon v. Newton, 3 Ohio, (N. S.) 495; Simpson v. Hart, 1 Johns. Ch. 91; Davenport v. Smith, 15 Iowa, 213; Hart v. Jewett, 11 Iowa, 276; Frazier v. Steenrod, 7 Iowa, 339; Myers v. McDougall, 47 Ill. 287; Carter v. Waugh, 42 Ala. 452; Merritt v. Horne, 5 Ohio St. 318; Rhode Island v. Massachusetts, 12 Pet. 657. The court, in the case of Grignon's Lessee v. Astor, add on this subject that, "The granting the license to sell is an adjudication upon all the facts necessary to give jurisdiction, and whether they existed or not is wholly immaterial, if no appeal is taken; the rule is the same whether the law gives an appeal or not; if none is given from the final decree, it is conclusive on all whom it concerns. The record is absolute verity, to contradict which there can be no averment or evidence, the court having power to make the decree, it can be impeached only by fraud in the party who obtains it. 6 Pet. 729. A purchaser under it is not bound to look beyond the decree, if there is error in it of the most palpable kind; if the court which rendered it have, in the exercise of jurisdiction, disregarded, misconstrued, or disobeyed the plain provisions of the law which gave them the power to hear and determine the case before them, the title of a purchaser is as much protected as if the adjudication would stand the test of a writ of error; so where an appeal is given but not taken in the time prescribed by law. These principles are settled as to all courts of record

III. There must not only be Power to take Jurisdiction of the Subject Matter, but there must be Actual Jurisdiction of the Particular Case.

§ 73. The power of the court, as we have seen, over the property or subject matter referred to in the proceeding must be invoked over the particular case by a petition good upon demurrer: and so it must, by personal notice, or service, where, by statute, the latter is essential to confer jurisdiction. [1]

§ 74. The action of the court and the notice of sale, as also the sale itself, must be of and concerning the same subject matter described in the petition. If the want of such conformity appears, as if the petition be in reference to one tract of land, and the decree, sale, or notice of sale, be of another and different one, then no title will pass by the sale. The proceedings, so far as the sale is concerned, will be a nullity. In *Frazier v. Steenrod*, the order of sale and the notice of sale were for entirely different tracts of land, and the court held the sale void, although the sale was of the tract described in the order, and the sale and deed had been approved by the probate court. [2]

§ 75. The principle of *caveat emptor* applies and the buyer must lookout for himself. [3] No mere error, however, or irregularity, will affect the validity of the sale on collateral inquiry. The remedy for these is by appeal, if one be by law allowed; and if not allowable, then the adjudication and proceedings are

which have an original general jurisdiction over any particular subjects; they are not courts of special or limited jurisdiction; they are not inferior courts, in the technical sense of the term, because an appeal lies from their decisions."

[1] Alabama Conference *v.* Price, 42 Ala. 49, and ante p. 33, n. 1; Cooper *v.* Sunderland, 3 Iowa, 114; Moore *v.* Niel, 39 Ill. 256; Frazier *v.* Steenrod, 7 Iowa, 339; Torrance *v.* Torrance, 53 Penn. St. 505; Long *v.* Burnett, 13 Iowa, 28; Sheldon *v.* Newton, 3 Ohio (N. S.) 495; Stokes *v.* Middleton, 4 Dutch. (N. J.) 32; Gerrard *v.* Johnson, 12 Ind. 636; Carter *v.* Waugh, 42 Ala. 452; Satcher *v.* Satcher's Admr. 41 Ala. 26.

[2] Frazier *v.* Steenrod, 7 Iowa, 340; Weed *v.* Edmonds, 4 Ind. 468; Wheatley *v.* Tutt, 4 Kan. 195.

[3] Vandevere *v.* Baker, 13 Penn. St. 126.

final, and so far as respects such errors or irregularities are valid;[1] then the record is absolute verity in all collateral proceedings if jurisdiction has properly attached.[2]

§ 76. If the court be one of general jurisdiction and the property be within its jurisdictional territorial limits, then it has power to take jurisdiction of the cause and of the subject matter. Or if it be a court of general jurisdiction, over subject matter of only a limited description, yet its jurisdiction is general *pro tanto,* and the same power exists in the court, over such subject matter, when jurisdiction has actually attached, as if the court were a court of unrestricted general jurisdiction; and the same presumptions then arise from the record as from the record of a court of full general jurisdiction.[3] And if there be no appeal, the adjudication is final.

§ 77. In either case, the court being thus clothed with legal capacity to take jurisdiction of the subject matter, then to give it actual jurisdiction and also jurisdiction of the particular case, whether *in personam,* or *in rem,* there must be filed a petition, or bill, or what else stands in lieu thereof, correctly describing and identifying the property sought to be affected, or sold, and also averring such facts as are necessary to the proper action of the court,[4] to enable it to make the

---

[1] Goudy v. Hall, 30 Ill. 109; Grignon's Lessee v. Astor, 2 How. 319, 340; Morrow v. Weed, 4 Iowa, 77; Thompson v. Tolmie, 2 Pet. 169; Todd v. Dowd, 1 Met. (Ky.) 28; Frazier v. Steenrod, 7 Iowa, 339; Pursley v. Hays, 22 Iowa, 128; Boswell v. Sharp, 15 Ohio, 447; Walker v. Morris, 14 Geo. 323; Elliott v. Piersol, 1 Pet. 340; Dingledine v. Hershman, 53 Ill. 288; Beauregard v. New Orleans, 18 How. 497.

[2] Grignon's Lessee v. Astor, 2 How. 340; Sheldon v. Newton, 3 Ohio St. 494; Beauregard v. New Orleans, 18 How. 341; Thompson v. Tolmie, 3 Pet. 165; Goudy v. Hall, 30 Ill. 109; Shriver's Lessee v. Lynn, 2 How. 43; Covington v. Ingram, 64 N. C. 123; Woods v. Lee, 21 La. An. 505; Southern Bank v. Humphreys, 47 Ill. 227; Parker v. Kane, 22 How. 14; Alexander v. Nelson, 42 Ala. 462; Dequindre v. Williams, 31 Ind. 444.

[3] Pursley v. Hays, 22 Iowa, 1; Grignon's Lessee v. Astor, 2 How. 339; Beauregard v. New Orleans, 18 How. 502, 503.

[4] Ib.; Jackson v. Robinson, 4 Wend. 436; Weed v. Edmonds, 4 Ind. 468; Finch v. Edmonson, 9 Texas, 504; Shriver's Lessee v. Lynn, 2 How. 43; Morrow v. Weed, 4 Iowa, 77; Elliott v. Piersoll, 1 Pet. 340; Satcher v. Satcher's Admr. 41 Ala. 26.

order of sale, and sale. The facts are sufficient, if good, on demurrer.

§ 78. If the proceedings be also *in personam*, with intent to bind the person of the party proceeded against, as well as to act *in rem* upon the property, as is some times the case, then there must be, to make a personal judgment valid, personal service on the owner of the property so as to get jurisdiction of the person. Without such personal service or notice, if there be no appearance, any judgment or decree *in personam* will be void. But the judgment or decree *in rem* will be binding notwithstanding.

§ 79. If however the proceeding be purely *in rem*, then such other notice, if any, as is required by the local law, must be given, and this too in addition to the filing of a petition. The latter is to confer jurisdiction of the particular case. But such notice will be inferred after decree if there is no statute requiring it to appear in the record and the contrary of its existence be not ascertainable from the record and proceedings of the case, and jurisdiction shall have actually attached by a petition with proper averments and allegations sustainable on demurrer.[1]

§ 80. If the proceedings be *in rem* for the sale of a decedent's lands, and no notice as a condition to the validity of the sale be by law required, then none is necessary to such validity, but only as against error, although a directory law may require notice. "The power of the court"[2] is over the property, or

---

[1] Grignon's Lessee v. Astor, 2 How. 319, 340; Simpson v. Hart, 1 Johns. Ch. 91; Cooper v. Sunderland, 3 Iowa, 114; Stokes v. Middleton, 4 Dutch. (N. J.) 32; Sheldon v. Newton, 3 Ohio St. 494.

[2] In Beauregard v. New Orleans, 18 How. 497, the court say: "And when the object is to sell the real estate of an insolvent or embarrassed succession, the settled doctrine is there are no adversary parties. The proceeding is *in rem*. The administrator represents the land. They are analogous to proceedings in admiralty where the only question of jurisdiction is the power of the court over the thing — the subject matter before them — without regard to the parties who may have an interest in it. All the world are parties. In the Orphans' Court and all the courts which have power to sell the estates of decedents, their action operates on the estate, not on the heirs of the intestate. A purchaser claims not their title, but one paramount. The estate passes by operation of law."

thing, before it, " without regard to the parties who may have an interest in it. All the world are parties." The estate passes then by operation of law. The power of the law lays hold of it through the court and passes the title by a right paramount to the right of heirs;[1] and as we conceive, a right which underlies all titles. The same right and power that enables the state to establish heirship and decide who shall be a dead man's heirs. That same power may well seize on, and first apply the property to payment of the decedent's debts, and leave the heirship or inheritence to be of the residue only, and to be holden by a right which the law postpones until the debts are paid.

§ 81. In Wisconsin, where the case of *Grignon's Lessee v. Astor* originated, the state courts, seemingly, repudiate the rulings in that and its kindred cases, and hold that in proceedings in probate by an administrator for sale of a decedent's lands to pay debts, the record should show notice to the heirs at law to have been given according to the requirements of the statute; and that in the absence of such showing the sale cannot be sustained, even in a collateral proceeding.[2]

[1] Grignon's Lessee *v.* Astor, 2 How. 319,338; Beauregard *v.* New Orleans, 18 How. 497, 503; Satcher *v.* Satcher's Admr. 41 Ala. 26; Sheldon *v.* Newton, 3 Ohio St. 494; McPherson *v.* Cunliffe, 11 S. & R. 432; Perkins *v.* Fairfield, 11 Mass. 227; Saltonstall *v.* Riley, 28 Ala. 164; Paine *v.* Morland, 15 Ohio, 442; Robb *v.* Irwin, 15 Ohio, 698; Benson *v.* Cilly, 8 Ohio St. 614; Borden *v.* The State, 6 Eng. 519; Tongue *v.* Morton, 6 Har. & J. 23; Rice *v.* Parkman, 16 Mass. 328; Williamson *v.* Leland, 2 Pet. 657; Sohier *v.* Mass. Genl. Hos. 3 Cush. 487.

[2] Gibbs *v.* Shaw, 17 Wis. 197. In this case, PAYNE, J., delivers the opinion of the Supreme Court of Wisconsin in the following terms: "Without passing upon any of the other objections to the validity of the sale of real estate by the first administrator, Wells, we think that sale must be held void, because the record fails to disclose any notice to the heirs at law of the time and place of hearing the application. The statute required such notice to be given before any such application should be heard. Statutes of 1839, p. 317, Sec. 29. The record offered to sustain that sale contains no proof whatever that any notice was given. The only thing upon which it could be assumed is a fragment of a recital in the order granting the license, to the effect that it appeared to the judge that the notice had been 'published in the Wisconsin Enquirer,' but leaving blanks at all the places where the facts should have been specified, show-

§ 82.   But the previous case of *Stark v. Brown*,[1] referred to in *Gibbs v. Shaw*, as basis for the latter ruling, does not accord with the latter.   It is not in point.   For although the court hold therein that to confer jurisdiction and make a valid decree and sale, the heirs must be made parties and must be brought into court by notice or by some legal means or other; yet, the case in 12th Wisconsin, in which this ruling is made, was a case of foreclosure of a mortgage, brought against the administrator of the deceased mortgagor, in which the heirs at law were not made parties, while the case of *Gibbs v. Shaw* was a proceeding in probate by the administrator to sell a decedent's lands under the statute for payment of debts.

The court expressly draw this distinction betwixt the two cases, in delivering the opinion in *Stark v. Brown*, and decline to discuss or decide upon the correctness of the ruling in *Grignon's Lessee v. Astor*.[2]   To illustrate which we subjoin in a note so much of the opinion in *Stark v. Brown* as bears upon that point.[3]

ing such publication to have been according to the statute.   And without determining whether a complete recital of all the facts necessary to show a proper notice in an order granting a license by a probate judge would be sufficient to sustain the proceedings, in the absence of any other proof of notice in the record, it seems clear that such a recital as this cannot be so, it being evidently incomplete on its face, and failing to show or even recite the necessary facts.   The question then is, whether an administrator's sale, under a license from the probate court, can be sustained where the record fails to show notice to the heirs at law as required by statute?   And we are of the opinion that it cannot be.   There may be some cases where it is intimated that such notice is not jurisdictional.   But we regard the opposite doctrine as established by the weight of authority, and resting upon the soundest principles, and that it is also established that the records of probate courts must show jurisdiction in order to sustain their proceedings."

[1] 12 Wis. 582.

[2] Stark v. Brown, 12 Wis. 572, 582, 583.   One class of these cases—sales in probate—rest on the paramount power of the courts and of the law; the other case—Stark v. Brown—rests in a mortgage contract.

[3] "Counsel relied upon the case of Grignon's Lessee v. Astor, 2 How. 319, as establishing the proposition 'that in a proceeding to sell the real estate of an indebted intestate, there are no adversary parties, the proceeding is *in rem*, and the administrator represents the land,' etc.   It is true that the court, in that case, asserted that doctrine, and held that the

§ 83. Now, the state court case, which seemingly overruled *Grignon's Lessee v. Astor*, is not a parallel case; being a case for foreclosure of a mortgage it rested in contract and was prosecuted in the court of general chancery jurisdiction according to the practice in adverse litigation, whilst that of Grignon's Lessee and its kindred cases are conducted in probate, under the special enactments conferring probate powers over the land of a decedent.

§ 84. Notwithstanding these rulings, some of which are by the highest court in the nation, and which we conceive to be the better doctrine, there are numerous decisions to the

provision in the statute requiring notice to be given to the parties interested before the court should pass upon the application, did not affect its jurisdiction. Whether that is the law or not in this state with respect to sales by administrators, we shall not now attempt to decide. It is certainly not in conformity with a long list of adjudications that might be cited, among which are the following: Bloom *v.* Burdick, 1 Hill, 130; Sherry *v.* Denn, 8 Blackf. 542; Given *v.* McCarrol, 7 S. & M. 351; Lessees of Adams *v.* Jeffries, 12 Ohio, 253; Messenger *v.* Kintner, 4 Bin. 97; Schneider *v.* McFarland, 2 Comst. 459; Bank *v.* Johnson and others, 7 S. & M. 449. But we do not feel called upon to discuss the correctness of that decision for the reason that it must be held to relate only to a proceeding by an administrator, under the statute, to sell the real estate for the payment of debts. When the court said that the administrator represented the land, they meant in that proceeding. And it would be entirely unwarrantable to say that they intended to assert that he represented it for all purposes, so that a foreclosure suit, to which he alone was a party, would divest the right of the heirs. There is a great difference between the two cases. In the one the statute expressly authorizes and requires him to proceed for the purpose of making a sale. The design is to pay the debts of the estate, which is one of his most important duties. In the other case it is conceded that there is no statute expressly requiring or authorizing him to be made a party to a foreclosure, and his character as a representative of the land for that purpose is sought to be derived entirely from the rights which the law gives him as to the possession and as to obtaining a license to sell on a certain contingency. Even if the case in 2d Howard should be held to establish the doctrine that on the direct statutory proceeding by him to effect a sale for the payment of debts, he is to be considered as the representative of the land for all the parties interested, so that the judgment would not be void, though such other parties had no notice, we do not by any means think it can have that effect with respect to foreclosure suits, or any other, by which the title to property is sought to be affected."

contrary, wherein it is held that jurisdiction is in all cases alike necessary over both the subject matter of the proceeding and of the persons of those in interest; and, therefore, decrees and sales without jurisdiction in some manner first obtained, as well of the person, as of the particular case, are simply void.[1]

§ 85.   This question as to the necessity of personal jurisdiction in probate for sale of a decedent's lands came up in the Iowa Supreme Court, at December term, 1869, in *Good v. Norley.*[2]

After great deliberation and a full investigation of the adjudications, the court were equally divided as to whether jurisdiction of the person of those in interest is necessary, under the Iowa statute, to the validity of an administrator's sale of lands for payment of a decedent's debts. By reason of such diversity of opinion the decree appealed from was affirmed, and, also, by one of the Justices deciding that jurisdiction had attached in the probate court over the persons of those now appealing to the Supreme Court.

IV.   The Title Passes by Operation of Law.

§ 86.   The title passes to the purchaser at judicial sale by operation of law.[3]   So it does from the ancestor to the heir,[4]

---

[1] French v. Hoyt, 6 N. H. 370; Dakin v. Hudson, 6 Cow. 222; Babbit v. Doe, 4 Ind. 356; Doe v. Anderson, 5 Ind. 34; Sibley v. Wells, 16 N. Y. 185; Doe v. Bowen, 8 Ind. 198; Bloom v. Burdick, 1 Hill. 140; Shelden v. Wright, 1 Seld. 518; Ridgway v. Coles, 6 Bosw. 486; Corwin v. Merritt, 3 Barb. 341; Stark v. Brown, 12 Wis. 572; Stelzman v. Pacquette, 13 Wis. 291; Gibson v. Shaw, 17 Wis. 197.

[2] Good v. Norley, 27 Iowa, 188. (See a more particular statement of this case, post. c. IV, No. 4.)

[3] 3 Bouvier, 131, 132; McPherson v. Cunliff, 11 S. & R. 423; Grignon's Lessee v. Astor, 2 How. 338; Shelden v. Newton, 3 Ohio St. 494; Holloway v. Richardson, 13 Ill. 171.

[4] Bank of Hamilton v. Dudley's Lessee, 2 Pet. 523; Drinkwater v. Drinkwater's Admr. 4 Mass. 358; Shelden v. Newton, 3 Ohio St. 474; Holloway v. Richardson, 13 Ill. 171.

but subject first to the paramount right of government, through its courts, to apply it to payment of ancestral debts,[1] without notice to any one, if such shall be the legislative policy.

§ 87. The government has the same power to direct the sale of lands for debts, before or after the owner's death, as it has to declare heirship by law, without which there would be no heirship and no inheritence. We conceive that the power to do the one and the other, and also to make sales in partition, is found in a paramount right in government which underlies all title, and to which all title is subject, for the public good.[2]

[1] Bank of Hamilton v. Dudley's Lessee, 2 Pet. 532; Nowell v. Nowell, 8 Greenl. 222; Drinkwater v. Drinkwater's Admr. 4 Mass. 358; Vansyckle v. Richardson, 13 Ill. 171; Wolf v. Robinson, 20 Mo. 459; Stillman v. Young, 16 Ill. 318; Shelden v. Newton, 3 Ohio St. 494; (twice) Wilkinson v. Leland, 2 Pet. 627; Watkins v. Holman, 16 Pet. 25; Gore v. Brazier, 3 Mass. 523.

[2] In Vansyckle v. Richardson, 13 Ill. 173, the court say: "The real estate descends to the heir with this charge resting upon it. He cannot incumber or alien it to the prejudice of the rights of creditors. He acquires a vested, but not an absolute interest in the land. He takes a defeasable estate, liable to be defeated by a sale made by the administrator in the due course of administration. He has no just claim to the land until the indebtedness of his ancestor is fully discharged. He acquires an absolute title only to what remains after the debts are extinguished."

CHAPTER IV.

THE SALE.

I. By whom to be Made.

§ 88. It is a general principle, applicable to all judicial sales, that they are to be conducted, unless differently provided by statute, by a person designated for that purpose in the license, order, or decree, or under his immediate direction and superintendence, but he may employ an auctioneer to cry the sale if it be done in his presence.[1]

§ 89. "Such sales," says the court, in *Blossom v. Railroad Company*,[2] "must be made by the person designated in the decree, or under his immediate direction and supervision, but he may employ an auctioneer to conduct the sale, if it be made in his presence."

§ 90. And a subsequent part of the same decision the court

---

[1] Williamson v. Berry, 8 How. 495, 544; Blossom v. R. R. Co. 3 Wall. 205; Reynolds v. Wilson, 15 Ill. 394; Heyer v. Deaves, 2 Johns. Ch. 154; Gould v. Garrison, 48 Ill. 260. The decree must be conformed to and the statute regulating execution sales does not apply. Blakely v. Abert, 1 Dana, 185.

[2] 3 Wall. 205.

say: "Judicial sales are always regarded as under the control of the court, subject to the power to set them aside, or to open the biddings at any time before the sale is confirmed, if there be proper ground for such interference;" and that " even after the sale is made, it is not final until a report is made to the court and it is approved and confirmed."[1]

II. How to be Made.

§ 91. The sale is to be at public auction, and to the highest real bidder[2] unless it be otherwise authorized by the court, as is sometimes done. It must be for cash, unless the court order other terms, which it may do if deemed more beneficial to those in interest.[3] But it must be for money, whether for cash in hand or on a credit. If the transaction should be for any other consideration it would be but a barter.[4]

§ 92. "Sale," say the Supreme Court of the United States, " is a word of legal import both at law and in equity. It means at all times a contract between parties to give and to pass rights of property for money, which the buyer pays, or promises to pay, to the seller, for the thing bought and sold."[5] In the same case, *Williamson v. Berry*, the court, further, as to the manner of selling, say:

"The usual mode of selling property under decree or order in chancery is a direction that it shall be sold with the approval of a master in chancery, to whom the execution of the decree

[1] Ibid.

[2] Veazie v. Williams, 8 How. 134; 2 Kent, Com. 537, 538.

[3] Foster v. Thomas, 21 Conn. 285; Reynolds v. Wilson, 15 Ill. 396; Sedgwick v. Fish, Hop. Ch. 594.

[4] Sedgwick v. Fish, Hop. Ch. 594; Wilson v. Reynolds, 15 Ill. 394; Maples v. How, 3 Barb. Ch. 611; Foster v. Thomas, 21 Conn. 285; Williamson v. Berry, 8 How. 496, 544; Noy, Max. Ch. 42; Bigley v. Risher, 63 Penn. St. 155; Hushmacker v. Harris' Admr. 2 Wright, Pa. 498; Hilliard, Sales, 1230; Shep. Touch. 244.

[5] Williamson v. Berry, 8 How. 496, 544; Noy, Max. Ch. 42, Risley v. Richer, 63 Penn. St. 155; Hushmacker v. Harris' Admr. 2 Wright, Pa. 498; Hilliard, Sales, 1230; Sedgwick v. Fish, Hop. Ch. 594. By the court: "The suggestion that credit may produce a higher price is equally applicable to all sales. But judicial sales are not in general made on credit without the consent of parties."

in that particular has been confided. It matters not whether the sale is public or private by a person authorized to make it. Not that the approbation of the master in either case completes a title to the purchaser. It is only the master's approval of the sale, and is one step towards getting a title. Before however, he can get a title, he must get a report from the master that he approves the sale, or that he was the best bidder, accordingly as the sale may have been made privately or at auction. That report then becomes the basis of a motion to the court by the purchaser that his purchase may be confirmed."[1]   *   *   *

§ 93.   The court then, after laying down certain premises not material to our immediate subject, adds, that "we have been thus particular," (in reference to the sale and the master's duties,) "for the purpose of showing the office of the master in relation to a sale, and what is meant by subjecting a sale to the approval of a master, and to show that such a sale until approved by the master and confirmed by the court, gives no title to a purchaser of an estate which he may have bargained to buy.   We do not mean to say that such cautionary proceedings upon sales under decrees and orders in chancery may not be dispensed with by a special order of the chancellor to pretermit them, but that such are the proceedings when no special order has been given."[2]

§ 94.   Several persons may join together and lawfully bid as a unit if done in good faith.   "It is not every joint bidder or partnership among bidders at a sale under a decree in chancery (say the court in *Holmes v. Holmes*,) that is corrupt and fraudulent.   Such joint or partnership bidding may be perfectly legitimate."[3]

---

[1] Williamson *v.* Berry, 8 How. 546.
[2] Williamson *v.* Berry, 8 How. 546.
[3] Holmes *v.* Holmes, 3 Rich. Eq. 61; Smith *v.* Greenlee, 2 Dev. 128; National Bank *v.* Sprague, 20 N. J. 159, 169. In the case of Holmes *v.* Holmes, it is said: "To render them unlawful and void, there must be a fraudulent intent to depress and chill the sale, to obtain the property at an under value, or to obtain other undue and unconscientious advantages. An estate might be offered for sale which neither of two joint bidders would be able separately to purchase.   Or, it might be that neither of two joint bidders, though able as to pecuniary means, would desire to pur-

§ 95. But combinations to advance or reduce the price of the property, and all by-bidding, is illegal and fraudulent.[1] A minimum price may be fixed and made public below which the property will not be allowed to go, and if made public it will not be legally objectionable. But without being made public it is in itself fraudulent.[2]

§ 96. By-bidding is fraudulent. It deceives. It misleads. It involves a falsehood. In the language of the United States Supreme Court, in *Veazie v. Williams*,[3] it "violates, too, a leading condition of the contract of sales at auction, which is that the article shall be knocked off to the highest real bidder without puffing,"

§ 97. The court will sometimes appoint a bidding to prevent an estate from going under value, on special showings to the court.[4]

§ 98. Judicial sales are in no wise subject to the operation of either valuation laws or redemption laws fixed by statute relative to sales at law on writs of execution,[5] unless the statute declare them so.

§ 99. In *Woods v. Monell*,[6] Chancellor KENT lays down the rule in execution sale, "that where a tract of land is in parcels, distinctly marked for separate and distinct enjoyment, it is in general the duty of the officer to sell by parcels, and not the whole tract, in one entire sale.

This rule had been previously asserted in *Rowley v. Webb*,

chase the whole of the estate offered for sale, though each would be desirous to become the owner of a part. Such persons, if not permitted to unite in their bidding would not enter into the competition at all. To adopt so stringent a rule as that contended for, in reference to sales in chancery, would, in many instances, have the effect of diminishing, instead of enhancing the prices."

[1] Veazie v. Williams, 8 How. 154; Holmes v. Holmes, 3 Rich. Eq. 61.
[2] Veazie v. Williams, 8 How. 153; 2 Kent, Com. 538, 539. Ross on Sales, 311.
[3] Veazie v. Williams, 8 How. 154; 2 Kent, Com. 538, 539.
[4] 2 Daniels Chy. 1448.
[5] Blakely v. Abert, 1 Dana, 185; Gould v. Garrison, 48 Ill. 258.
[6] 1 Johns. Ch. 505.

in *Executors of Stead v. Course*, and is referred to by Chancellor Kent with approbation in Woods *v.* Monell.[1]

§ 100. Unless there be special reasons to the contrary, (or the court otherwise direct,) the sale, when made in parcels, should be made in such order as the debtor may desire.[2]

§ 101. It is the duty of the person selling to sell in such order as will be likely to produce the largest amount for the smallest quantity of lands, in his best judgment. But he must exercise a sound discretion.

Ordinarily, where a judicial sale of several lots or parcels of land is being made to satisfy a money decree, it is the duty of the referee or person conducting the sale, not only to sell in parcels, but to also respect the wishes of the debtor as to the order in which the lots should be sold, if there is no good reason to believe such order of sale will prove injurious.[3]

§ 102. And if the debtor and creditor cannot agree upon the order in which the property shall be sold, either party may apply to the court for instructions to the referee, and if deemed proper they will be given.[4] Such sales proceed under the control and supervision of the court, and it will "scrutinize the conduct of a party" placed in a position where he may sacrifice the interest of another in a manner not easily to detect. "The unfortunate debtor," say the court, in *King v. Platt*, "is not beneath its protection." And, "it will not tolerate the slightest advantage over him."[5]

§ 103. "It is clearly competent for the court to prescribe the mode and terms" of sale, "provided it requires as much of the executor or administrator as the statute contemplates," and these requirements must be conformed to by the person

---

[1] Am. Ins. Co. *v.* Oakly, 9 Paige, 259; Wood *v.* Monell, 1 Johns. Ch. 505; Runyon *v.* N. Ark. In. Rub. Co. 4 Zabr. 473; Penn *v.* Craig, 1 Green. Ch. 495; Mohawk Bk. *v.* Atwater, 2 Paige, 54; Meeker *v.* Evans, 25 Ill. 322; Rowley *v.* Webb, 1 Binney, 61; Executors of Stead *v.* Course, 4 Cranch, 309; Laughlin *v.* Schuyler, 1 Neb. 409.

[2] King *v.* Platt, 37 N. Y. 155.

[3] King *v.* Platt, 37 N. Y. 155; Cauffman *v.* Sayre, 2 B. Mon. 309.

[4] King *v.* Platt, 37 N. Y. 155,

[5] Ibid. and Collier *v.* Whipple, 13 Wend. 229, 230.

conducting the sale.[1] And so, also, in regard to the place of sale.[2] If made at a different place than the one ordered, it will be invalid; the purchaser cannot enforce it, if opposed, and will not be compelled to perfect it if he objects.[3] And, quere, if even confirmation of a sale so made at an unauthorized place, will render it valid.[4] If the manner and time of sale are not prescribed by the decree, then they are vested in the sound discretion of the person or officer selling.[5]

§ 104. So far as the terms and conditions of sale are not regulated by the decree, the master or person charged with the conduct of the sale may "adopt such means to prevent sham bidding" as have a tendency to promote fairness and to prevent fraud, and which may give confidence to fair and honest bidders as to their being justly dealt with.[6]

But all such regulations, as also the action and conduct of the person conducting the sale, are subject to the scrutiny of the court, whose judicial sanction thereof may be given, or denied, at discretion, and confirmation ordered or refused accordingly.

§ 105. A sale made under the statute of Indiana which submits the matter of selling in parcels to the judgment of the officer or person conducting the sale, will not be set aside by reason of the land not being sold in parcels, unless it be made to appear that the action of the officer was in that respect fraudulent.

Unless it be made to appear that the officer selling acted otherwise than in accordance with his honest judgment, and in a fraudulent manner, the purchaser has a right to the benefit of his purchase.[7]

§ 106. When separate parcels of land are contiguous to

[1] Reynolds v. Wilson, 15 Ill. 394; Wheatly v. Tutt, 4 Kan. 195; Gould v. Garrison, 48 Ill. 258; Williamson v. Berry, 8 How. 544.
[2] Tally v. Starke, 6 Gratt. 339.
[3] Tally v. Starke, 6 Gratt. 339; Bethel v. Bethel, 6 Bush (Ky.) 65, 69.
[4] Minnesota Co. v. St. Paul Co. 2 Wall. 609; Bethel v. Bethel, 6 Bush (Ky.) 65.
[5] Blossom v. R. R. Co. 3 Wall. 196, 208.
[6] National Bank of the Metropolis v. Sprague, 20 N. J. Eq. 159, 165, 166.
[7] Wright v. Yetts, 30 Ind. 185, 188.

4

each other, and being properly offered, no bid is received for them separately, they may then be sold together; but subject to the discretion of the court ordering the sale.[1]

III. Who may not Buy.

§ 107. The person selling may not buy. Nor any person concerned or employed in selling, unless by leave obtained from the court.

The rule is sweeping, and extends to all agents, commissioners, trustees, guardians, administrators, executors, and others, whether selling under decree, or order of court, or otherwise, where others are interested in the property or in the proceeds of sale. They cannot be buyer and seller; bidder and crier; or combine other like incompatible capacities in one and the same transaction; common honesty and morality forbid it.[2]

§ 108. In *Michoud v. Girod*,[3] the Supreme Court of the United States characterize this principle in the following language: "The rule, as expressed, embraces every relation in which there may arise a conflict between the duty which the vendor, or purchaser, owes to the person with whom he is dealing, or on whose account he is acting, and his own individual interest." The general rule, the court say, "Stands upon the great moral obligation to refrain from placing ourselves in relations which ordinarily excite a conflict between self-interest and integrity." In such conflict the law interposes

---

[1] Martin v. Hargadine, 46 Ill. 322.

[2] Davoe v. Fanning, 2 Johns. Ch. 252; Michoud v. Girod and others, 4 How. 555; Wormsley v. Wormsley, 8 Wheat. 421; Ringo v. Binns, 10 Pet. 269; Oliver v. Piatt, 3 How. 333; Kruse v. Steffens, 47 Ill. 114; McConnell v. Gibson, 12 Ill. 128; Thorp v. McCullum, 1 Gilm. 627; Pensonneau v. Bleakly, 14 Ill. 15; Wickliff v. Robinson, 18 Ill. 145; Robbins v. Butler, 24 Ill. 387; Dennis v. McCagg, 32 Ill. 429; Miles v. Wheeler, 43 Ill. 123. "The fact that the person entrusted by the law to make the sale becomes the purchaser, whether by direct or indirect means, creates such a presumption of fraud as requires the sale to be vacated if application is made in proper time. The rule is regarded as firmly established by this court, and it is deemed unnecessary to review the authorities or to discuss the reason of the rule." Kruse v. Steffens, 47 Ill. 114, 115.

[3] Michoud v. Girod, 4 How. 503. See, also, Wormsley v. Wormsley, 8 Wheat. 421; Prevost v. Gratz, 6 Wheat. 481.

and prohibits the party from selling to himself, and buying from himself, that which his duty requires him to sell for account of others.

§ 109. Such is the doctrine laid down in the case of *Michoud v. Girod* after a careful examination and review of the conflicting cases, and which the court lay down as not only the rule in England, but that which, since the decision in *Davoe v. Fanning*,[1] has triumphed "over all qualifications and relaxations in the United States to the same extent that has been achieved for it in England by the great chancellor, Lord ELDON." Such purchases are now uniformly regarded by courts, both of law and equity, as not only against the policy of the law, as has been said, but also as against the law itself, and as totally inconsistent with fair dealing.

They can in no case be maintained unless made by leave of the court, on formal application therefor.[2]

§ 110. One whose duty it is to discharge a debt, or any portion thereof, may not buy at a sale brought about by his own dereliction of duty in not paying as his obligation requires.

Thus, where the cashier of a bank bought, at the sale for a debt which the bank was bound to pay for the debtor, it was held, that whether he purchased for himself, or for the bank, the sale could not stand. The court, in disposing of the question, say: "The general interests of justice" require "that purchases made by persons holding a fiduciary situation in relation to the sale, should be set aside in all cases, if application is made in a reasonable time," and that the purchaser could not be permitted to hold his purchase.[3] It were a fraud upon the debtor for those whose duty to him required them to pay the debt, to buy at a sale caused by their own default.

[1] 2 Johns. Ch. 252.
[2] Michoud v. Girod, 4 How. 503; Wormsley v. Wormsley, 8 Wheat. 241; Prevost v. Gratz, 6 Wheat. 481; Benedict v. Butterfield, 11 Foster (N. H.) 70; Beeson v. Beeson, 9 Barr. 297.
[3] Torrey v. The Bank of Orleans, 9 Paige, 649.

IV. Notice of Sale. Adjournment.

§ 111. The notice of sale, as to manner and time, must be such as the order and statute directs, and must correctly describe the property. If given different in manner, or for less time than required by the law or the decree, the sale will be void; and so, if there be a substantial misdescription of the property.[1]

§ 112. But if the discrepancy is not apparent in the proceedings, or is not made to appear by other evidence, the presumption of law is, after the sale is confirmed, that no such discrepancy existed; and, therefore, this presumption, after confirmation, may not be rebutted in a collateral proceeding.[2]

§ 113. Notices by posting up in public places, are presumed to perish as soon as they have "discharged their office." Therefore, secondary evidence of them and their purport is admissible.[3]

§ 114. Where notice was given in the particular manner required, and there were no bidders, an adjourned sale made on a slightly variant notice, but from fair motives, was held valid.[4]

§ 115. But if there is no particular notice prescribed by the decree, then such reasonable notice should be given as will be calculated to give publicity and secure fair competition; and if the character of the notice given be of doubtful sufficiency the court should refuse confirmation.[5]

[1] Reynolds v. Wilson, 15 Ill. 394; Frazier v. Steenrod, 7 Iowa, 339.

[2] Thompson v. Tolmie, 2 Pet. 157; Parker v. Kane, 22 How. 14; Beauregard v. New Orleans, 18 How. 497; Grignon's Lessee v. Astor, 2 How. 319; Morrow v. Weed, 4 Iowa, 77; Little v. Sennett, 7 Iowa, 324; Long v. Bennett, 13 Iowa, 28.

[3] Brown v. Redwyne, 16 Geo. 67.

[4] Farmers' Bank v. Clarke, 28 Md. 145.

[5] Sowards v. Pritchett, 37 Ill. 517, 524; Trustees of Schools v. Snell, 19 Ill. 156. "It is a cherished object of courts to give stability to judicial sales, and at the same time, as far as possible, protect and guard the rights of the owner. In all such cases the chancellor is necessarily vested with a large discretion, and he must so exercise it as will promote justice and protect the rights of parties. And in the exercise of that discretion this court will not interfere if it seems to have been soundly exercised." Sowards v. Pritchett, 37 Ill. 524.

§ 116. The officer making the sale may adjourn it, in the exercise of a reasonable discretion, with honest intent and in good faith, and with a view to a faithful performance of his duty (unless restricted by law).[1]

§ 117. In the leading case cited, *Blossom v. The R. R. Company*, the court say that such is the rule in execution sales at law, "and no reason is perceived why the same rule may not be safely applied in judicial sales made under the decretal order of a court of chancery."[2] And in *Richards v. Holmes*, they hold that a sale, "regularly adjourned, so as to give notice to all persons present of the time and place to which it is adjourned, is, when made, in effect the sale, of which previous public notice was given."[3]

§ 118. That the person or officer who is authorized to sell at public auction, after proper notice of the time and place of sale, may regularly and legally adjourn the sale to a different time and a different place, when in his fairly exercised discretion it shall seem necessary, in order to obtain a fair auction price for the property, is too well settled to remain a matter of doubt, subject always, however, to the scrutiny and wise discretion of the court ordering the sale, as to the confirmation thereof.[4]

§ 119. In the language of the United States Supreme Court, "If he has not this power, the elements, or many unexpected occurrences, may prevent an attendance of bidders and cause an inevitable sacrifice of the property. It is a power which every prudent owner would exercise in his own behalf, under the circumstances supposed, and which he may well be presumed to intend to confer on another." And in the same case, "The courts of the several states have gone further in this direction than we find it necessary, though we do not intend to intimate any doubt of the correctness of their decisions. They

[1] Blossom v. R. R. Co. 3 Wall. 209; Collier v. Whipple, 13 Wend. 229; Brown v. Redwyne, 16 Geo. 67.

[2] Blossom v. R. R. Co. 3 Wall. 209.

[3] 18 How. 147; Tinkom v. Purdy, 5 Johns. 345; Russell v. Richards, 11 Maine, 371; Warren v. Leland, 9 Mass. 265; Lautz v. Worthington, 4 Barr, 153.

[4] Richards v. Holmes, 18 How. 147.

have held that a public officer, upon whom a power of sale is conferred by law, may adjourn an advertised public sale to a different time and place, for the purpose of obtaining a better price for the property. *Tinkom v. Purdy*, 5 Johns. 345; *Russell v. Richards*, 11 Maine, 371; *Lautz v. Worthington*, 4 Barr, 153; *Warren v. Leland*, 9 Mass. 265.[1] "

§ 120. The case of *Richards v. Holmes* arose on a sale by a trustee, under a deed of trust and not on a judicial decree. But the United States Supreme Court distinctly therein recognize the rule that officers selling under proceedings in court may adjourn the sale, and therefore the court assume that the trustee selected by the debtor himself may, by inference, do the same. But we would not be understood as claiming that the officer may, as a general rule, adjourn to a different place than the one named in the decree, if a place be named therein. Yet, even under such circumstances, sales have been allowed and confirmed by the courts.[2]

§ 121. The notice of a judicial sale, if no time be fixed by the decree, should name the hour of the day at which the sale is to be made, or certain hours betwixt which it will take place, fixing the time in the ordinary business hours of the day; and the place of sale should be a convenient or public place, accessible to bidders.

When sale has been made under a notice which did not specify any hour or certain time of day for the sale, and the property was sold for a nominal sum, the sale was set aside.[3]

---

[1] Richards *v.* Holmes, 18 How. 144, 147.

[2] Farmers' Bank *v.* Clarke, 28 Md. 145.

[3] Trustees of Schools, etc., *v.* Snell, 19 Ill. 156. In this case, SKINNER, Justice, said: "This was a motion to set aside a sale of land made on foreclosure of a mortgage. The Circuit Court set the sale aside. The decree directed the master to sell upon four weeks' notice of the time, terms, and place of sale, published in a newspaper printed in the city of Pekin. The notice, published on the 4th of December, 1856, stated that the sale would be made on 'the 2d day of January next.' The proof showed that the property was sold at an enormous sacrifice. The notice as to the time of sale was insufficient. The 2d day of January included the astronomical period of a revolution of the earth upon its axis twenty-four hours. 2 Blackstone's Com. 141, and notes; 1 Cowen's Treatise, 297. The sale, therefore, might, consistently with the notice, have been made

V. Confirmation.

§ 122. Confirmation is the judicial sanction of the court. Until then the bargain is incomplete. When made it relates back to the time of sale and " supplies all defects,"[1] except those founded in defect of jurisdiction or in fraud.

§ 123. A sale of lands under a decree of a court not having jurisdiction of the subject matter is void and is not the less so for being confirmed.[2]

§ 124. Until confirmed by the court, the sale confers no rights. Until then it is a sale only in a popular, and not in a judicial or legal sense. The chancellor has a broad discretion in the approval or disapproval of such sales. "The accepted bidder," (say the Supreme Court of Kentucky,) "acquires by the mere acceptance of his bid no independent right, as in the case of a purchaser under execution, to have his purchase completed;" but is merely a preferred proposer, until confirmation of the sale by the court, as agreed to by its "ministerial agent." In the exercise of this discretion a proper regard is had to the interest of the parties and the stability of judicial sales.[3] By sanctioning the sale the courts make it their

immediately before midnight of that day, and if it was so made, it is voidable. The object of a public sale is, by fairness and competition, to evolve the full value of the property exposed, and produce that value in the form of money. This can, as a general rule, only be done by making the sale at a convenient or public place, accessible to bidders, and during the ordinary business hours of the day. The notice should have stated the hour of sale, or that the sale would be made between certain named hours of the business portion of the day. Decree affirmed."

[1] Branch's *Principia*, 28; Cockey *v.* Cole, 28 Md. 276; Koehler *v.* Ball, 2 Kan. 160, 172; Williamson *v.* Berry, 8 How. 546.

[2] Shriver's Lessee *v.* Lynn, 2 How. 43, 59, 60; 2 Bouvier, 415; Minnesota R. R. Co. *v.* St. Paul, 2 Wall. 609.

[3] Bussey *v.* Hardin, 2 B. Mon. 407; Taylor *v.* Gilpin. 3 Met. (Ky.) 544: Southern Bank *v.* Humphreys, 47 Ill. 227: Williamson *v.* Berry, 8 How. 547; Thorn *v.* Ingram, 25 Ark. 52; Mason *v.* Osgood, 64 N. C. 467; Moore *v.* Shultz, 13 Penn. St. 102; Hays' Appeal, 51 Penn. St. 58; Sowards *v.* Pritchett, 37 Ill. 517; Young *v.* Keogh, 11 Ill. 642; Ayres *v.* Baumgartner, 15 Ill. 444; Foreman *v.* Hunt, 3 Dana, 622; Campbell *v.* Johnson, 4 Dana, 186. In Hays' Appeal, 51 Penn. St. 61, the court say: "Even the highest bidder, whose bid has been returned to the court as the best offered, has acquired no right which debars the heirs or the counsel from endeavoring

own. There is a difference between such sales and ordinary auction sales and sales by private agreement. In the latter, says Daniel in his Chancery Practice, "the contract is complete when the agreement is signed; but a different rule prevails in sales before a master. In such cases the purchaser is not considered as entitled to the benefit of his contract till the master's report of the purchaser's bidding is absolutely confirmed." Such is the rule whether the sale be by a master, commissioner, or other person or functionary authorized by the court to conduct the sale. The bargain is not ordinarily considered as complete until the sale is confirmed and the conveyance is made.[1]

§ 125. But, although there be no confirmation, if the deed be made and delivered, accompanied by possession of the premises, time may, and if sufficiently long will operate to confirm and ratify the sale, and will cure the title of the purchaser.[2]

§ 126. The court is clothed with an unlimited discretion to confirm a judicial sale or not, as may seem wise and just. Confirmation is final consent; and the court being the vendor,

to have his bid rejected and a resale ordered. It is their right to have as much obtained for the property as can be, and until a sale has been made and confirmed, they may seek for purchasers who are willing to give more than was offered at the public auction. They may ask the court to open the biddings, to order a new exposure of the property at auction. His bid, though the highest, was but an offer to purchase, subject to the approval or disapproval of the court, and in approving sales made in partition it is the duty of the court to regard primarily the interest of the heirs."

[1] 2 Daniel, Ch. 1454; Rawlings v. Bailey, 15 Ill. 178; Blossom v. R. R. Co. 3 Wall. 207; Childress v. Hust, 2 Swan (Tenn.) 487; Williamson v. Berry, 8 How. 496; Vallee v. Fleming, 19 Mo. 454; Webster v. Hill, 3 Sneed (Tenn.) 333; Henderson v. Herrod, 23 Miss. (1 Cush.) 434; Gowan v. Jones, 10 S. & M. 164; Young v. Keogh, 11 Ill. 642; Wallace v. Hale, 19 Ala. 367; Robinson's Appeal, 62 Penn. St. 216; Hays' Appeal, 51 Penn. St. 58; Koehler v. Ball, 2 Kan. 160, 172; Young v. Keogh, 11 Ill. 642; Ayres v. Baumgartner, 15 Ill. 444; Lischy v. Gardner, 3 W. & Sergt. 314; Erb v. Erb. 9 W. & Sergt. 147; Webster v. Hill, 3 Sneed (Tenn.) 333; Dickenson v. Talbot, 14 B. Mon. 60; Rawlings v. Bailey, 15 Ill. 178; Ayres v. Baumgartner, 15 Ill. 444.

[2] Gowan v. Jones, 10 S. & M. 164.

it may consent or not, at its discretion;[1] but it cannot change the terms of sale and then confirm. Such act would have no validity.[2]

§ 127. But confirmation, when made by the court, though subsequent to the day of sale, relates back to the date of the sale, if the date of sale is apparent of record or in the deed, and carries title as from that date.[3] Confirmation cures all mere irregularities.[4] Such relation, however, as well as the validity of the transaction is dependant upon the jurisdiction of the court; for if the court has not obtained jurisdiction so as to enable it to decree, or having jurisdiction, and the sale be of lands not decreed to be sold or described in the decree, then, in either event, confirmation will not give validity; the sale will be void.[5]

§ 128. The matter of confirmation rests so peculiarly upon the wise discretion of the court, in view of all the surrounding facts and circumstances, to be exercised in the interest of fairness, prudence, and the rights of all concerned, that it is difficult to come at any absolute legal rule on the subject other than that of a sound legal discretion.[6]

§ 129. Any mistake or misunderstanding between the persons conducting the sale and intended bidders or parties in interest, and any accident, fraud, or other circumstance by which interests are prejudiced without the fault of the injured party or parties, or by reason whereof property is sold at an under price considerably disproportioned to its real value, will be deemed sufficient cause for refusing confirmation and for ordering a resale.[7] And so, generally, whatever, and even

---

[1] Ohio L. and T. Co. v. Goodin, 10 Ohio St. (N. S.) 557; Davis v. Stewart, 4 Texas, 223; Henderson v. Herrod, 23 Miss. (1 Cushm.) 434; Glenn v. Wotten, 3 Md. Ch. Decis. 514; Andrews v. Scotten, 2 Bland, 643; Cunningham v. Schley, 6 Gill, 207; Harrison v. Harrison, 1 Md. Ch. Decis. 331.

[2] Ohio L. and T. Co. v. Goodin, 10 Ohio St. (N. S.) 557; Benz v. Hines, 3 Kansas, 390.

[3] Evans v. Spurgin, 6 Gratt. 107; Wagner v. Cohen, 6, Gill, 97.

[4] Harrison v. Harrison, 1 Md. Ch. Decis. 331.

[5] Schriver's Lessee v. Lynn, 2 How. 43; Townsend v. Tallant, 33 Cal. 45.

[6] Henderson v. Herrod, 23 Miss. (1 Cushm.) 434; Sowards v. Pritchett, 37 Ill. 517.

[7] Cohen v. Wagner, 6 Gill, 236; Latrobe v. Herbert 3 Md. Ch. Decis. 375.

less, than is sufficient to set a sale aside after its consummation will of course, upon the same principle, (if known,) cause confirmation to be denied.

§ 130. In California, where, it seems, that personal jurisdiction of those in interest, is required in procuring decrees in probate for sale of a decedent's land by the administrator, it is held that without such jurisdiction the sale is void,[1] and will be so held in a collateral proceeding. So likewise is void any order of confirmation of such a sale, the order of sale itself being void.[2]

§ 131. In an application of the administrator to sell lands of an estate wherein he is also guardian of the heir, if personal notice to the heir is necessary by law, then the relations of administrator and guardian are antagonistic, and he cannot perfect a legal sale in acting for both.[3]

§ 132. The order of confirmation is in the nature of a final order, judgment or decree, and may be appealed from.[4] If there is jurisdiction, and the law allows no appeal, then it is final to the like extent as other judgments and decisions from which no appeal is allowed, are final. It cannot be assailed in a collateral proceeding. It is a judicial decision that the sale is properly made so far as facts appear on the officer's return.

§ 133. In some of the States, as in Kansas, the legal and the equitable jurisdictions and practice are so mingled into a

---

[1] Townsend v. Tallant, 33 Cal. 45.

[2] Townsend v. Tallant, 33 Cal. 45. By the court: "Again, the defendants insist that the sale having been confirmed by the probate court, cannot be collaterally attacked in this action, but that as against the plaintiff the confirmation is conclusive that the court had jurisdiction of both subject matter and parties. But if the order of sale was *coram non judici*, then the 'sale' was no sale, and it could not be made valid and binding by any number of so-called confirmations. The sale being void, there was no subject matter upon which the order of confirmation could act. If the court had no jurisdiction to order the sale it had none to confirm it. Where there is no power to render a judgment, or to make an order, there can be none to confirm or execute it; or none at least without the help of legislation."

[3] Townsend v. Tallant, 33 Cal. 45; Gregory v. Tabor, 19 Cal. 410; Haynes v. Meeks, 20 Cal. 317.

[4] Kœhler v. Ball, 2 Kansas, 160.

sort of hybrid system as to partake alike sometimes of each, and seldom exclusively of either. Thus, in that state, even in cases at law, instead of an ordinary writ of execution, an order of sale goes to the officer, partly under the control of the court and partly directed by statute, and the sale is to be reported for confirmation as well on legal as on equitable findings; but when so reported, instead of being confirmable at the discretion of the court, the court is by statute required to confirm them, "if made in conformity to the provisions" of the statute. This renders the sale partly judicial and partly ministerial,[1] and is a finding that the statute is complied with.

VI. WHEN THE TITLE PASSES.

§ 134. The contract of sale is only executed so as to pass the title by payment of the money, and the execution and delivery of the deed, duly approved or confirmed by the court, as the practice may be.[2]

In the mean time, and until then, the title in administration, executors and guardian sales remains in the ward or in the heirs, as the case may be, and in other cases it remains until then, in the former owner.[3]

§ 135. But if the deed be executed and delivered, and the consideration be paid, and the proceedings and sale are correct in all things other than report of the selling and order of confirmation, yet the title, by long possession of the premises, without question of its validity, will ripen into a valid one by lapse of time, as is herein before stated.[4]

VII. WHEN NOT AIDED IN EQUITY.

§ 136. A purchaser of real estate at a guardian's sale, where

[1] Koehler v. Ball, 2 Kansas, 160, 172, 171; Chick v. Willetts, 2 Kansas, 384, 390.

[2] Lischey v. Gardner, 3 W. and Sergt. 314; Williamson v. Berry, 8 How. 547; Moore v. Shultz, 13 Penn. St. 102; Bussey v. Hardin 2 B. Monroe, 407; Thorn v. Ingram, 25 Ark. 52; Sowards v. Pritchett, 37 Ill. 517; Campbell v. Johnson, 4 Dana, 186; Foreman v. Hunt, 3 Dana, 622.

[3] Ibid. and Erb v. Erb, 9 W. and Sergt. 147.

[4] Gowan v. Jones, 10 S. and M. 164.

the sale has not been reported, confirmed, or approved, as required by statute, will not be aided in equity by injunction against an action at law for the premises, nor by a decree confirming the sale, or quieting title, although such purchaser has paid the purchase money.[1]

§ 137. If an administration sale of lands be void at law, equity cannot ordinarily interfere to set up or maintain it.[2]

Nor has the purchaser a lien on the land on failure of title, which chancery can enforce against the heirs for the purchase money.[3]

VIII. NOT AFFECTED BY REVERSAL OF THE DECREE.

§ 138. The title acquired at a decretal sale of lands made by a court in the exercise of competent jurisdiction, is not rendered invalid by the reversal of the decree for mere irregularity or error.[4] This, too, although the purchaser was a party to the suit in which the decree was made.[5] Nor if notice be given to the purchaser at the time of the sale and before he purchased that an effort would be made to reverse the decree.[6]

§ 139. In the case above cited from the first of Wallace, the Supreme Court of the United States lay down the rule to be,

---

[1] Young v. Dowling, 15 Ill. 481; Bright v. Boyd, 1 Story, 478; Dickey v. Beaty, 14 Ohio St. 389. In Bright v. Boyd, STORY, Justice, says: "Now it is a well settled doctrine that although courts of equity may relieve against the defective execution of a power created by a party, yet they cannot relieve against the defective execution of a power created by law, or dispense with any of the formalities required thereby for its due execution, for otherwise the whole policy of the legislative enactments might be overturned. There may be exceptions to this rule, but if there be the present case does not present any circumstances which ought to take it out of the general rule."

[2] Lieby v. Parks, 4 Ohio, 469, 493; Young v. Dowling, 15 Ill. 481; Bright v. Boyd, 1 Story, 478.

[3] Lieby v. Parks, 4 Ohio, 469, 493.

[4] Ward v. Hollins, 14 Md. 158; Irwin v. Jeffers, 3 Ohio, (N. S.) 389; Gossom v. Donnaldson, 18 B. Monroe, 230; Gray v. Brignardello, 1 Wall. 627, 634; Clark v. Bell, 4 Dana, 20; Fergus v. Woodworth, 44 Ill. 374; Goudy v. Hall, 36 Ill. 319; McLagan v. Brown, 11 Ill. 637; Iverson v. Loberg, 26 Ill. 179.

[5] Gossom v. Donaldson, 18 B. Mon. 230.

[6] Irwin v. Jeffers, 3 Ohio, (N. S.) 389.

"that although the judgment or decree may be reversed, yet all rights acquired at a judicial sale while the decree or judgment were in full force, and which they authorized, will be protected. It is sufficient for the buyer to know that the court had jurisdiction and exercised it, and that the order on the faith of which he purchased was made, and authorized the sale." With the errors of the court he has no concern.[1] This doctrine applies however to sales where present power to make them is clearly given to the person selling by the decree or order of the court, and not to sales made on interlocutory orders not yet ripened into full authority to sell, and which contemplate and require further action of the court in reference thereto before the authority to sell can be exercised. Sales under such interlocutory order before further action by the court are invalid and will not be protected from the effect of reversal even by a curative entry made *nunc pro tunc*.[2]

§ 140. But where one only of several creditors, parties to the proceedings and entitled to the proceeds of sale, becomes the purchaser, applying only his own portion of the purchase money on his purchase, and paying the residue into court, and the same is distributed among the other claimants by a decree of distribution and paid over to them, some of whom are insolvent, it is holden in Ohio, that such purchaser, on a bill of review, is entitled to the protection of the statute of that state of 1841, which provides, "that if any judgment or judgments in satisfaction of which any lands or tenements belonging to the party hath or shall be sold, shall, at any time thereafter be reversed, such reversal shall not affect or defeat the title of the purchaser or purchasers; but in such case restitution shall be made of the monies by the judgment creditor, for which such lands or tenements were sold, with lawful interest from the day of sale." And in the same case

---

[1] Gray *v.* Brignardello, 1 Wall. 634; Vorhees *v.* Bank of the United States, 10 Pet. 449; Blanc *v.* Carter, 4 Cranch, 328; Taylor *v.* Thompson, 5 Pet. 370; Wright *v.* Hollingsworth, 1 Pet. 169; Elliott *v.* Piersol, 1 Pet. 340.

[2] Gray *v.* Brignardello, 1 Wall. 634, 636; Southern Bk. *v.* Humphreys, 47 Ill. 227.

an improper distribution of proceeds was afterwards corrected on bill of review.[1]

§ 141. In the case of *McBride v. Longworth*,[2] the previous case of *Hubbell v. The Administrator of Broadwell*[3] was adverted to and approved, as not in conflict with the decision in *McBride v. Longworth*, as in the case from 8th Ohio, the purchaser was the sole creditor; purchased in discharge of his own mortgage decree; received the entire proceeds, and was still the holder of the premises so purchased by him, and "no new rights had intervened." The court there held that such sole purchaser was to be regarded as a party merely and not as a *bona fide* purchaser; and that on reversal of the decree of sale the mortgagor had a right to redeem. That as "there were no other parties in interest but the mortgagor and mortgagee," and that "between them full justice could be done" after such reversal.

IX. How Affected by Statute of Limitation.

§ 142. The special statute of limitations limiting the time to five years, or other term, in which the validity of sales in probate made at the instance of guardians and administrators may be questioned, is not construed to apply to such sales made under decrees or orders that are void for the want of jurisdiction of the court; or in cases where jurisdiction had not attached; nor to sales made as if by a guardian, by one assuming to be, but in reality not such. If the order be void, or if the sale be made by one having no authority whatever, nor semblance thereof, the statute will not apply. In all such cases the heir at law will not be estopped by the limitation of time named in the statute, from asserting his title.[4] Nor will the statute apply to sales made before its enactment.[5]

§ 143. But the defendant, in an action for real estate, who

---

[1] McBride v. Longworth, 14 Ohio St. 344, 351, 352.

[2] McBride v. Longworth, 14 Ohio St. 349, 351, 352.

[3] 8 Ohio, 120.

[4] Purley v. Hays, 22 Iowa, 1; Holmes v. Beal, 9 Cush. 223; Chadbourne v. Radcliff, 30 Maine, 354.

[5] Cooper v. Sunderland, 8 Clarke, 14.

makes title under an administrator's sale in probate and conveyance, and having had possession for more than five years, the time limited in which to question such sales, and who pleads and relies on such limitation, will not be required in such action to first show a *prima facie* valid sale before he can take the benefit of the statute.[1]

§ 144. To require the defendant to first establish a valid sale before he can have the benefit of the limitation, would effectually do away with the statute, for if the sale be shown to be valid, such showing is a full defense and the statute is useless.

§ 145. But ordinarily a defendant thus defending must show a sale in fact and a deed thereon, and that the same was confirmed by the court, so as to amount to color of title under which to claim the protection of the statute of limitation.[2]

X. How Affected by the Statute of Frauds.

§ 146. The prevailing rule is, that after confirmation, judicial sales are not within the statute of frauds. Lord Hardwicke seems to have first asserted this principle in the case of the *Attorney General v. Day*.[3] His Lordship, in that case, lays down the rule that judicial sales, unlike ministerial sales of a sheriff on execution, are not within the statute of frauds, and, therefore, his Lordship declared that after the master's report and confirmation, he did not doubt the propriety of carrying into execution a purchase made by oral bid, although the purchaser had subscribed to no agreement. Judge Story assented to the same principle in *Arnold v. Smith*, but did not consider the sale involved in that case a judicial sale, for the reason, as he states, that in Rhode Island such sales are not by law required to be reported to the court for confirmation.[4]

§ 147. In New York it is held that if a judicial sale is within the statute at all, the report of the master or officer, or

---

[1] Holmes v. Beal, 9 Cush. 223; Vancleave v. Millikin, 13 Ind. 105.

[2] Rawlings v. Bailey, 15 Ill. 178; Vancleave v. Millikin, 13 Ind. 105.

[3] 1 Vez. Senr. 218; Brown, Statute of Frauds, Secs. 624, 625; King v. Gunnison, 4 Barr, 171.

[4] Arnold v. Smith, 5 Mason C. C. 414, 420, 421.

the memorandum of the auctioneer employed by him is sufficient to take it out.[1]   In Missouri the ruling is substantially
the same as to the effect of the master's report.[2]   In Alabama
the sale is held to be out of the statute by confirmation, not
before.[3]   These rulings, though some of them go further, sustain the principle laid down by Lord HARDWICKE, which is that
after confirmation the sale is out of the statute.

In Pennsylvania and California, the authorities go to a still
greater length, and the rule is, that judicial sales are not within
the statute of frauds at all.[4]

§ 148.   In Illinois the ruling is, that administrator's sales
are within the statute, and that even judicial sales by a master
are not binding "until approved by the court," which, of
course, carries the inference that after approval or confirmation
those made by a master are no longer within the statute.[5]

XI.   WHEN VALID BY LAPSE OF TIME

§ 149.   There is a defense, founded alike in benevolence,
equity, and sound policy.   It is lapse of time.   Time, which
destroys all things else, serves but to render one's landed possessions and titles more sacred and more secure.   Time or
accident destroy records and muniments of title, yet time
itself, when sufficiently long, repairs the loss.   Errors, irregularities, and judicial insufficiencies may intervene after a series
of years to avoid a title and destroy a right; but time supplies
the presumption that in the inception of the possession the
attributes of title were all right, a presumption growing out
of long possession and out of the negligence of the adverse
claimant in prosecuting his claim.   Benevolence and good
conscience alike forbid the disturbance of possessions and fire-

---

[1] Hageman v. Johnson, 35 Barb. (N. Y.) 200.   The case here cited from
New York was a case of sale on mortgage foreclosure.   National Fire
Ins. Co. v. Loomis, 11 Paige, 431.

[2] Stewart v. Garvin, 31 Mo. 36.

[3] Hutton v. Williams, 35 Ala. 503.

[4] Fulton v. Moore, 25 Penn. St. 468; Halleck v. Guy, 9 Cal. 181; King v.
Gunnison, 4 Barr, 171.

[5] Bozza v. Rowe, 30 Ill. 198.

sides by demands, which if earlier presented, might possibly have been explained away.

§ 150. Equity will discountenance them when time has carried away those who are presumed to have had knowledge of the transactions and rights thus sought to be questioned, and will refuse such claimants equitable aid. A like refusal is also based on what is called "analogy" to limitations of statutes at law, where a less time has run than is ordinarily deemed curative in itself.[1] So, that in titles founded on judicial sales, if there be defects and irregularities, by lapse of time the presumption arises that in the inception of the title the deficiencies were all supplied, and that their evidences have passed away.

But no length of time will within itself raise a presumption in contradiction to an express showing of the record Thus, where the record and proceedings show affirmatively that a guardian *ad litem* did not, as such, or otherwise, appear in an action, and was not in any manner brought into court in the course of the proceedings, and the proceedings are fatally defective by means of such showing, mere lapse of time will not cure the defect, or raise a presumption contradictory to, the record in order to uphold a sale or to supply the deficiency.[2]

§ 151. The affirmative showings of the record are to be received as absolute verity. Presumptions will supply such irregularities only as do not involve the question of jurisdiction, and whereof the record is silent.

[1] 2 Story, Eq. Jur. Secs. 1620, 1622; Slicer v. Bank of Pittsburgh, 16 How. 571; Beauregard v. New Orleans, 18 How. 502; Newson v. Wells, 5 McLean, 22; Shafer v. Gates, 2 B. Mon. 457; Gray v. Gardner, 3 Mass. 399; Leverett v. Armstong, 15 Mass. 27; Scott v. Freeland, 7 S. & M. 409; Bostwitch v. Atkins, 3 Comst. 53; Laughman v. Thompson, 6 S & M. 9; Moore v. Green, 18 How. 69; Watts v. Scott, 3 Watts. 79; Evans v. Spurgin, 11 Gratt. 615.
[2] Shaefer v. Gates, 2 B. Mon. 457, 458.

XII. How Enforced against the Purchaser.

§ 152. By the purchase, the purchaser at a judicial sale becomes a party to the proceedings in which the sale is made.[1]

§ 153. Now, whoever makes himself a party to the proceedings of a court of general equity jurisdiction, and undertakes to do a particular thing under its decretal orders, may be compelled to perform what he has undertaken.[2] The proper tribunal to compel it is the same court, and by motion in the same cause in which the undertaking occurred.[3] This rule applies to purchasers at judicial sales in courts of chancery, and the proper method of compulsion is by attachment.[4]

§ 154. Nor does it matter that there is a right, on default of payment, to re-sell the lands or bring suit; for the right is optionary, not with the purchaser, but with the court or party selling.[5] The very point was decided by Lord Eldon, in *Leaton v. Slade*,[6] in which case the court said: "If you make out that the seller would have been at liberty to re-sell, that does not make out that he lets the other off."

§ 155. But such purchaser at a judicial sale may not be thus compelled to complete the sale if the title be defective, nor to pay the consideration money until the defect, if there be one, is obviated; for although the rule *caveat emptor* applies after the sale is closed by payment of the purchase money and delivery of the deed, if there be no fraud, yet the buyer, if he

---

[1] Cazet *v.* Hubble, 36 N. Y. R. 677; Requa *v.* Rea, 2 Paige, 339; Dedrick *v.* Watkins, 8 Humph. 520.

[2] Wood *v.* Mann, 3 Sumn. C. C. 318, 326; Gross *v.* Pearcy, 2 P. and H. (Va.) 483; Planter's Bk. *v.* Fowles, 4 Sneed, (Tenn.) 461; Blackmore *v.* Barker, 2 Swan, (Tenn.) 340; Stimson *v.* Meed, 2 Rhode Island, 541; Cazet *v.* Hubble, 36 N. Y. 677.

[3] Wood *v.* Mann. 3 Sumn. C. C. 318, 325; Cazet *v.* Hubble, 36 N. Y. 677.

[4] Wood *v.* Mann, 3 Sumn. C. C. 318, 326; Landsdown *v.* Elderton, 14 Ves. 512. In the matter of Yates, 6 Jones Eq. (N. C.) 212. Brasher *v.* Cortland, 2 Johns. Ch. 505.

[5] Wood *v.* Mann, 3 Sumn. C. C. 318; Cazet *v.* Hubble, 36 N. Y. 677.

[6] 7 Ves. 265; Wood *v.* Mann, 3 Sumn. C. C. 331.

discover the defect beforehand, will not be compelled to complete the sale.[1]

§ 156. And therefore if a rule be made against him with a view to enforcing compliance with his bid, he may, on appearance thereto, have an order of reference to inquire into and report the state of the title to the property, and if the title prove to be doubtful and incurably defective, he will not be coerced into completion of the purchase.[2]

XIII. How Carried into Effect in favor of Purchaser.

§ 157. In judicial sales, by courts of ordinary general chancery jurisdiction, the better course is for the decree or order of sale to include also an order to put the purchaser into possession to save a resort to an action at law for that purpose. But whether there be such order inserted in the decree or not, the court has full power to enforce its sale by putting the purchaser into possession of the premises against the possession of a party to the suit, or any one holding under such party, who came into the possession during the pendency of the suit and refuses to render up the premises to the purchaser.[3]

§ 158. The mode of proceeding is, first by a judicial order to the defendant in possession to deliver up the premises to the purchaser, according to the intent of the decree. Or when the decree of sale includes an order for possession, then a formal writ of possession or decretal order for possession is proper. If ineffectual, the next step is an injunction, and then a writ of assistance.[4]

§ 159. But these summary methods of putting a purchaser

[1] Ormsby v. Terry, 6 Bush. (Ky.) 533.

[2] Graham v. Bleakie 2 Daly, (N. Y.) 55.

[3] Kershaw v. Thompson, 4 Johns. Ch. 609; Gowan v. Sumevalt, 1 Gill and J. 511; 1 Bland, 363; Frelinghuysen v. Colden, 4 Paige, 204; Van Hook v. Throgmorton, 8 Paige 33; McGowan v. Wilkins, 1 Paige, 121; Creighton v. Paine, 2 Ala. 158; Planter's Bk. v. Fowlkes, 4 Sneed. (Tenn.) 461; Oliver v. Caton, 2 Md. Ch. Decis. 297; Trabue v. Ingles, 6 B. Mon. 84; Applegate v. Russell, 25 Md. 317.

[4] Kershaw v. Thompson, 4 Johns. Ch. 609; Frelinghuysen v. Colden, 4 Paige Ch. 204; Van Hook v. Throgmorton 8 Paige, 33; McGowan v. Wilkins, 1 Paige, 121

at judicial sale into possession, or of forcing him to comply
with his purchase, are not understood to be within the powers
of a mere probate court making sales of a decedent's lands
under the statute. The purchaser at such sales will be left to
his remedy at law by action of ejectment, or whatever legal
remedy by action stands in lieu thereof, in case, as in some of
the States, the action of ejectment be abolished.[1]

§ 160. If, on the other hand, the purchaser at a sale of
lands in probate, refuse to complete the purchase and pay the
purchase money, then, instead of the coercive process which a
chancery court of general jurisdiction might resort to, and
which is not among the powers of the probate court, the
property may be sold over again, and if for a less sum the
administrator may recover the difference from such first purchaser, and if it amounts to more than what will pay the debts,
the residue is a trust fund for the widow and heirs of the
deceased.[2]

XIV. RATIFICATION BY THE PARTY AFFECTED, OR BY LAPSE OF TIME.

§ 161. Though a sale be not legally binding in the first
instance, yet it may become so by ratification, either express
or implied, of the party whose property is sold.[3]

§ 162. Thus a sale by guardian, of a ward's lands, is ratified,
if the ward, when of full age, receive and accept the proceeds
of the sale with knowledge of the circumstances.[4]

And so of an acceptance by the heirs at law of their respective
shares of the purchase money of land sold by the administrator of a decedent with full knowledge of the condition of
things; they thereby ratify the sale and may not thereafter

[1] Butler v. Emmet, 8 Paige, 12,
[2] Cobb v. Wood, 8 Cush. 228; Mowry v. Adams, 14 Mass. 327.
[3] Michoud v. Girod, 4 How. 503, 561; Scott v. Freeland, 7 S. and M. 409,
420; Tooley v. Gridley, 3 S. and M. 493; Henderson v. Herrod, 23 Miss. 434.
[4] Scott v. Freeland, 7 S. and M. 409, 420.

contest its validity,[1] unless for fraud unknown to them when they received the proceeds.[2]

§ 163. Where the widow of an intestate sold the equitable interest of the deceased, in a parcel of land, without any authority, it was holden that the heirs at law, by receiving the purchase money affirmed and ratified the sale.[3]

[1] Lee v. Gardner, 26 Miss. 521: Jennings v. Kee, 5 Ind. 257, 259: Maple v. Kussart, 53 Penn. St. 348: Michoud v. Girod, 4 How. 503, 561.

[2] Michoud v. Girod, 4 How. 503.

[3] Jennings v. Kee, 5 Ind. 257, 259.

CHAPTER V.

JUDICIAL SALES TO ENFORCE LIENS ON REAL PROPERTY.

 I. Municipal Liens for Street Improvements.
 II. Mechanic's Liens.
 III. Mortgage Liens.
 IV. Vendor's Liens.

I. Municipal Liens for Street Improvements.

§ 164. Sales in equity for the enforcement of municipal liens on land, arising under ordinances or statutes for street improvements, are regarded as judicial sales.[1] If there be no special method provided for the enforcement of liens of a municipal corporation for street improvements, or if there be a method prescribed, but not prescribed as exclusive, then, in either case, the remedy may be sought and the enforcement had by decree and sale, in equity, on application by bill or petition, upon the general principle of equity jurisdiction for the enforcement of liens.

§ 165. In *McInerny v. Read*,[2] the Supreme Court of Iowa, Dillon, Justice, lay down the rule in the following language: "We take a view of the matter which upholds the power granted and makes it effective, but which duly guards and preserves the rights of the property owner. The expenditure is declared to be a lien, and liens may be enforced in equity, and the power 'to collect' given by the charter may be exercised by commencing an action in court to have the lien enforced." And again, in the same case, the court say the city or corporation may, " if its right is not barred, commence a suit in equity to collect its tax and enforce its lien, we have no doubt, and it was so expressly adjudged in the case of the *Mayor, etc., v. Colgate*, above cited."

---

[1] Ohio Life Ins. & Trust Co. *v.* Gibbon, 10 Ohio St. 557; Hamilton *v.* Dunn, 22 Ill. 259.

[2] McInerny *v.* Read, 23 Iowa, 410; Mayor *v.* Colgate, 12 N. Y. 140.

§ 166. And we may not regard the use of the word "action" in this opinion as applied in its ordinary and original legal sense, and, therefore, as importing a proceeding at law, but rather in the extended sense in which the Revision of Iowa has used it, alike in reference to both equitable and legal proceedings. This is clearly apparent by the subsequent reference to a "suit" in "equity" in the opinion of the learned judge.

§ 167. Such liens and sales are the creatures of the statute —are regulated thereby—and the power of the court is said to be limited to a confirmation or rejection of the sale when made, whether the sale be by virtue of a judgment at law or decree in chancery. The court cannot modify, but must confirm or reject the sale.

The principle, in either case, is the same. The right and lien are purely statutory, were unknown to the common law and ordinary chancery jurisdiction. The statute in the several states is the judicial guide as to the extent and enforcement of such liens, although, in the very nature of the case, the exercise of more or less of chancery powers is involved in the proceeding, as in addition to the ordinary judgment, if the proceeding be at law, an order or decree of condemnation and sale of property specified and described therein is necessary.[1]

§ 168. In *Ohio Life Ins. and Trust Co. v. Gibbon*,[2] arising on street improvements, the sale was made on decree and under the appraisement law of that state. The ground and a building thereon were appraised together and sold as an entirety. After confirmation of the sale and payment of the purchase money, it was discovered that there was less ground by three feet frontage than the quantity sold. It was holden that a corresponding deduction from the price could not be made by the court. That there was no rule by which the discrepancy in

---

[1] Ohio Life Ins. & Trust Co. v. Gibbon, 10 Ohio St. 557; Canal Co. v. Gordon, 6 Wall. 561, 568; McInerny v. Read, 23 Iowa, 410; Dillon, Municipal Corps. Sec. 660. A personal action will, in some cases, lie for the money, as for instance an ordinary action at law where the party has petitioned for or otherwise acquiesced in the improvement, but this will not reach the lien. Eschbach v. Pitts, 6 Md. 71.

[2] 10 Ohio St. 557.

value could be arrived at, as the purchaser had lost no part of
the building, but a part of the ground only which he had
contracted for, and the whole had been appraised and sold
together. Moreover, that were it otherwise, the court could only
confirm, or vacate, the sale as it was made, and could not alter
or modify it in any substantial particular. It might correct
mistakes in computation and other errors, but not change the
terms of the sale when made. In this case, the court say:
"The purchaser gets, with his twenty-seven feet, all the improvements which entered into their estimate of the value of the
entire lot. How much of this estimate was for the 'ground'
and how much for the 'improvements' does not appear, and
no computation could have ascertained it." The court add,
that the improvements "may have been very valuable;" that
there "was no previous measurement to ascertain the frontage
of the lot, and no express reservation of a right to do so,
before or at the time the money was paid, which was several
days prior to filing the motion at special term, one month
after the sale;" that "judicial sales should always be certain,
and not subject to any future contingencies, so that all bidders
may have equal advantages;" that the power of the court is
"to confirm or set aside, but not to modify the sale or its
terms;" that if "the sale ought not to be confirmed as it was
made, the best, and only proper remedy, is a resale, with or
without valuation, as justice may require." [1]

§ 169. To enable a municipal corporation to enforce payment of a tax levied for street improvements by judicial proceedings against the property or owner, the ordinance under
which the proceedings are had, must have been duly published
as required by law. Until such publication no liability to pay
is incurred. In the case of *Dubuque v. Wooton*, [2] a suit in
chancery, commenced by the city of Dubuque to enforce payment for street improvements, the Supreme Court of Iowa
held, that for want of such publication, the complainant was
not entitled to relief. That court, BECK, Justice, say: "The
publication required by the second section of the ordinance is

---

[1] Ohio Life Ins. & Trust Co. v. Gibbon, 10 Ohio St. 565, 566.
[2] Dubuque v. Wooton, 33 Iowa, 571, 574.

undoubtedly necessary in order to fix the liability of the tax-payer, for, by the terms of the ordinance, the tax is declared to be due and payable after the publication is completed. We do not think the tax can become 'due and payable' until this requirement is complied with. The city has chosen to fix this condition to its right to enforce the tax, it must be complied with."

II. MECHANIC'S LIENS.

§ 170. Mechanic's liens are of modern date, and are creatures of the statute.[1] Though given by law, the enforcement of them usually involves the exercise of equitable powers, however in form of law merely such proceedings may be conducted. Thus the courts have held that the proceeding itself, when not otherwise required by the statute, should be in chancery or according to equity principles and practice.[2]

§ 171. In the case of *Hamilton v. Dunn*, the Supreme Court of Illinois, BREESE, Justice, lay down the rule that "suits to enforce 'such liens' although by statute placed on the common law docket, are yet proceedings in chancery, and governed by the rules of that where they apply and where the act giving the lien has not prescribed different rules."[3] They are regarded in Connecticut as conferring the same rights as a mortgage.[4]

§ 172. In the case of *Canal Co. v. Gordon*,[5] the court say: "They were unknown to the common law and equity jurisprudence both of England and of this country. They were clearly defined and regulated in the civil law.[6] Where they exist in this country they are the creatures of local legislation They are governed in everything by the statutes under which

---

[1] Canal Co. v. Gordon, 6 Wall. 561, 571,

[2] Hamilton v. Dunn, 22 Ill. 259; Rose v. Persse, 29 Conn. 256; Goodman v. White, 26 Conn. 317, 319, 329; McInerny v. Read, 23 Iowa, 410.

[3] Hamilton v. Dunn, 22 Ill. 259, 261; Clark v. Boyle, 51 Ill. 104; Marvin v. Taylor, 27 Ind. 73.

[4] Goodman v. White, 26 Conn. 317, 319, 320.

[5] 6 Wall. 561, 571.

[6] Domat, Secs. 1742, 1744.

they arise." This was a case coming up on appeal in chancery
from the decree of the circuit court of the United States for
the northern district of California. It involved the question
as to whether the mechanic's or builder's lien for constructing
one section of a canal flumes and acqueducts, attached to the
whole canal or only to the section on which the work was
bestowed. The Supreme Court held that the lien attached
only to the section on which the work was done. That court
says: "The lien is given to contractors and laborers upon the
ditch or flume 'which they may have constructed or repaired,
*   *   *   *   * to the extent of the labor done and materials
furnished.' The work of Gordon was all done upon the upper
section. He had nothing to do with the lower section. So far
as he was concerned and for all the purposes of this litigation
they were distinct and independent works. A different principle would produce confusion and lead to serious evils."[1]

§ 173. By analogy to the general doctrine of relation, such
sales and conveyances made thereon bear relation to the time
of the inception of the lien if the statute be conformed to,
and such date be agreed and fixed by the order or decree of
sale as against subsequent lien-holders and purchasers.[2]

§ 174. In Indiana the practice is to render a judgment at
law for the debt against the owner of the property who was
such at the time of executing the work, and also to make a
decree in equity against the property itself, condemning it to
be sold for the amount found due to the plaintiff. Thus the
proceeding, as is necessarily the case where the proceeding is
in *personam* as well as *in rem*, becomes a mixed one of law
and equity.[3]

§ 175. In such cases it follows that if the amount be not
realized on the decree, a writ of ordinary execution can go
against the property generally of the defendant to enforce the
personal judgment for the unsatisfied residue of the judgment. A sale on the latter would be a ministerial one, whilst

[1] Canal Company v. Gordon, 6 Wall. 572.
[2] Jackson v. Davenport, 20 Johns. 537; Jones v. Swan, 21 Iowa, 184;
Redfield v. Hart, 12 Iowa, 355; State v. Lake, 17 Iowa, 215.
[3] Marvin v. Taylor, 27 Ind. 73.

a sale on the decree in equity would partake of the character of a judicial sale.

§ 176. To make a valid sale of lands under a decree to enforce a mechanic's lien, all persons in interest in the premises are to be made parties. Therefore if the debtor who procured the work to be done upon the premises convey the property to a *bona fide* purchaser after the execution of the work, and before commencement of proceedings to enforce the lien, and the conveyance be recorded, (or come otherwise to the knowledge of the creditor,) the grantee must be made a party defendant, else he will not be affected in his rights under his conveyance by the decretal sale.[1]

§ 177. In the leading case cited from Indiana, the decree expressly reserved the rights of all persons not made parties to the suit, but such would be the general effect without the reservation. A party in interest (not buying *lis pendens*) must have his day in court in adversary proceedings.

§ 178. As betwixt a prior mortgage lien and a mechanic's lien on one and the same property, the rule in Illinois is to give the mechanic's lien its *pro rata* proportion of the increased value caused to the property by the improvement when the fund arising from the sale is insufficient to satisfy both. Not the *cost* of the improvement, but such part of the proceeds of the sale as bears a just proportion to the increase thereof caused by the betterments placed on the property by the mechanic.[2] And in the same state, as betwixt two or more mechanic's liens against the same property, and of equal priority, the proceeds of sale are equally distributed among them.[3]

§ 179. In Nevada it is held that a purchase and deed under a mortgage foreclosure and sale, made and perfected before proceedings were commenced for enforcing a mechanic's lien on the same premises, carries the title as against the pur-

---

[1] Marvin *v.* Taylor, 27 Ind. 73; Brown *v.* Wyncoop, 2 Blackf. 230; Holland *v.* Jones, 9 Ind. 495; Shaw *v.* Hoadley, 8 Blackf. 165.

[2] Crosby *v.* N. W. Manf. Co. 48 Ill. 481; Howett *v.* Selby, 54 Ill. 151; Dingledine *v.* Hershman, 53 Ill. 280.

[3] Buchter *v.* Dew, 39 Ill. 40.

chaser under the mechanic's lien, when in the proceedings to
enforce it the purchaser under the mortgage decree was not
made a defendant, although the mortgage deed be junior in
point of date to the inception of the lien of the mechanic.
For, by the purchase and deed under the decree foreclosing
the mortgage, the legal estate passed to the grantee in such
deed, and could not be divested by the sale under the mechanic's
lien without having made the mortgage purchaser a party so
as to give him a day in court, and an opportunity to contest
the lien of the mechanic.[1]

§ 180. Nor does it matter that the deed under the mortgage
sale was made to an assignee of the purchaser. The effect is
the same as if made to the purchaser himself. "The sheriff
had a right, on sufficient evidence of the assignment of the
certificate of sale, to make the deed" to the assignee.[2]

The same principle as to priority is asserted in Illinois,
under the statute respecting mechanic's liens. In *Williams
v. Chapman and others*,[3] the court say: "The right of those
not made parties are not affected by the decree, or any proceeding under it;" and hold that the purchaser, in that case,
under a mortgage foreclosure not having been made a party to
the suit on the mechanic's lien, had the superior title even if
the mechanic's lien were the oldest, though it was not.

§ 181. In Iowa, the lien of the mechanic attaches from the
commencement of the work. It continues without any effort
to perpetuate it until ninety days after the work is completed
and materials furnished. Within the ninety days it is the
duty of subsequent incumbrancers to ascertain if such lien
exists. In default thereof, the lien of the mechanic will override such incumbrances originating within the ninety days.
Within the ninety days the mechanic must file with the clerk
of the court notice of his lien and the amount thereof. After
that time, and after such filing, such notice is notice to sub-

[1] The Matter of Smith, 4 Nevada, 254; but see State *v.* Eads, 15 Iowa,
114, where the contrary doctrine is substantially holden.
[2] The Matter of Smith, 4 Nev. 254, 260.
[3] Williams *v.* Chapman, 17 Ill. 423; Kimball *v.* Cook, 1 Gilm. 427; Kelly
v. Chapman, 13 Ill. 531.

sequent incumbrancers, and they take subject to the mechanic's lien. Omission to file the notice will postpone the mechanic's lien in favor of such subsequent incumbrancers and purchasers.[1] Not, however, if they otherwise have notice of the lien.[2]

§ 182. In the same state it is held that the erection of such a structure on land at the request of the purchaser thereof, who is in possession under a contract of purchase which is yet executory, and is never afterwards completed by payment of the purchase money and procurement of a conveyance, entitles the mechanic to a lien against the building so erected.[3]

Such is the ruling under the statute which declares that, "The lien for the things aforesaid, or work, shall attach to the buildings, erections, or improvements, for which they were furnished or the work was done, in preference to any lien," etc., and that such building may be "sold under execution, and the purchaser may remove the same."

§ 183. In Iowa, judgments given for mechanic's liens are enforcible by special execution.

By statute such special execution is to conform to the judgment; and the sale shall be made as on ordinary writs of execution.[4] The statute also declares that the "lien shall attach to the building, erections, or improvements, for which they were furnished or the work was done, in preference to any prior lien, or incumbrance, or mortgage upon the land upon which said building, erections, or improvements have been erected or put, and any person enforcing such lien may have such building, erections, or improvements sold under execution, and the purchaser may remove the same within a reasonable time thereafter." Under this statute it is holden that a sale on special execution running against a house and ground, issued on a mechanic's lien, judgment entered against the house alone

[1] Jones v. Swan, 21 Iowa, 181.
[2] Noel v. Temple, 12 Iowa, 276, 281.
[3] Stockwell v. Carpenter, 27 Iowa, 119.
[4] Revision of 1860, Sec. 1864.

is void[1] in a contest between the purchaser under the special execution and a prior mortgagor.[2]

§ 184. On a proceeding to enforce by foreclosure such prior mortgage, the court will treat the execution sale as void, and will provide for discharge of the mechanic's lien out of the proceeds of the mortgage sale; and although the priority of the mechanic's lien attaches only to the house or proceeds of sale thereof, yet if the court award to such lien a general priority of payment from the proceeds of both house and ground, it is not a matter of such error as the holder of the mechanic's lien can complain of. If there be error, the error is in his favor.[3]

III. Mortgage Liens.

§ 185. Foreclosure sales in equity of mortgaged premises are an innovation on the original remedy of the mortgagee. He had a right at common law, on breach of condition, to take possession of the property, and to a prudent use of the same, but subject to an accounting for the rents and profits thereof. He was moreover bound to deliver back possession when out of such income the debt, interest and charges were satisfied. Or, as an alternative remedy, he might proceed by bill in chancery and foreclose the debtor's equity of redemption by a decree cutting off the right to redeem and vesting in the mortgagor the entire property and estate.[4] This latter is termed a strict foreclosure. This procedure, however, was liable to impose great hardship on one or other of the parties, as the property might be of much less or much greater value than the amount of the mortgage debt. If the former, the creditor got too little, and if the latter, he got too much for his debt. The creditor being now the owner of the property might sell the same. If by fair sale, the amount produced was less than his debt, he could then proceed, according to some rulings, on his bond, at

---

[1] Wilson v. Reuter, 29 Iowa, 176.

[2] Ibid.

[3] Ibid.

[4] 4 Kent, Com. 166, 167; Bradley v. R. R. Co. 36 Penn. St. 141, 150, 151; Robertson v. Campbell, 2 Call. 423.

law, against his debtor for the residue. To obviate these results, and assure a more equitable adjustment of the rights of parties, the most of the American States adopted the system of foreclosure and sale in chancery and causing the fund to be brought into court and applied on the debt, interest and costs, and the overplus, if any, to be paid over to the mortgage debtor;[1] but in case of a deficiency in amount to discharge the debt, interest and costs, the residue of the debt remained against the debtor for which he was proceeded against at law by an action, judgment, and execution sale if other property were found. A still further progress was then made in many of the States to avoid the suit at law by allowing a decree or judgment in the same proceeding for the remaining balance of the debt and awarding execution thereon, thus avoiding circuity of action. Sales in each of these proceedings in chancery (but not sales on the judgment and execution for the residue,) are judicial sales. Of these only it is our purpose, under this head, briefly to treat. Mortgage sales, on writ of *scire facias* and other proceedings at law, and in proceedings of a mixed nature, under various statutory innovations as adopted in some of the States, do not properly come under our present title. They are not purely judicial sales. Some are purely ministerial, and others again are of so dubious a character, though made in obedience to judicial decrees as at most to be but *quasi* judicial. As for instance, where the enforcement is by special writ of execution issued to the sheriff, and no report or confirmation of the sale being by law required.

§ 186. In Pennsylvania and some other of the States, equitable foreclosure and sale does not exist, unless a trust be connected with the mortgage and be abused.[2] The procedure is at law by *scire facias* or other legal process.[3]

§ 187. But the powers of courts of equity to decree a foreclosure and sale of mortgaged premises in general, on a proper case made by bill or petition, and to enforce such decree by

---

[1] Story, Eq. Jur. Sec. 1025; Bradley v. R. R. Co. 36 Penn St. 147, 1848.

[2] Bradley v. R. R. Co. 36 Penn. St. 141, 148; Willard v. Norris, 2 Rawle, 56.

[3] Bradley v. R. R. Co. 36 Penn. St. 141, 151.

judicial sale, and distribute or order the application of the proceeds, is now finally established in most of the States.[1]

§ 188. Mortgage sales in equitable proceedings are ordinarily made for cash; but by consent of parties the court will sometimes order the sale to be made on a credit; and may, on complainant's request alone, so direct as to the amount of the debt and interest of the complainant. In the case of *Sedgwick v. Fish*, the court say, "Judicial sales are not, in general, made on credit without the consent of the parties."[2]

§ 189. The proper person to make them, where there is no statutory regulation to the contrary, is a master or commissioner, appointed by the court and designated in the decree.[3] They must be made by him in person, and not by deputy, but he may depute another person to make the same, if such deputed person act in his immediate presence and under his control.[4]

§ 190. The purchaser will not be forced to complete the purchase when the sale was not made at his risk, and he cannot be placed in possession without resorting to an action of ejectment, or where he cannot have a clear title.[5]

§ 191. After the sale the court, when necessary, will retain control of the case to the perfecting of the ends of justice, and will coerce, by proper process, the delivery of possession of the premises to the purchaser, in case the mortgagor or any person claiming, or coming in under him subsequently to the commencement of the suit, withhold the same from the purchaser. The court will not, in such case, leave the purchaser to his remedy at law.[6]

[1] Story, Eq. Jur. Sec. 1025; Brownson v. Kinzie, 1 How. 318; Lansing v. Goelet. 9 Cow. 346; 4 Kent, Com. 181; Rogers v. Jones, 1 McCord, Ch. 221; Pannell v. The Bank, 7 Har. and J. 202; Bradley v. R. R. Co. 36 Penn. St. 141, 148.

[2] Sedgwick v. Fish, Hopkins, Ch. 594.

[3] Heyer v. Deaves, 2 Johns. Ch. 154.

[4] Heyer v. Deaves, 2 Johns. Ch. 154.

[5] McGowan v. Wilkins, 1 Paige, 120; Seaman v. Hicks, 8 Paige, 655.

[6] Suffern v. Thompson, 1 Paige, 450; Williams v. Waldo, 3 Scam. 264; Kershaw v. Thompson, 4 Johns. Ch. 609; Frelinghuysen v. Colden, 4 Paige, 204; Van Hook v. Throgmorton, 8 Paige, 33; Creighton v. Payne, 2 Ala. 158; McGowan, v. Wilkins, 1 Paige, 131.

§ 192. The proper remedy is first an order, in case of dis-obedience thereof, then an injunction, and if need be, a writ of assistance.[1] Such proceedings, however, will not be awarded, usually, to a purchaser from the purchaser at the judicial sale, nor as against one entering though during the pendency of the suit, yet not entering under the mortgage debtor, or other party defendant to the suit.[2]

§ 193. In case there be a judgment or judgments against the mortgage debtor, prior in date to the mortgage, and a lien on the premises, then such judgments are to be first extin-guished out of the proceeds of the mortgage sale.[3]

§ 194. If there be conflicting claimants to the proceeds of a sale, the court should settle the priorities and rights of the parties before the sale is made, which it will do, on application for that purpose. Such a course not only enables the parties and the master or person selling to act intelligibly as to application of the fund, but also enables the interested parties to bid with knowledge of their rights as to receipt of the pro-ceeds.[4]

§ 195. In case a part of the mortgaged lands be sold by the mortgagor after date of the mortgage, then equity charges the residue in the hands of the debtor with the whole debt, as in favor of the purchaser, or purchasers, and on foreclosure thereafter such residue is first to be sold, under the decree, before resorting to the part conveyed away by the debtor.[5] If several portions be so sold by the debtor after making the mortgage then by some of the authorities, the piece last sold by the mortgagor is the first to be sold under the decree, and so on in succession, each piece successively, in the inverse order of their sale by the debtor, until the whole are exhausted or

[1] Kershaw v. Thompson, 4 Johns. Ch. 609; Frelinghuysen v. Colden, 4 Paige, 204; Van Hook v. Throgmorton, 8 Paige, 33; McGowan v. Wilkins, 1 Paige, 131.
[2] Van Hook v. Throgmorton, 8 Paige, 33.
[3] Bell v. Brown, 3 Har. and J. 484.
[4] Snyder v. Stafford, 11 Paige, 71.
[5] Massie v. Wilson, 16 Iowa, 390; McWilliams v. Myers, 10 Iowa, 325; Clowes v. Dickenson, 5 Johns. Ch. 235; James v. Hubbard, 1 Paige, 226; Gill v. Lyons, 1 Johns. Ch. 447.

6

the decree and costs are satisfied. With this exception, however, that so long as any part still remains in the debtor, such part so remaining unsold by him is to be disposed of under the decree before either one of the portions conveyed away by him can be sold under the decree. For as long as any part remains the property of the debtor equity charges it with the debt to the exemption of the part sold, as between the debtor and his vendee; and the vendee of the residue or of any part thereof takes it subject to such equity, and yet with a like equity in his favor as between him and his vendor to have the residue, if any, belonging to his vendor sold first.[1]

§ 196. In the language of the chancellor, in *Clowes v. Dickenson*, each subsequent purchaser in turn "sits in the seat of his grantor and must take the land with all its equitable burdens."

And so likewise in regard to subsequent incumbrances of the mortgaged estate. The incumbrances vesting last will first be postponed, and so on in succession in an order inverse to their respective dates, in like manner as above stated in reference to sales of the mortgaged property in parcels.[2]

§ 197. But by other authorities the contrary is holden, both in reference to subsequent sales and subsequent incumbrances of mortgaged premises, and the ruling is that although in case the mortgage debtor only dispose of a part of the mortgaged premises, the mortgagor is in equity to look to the remainder of the mortgaged property still held by the debtor for satisfaction of his debt, as far as it will go, before following the property disposed of; yet, in case it be all sold or incumbered

---

Stuydevant v. Hall, 2 Barb. Ch. 151; Marshall v. Moore, 36 Ill. 321; Clowes v. Dickenson, 5 Johns. Ch. 235. "That where tenants in common, mortgaged for a joint debt due from both, for the payment of which debt both were equally liable as between themselves, and afterwards made partition, and aliened their several shares in different parcels, the share of the premises set off to each was chargeable primarily with one-half of the debt and costs, and should be sold to raise that half in the inverse order of the alienation of the several portions thereof." Rathbone v. Clark, 9 Paige, Ch. 649.

[2] Stuydevant v. Hall, 2 Barb. Ch. 151; Conrad v. Harrison, 3 Leigh, 532; Ins. Co. v. Miller, 1 Barb. Ch. 353.

by him subsequently to the mortgage, then those taking under him, though taking at different dates, hold their several interests subject equally to the mortgage debt in proportion to the respective values of their several interests. In other words, that they are to contribute equally and not in the inverse order above referred to, and that their several interests are equally liable to the extent of their proportionate values, or in the whole, if necessary, for the mortgage debt.[1] The former ruling of liability in the inverse order of dates of purchase or incumbrance, seems to us the more correct and equitable, as not leaving the rights of subsequent purchasers and incumbrancers dependent on the subsequent conduct of the mortgage debtor as to selling the mortgaged estate.

§ 198. Every community has power to declare the legal obligation of contracts being made within its jurisdiction, and may impose such conditions, restrictions, and exemptions, within constitutional limits, as may be most politic, as to all contracts made in the future. Hence mortgage sales are to conform to the laws in force at the date of the contract, so far as regards valuation and redemption laws.[2]

§ 199. The sale under a mortgage decree confers title only as against the parties to the suit. The proceeding cannot be enforced to cut off subsisting equities of incumbrancers who have not had their day in court as parties to the proceedings resulting in the sale.[3]

§ 200. In case of a sale under representations that the property is clear of incumbrances, and it transpires that incumbrances actually exist, the proper course is for the court to order the incumbrances to be removed by so much of the proceeds of the sale as shall be necessary to effect the removal thereof, so as to make good to the purchaser an unincumbered estate, according to the terms of his purchase.[4]

In *Brobst v. Brock*, the Supreme Court of the United States

Bates r. Ruddick, 2 Iowa, 423; Massie v. Wilson, 16 Iowa, 391; Barney r. Myers, 28 Iowa, 427.

[2] Bronson v. Kenzie, 1 How. 311, 321, 319.

[3] Haines v. Beach, 3 Johns. Ch. 459.

[4] Lawrence r. Carnell, 4 Johns. Ch. 542.

hold that an irregular, judicial sale, that is even void for want of notice as to the mortgagor, made at the instance of the mortgagee, passes to the purchaser all the rights of the mortgagee, although it may not bar the mortgagor's equity of redemption.

§ 201. The purchaser having paid the purchase money would seem to be subrogated to all the rights of the mortgagee as creditor, leaving the right to redeem still in the mortgagor.[1] The sale being made by procurement of the mortgagee he is estopped to deny its validity.

§ 202. In Illinois the rule of priority as betwixt a mortgage lien and lien of a mechanic, where the mortgage lien is the senior, is to ascertain the value of the premises at the time the mechanic's lien accrued, and the comparative value thereof as increased by the betterments made by the mechanic, and then in the decree of sale, give priority to the mortgage as to that proportion of the fund arising from the sale, which represents its comparative interest, and to the mechanic's lien priority as to the amount that represents the increased value caused by the improvements to the premises.

§ 203. The lien of the mechanic, so far as its priority is concerned, is commensurate only with the increased value of the property, and, in that respect, is not to be measured "by the cost of the material or labor actually furnished."[2]

§ 204. In Kansas an unrecorded mortgage, or mortgage made and recorded for the wrong land by mistake, takes priority over the mere lien of a junior judgment on the lands really agreed to and intended to have been subjected to the mortgage. Such mortgage may be reformed and the lien of the judgment before sale on such judgment will be postponed to that of the

---

[1] Brobst v. Brock, 10 Wall. 534; Gibert v. Cooley, Walker, Ch. 404; Jackson v. Bowen, 7 Cow. 13.

[2] Croskey v. N. W. M. Co. 48 Ill. 481. See also Raymond v. Ewing, 26 Ill. 343; Smith v. Moore, 26 Ill. 396; North Pres. Church v. Jevne, 32 Ill. 219.

mortgage.[1] And so does an unrecorded mortgage in Illinois overreach a prior judgment lien with notice.[2]

§ 205. Under the Ohio Statute of 1831, a recorded junior mortgage takes precedence against an unrecorded senior mortgage; and so does an execution sale, under a judgment junior to an unrecorded mortgage. A purchaser at such execution sale, or at such junior mortgage sale, takes the superior title over the senior unrecorded mortgage, although the purchase be made with full knowledge of the existence of the unrecorded senior mortgage. Such unrecorded instrument in Ohio, though valid as between the parties when such validity does not affect the rights or interests of third persons, is, by the statute of Feb. 22, 1831, void as to third parties until filed for record.[3]

§ 206. Where a mortgagor sells and conveys the mortgage premises with a stipulation in the deed that the vendee shall pay off the mortgage debt as a part of the purchase money to be paid for the premises, it is holden under the statute of Missouri that the mortgagee cannot, in a statutory foreclosure, extend the remedy so as to include the rendition of a judgment against the vendee for the amount so agreed by him to be paid. The Missouri statute is not comprehensive enough for such a proceeding; it provides for merely a foreclosure at law against the property and the original mortgage debtor. Any judgment rendered therein against the vendee personally, is not only void, but an execution sale and conveyance thereunder are also void, and may be so treated in a collateral pro-

[1] Swarts v. Steere, 2 Kansas, 236; Gouverneur v. Titus, 6 Paige, Ch. 347.

[2] Williams v. Tatnal, 29 Ill. 553. But in Ohio the reverse is the rule, under the statute of 1831; see, Pt. 2 Chap. VII. title Priority; and Fordick v. Barr, 3 Ohio St. 471; and Brown v. Kirkman, 1 Ohio St. 116; White v. Denman. 1 Ohio, 110

[3] Stansel v. Roberts, 13 Ohio, 148, 156; Fosdick v. Barr, 3 Ohio St. 471; Holiday v. Franklin Bank, 16 Ohio, 533; White v. Denman, 16 Ohio, 59; Jackson v. Luce, 14 Ohio, 514; Mayham v. Combs, 14 Ohio, 428; Stansel v. Roberts, 13 Ohio, 148. Before the recording act of 1831, the recording of mortgages was placed on the same footing as absolute deeds; and notice of a mortgage, though unrecorded, operated to prevent priority of the subsequent judgment lien or junior mortgage. The ruling then was different. Fosdick v. Barr above cited.

ceeding.[1] If the mortgagee would, in one and the same suit, seek a remedy by foreclosure against the mortgagor, the property, and against the vendee as on his agreement to pay the purchase money, or part thereof, as the case may be, he must resort to the concurrent remedy of a foreclosure in chancery, making the vendee a party and seeking his remedy against both the land, the mortgagor, and his vendee.[2]

§ 207. The equitable powers of a chancery court, when once in possession of the case, and jurisdiction has attached by proper service, are sufficiently broad and searching to reach all the equities and all the rights and liabilities of all the parties, and will settle, dispose of, and enforce the whole in one suit.[3]

§ 208. In New York the practice is, on a bill in chancery, filed to obtain satisfaction of a mortgage, to decree not only as against the mortgagor for payment of the mortgage debt and sale of the land, but also for payment as against any other person who may have become surety for, or have assumed to pay the debt. This is done under the provisions of the New York statutes. This statutory foreclosure in New York is a proceeding in chancery, and in addition to the ordinary decree of foreclosure the court renders a personal judgment against the vendee of a mortgagor, upon the equitable undertaking that by virtue of his contract with the mortgagor, rests upon him to pay the amount, and which inures to the benefit of the mortgagee by subrogation, and which will thus be enforced to avoid circuity of action should the land not sell for the amount of the mortgage debt.[4]

§ 209. When the foreclosure is for interest only, or for one or more over-due installments of principal payable in installments, whilst others yet remain unmatured, the court will

[1] Fithian v. Monks, 43 Mo. 502; Janney v. Spedden, 38 Mo. 395; Shaw v. Gregoire, 41 Mo. 407.

[2] Fithian v. Monks, 43 Mo. 502.

[3] Fithian v. Monks, 43 Mo. 502, 519, 520; Clapworth v. Dressler, 2 Bessley, Ch. (N.J.) 62.

[4] Fithian v. Monks, 43 Mo. 502; Blyer v. Mulholland, 2 Sandf. Ch. 478; King v. Whitely, 10 Paige, 465; Belmont v. Cowan, 22 N.Y. 438; Burr v. Beers, 24 N.Y. 178; Curtis v. Tyler, 9 Paige, 432; Vail v. Foster, 4 Comst. 312.

decree a sale of part, or of the of whole the mortgaged premises, at its discretion, as may seem most conducive to equity and the rights and interests of the parties, especially if the property cannot be advantageously divided.[1] Or it may make a decree as for the whole debt, with an order to sell for the amount then due and retain the cause upon the docket with leave to take additional orders of sale of a part of the premises, from time to time, to satisfy other installments or interest, as the same becomes due.[2] If sale be made of the whole of the property, the court will see that the proceeds of the sale are so applied upon the several liabilities as will protect the rights and equities of the parties in interest.[3]

§ 210. In case of conflicting claimants to the surplus proceeds, or to any part thereof, the court will settle the rights of all such claimants after the surplus fund is brought into court, so as to protect the rights of all; and if not known to the court, then they should make known their rights before disposal of the proceeds and apply to have them settled and respecte

IV. VENDOR'S LIEN.

§ 211. The vendor's lien arises by implication of law. It attaches to the land sold for the unpaid purchase money, as against the vendee and all persons holding under him, with notice that purchase money remains unpaid. It is good as against the heirs or devisees of the vendee, or others, holding by voluntary conveyance, whether they have notice or not; for having paid no consideration, their equity is inferior to that of the original vendor. In fact, as against him, they have no equity at all.[5]

[1] Brinkerhoff v. Thalhimer, 2 Johns. Ch. 486; Ellis v. Craig, 7 Johns. Ch. 7.
[2] Ellis v. Craig, 7 Johns. Ch. 7, 14; Brinkerhoff v. Thalhimer, 2 Johns. Ch, 489.
[3] Brown v. Stewart, 1 Md. Ch. 87; Astor v. Miller, 2 Paige, 68.
[4] Snyder v. Stafford, 11 Paige, 71.
[5] 2 Story, Eq. Jur. Sec. 1217; 4 Kent, Com. Sec. 51; Garson v. Green, 1 Johns. Ch. 308; Bailey v. Greenleaf, 7 Wheat. 46, 50; Watson v. Wells, 5 Conn. 468; Greenup v. Strong, 1 Bibb, 590; Hundley v. Lyons, 5 Mumf. 842; Pierce v. Gates, 7 Blackf. 162.

§ 212. This lien can only be enforced in equity;[1] and a sale in chancery to enforce a vendor's lien is a judicial sale.

§ 213. Such lien overrides a mechanic's lien where the debtor has only an executory contract of purchase. And so it will if the purchase is executed, provided the mechanic works with notice that the purchase money is unpaid.[2]

§ 214. The court assert the preference of the vendor's lien in *Stoner v. Neff*,[3] after reviewing former cases, in the following language:

"Now, although as decided in *Lyon v. McGuffey*, 4 Barr, 126, a mechanic's lien upon an equitable estate attaches to the subsequently acquired legal estate, which takes place by operation of law, yet it does not thereby take precedence of the vendor's claim." The court say: "The latter had an estate upon which the former had no lien, and when he transmitted it to his vendee he never let go his grasp upon his purchase money."

§ 215. If a vendor sell land by a contract merely executory and on a credit, retaining the legal title as security for the purchase money, and then takes judgment at law for the purchase money, and executes and sells the land generally to satisfy the judgment, the purchaser, under the execution, takes the whole title, legal and equitable, to the land, leaving no interest therein whatever in either vendor or vendee, unless there be right of redemption in the judgment debtor.[4]

§ 216. And if on such judgment the vendor cause to be

---

[1] 2 Story Eq. Jur. Sec. 1217; Pierce *v.* Gates, 7 Blackf. 162.

[2] Stoner *v.* Neff, 50 Penn. St. 258.

[3] 50 Penn. St. 261. We are aware that in Lyon *v.* McGuffey, 4 Barr, 126, it is holden that the mechanic's lien has preference of the vendor's judgment for the purchase money; but the decision in that case is put upon the omission of the vendor to file his judgment as by law required within ten days after parting with his title, by which omission the vendor lost his priority. Lyon *v.* McGuffey, 6 Barr, 126, and Stoner *v.* Neff, 50 Penn. St. 258, 261. In Illinois, as we have seen, the court apportions the proceeds of sale, where the mortgage lien is the oldest, betwixt the two, according to their respective equity, taking into consideration the increased value of the property occasioned by the betterments added thereto by the mechanic. *Ante*, and Crosky *v.* N. W. M. Co. 48 Ill. 481.

[4] Pittsburgh & Steubenville R. R. Co. *v.* Jones, 59 Penn. St. 433, 436, 437.

executed and sold the equitable right only of the vendee or judgment debtor, then the sale will be valid to extinguish or transfer such right, and the purchaser will stand in the place of the vendee, if a third person, although there be no statute authorizing such proceedings.[1]

§ 217. By statute in Iowa, it is provided that "when part or all of the purchase money remains unpaid after the day fixed for payment, whether time is or is not of the essence of the contract, the vendor may file his petition asking the court to require the purchaser to perform his contract, or to foreclose and sell his interest in the property."[2] And so may his assignee if he assign the note given for the purchase money.

Thereupon the court may decree a rescission of the contract, or may by decree of foreclosure, as in case of a mortgage, cause the premises to be sold for payment of the unpaid purchase money.

§ 218. In case a note, or other security, is taken for such purchase money, the right to thus foreclose will follow the note into the hands of an assignee or indorser thereof, if so agreed by the vendor, or, without such agreement, by analogy to the equitable principle by which security for the payment of a debt passes with the debt to the assignee thereof.[3]

§ 219. Under the provision of the Iowa statute the vendor, where he retains title to the property sold, may file his petition on default of payment, tender a deed, and proceed for the two-fold purpose of a judgment *in personam* on the note or debt for the purchase money, and a decree of foreclosure declaring

---

[1] Gaston v. White, 46 Mo. 486.

[2] Revision of 1860, Secs. 3671, 3672; Blair v. Marsh, 8 Iowa, 144; Pierson v. David, 1 Iowa, 31; Page v. Cole, 6 Iowa, 154; Hartman v. Clarke, 11 Iowa, 510.

[3] Blair & v. Marsh, 8 Iowa, 144, 147. In Adams v. Cowherd, the Supreme Court of Missouri assert the rule as follows: "The doctrine in those states, in which it is admitted to be law, that the assignee of a note given for the purchase money does not acquire by such assignment the lien which the vendor himself had, has no application in cases where the vendor retains the legal title. It is only applicable where the vendor makes a full conveyance which passes away absolutely his legal title. This seems to be well settled law. 1 Lead Cas. Eq. 274, 275." Adams v. Cowherd, 30 Mo. 458.

such judgment a lien on the land, and ordering it to be sold to satisfy the judgment and costs; and there will be no missjoinder of causes of action or remedies.[1]

§ 220. Such foreclosure as of a mortgage being provided for by statute, is of a mixed nature of law and equity; is not purely either a legal or a chancery remedy or procedure; but partakes of the nature of each. It is a union of the powers of both law and equity jurisdictions.[2]

§ 221. But the remedy of the vendor is not confined to the proceeding provided by the Iowa statute. He may proceed at law exclusively, taking a judgment *in personam* for the debt;[3] or he may proceed by the mixed procedure and jurisdiction for a judgment *in personam* at law, and a decree of foreclosure *in rem* against the land, with an order of sale of the same to pay the judgment;[4] or he may, at his election, proceed purely under the statute for a foreclosure and sale of the land by a proceeding *in rem*, partaking partly of law and partly of chancery jurisdiction in its nature;[5] or he may proceed by original bill in equity for a specific performance of the contract just as if no statutory provisions were ever enacted on the subject. These several remedies are concurrent and neither of them is exclusive. The statutory remedy being merely cumulative, does not extinguish the others.

[1] Hartman v. Clarke, 11 Iowa, 510.
[2] Cramer v. Redman, 9 Iowa, 114; Hartman v. Clarke, 11 Iowa, 510.
[3] Hershey v. Hershey, 18 Iowa, 24.
[4] Hartman v. Clarke, 11 Iowa, 510.
[5] Hershey v. Hershey, 18 Iowa 24; Cramer v. Redman, 9 Iowa, 114.

CHAPTER VI

SALES OF LANDS IN PROBATE FOR PAYMENT OF DEBTS.

I. WHAT LANDS MAY BE SOLD.

§ 222. Sales in probate for payment of a decedent's debts can, as a general rule, only be made of those lands, or interests therein, whereof the debtor dies seized.[1]

The law fixes the status of property and renders it liable to sale or not, as may be enacted, for the payment of the owner's debts, whether such owner be living or dead, and if made liable, also regulates the method of subjecting it to sale. It follows, therefore, that in the absence of statute law rendering lands liable to sale in probate for the payment of debts, no such sales can be made.[2]

§ 223. In Texas, it has been held that head right certificates for land are such an interest in real estate as may be sold by

---

[1] Torrence v. Torrence, 53 Penn. St. 505, 511, 512; Williard v. Nason, 5 Mass. 240, 244; Johnson v. Collins, 12 Ala. 322; George v. Williams, 26 Mo. 190; McCandish v. Keene, 13 Gratt. 615.

[2] Ticknor v. Harris, 14 N. H. 272; Drinkwater v. Drinkwater, 4 Mass. 358; Bergin v. McFarland, 6 Foster (N. H.) 536; Moore v. The Widow, 11 Humph. 512; Pelletreau v. Smith, 30 Barb. 494; Washington v. McCaughan, 34 Miss. 304; Haynes v. Meeks, 20 Cal. 228; Petit v. Petit, 32 Ala. 288; Ikelheimer v. Chapman, 32 Ala. 676.

the administrator under an order in probate for payment of a decedent's debts.[1]

§ 224. In Alabama, it is held that lands purchased from the United States in the name of the widow and heirs of a decedent, and with the monies of the estate, under a pre-emption right which had enured to the decedent in his life time as a settler on the public lands, are not liable to sale in probate for payment of the decedent's debts. Nor can the investment be treated in a court of equity as a trust so as to enable the creditors to follow the fund and subject the lands in a court of equity. The pre-emption right descends, under the act of Congress, to the widow and heirs and not to the creditors or to the administrator. The court, GOLDTHWAITE, Justice, say, that "such a trust would be directly against the policy of the pre-emption acts, as the bounty of the government was obviously intended for the settler and his heirs. A construction, therefore, which would make him or them trustees for the person advancing the purchase money, is not to be tolerated, as it would, in effect, transfer the bounty of the government from the settler to the lender of the money.[2]

§ 225. In the case above referred to from Alabama, the court were disposed to regard the investment of the monies of the estate as a payment to the widow and heirs, and, therefore, as not calculated to create a trust were the question ruled under the pre-emption laws out of the way. If regarded as a payment, then, however liable to refund for payment of debts, such payment would not create a lien on the lands in which the monies were invested, but would create only a personal liability for the amount. If, however, the monies of the estate be diverted from their ordinary course by the administrator and be vested in realty by him, it seems that in whosesoever name it may be, that creditors and heirs would alike be able, on ordinary principles of equity, to treat the investment as a trust for their benefit or for either, as the necessities of the case should require. And such seems to be the doctrine in Tennessee, where the ruling is contrary, to some extent, to

[1] Soye v. Maverick, 18 Texas, 100.
[2] Johnson v. Collins, 12 Ala. 322, 337; Cothran v. McCoy, 33 Ala. 65.

that in Alabama. The heirs in Tennessee are regarded as holding lands in trust for the payment of debts of a decedent, where monies of the estate are invested in lands in their name and will be so considered to the extent of the debts, as far as the property will go towards payment of the same, if there be no other fund for payment thereof. But in such cases the jurisdiction is in the ordinary court of general chancery jurisdiction and not in the court of probate.[1]

§ 226. In the case of *Moore v. The Widow*,[2] the Supreme Court of Tennessee say: "By our law all the real estate of a deceased debtor, whether of a legal or equitable character, is liable to satisfaction of his just debts, subject to the widow's right of dower, which has preference over the rights of creditors. II. Humph. 512."

§ 227. In Alabama, if, at his death, the decedent is seized of an inchoate title (other than a government pre-emption) to lands, such interest may be sold in probate for payment of debts.[3]

§ 228. In Massachusetts the jurisdiction of the probate court is, by statute, extended so as to enable it to subject to sale for payment of debts, lands fraudulently conveyed away by the debtor in his lifetime.[4] But this is contrary to the general rule in the several states. Prior to this statute the contrary seems to have been the law in Massachusetts.[5]

§ 229. In *Vaughan v. Holmes*,[6] the Supreme Court of Alabama say that if the question was before them for the first time they should be disposed to hold that the probate court could not, under the authority given it for the sale of lands, direct the sale of an inchoate equity like the one then under consideration; but that the rule was too firmly established to allow a departure therefrom.

---

[1] Moore v. The Widow, 11 Humph. 512.

[2] Ibid.

[3] Vaughan v. Holmes, 22 Ala. 593; Perkins v. Winters, 7 Ala. 855; Duval v. The Bank, 10 Ala. 636; Duval v. Losky, 1 Ala. 708; Jennings v. Jenkins, 9 Ala. 285.

[4] Norton v. Norton, 8 Cush. 524.

[5] Bancroft v. Andrews, 6 Cush. 493.

22 Ala. 593.

§ 230. Thus it is settled in Alabama that equitable interest or title to lands, or inchoate interest therein of any kind, may be sold in probate for payment of debts, on application and proper showing of the administrator, and that the purchaser will take the title of the decedent, whatever it may be, and will in that respect stand in lieu of the heirs.[1]

§ 231. The power to subject lands of a decedent for payment of debts, conferred on the courts, is holden to be remedial, and applicable " as well in relation to estates where the decedent had died before as after its enactment."[2]

§ 232. In *McDonald v. Allen*,[3] it is said that, " Upon the death of a debtor, his estate, of whatever description, stands for the payment of all his general creditors alike." The executor or administrator is a trustee for the creditors and for the lien, to administer and apply the proceeds under the order and as the instrument of the court; and the order of sale can ordinarily only be made on his application. The contrary, we have seen, is the rule as to application in Texas. The order, when made, operates not on the persons of the heirs, but on the paramount title of the ancestor on which the debts operated as an implied lien.[4]

§ 233. But sales in probate may not be made of a decedent's lands, to pay debts which are not presented within the time allowed by statute for presentation of claims.[5]

§ 234. The administrator or executor must interpose the statute in such case in bar of claims, and may not waive it.[6]

§ 235. And though it has been held that he is not bound to plead the general statute of limitations in bar of debts presented for allowance, and that sales of lands may be made to

---

[1] Evans v. Matthewson, 8 Ala. 99.

[2] Fitzhugh v. Fitzhugh, 6 B. Mon. 4.

[3] 10 Ohio St. 297; Sheldon v. Newton, 3 Ohio St. 494; Lane v. Thompson, 43 N. H. 320.

[4] Sheldon v. Newton, 3 Ohio St. 494; Grignon's Lessee v. Astor, 2 How. 319; Beauregard v. N. Orleans, 18 How. 502.

[5] Hogan v. White, 1 N. H. 208; Nowell v. Nowell, 8 Greenl. 220; Fitch v. Witbeck, 2 Barb. Ch. 161; Moore v. White, 6 Johns. Ch. 360; Brown v. Foster, 7 Humph. 373.

[6] Brown v. Foster, 7 Humph. 373; Hogan v. White, 11 N. H. 208.

pay debts so subject to be barred; yet in some cases it is held
that any one or more of the heirs may interpose the general
statute to bar claims and prevent sales of their patrimonial
lands.[1]

II. WHAT DEBTS LANDS OF A DECEDENT MAY BE SOLD TO PAY.

§ 236. As sales of land under the statute to pay a decedent's
debts can only be made in probate, as a general rule, of land
whereof he died seized; so, by a like rule, the lands of a
decedent can only be sold to pay such debts as he owed at the
time of his death, and was legally liable to pay.[2]

§ 237. In other words, they cannot be sold to pay costs or
expenses of the administration, or liabilities created or incurred by the administrator. Such a sale would be illegal and
void.[3]

---

[1] Moore v. White, 6 Johns. Ch. 360, 389; Rizor v. Snoddy, 7 Ind. 442;
Bond v. Smith, 2 Ala. 660.

[2] Torrence v. Torrence, 53 Penn. St. 505, 511, 512; Dubois v. McLean,
4 McLean, 486, 489; Carnan v. Turner, 6 Har. and J. 65; Baker v. Kings-
land, 10 Paige Ch. 366; Farrar v. Dean, 24 Mo. 16.

[3] Dubois v. McLean, 4 McLean, 486, 489; Sumner v. Williams, 8 Mass.
199, 200; Farrar v. Dean, 24 Missouri, 16; Wood v. Byington, 2 Barb. Ch.
387; Fitch v. Whitbeck, 2 Barb. Ch. 161; Carnan v. Turner, 6 Har. and J.
65. In Farrar v. Dean, the Supreme Court of Missouri, in the delivery of
their opinion, held the following language: "The administrator has no
power over the real estate, except so far as to hold it for the payment of
the debts of the deceased; and when there are no debts the lands descends
to the heirs, or escheats to the State; and it is not in the power of the
administrator to hinder this legally; nor can the probate court direct or
order a sale of real estate for the costs accrued after the administration
begins, and only because it did begin. Such costs are not debts due by
the deceased, nor debts at the time of the death of the intestate." * * *
And again, in the delivery of the same opinion: "It is beyond doubt
that the debts to be paid by the sale of the real estate of a deceased person,
were debts and liabilities of that person only—debts due or to become
due by him. No one ever imagined that the legislature designed to place
the power in the hands of the administrator to create the debt, and then
to sell the real estate of the decedent to pay for it. When there is no
debts there is no law to sell the real estate. The administrator cannot
procure, in such a case, an order for its sale without a violation of
law." * * * * "We must hold such sales invalid." Farrar v. Dean,
24 Mo. 16, 18, 19, 20.

§ 238. Nor to pay costs of suit recovered against the administrator or estate, nor other cost not incurred by deceased during his life time.[1] But if a valid sale be made for the *bona fide* purposes of paying debts, and there remains of the proceeds a surplus fund, then this remnant may be applied to pay costs, charges and expenses of administration, or of litigation, under discretion of the court.[2]

§ 239. In *Dubois v. McLean*,[3] the court illustrate the principle of the text in the following terms: "Again, the only debt shown to support the sale in 1828, was one of two hundred and fifty-seven dollars, contracted by the executors in August, 1824. * * * * The land was sold, not for a debt of Dubois, but for a debt contracted by the executors. * * It is no answer that this debt was contracted by the executors in due course of administration, and for the benefit of the estate."

§ 240. So far as the estate is concerned, this supposed debt was not a debt, but only a liability, as costs, arising incidentally in the course of administration, and whether rightfully or wrongfully incurred, was not one for which, under the ordinary statutes, real estate may be sold.

§ 241. In the language of the court, in *Carnan v. Turner*,[4] to subject lands of a decedent for payment of debt, by an order of sale in probate, "the claimants must prove themselves creditors of the deceased ancestor."

§ 242. The debt must be, as is held in *Wood v. Byington*,[5] a "debt due from the testator." And in the more recent case of *Sanford v. Granger*,[6] it is holden that *Wood v. Byington*, is authority for saying, "that the costs awarded against executors can in no event be a charge on real estate in the hands of the heir."

§ 243. The individual lands of a decedent cannot be sold to pay a copartnership debt until after the individual debts of the

---

[1] Sandford *v.* Granger, 12 Barb. 392; Farrar *v.* Dean, 24 Missouri, 16, Wood *v.* Byington, 2 Barb. Ch. 387; Carey *v.* Dennis, 13 Md. 1.

[2] Drinkwater *v.* Drinkwater, 4 Mass. 358, 359.

[3] 4 McLean, 489.

[4] 6 Har. and J. 65, 67.

[5] 2 Barb. Ch. 387.

[6] 12 Barb. 392, 403.

decedent are all satisfied and the copartnership assets are exhausted.[1]

§ 244. The individual creditors have a right to be first paid out of the individual assets; and copartnership creditors have the same preference as to the copartnership assets. When the latter are all exhausted, then if the copartnership debts be not all paid, the creditors of the copartnership may pursue the individual property of the deceased member or members of the copartnership, may cause their claims to be allowed in probate, and in default of personal assets the administrator may obtain a license or decree for sale of lands to pay the same; but not until the individual debts of the decedent are all provided for.[2]

III. Who may Conduct the Sale.

§ 245. Under the common law lands were not sold by proceedings in probate for payment of debts.[3]

§ 246. Under the enactments of the several American States, in which such sales are made, they are conducted and made under the supervision and approbation of the court by the executor or administrator; and in nearly all cases on his application. A stranger, the sheriff as such officer, or other person, cannot, in probate, be authorized to sell. Their sale would be void.[4] And so of a special administrator.[5]

§ 247. In *Long v. Burnett*,[6] the Supreme Court of Iowa. Lowe, Justice, in treating of the powers of a special administrator, in reference to sales of land in probate say, " His functions are limited to a few described duties, in relation to the preservation of the personal assets, and these cease as soon as a regular administrator is appointed. He cannot be sued. The statute of limitations does not run against the creditors

[1] Moline *v.* Webster, 26 Ill. 233, 239.

[2] Pahlman *v.* Graves, 26 Ill. 405; 1 Story Eq. Jur. Sec. 675; 3 Kent, Com. 64; Wilder *v.* Keller, 3 Paige, 167; Story, Part. Sec. 363; McCulloh *v.* Dashiell, 1 Harris & Gill, 96; Moline *v.* Webster, 26 Ill. 239.

[3] Bergin *v.* McFarland, 6 Foster, N. H. 536.

[4] Crouch *v.* Eveleth, 12 Mass. 503; Swan *v,* Wheeler, 4 Day, 137; Jarvis *v.* Kusick, 12 Mo. 63; Long *v.* Burnett, 13 Iowa, 28

[5] Long *v.* Burnett, 13 Iowa, 28.

[6] 13 Iowa, 28, 33, 34.

of the estate during the period of his agency. He is simply an agent, and not an administrator. He has no power to settle the estate; much less power to sell land for any purpose. It was no more competent for the judge of probate to grant him license to sell land than that of any third person. His act in doing so was extra judicial and void. The Judge's power over real estate of deceased persons is derived through the medium of regular administration. This was wanting in the case before us. Hence the jurisdiction did not, as it could not, under the circumstances, attach." The court then lay down the rule, in that case, that for such want of a regular administrator, and of jurisdictional power in the probate court making the order of sale, such sale should be treated as void in a collateral proceeding. That "the power to grant a license to sell real estate to pay debts does not arise till a petition, as the law directs, is presented by a legal administrator." That "when such a petition is presented, jurisdiction over that particular subject is acquired, and the subsequent proceedings, although those of a court of inferior and limited powers, will be presumed as regular and conclusive as those of courts of general jurisdiction, and shall not be collaterally assailed."

§ 248. A sale of lands in probate, based on a special act of the legislature authorizing such order and sales, is to be made by the administrator, and when made will be holden to have been made by him in his capacity of administrator, and not as a commissioner of the courts.[1]

§ 249. But although no one but the administrator or executor may be authorized by order in probate to sell; yet, *quere*, if any one or more of several executors or administrators of an estate may not be empowered by such order to sell instead of their whole number.[2]

IV. APPLICATION TO SELL: How, AND IN WHAT TIME TO BE MADE.

§ 250. As no one but the executor or administrator can,

---

[1] Corbell v. Zeluff, 12 Gratt. 226, 335.

[2] Jackson v. Robinson, 4 Wend. 437; Wortman v. Skinner, 1 Beasley, (N. J.) 538.

under the statute, as a general rule, be authorized in probate to sell the lands of a decedent for payment of debts,[1] so it follows, as a general rule, that the application for the order to sell is to be made by the executor or administrator, which ever there be.

§ 251. But to this rule there are some exceptions. In Texas an heir, legatee or creditor, must join in the application under the act of February 25th, 1843. Prior to the passage of that act the administrator alone might apply.[2]

§ 252. It is held that where there are several administrators or executors of an estate any one or more of them may apply, and may be authorized by the court of probate to sell.[3]

§ 253. In Iowa the term administrator is by statute made to apply alike to executors and administrators.[4]

§ 254. The application of the administrator or executor for an order of sale of lands to pay debts must be a timely one,[5] and the court are the judges in all cases of the reasonableness of the time, when no time is fixed by law.[6]

§ 255. In some cases, one year from the grant of administration has been adjudged a suitable time within which to apply.[7]

But we apprehend that there are cases in which one year would not be a reasonable time.

Much depends upon the time allowed for presenting and proving up debts, and for settling the estate. The court are to judge, if there be no time limited, taking all circumstances into consideration.

---

[1] Chapt. IV. No. 3; Crouch v. Eveleth, 12 Mass. 503; Swan v. Wheeler, 4 Day, 137; James v. Kusick, 12 Mo. 63; Florithe v. Barton, 2 Wall. 210, 216; Long v. Burnett, 13 Iowa, 28; Palmer v. Palmer, 13 Gray, 326.

[2] Miller v. Miller, 10 Texas, 319.

[3] Jackson v. Robinson, 4 Wend. 436. But see to the contrary, Gregory v. McPherson, 13 Cal. 562; Wortman v. Skinner, 1 Beasley, (N. J.) 538.

[4] Revision of 1860, Sec. 2333.

[5] Moore v. White, 6 Johns. Ch. 376; Ricard v. Williams, 7 Wheat. 59, 115; Smith v. Dutton, 4 Shep. 308; Langworthy v. Baker, 23 Ill. 484.

[6] Moore v. White, 6 Johns. Ch. 376; Jackson v. Robinson, 4 Wend. 436, 442.

[7] Moore v. White, 6 Johns. Ch. 376, 377.

In *Palmer v. Palmer*[1] four years is held not to be an unreasonable time in which to make the application to sell.

§ 256. Orders of sale made after an unreasonable length of time from the grant of administration, and sales made thereon, are held to be absolutely void.[2]

§ 257. In *Hyde v. Farmer*,[3] it is held that three years, under the statute, is the time limited in which to pass the title by a sale of lands in probate, as against a *bona fide* purchaser from the heirs, and that after that time the land is discharged from the statutory lien, and that the functions of the probate court over the same then cease.

§ 258. The application should be accompanied with a show of diligence on the part of the administrator in first administering and exhausting the personalty.[4]

§ 259. If one order of sale prove insufficient, as to the sum raised, another order or orders may be made, as may be necessary, from time to time.[5] The debts should first be allowed of record; but if omitted the entry may be made *nunc pro tunc*.[6]

§ 260. The application must be by petition, identifying the lands intended to be sold, and setting forth whatever under the statute is required to give the court jurisdiction of the particular case and subject matter thereof, which should be so set forth as to be good upon demurrer.[7]

§ 261. The action of the court or decree, the notice of sale, and the sale itself, must all conform to the same subject matter

[1] 13 Gray (Mass.) 326.

[2] Langworth v. Baker, 23 Ill. 484.

[3] 1 Barb. 75; Fitch v. Witbeck, 2 Barb. Ch. 161; Furguson v. Brown, 1 Bradf. 10.

[4] Furguson v. Brown, 1 Bradf. 10.

[5] Farrington v. King, 1 Bradf. 182.

[6] Farrington v. King, 1 Bradf. 182, 191, 192.

[7] Grignon's Lessee v. Astor, 2 How. 319; Beauregard v. New Orleans, 18 How. 592; Alabama Conference v. Price, 42 Ala. 39; Cooper v. Sunderland, 3 Iowa, 114; Moore v. Neil, 39 Ill. 256; Frazier v. Steenrod, 3 Iowa, 339; Long v. Burnett, 13 Iowa, 28; Sheldon v. Newton, 3 Ohio (N. S.) 493; Coates v. Loftus, 4 Mon. 411; Gerrard v. Johnson, 12 Ind. 636; Morris v. Hogle, 37 Ill. 150; Morrow v. Weed, 4 Iowa, 77; Florentine v. Barton, 2 Wall. 210, 216; Gregory v. McPherson, 13 Cal. 562, 570.

or land described in the petition as the land sought to be sold. No title will pass if the petition be in reference to one tract of land, and the decree, sale, or notice of sale, be in reference to another and different one.[1]

§ 262. The petition should also show the death of the decedent;[2] that the land sought to be sold was owned by him at his decease;[3] should show the state of the personal assets, and the insufficiency thereof to pay the debts;[4] and all such other matters, if any, that by local statute may be required. It must likewise be sworn to as may by statute be required.[6] It is not necessary, as a general rule, to specify the several debts, yet a statement of the aggregate amount is required.[5]

§ 263. In Tennessee, a report showing the state of the assets is first to be made and affirmed by the court as a basis for the application.[7]

---

[1] Frazier v. Steenrod, 7 Iowa, 340; Weed v. Edmonds, 4 Ind. 468; Williams v. Blair, 25 Miss. 78. In Schnell v. Chicago, 38 Ill. 382, there is ruling seemingly to the contrary, but in that case the land sold was the same as the description in the petition, whereas the order of sale was that the land described in the petition be sold, naming it by a wrong number. And if application be made and exhausted by a decree and sale of real estate to pay the then known debts of a decedent, and afterwards other debts appear against the estate requiring a further sale for their payment, then there must be a new application for such additional decree and sale, substantially as if none before had ever been made. Gilchrist's Admr. v. Rea, 9 Paige Ch. 66.

[2] Comstock v. Crawford, 3 Wall. 396, 403; Florintine v. Barton, 2 Wall. 210, 216; Griffith v. Frazier, 8 Cranch, 9, 23. In Illinois it should give also the names of the heirs. Turney v. Turney, 24 Ill. 625.

[3] Wood v. Nason, 5 Mass. 243, 358; McCandish v. Kern. 13 Gratt. 615; Johnson v. Collins, 12 Ala. 322; George v. Williams, 26 Mo. 190, 193; Drinkwater v. Drinkwater, 4 Mass. 354; Hathaway v. Valentine, 14 Mass. 500; Griffith v. Frazier, 9 Cranch, 23.

[4] Van Nostrand v. Wright, Hill & D. (N. Y.) 260; Small v. Cromwell, Ib. 154; Cralle v. Meem, 8 Gratt. 196; Gregory v. McPherson, 13 Cal. 562; Crippin v. Crippin, 1 Head. (Tenn.) 128.

[6] Cooper v. Sunderland, 3 Iowa, 114, 137, 138; Babbitt v. Doe, 4 Ind. 355; Thornton v. Mulquinne, 12 Iowa, 549, 554; Parker v. Nichols, 7 Pick, 111. 116; Campbell v. Knight, 26 Maine, 244; Little v. Sennett, 7 Iowa, 324; Morrow v. Weed, 4 Iowa, 77.

[6] Collins v. Farnesworth, 8 Blackf. 575.

[7] Frazier v. Pankey, 1 Swan (Tenn.) 75.

§ 264. In Mississippi, the personal estate must first be
found insufficient to pay the debts; and this fact is required
to be found by the verdict of a jury, before any order for the
sale of a decedent's lands can be made.[1] And if the personalty
be wasted by the administrator, by reason of which the personal assets are insufficient to pay the debts, it does not follow
that there is to be a sale of the realty for that purpose; but
the remedy, in such case, is against the administrator and his
sureties on their bond. The heirs may set up such waste, and
thereby prevent an order of sale.[2]

§ 265. Some of the cases vest the jurisdiction in an application by the administrator to sell a decedent's lands on a proper
petition alone;[3] others on notice and petition.[4] In either
case, when jurisdiction has attached, the decree is regarded as
an adjudication of all previous questions, both as to jurisdiction and merits, and as shutting out all subsequent inquiry
into the same, or as to their sufficiency, except on an appeal.[5]
In all cases the power of the court to decree and sell is the
creature of the statute, and its requirements must be con-

[1] Turner v. Ellis, 24 Miss. 173, 179.

[2] Turner v. Ellis, 24 Miss. 173, 180; Paine v. Pendleton, 32 Miss. 320.

[3] Grignon's Lessee v. Astor, 2 How. 369, 338; Beauregard v. New Orleans,
18 How. 502, 503. See Part 1st. Chap. 2, notes, and George v. Watson,
19 Texas, 354, 370, 371; McPherson v. Cundiff, 11 Sergt. & R. 422; Alexander v. Maverick, 18 Texas, 179.

[4] Morrow v. Weed, 4 Iowa, 77; Davenport v. Smith, 15 Iowa, 213; Frazier
v. Steenrod, 7 Iowa, 339; Myers v. McDonald, 47 Ill. 278; Moore v. Neil.
39 Ill. 256; Morris v. Hogle, 37 Ill. 150; Hawkins v. Hawkins, 28 Ind. 66;
Stow v. Kimball, 28 Ill. 108; Doe v. Anderson, 5 Ind. 33. But the notice
need not name the heirs by name under the statute in Illinois. Stow v.
Kimball, 29 Ill. 93. So much of Turney v. Turney, 24 Ill., as rules differently is disavowed.

[5] Grignon's Lessee v. Astor, 2 How. 319; Morrow v. Weed, 4 Iowa, 77,
87; Sheldon v. Newton, 3 Ohio (N. S.) 493; Simpson v. Hart, 1 Johns. Ch.
91; Beauregard v. New Orleans, 18 How. 502; Carter v. Waugh, 42 Ala.
452; Paul v. Hussey, 35 Maine, 97; Comstock v. Crawford, 3 Wall. 396.
And if there be on file a defective or insufficient notice, purporting to be
the one given, yet where the decree states that "notice according to law
was given of the pendency of the cause," it will be intended that such
was the case, and that other proof was received thereof by the court.
Moore v. Neil, 39 Ill. 256.

formed to; such conformity, however, is presumed to have existed after decree, where jurisdiction has attached.

§ 266. In a probate proceeding *in rem*, by an administrator or executor for the sale of a decedent's lands to pay debts, if no notice is required by the statute, then none need be given; such proceeding is the creature of the statute;[1] and it is sufficient if the statute be conformed to. If notice be left to the discretion of the court, then a reasonable notice will be necessary, to avoid reversal on error.

§ 267. If notice or other thing be by the statute or local practice required, and the statute or local decisions declare the decree, or sale *invalid* if conformity to such requirements does not in the record appear to have existed, then such conformity must appear from the record, in order to support the sale.[2] But if such statute be only *directory*, then, although notice is necessary to avoid error on an appeal, yet it is not absolutely essential to the validity of the decree and sale, when they are questioned in a collateral proceeding. The presumption of law is, after decree and sale, that the statute was conformed to; and the proceedings are binding, if the jurisdiction of the court had attached over the particular case, by a petition good upon demurrer.[3] Nor does it follow that the proceedings are not binding, where the statute is but directory, even if it appear that notice is wanting; for though the omission may be error, yet if not reversed, or set aside, the decree is binding, even if it appear from the record that such notice had not

[1] Bergin v. McFarland, 6 Foster (N. H.) 536; Clark v. Thompson, 47 Ill. 25, 28; Florentine v. Barton, 2 Wall. 210, 216.

[2] Guy v. Pierson, 21 Ind. 18; Gelstrop v. Moore, 26 Miss. 206; Cooper v. Sunderland, 3 Iowa, 144, 137, 138; Thornton v. Mulquinne, 12 Iowa, 549, 554; Babbit v. Doe, 4 Ind. 355.

[3] Morrow v. Weed, 4 Iowa, 77; Shelden v. Newton, 3 Ohio, (N. S.) 495; Reeves v. Townsend, 2 Zab. 396; Wilson v. Wilson, 18 Ala. 176; Clark v. Blacker, 1 Ind. 215; Paul v. Hussey, 35 Maine, 97; Fox v. Hoit, 12 Conn. 491; Raymond v. Bell, 18 Conn. 81; Wright v. Warner, 1 Doug. 384; Grignon's Lessee v. Astor, 2 How. 319; McPherson v. Cunliff, 11 Sergt. & R. 422; Clarke v. Holmes, 1 Doug. 390; Elliott v. Piersol, 1 Pet. 328; Thompson v. Tolmie, 2 Pet. 157; Vorhees v. The Bank, 10 Pet. 473; Wright v. Marsh, G. Green, 111; Florentine v. Barton, 2 Wall. 210, 216; George v. Watson, 19 Texas, 354.

been given; for the power of the court is over the property sought to be affected by the order, or decree, when the case is *in rem*, " without regard to the parties who may have an interest in it. All the world are parties." By the decree and sale. " the estate passes by operation of law." The court lays hold of, and passes the title, by a right paramount to that of the heirs. It does this under the same authority that confers the heirship: The authority of the legislature, which has full power to control the property of decedents.[1]

Such seems to be the settled rule of decision in the Supreme court of the United States, in the absence of a positive statute declaring sales void if notice be required, and does not from the record, appear to have been given; and such we conceive to be the more correct doctrine. The same power that confers heirship may postpone it, and hold the property first liable for the decedent's debts, and as a consequence may confer the power to so apply it on the probate court without notice to the intended heir, whose right attaches to the residue and not to the estate generally, in its unadministered condition. True the legal title descends to the heir at once, as it can not be in abeyance; but so descends, subject to a prior lien in law for the ancestor's debts—a lien which the power that creates both it and the heirship, may enforce in its own way. The probate court acts upon the title of the ancestor, subject to which action the lien takes title. "The administrator represents the land,"[2] and no notice is ordinarily necessary to the validity of the sale in proceedings *in rem*.

[1] Florentine v. Barton, 2 Wall. 210.

[2] Moore v. Stark, 1 Ohio St. 369; Grignon's Lessee v. Astor, 2 How. 319; Beauregard v. N. Orleans, 18 How. 497; Williamson v. Leland, 2 Pet. 657; Satcher v. Satcher's admr. 41 Ala. 26; Sheldon v. Newton, 3 Ohio, St. 494; McPherson v. Cunliff, 11 Serg. & R. 422; Perkins v. Fairfield, 11 Mass. 227; Saltonstall v. Riley, 28 Ala. 164; Paine v. Moorland, 15 Ohio, 442; Robb v. Irwin, 15 Ohio, 698; Benson v. Cilley, 8 Ohio, St. 614; Borden v. The State, 6 Eng. 519; Tongue v. Morton, 6 Har. & J. 23; Rice v. Parkman, 16 Mass. 328; Sohier v. Mass. Genl. Hos. 3 Cush. 487; Ludlow's heirs v. Johnson, 3 Ohio, 560; Adams v. Jeffries, 12 Ohio, 253; Voorhees v. Bk. United States, 10 Pet. 473; United States v. Aredondo, 12 Pet. 709; Rhode Island v. Mass. 12 Pet. 718; Stow v. Kimball, 28 Ill. 93; Florentine

§ 268. This question of notice and personal jurisdiction in probate sales came before the Iowa Supreme Court in *Good v. Norley*, at December term, 1869. Good filed a petition in chancery in the District Court of Polk county to quiet title to

v. Barton, 2 Wall. 210, 216; Lane *v*. Thompson, 43 N. H. 320. In Sheldon *v*. Newton, above cited, the supreme court of Ohio review the subject of such sales, and of judicial sales generally, with great ability, and say: " 1. A settled axiom of the law, furnishes the governing principle, by which these proceedings are to be tested. If the court had jurisdiction of the subject matter, and the parties, it is altogether immaterial how grossly irregular, or manifestly erroneous, its proceedings may have been; its final order can not be regarded as a nullity, and can not therefore be collaterally impeached. On the other hand, if it proceed without jurisdiction, it is equally unimportant how technically correct, and precisely certain, in point of form, its record may appear; its judgment is void to every intent and for every purpose, and must be so declared by every court in which it is presented. In the one case the court is invested with the power to determine the rights of the parties, and no irregularity or error in the exe. cution of the power, can prevent the judgment while it stands unreversed, from disposing of such rights as fall within the legitimate scope of its adjudication; while in the other its authority is wholly usurped, and its judgments and orders, the exercise of arbitrary power, under the forms but without the sanction of law. The power to hear and determine a cause, is jurisdiction; and it is *coram judice* whenever a case is presented which brings this power into action. But before this power can be affirmed to exist it must be made to appear that the law has given the tribunal capacity to entertain the complaint against the person or thing sought to be charged or affected; that such complaint has actually been preferred; and that such person or thing has been properly brought before the tribunal to answer the charge therein contained. When these appear the jurisdiction has attached; the right to hear and determine is perfect; and the decision of every question thereafter arising is but the exercise of the jurisdiction thus conferred; and whether determined rightfully or wrongfully, correctly or erroneously, is alike immaterial to the validity-force, and effect of the final judgment, when brought collaterally in ques, tion. United States *v*. Aredondo, 6 Pet. 709; Rhode Island *v*. Mass. 12 Pet. 718. We wholly dissent from the position taken in argument, that the jurisdiction of the court, or the effect of its final order, can be made to depend upon the records disclosing such a state of facts, to have been shown in evidence, as to warrant the exercise of its authority. To adopt the language of the court, in answer to the same position, in Voorhees *v*. The U. S. Bank, 10 Pet. 473: 'We cannot hesitate in giving a distinct and unqualified negative to this proposition, both on principle and authority too well and long settled to be questioned.' It was distinctly repudiated in the early case of Ludlow's heirs *v*. Johnson, 3 Ohio 560; and has been

a tract of land, claiming that in 1852 it was purchased at a
sale thereof, in probate, for payment of debts, made under
order in probate by the administrator of John Norley, deceased.
That a deed therefor was duly executed and by the court

no less positively denied in every subsequent case, including Adams *v.*
Jeffries, 12 O. R. 253. The tribunal in which these proceedings were had,
was a court of record of general common law and chancery jurisdiction;
and while it is true, that in the exercise of this particular authority, it may
be regarded as a tribunal of special and limited powers prescribed by
statute, it is still to be remembered that it was the tribunal created by the
constitution with the exclusive jurisdiction over probate and testamentary
matters, and had no one single characteristic of those inferior courts and
commissions to which the rule insisted upon has been applied by the
English and American courts. All its proceedings are recorded and constitute records, in the highest sense of the term, imparting absolute verity,
not to be impaired by averment or proof to the contrary, and conclusively
binding the parties, and all who stand in privity with them. The distinction is not between courts of general and those of limited jurisdiction,
but between courts of record that are so constituted as to be competent to
decide on their own jurisdiction, and to exercise it to a final judgment
without setting forth the facts and evidence on which it is rendered, and
whose records when made import absolute verity; and those of an inferior
grade, whose decisions are not of themselves evidence, and whose judgments can be looked through for the facts and evidence which are
necessary to sustain them. McCormick *v.* Sullivant, 10 Wheat. 199; Griswold *v.* Sedgwick, 1 Wend. 131; Baldwin *v.* Hale, 17 J. R. 272; Grignon's
Lessee *v.* Astor, 2 How. 341; 2 Bin. R. 255; 4 Ib. 187. Orphans' courts, and
courts of probate, when constituted courts of record, have uniformly been
held of the former description. Thompson *v.* Tolmie, 2 Pet. 165; Grignon's Lessee *v.* Astor, supra; 11 Serg. & Rawle, 429; 11 Mass. 221. In
respect to them, when it appears that they have proceeded with jurisdiction over the subject matter and the parties, we fully agree with the
supreme court of Pennsylvania in saying: 'If the purchaser was responsible for their mistakes in point of fact, after they had adjudicated upon
the facts, and acted upon them, those sales would be snares for honest
men;' and with the supreme court of the United States, in affirming that
the reasons upon which their decisions have rested 'are founded on the
oldest and most sacred principles of the common law. They are rules of
property, on which the repose of the country depends; titles acquired
under the proceedings of courts of competent jurisdiction must be deemed
inviolable in collateral actions, or none can know what is his own; and
there are no judicial sales around which greater security ought to be
placed, than those made of the estates of decedents, by order of those
courts to whom the laws of the States confide full jurisdiction over the
subjects.' The purchaser is bound to look no further back than the order

approved; but that the same was lost before recording. In the proceeding in probate under which the sale occurred, the administrator made the widow (whose dower had already been assigned) and the infant heir—the only child of the decedent—

of the court, made in a proceeding which the law has empowered it to entertain, and with the proper parties, or subject matter before it. All else, we are bound to presume in favor of its action; and neither in judgment of law, nor in fact, is it to be treated with the least distrust. The proper application of this principle disposes of all the exceptions taken to these proceedings, arising after the jurisdiction of the court should have attached. * * * * As it is not denied that the court was invested with power to entertain the proceeding, and as the lands were situated within the limits of its jurisdiction, it only remains to consider whether notice to the heirs was indispensible to the jurisdiction of the court; and if so, whether such notice was substantially given. These questions can only be answered in the light of a proper construction of the act of February 11th, 1824, (2 Ch. Stat. 1308,) under which these proceedings were had. From a very early period in our history, lands have been made assets, in the hands of executors and administrators, for the payment of debts; but at no time could they be converted into money for this purpose until the personal property was exhausted, nor without the special leave of the proper court of probate. Prior to the passage of the act of 1824, the leave was obtained upon the petition of the personal representative, showing a deficiency of personal assets. No parties defendant was required to be made, and the proceeding throughout was wholly *ex parte* and strictly and technically *in rem*. That act effected no further change than to require 'the person having the next estate of inheritance of the testator or intestate,' to be made defendant to the petition. What effect did this have upon the proceeding? Did it make it an adversary proceeding *in personam* in such sense as to make actual notice to the heir indispensible to the jurisdiction of the court? These questions have not been answered in any of the cases that have been decided, and they are not of easy solution. As the interests of the owner of the property sought to be appropriated are involved in either form of proceeding, neither is supposed to be pursued without notice to him. Proceedings *in rem* have their own essential and distinguishing characteristics. They are usually brought to enforce some liability which the thing itself has incurred—the law treating the thing itself as the debtor or delinquent, or some specific lien upon it. The seizure of the thing and taking it from the possession of the owner and into the custody of the law, is deemed to be implied notice to him, and while the proceedings were confined to the pursuit of personal property, was often quite as effectual as actual notice by the service of a summons would have been. Other means for giving notice were usually prescribed, but a failure to comply with them only goes to the regularity of the proceeding, and has never been held necessary to give the court

defendants, and asked for the appointment of a guardian *ad litem* for the infant. A guardian *ad litem* was appointed. The guardian appeared in person and the widow by an attorney, and severally waived notice and filed answers, consenting

jurisdiction. When the property charged with the liability is taken into the custody of the law and brought within the power of the tribunal, and the judgment spends its whole force upon the property,—creating no personal liability upon the owner—it has never been doubted that a judgment of condemnation was effected to vest a perfect title in the purchaser, however irregularly or erroneously the court may have proceeded. But when the liability is not upon the thing and it is seized only to secure and satisfy such judgment as may be recovered against the owner, there is much difficulty in seeing how the proceeding can be said to be *in rem*, or how a judgment *in personam* can be rendered until the party has been personally brought into court by such notice as the law may have provided. I do not doubt that the validity of judgments strictly *in rem*, may, by positive provision of law, be made to depend upon the service of process or other notice upon the owner; but in the absence of such expressed legislative intention, the omission to serve the process or give the notice, makes the proceeding only erroneous, but not void. The thing itself being in the custody of the law and within the power of the court, is subject to its action and effectually disposed of by its judgment. The proceeding authorized by the act of 1824, tested by its nature and essential qualities would seem to be clearly enough a proceeding *in rem*. Upon the death of the owner the law charged his debts as a specific lien on all his property, real and personal, and held it subject to their payment. The legal title to the real estate, it is true, descended to the heir, but it descended to him subject to this paramount lien. The executor or administraior was a trustee alike for creditors and heir, and the order of sale upon his petition operated on the estate and not on the heir; and the purchaser by operation of law, took the paramount title of the ancestor and did not claim through or under the heir. 2 How. 338; 11 Serg. & Rawle, 430. The heir was required to be made a party to the proceeding with a view to his having notice; but it is nowhere intimated that a failure to give the notice should deprive the court of jurisdiction over the property. I am, therefore, strongly inclined to the opinion that such an omission goes only to the regularity of the proceeding and not to the jurisdiction of the court; and that its final order can only be set aside for irregularity or reversed on error, and cannot be treated as a nullity in a collateral action. The proceeding was distinctly declared to be *in rem* in the case of Robb *v.* Irwin's Lessee, 15 O. R. 698; and, although READ, J., in his dissenting opinion, characterizes it as a 'nickname,' in the case of Paine's Lessee *v.* Mooreland, 15 O. R. 435, decided at the same term, he not only concurred with the court, but delivered their opinion in holding proceedings in attachment to be *in rem*, in which jurisdiction was acquired by the seizure of property,

to the sale of the property. An order of sale was accordingly made and the property was sold, deed executed, and by the court approved. To set up this title and to quiet the same, the petition in chancery in Polk District Court was filed. To

and that a judgment rendered without notice could not be treated as a nullity, although such proceedings are founded upon no liability or lien, resting upon the property itself; have adversary parties and are consummated by a judgment *in personam*, and the statute expressly declaring that the suit shall be dismissed at the cost of the plaintiff, if the notice is not given.

" But it does not become necessary to place this case upon that ground, as the court are of the opinion that notice was given in such manner as substantially complied with the law. This, we think, has been in effect settled for more than by the court of last resort in the state. The statute provided for no particular form of process or mode of giving notice to the defendants. The necessity of giving any notice is only to be inferred from the fact that the heirs are required to be made defendants. This omission in the law had to be supplied by a course of practice in the several courts invested with the jurisdiction, and it is in no way surprising that entire uniformity was not secured. This fact demonstrates the propriety of upholding any form of notice that afforded a reasonable opportunity to the heirs to interpose their objection to the sale. In the case of minor heirs the practice was general to serve the process upon the general guardian, or a guardian *ad litem*, or to permit an appearance without by either. The correctness of this practice was first drawn in question in Ewing's Lessee *v.* Higby, 7 O. R. 198, part 1. In that case the heirs were minors, and two of them were not named in the petition; but their guardians, during its pendency, entered their appearance. The court held them bound by the order of sale, and decided that the proceedings could not be collaterally impeached. And in Ewing *v.* Hollister, 7 O. R. 138, part 2d, the same order was affirmed on writ of *certiorari*. In Robb *v.* Irwin's Lessee, no process was served or issued, but the court appointed a guardian *ad litem* for the infant defendants, who appeared and answered. This was held sufficient to give the court jurisdiction and the title of the purchaser was protected. In Snevely *v.* Lowe, 18 O. R. 368, one of the minor heirs was not made a party to the petition, nor was any process issued or served. A guardian *ad litem* was appointed who filed an answer for the minor heirs, without specifying whether for those named in the petition alone, or for all the minor heirs of the decedent. But the court construed the answer to include them all, and held the proceeding effectual to transmit the title to the purchaser. Thus has the Supreme Court of the state, from the first to the last, uniformly decided that an actual service of process upon the minor heirs was not necessary to give the court jurisdiction, or even to the regularity of the proceedings. That it was enough that a guardian, either especially appointed for the purpose, or having the care

this petition one of the defendants answered. The others made default. The District Court decreed in favor of the petitioner, according to the prayer of the petitioner, and Mary Norley, the defendant who had appeared and answered, appealed. On this state of the case the cause came up for hearing on the appeal, and the judges of the Supreme Court were divided equally on the question as to whether personal jurisdiction of the infant defendant was essential in the probate court to the validity of the decree and sale. WRIGHT, Justice, was of opi-

and custody of the infants, person or estate, was before the court when the order was made. That it was not even indispensable that the infant should be named as a party in the petition; and without directly affirming that the court could obtain jurisdiction, without having him in some way before them, I must think that the case of Snevely v. Lowe can be supported on no other grounds. In my opinion it cannot be upon reasons assigned in the opinion. These decisions have stood as the law of the state for more than twenty years. During all that time they have constituted rules of property, and upon the faith of them men have invested their money. If ever an urgent case for the application of the maxim *stare decisis* existed, this is one. It is not enough that we should doubt their correctness, or that we should decide differently, if the question was now for the first time presented. It must be made to appear clearly and unquestionably that the rules of law have been violated, and the rights of the parties disregarded, before we could justify ourselves in questioning their authority. No such case is made; the question was a doubtful one, and has been settled, and one plain duty is to let it remain settled. In no one of these cases has the court gone further than the Supreme Court of the United States in Grignon's Lessee v. Astor, 2 How. 335, as will be seen by a particular examination of that case. I have not referred to the case of Adams v. Jeffries, 12 O. R. 253, cited and relied upon by the plaintiff's counsel, because the order of sale there involved was not made under the act of 1824, but under that of 1831, which specially provided the mode in which service should be made. These principles seem to us conclusively to settle the case in hand. In this case the heirs were all made parties to the petition, and service of process was regularly upon the guardian appointed for them. If the court had power to appoint them a guardian, it had power to bring him into court in this manner; and if he was in court when the order was made, the jurisdiction of the court over him and those he represented cannot be questioned. It is true he filed no answer, nor does the record show that he accepted the appointment; but the want of an answer could not affect the jurisdiction, and we are bound to presume the court were advised of his acceptance of the trust before proceeding to make the final order in the case." Shelden v. Newton, 3 Ohio St. 494.

nion, however, that there was jurisdiction of the person, and, therefore, as well as for account of the division of the court, the decree appealed from was affirmed, and the sale, as a legal result of such division, was held valid.[1]

§ 269. When jurisdiction has fully attached, by petition, if notice be not a condition to the validity of the proceedings, or by petition and notice, when such notice is thus required as a condition to validity, then, after decree, all things else as to regularity of the proceedings and necessary to their validity, is presumed; and after confirmation are no longer open to collateral inquiry.[2]

§ 270. Again, in *Florentine v. Barton*,[3] the Supreme Court of the United States, adhering to all its former decisions on this subject, Justice GRIER, delivering the opinion, hold the following language: "The petition of the administrator setting forth that the personal property of the deceased is insufficient to pay such debts, and praying the court for an order of sale, brought the case fully within the jurisdiction of the court. It became a case of judicial cognizance, and the proceedings are judicial. The court has power over the subject matter and the parties. It is true in such proceedings there are no adversary parties, because the proceeding is in the nature of a proceeding *in rem*, in which the estate is represented by the administrator, and, as in a proceeding *in rem* in admiralty, all the world are parties."

§ 271. In the same case the court say that in making the order of sale the probate court are "presumed to have adjudged every question necessary to justify such order or decree, viz.: the death of the owner; that the petitioners were his administrators; that the personal assets was insufficient to pay the

---

[1] Good *v.* Norley, 27 Iowa, 188.

[2] Morrow *v.* Weed, 4 Iowa, 77, 87; Carter *v.* Waugh, 42 Ala. 452; Myers *v.* McDonald, 47 Ill. 278; Frazier *v.* Steenrod, 7 Iowa, 339; Hart *v.* Jewett, 11 Iowa, 276; Davenport *v.* Smith, 15 Iowa, 213; Shelden *v.* Newton, 3 Ohio (N. S.) 495; Simpson *v.* Hart, 1 Johns. Ch. 91; Grignon's Lessee *v.* Astor, 2 How. 319, 340; Fox *v.* Hoit, 12 Conn. 491; Paul *v.* Hussey, 25 Maine, 97; Goudy *v.* Hall, 36 Ill. 313; Moore *v.* Neil, 39 Ill. 256, 262; Comstock *v.* Crawford, 3 Wall. 396.

[3] 2 Wall. 216.

debts of the deceased; that the private act of assembly as to
the manner of sale was within the constitutional powers of the
Legislature, and that all the provisions of the law as to notices,
which are directory to the administrators, have been complied
with."

§ 272. The court moreover holds substantially and expressly,
in the same case, that such order, whether correct or incorrect,
is final and binding, unless reversed for error, and is everywhere, in every court, binding in every collateral proceeding;
and that a purchaser under the same is not bound to look
further than the order of the court, or to "inquire into its
mistakes." That the court ordering the sale is not bound to
enter all things on its record; and that "a different doctrine"
would render "titles under a judicial sale worthless and a
'mere trap for the unwary.'"

§ 273. The court thus reaffirm the doctrine and the case of
Grignon's Lessee v. Astor, and so they do again in the case
of *Comstock v. Crawford*,[1] wherein the same principles are
reiterated and affirmed, as in *Florentine v. Barton*, above
referred to; and the latter case is cited and relied on as in
point.

§ 274. But the ruling is uniform that in chancery proceedings, in a regular court of chancery, if it appear affirmatively,
where there are litigant parties, that there was no service of
notice on the defendant, and there be no appearance, a decree
and sale disposing of the defendant's rights are void.[2] In
Ohio, it is said that the appointment of a guardian *ad litem*
for minor defendants is to enable them to defend and is after
they are in court, in a regular chancery cause, and not to bring
them in.[3] But in the probate court, in administrations, the
property is assets in the control of the court, first for payment of debts; remainder to the heirs. The latter are not
absolutely necessary as parties, unless made so by express
statute as a condition to validity of the decree.

§ 275. And where by statute, in proceedings in probate by

[1] 3 Wall. 396, 406.
[2] Moore v. Starks, 1 Ohio St. 369.
[3] Ibid.

an administrator to sell a decedent's lands for the payment of debts, the heirs are required to be made parties and no particular mode is prescribed for making them such, the law is complied with by the appointment of a guardian *ad litem* for infant heirs, so far as to them.[1]

§ 276. Notwithstanding the diversity of decisions and statutory regulations of the different states upon this subject, we think the following conclusions are borne out as general principles by the rulings of the courts in relation to sales of lands in probate for payment of debts: First—That all property of a decedent, which was liable to execution sale while he lived, is subject to an implied lien in favor of his creditors for payment of his debts at his death, which lien is paramount to the rights acquired by bequest or by heirship. Second—The enforcement of this lien is against the title of the ancestor or testator, as the case may be, and may be enforced in any manner which the law-making power may prescribe. Third—That both legatees and heirs take subject to this lien, and also subject to this paramount power of the state to enforce the lien in its own way, before its benefits, conferred on the heirs and permitted to be conferred by will upon legatees, shall unconditionally and absolutely inure to them. Fourth—That in the proceedings to enforce such lien by sale of lands, jurisdiction over the particular case and lands must attach by a petition good upon demurrer. Fifth—That if, by statute, no notice to the heirs or legatees be required, then none need be given. The power of the court is over the property and title of the ancestor. Sixth—That if by law a notice is required, and the law in that respect is directory only, then the omission thereof, though error for which a decree will be reversed, will not invalidate a sale thereon if the decree is permitted to stand; but if it is not apparent whether notice was given or not, then in such case, after decree, the law presumes the notice to have been given, and a sale thereon is valid. Seventh—That if by law a notice is required, and the law provides that unless it appear from the records to have been given, then it

---

[1] Robb *v.* Irwin, 15 Ohio, 689; Lewis *v.* Lewis' Admr. 15 Ohio, 715.

must so appear from the records, else the decree and sale will be void. Eighth—That where notice is required, as in either of the cases above stated, if it appear that there was what stands for notice, and that it was in the right case as to the lands described and against the right persons, if notice be required to the persons, that the proceedings and sale will be valid in that respect, although the notice or service thereof be irregular or defective, for the matter after decree is *res judicata* and at most but error of judgment.

§ 277. If notice of application be by law required, then the petition must be presented at the term of court named in the notice; but not necessarily on the first day of the term. The term in law is but one day in that respect. If a term intervene, that is, if the notice be of one term, and the petition be not presented then, but is presented at the succeeding term, it is *coram non judice*, and the proceeding will be void.[1] There cannot be a continuance of the application until the petition is filed, for until then there is no cause to continue. The proceedings, if a term intervenes without a petition being filed, abate by operation of law. Any subsequent proceedings based thereon are void.[2]

§ 278. But if the petition be presented at the term designated in the notice, and the case be docketed, and continued by the court until the next term, and such facts appear of record, then the action of the court at such subsequent term will be of like validity as if had at the time the petition is presented.[3] By failure to file the application at the time

---

[1] Schnell *v.* Chicago, 38 Ill. 382; Morris *v.* Hogle, 37 Ill. 150; Turney *v.* Turney, 24 Ill. 625; Goudy *v.* Hall, 16 Ill. 316.

[2] Schnell *v.* Chicago, 38 Ill. 394.

[3] Schnell *v.* Chicago, 38 Ill. 382. In this case the court say: "The question then is, was such presentation of the petition at the September term, when notice had been given, it would be presented at the August term, a compliance with the statute, and if not such compliance, does it not render the proceedings void? This question has already been determined by this court. The case of Turney and others *v.* Turney's Admr. 24 Ill. 625, is in point. In that case notices was given by the administratrix that she would apply by petition to the circuit of Jo Daviess county, at the July term, 1847, for an order to sell the real estate of the intestate. The petition was not filed until the following September term, and this court

designated in the notice the proceedings abate, and to give the
court proper jurisdiction, where notice is required, a new notice
is necessary.[1]

§ 279. As a pre-requisite to making the order of sale, the
claims of the creditors should first be adjudicated so as to
exhibit or show what is chargeable against the lands.[2] And in
some of the States the petition is required to state the names
of the heirs, or else the order or decree will be void.[3] Unless
the proceedings be entitled against the *unknown* heirs, under
the statute, and it be therein stated that the heirs are unknown.[4]

§ 280. It is held in New Hampshire that if the sale be void,
a new order and sale may be made, although the proceeds of
the first sale went to the creditors.[5]

§ 281. In Mississippi it must affirmatively appear in the
proceedings that the statutory requirements are conformed to,
else the sale will be void.[6]

§ 282. In Texas the application is to be made by a creditor,
heir, or legatee. An order of sale made on the application of
the administrator alone, is invalid to confer title by sale under
it, and if a sale be made thereon, it will be set aside on application for that purpose, although a lapse of more than five
years time intervene between the time of such application and
the day of sale.[7]

§ 283. The court has power to order the sale to be made on
a credit and may prescribe the terms thereof.[8]

§ 284. The order of sale must be confined to the lands

held that the failure to file the petition at the time specified in the notice
and petition, and to have the cause docketed at the July term, abated the
proceeding, and before any other steps could be taken the heirs and
parties in interest should have been again brought in to court by another
notice, as if none had been previously given.

[1] Turney *v.* Turney, 24 Ill. 625; Schnell *v.* Chicago, 38 Ill. 382.
[2] Cralle *v.* Meem, 8 Gratt. 496.
[3] Taliy *v.* Starke, 6 Gratt. 339; Guy *v.* Pierson, 21 Ind. 18.
[4] Guy *v.* Pierson, 21 Ind. 18.
[5] Wilson *v.* Bergin, 8 Foster, (N. H.) 96.
[6] Getstrop *v.* Moore, 26 Miss. 206.
[7] Miller *v.* Miller 10, Texas, 319.
[8] Reynolds *v.* Wilson, 15 Ill. 304.

described in the petition as those which it is desired to sell.[1] The order may be that the sale be public, or that it be private, at the discretion of the court.[2] No more land should be sold than is required to pay the debts, unless the sale of part only will injure the residue.[3] But selling a larger quantity will not always invalidate the sale.[4]

§ 285. In Illinois the court must have jurisdiction of the persons of the heirs in proceedings by an administrator to sell the land of a decedent to pay debts, and a decree made on the mere answer of the guardian *ad litem*, where no such jurisdiction had attached, is void, and so is a sale made thereon.[5]

§ 286. But if the court obtains jurisdiction of the case, and the subject matter and parties thereof, where jurisdiction of the persons is required, it matters not that errors or irregularities may intervene in the course of the proceedings. They will neither be void, nor will the court, for such irregularity or errors, without other cause, set the sale aside.[6] The sale, when confirmed, will be valid, irrespective of mere irregularities or errors in the proceedings. So, too, in Arkansas; mere irregularities will not vitiate the proceedings or the sales.[7] When the sale is confirmed by the court, all anterior questions arising collaterally, are precluded. But, until confirmation, the sale is incomplete and confers no rights.[8]

§ 287. The purchaser at an administrator's sale of lands in probate is not bound to look behind the decree more than to see if there was jurisdiction in the court making it of the subject matter and of the parties in interest.

§ 288. And though the sale be for the payment of debts some of which were fraudulent and the administrator may

---

[1] Williams v. Childress, 25 Miss. 78.

[2] Ex parte Couzins, 5 Greenl. 240.

[3] Black v. Meek, 1 Ind. 810; Merrill v. Harris, 6 Foster, (N. H.) 142.

[4] Runyon v. Rubber Co. 4 Zabr. 469.

[5] Clark v. Thompson, 47 Ill. 25; Herdman v. Short, 18 Ill. 59; Johnson v. Johnson, 30 Ill. 215.

Carter v. Waugh, 42 Ala. 452; Madden v. Cooper, 47 Ill. 362.

[7] Thorn v. Ingram, 25 Ark. 52.

[8] Mason v. Osgood, 64 N. C. 467; Rawlings v. Bailey, 15 Ill. 178; Ayres v. Baumgartner, 15 Ill. 444, 446; Young v. Keogh, 11 Ill. 642.

have been party to their fraudulent admission, yet such circumstance will not avoid the sale in collateral proceedings when a portion of the claims were just; at most it would only be voidable after confirmation, in a direct proceeding in chancery to set it aside. Nor will it alter the case if the purchaser have notice of or participate in the fraud. After confirmation the remedy is, in either case, by original bill. The sale cannot be attacked successfully in a collateral proceeding.[1]

§ 289. It is well settled in Indiana, first upon general principles, and subsequently under the statutes of that State, that a sale of the realty, by an administrator, without notice to the heir, though ordered and confirmed by the court, is absolutely void.[2] This is not only upon the general principle that to give validity to the proceedings the court must have jurisdiction of the parties by service or appearance, as well as of the subject matter,[3] as originally holden in that State previous to the enactment of 1843. But, as ruled subsequently under said statute which declares that the petition must state the names and age of the heirs or others in interest, if known, and if unknown, that such want of knowledge should be stated. That no order of sale shall be made without notice to such heirs or others in interest; personal notice if residents of the State, and by publication if non-residents.[4]

§ 290. But every reasonable intendment or presumption is made in favor of the proceedings where the record comes collaterally in question and there is no disclosure whatever in the same negativing jurisdiction of the person.[5]

§ 291. And where the petition for leave to sell lands of minor heirs was filed, and a guardian *ad litem* for the heirs appointed all at the same time, without actual notice to the

[1] Myers v. McDougal, 47 Ill. 278.
[2] Hawkins v. Hawkins, 28 Ind. 70, 71; Babbitt v. Doe, 4 Ind. 355; Doe v. Anderson, 5 Ind. 33; Doe v. Bowen, 8 Ind. 197; Gerrard v. Johnson, 12 Ind. 636; Wart v. Finley, 8 Blackf. 335; Bliss v. Wilson, 4 Blackf. 169.
[3] Hawkins v. Hawkins, 28 Ind. 66, 71.
[4] Hawkins v. Hawkins, 28 Ind. 70.
[5] Hawkins v. Hawkins, 28 Ind. 66, 71; Homer v. Doe, 1 Ind. 130; Doe v. Harvey, 5 Blackf. 487.

heirs, but in which proceeding the guardian *ad litem* appeared
and answered admitting the truth of the petition, and the
court ordered a sale which was made and confirmed, it was
holden that though the order of sale was erroneous, it was not
a nullity, and that the sale and purchase under it were valid.[1]

§ 292.   Where, however, in a like case, under the act of 1843,
the general guardian of the minor heirs appeared and filed an
answer stating that he neither admitted nor denied the matters
charged in the petition, and waived service of notice on his
wards, the court decreed an order of sale upon such petition
and answer, and the sale was made, it was held that the sale
and the order of sale were nullities when the same came in
question in a collateral proceeding.[2]

§ 293.   The infancy of the heirs does not excuse the service
of process or notice on them, where the statute makes notice
necessary to the validity of the proceeding.[3]   Such service
being omitted, seems not to render the order void, where a
guardian *ad litem* is appointed and appears for the minors;
still, as we have seen, its omission is error.[4]

§ 294.   Where a creditor of a deceased debtor would otherwise have a right to an order in probate for sale of the realty
to pay his debt, but has been prevented by destruction of the
records by fire or by other circumstances not arising from any
fault of his own, from enforcing his claim by administrator's
sale of the realty, and the estate of the decedent still remains
unsettled without any evidences or basis in the probate court
of assets or data from which to procure a settlement, decree
of sale or payment, such creditor may, upon the general principles of equity jurisdiction, obtain relief in the ordinary court
of chancery by bill in equity, and a decree for the sale of the
real estate to pay his debt in a direct proceeding against the
heirs for discovery of assets and for relief; and in such case

[1] Thompson *v.* Doe, 8 Blackf. 336.

[2] Doe *v.* Anderson, 5 Ind. 33.

[3] Hawkins *v.* Hawkins, 28 Ind. 66, 72; Hough *v.* Canby, 8 Blackf. 301;
Peoples *v.* Stanley, 6 Ind. 410; Martin *v.* Starr, 7 Ind. 224; Pugh *v.* Pugh,
9 Ind. 132; Abdill *v.* Abdill, 9 Ind. 287.

[4] Thompson *v.* Doe, 8 Blackf. 336.

eight years is not deemed an unreasonable time in which to commence such proceeding.[1]

§ 295. But it is also held in New York, that although sufficient time has elapsed between the grant of administration and the time of the application to the surrogate's court for the order of sale to cause the court to reject the application, that nevertheless if the court grant the order, it is but error, and can be corrected only by appeal. That until reversed the proceeding will be valid, and being so, of course a sale, in accordance with it, and in other respects sufficient, would also be valid. The erroneous judgment of the surrogate, given in a proceeding wherein jurisdiction has attached, will not be void, and cannot be treated as such in a collateral proceeding. The court having obtained jurisdiction its order is not a nullity.[2]

V. WITHIN WHAT TIME THE SALE IS TO BE MADE AND PERFECTED BY DEED.

§ 296. The general ruling is, that where the life, or validity of the license to sell is limited to one year, or other time, the sale must be made and perfected within the limited time.[3] In Michigan, however, a sale was made on the last day limited by law, and the deed was executed eighteen days thereafter, and the court held the same to be valid.[4]

§ 297. Though there be no limit of time by law in which to sell a decedent's lands to pay debts, yet the power may

---

[1] Clark v. Hogle, 52 Ill. 427. And one creditor alone may file such bill. Ib. and 1 Story, Eq. Jur. 603, Sec. 546.

[2] Jackson v. Robinson, 4 Wend. 436. But this decision was made previous to the passage of the revised statutes limiting the time to three years. The statutory limit is arbitrary and cuts off the power of the surrogate at the end of the time limited. If there be a remedy afterward, it must be under suitable circumstances in a court of general chancery jurisdiction.

[3] Marr v. Boothy, 19 Maine, 150; Mason v. Hain, 36 Maine, 573; Macy v. Raymond, 9 Pick, 285; Welman v. Lawrence, 15 Mass. 326, 329; Chadbourne v. Ratcliff, 30 Maine, 354, 359; Dubois v. Dubois, 4 McLean, 486, 489.

[4] Howard v. Moore, 2 Mich. 226.

expire by analogy to the statute of limitations.[1] But where circumstances require it, an ordinary court of chancery, having jurisdiction of the subject matter, will not be restricted by the time allowed in probate.[2]

§ 298. In the case of *Clark v. Hogle*,[3] the ordinary court of chancery jurisdiction, assumed jurisdiction and afforded relief by decree and sale of real estate of a decedent at the suit of creditors who had been prevented by accident and burning of the probate records from obtaining satisfaction of his debt by proceedings and sale in probate in the ordinary manner. In that case the proceedings was a direct one by bill in equity against the heirs of the decedent; and though the term of eight years had intervened, chancery did not consider that a sufficient time to preclude the creditor under the circumstances of the case. In such cases, equity courts have jurisdiction upon the general principles of affording relief against accidents.

VI. Not after Repeal of the Law or Abolition of the Court Allowing the Order.

§ 299. The power to make or carry out the sale, or to enforce the decree, ceases with the abolition of the court in which the decree is made in case such court be abolished by law between the time of making the decree and the completion of the sale. In such case no authority remains to perfect the same, or to enforce the decree.[4]

§ 300. And so a sale under an order or decree made after repeal of the law under which the proceedings and decree were had. The repeal of the law, if there be no saving clause, puts an end to the authority of the decree, and the sale is void.[5]

§ 301. It follows from these principles that if the decree itself be made under a supposed law, but which was then

---

Dubois *v.* McLean, 4 McLean, 486; *In re* Godfrey 4 Marsh, 308.

[2] Clark *v.* Hogle, 52 Ill. 427.

[3] Clark *v.* Hogle, 52 Ill. 427.

[4] McLaughlin *v.* Janney, 6 Gratt. 609, 614.

[5] Perry *v.* Clarkson, 16 Ohio, 571; Campan *v.* Gillett, 1 Man. (Mich.) 416; Bank of Hamilton *v.* Dudley, 2 Pet. 494.

already repealed and had ceased to exist, both the decree and any sale made thereon are void.[1]

§ 302. In the case of *McLaughlin v. Janney*,[2] the court hold the following language: "It would be a solecism, in law, to assert that persons appointed by a court to act as its commissioners can exercise that authority as commissioners of that court after the court itself has been abolished, or has ceased to exist."

§ 303. And in the *Bank of Hamilton v. Dudley*,[3] that very learned Justice, MARSHALL, says, in reference to the effects of a repeal: "If the law which authorized the court to make the order be repealed, the power to sell can never come into existence."

§ 304. Thus it is well settled that abolishing the court, or repealing the law before enforcement of the order or decree, destroys the power to execute it, if there be no saving clause, and terminates the proceedings.

VII. THE OATH.

§ 305. When, by law, an oath is required to be taken by the administrator or executor, in reference to selling, it should be taken before fixing the time and place and giving notice of sale, and not merely before the act of selling, or the execution of the deed. The taking of the oath in such cases should be the first step taken in proceeding to sell.[4]

§ 306. If the law requiring the oath is only directory, and it does not appear from the proceeding whether it was taken or not, then the presumption of law is that it was taken, if jurisdiction had attached; and the question will not be open to collateral inquiry.[5] And so, too, though the validity of the proceedings are, under the statute, dependent on the taking of

[1] Ludlow *v.* Wade, 5 Ham, 494.
[2] 6 Gratt. 609, 614.
[3] 2 Pet. 492.
[4] Parker *v.* Nichols, 7 Pick. 111, 116; Cooper *v.* Sunderland, 3 Iowa, 114; Campbell *v.* Knight, 26 Maine, 244; Thornton *v.* Mulquinne, 12 Iowa, 549, 554; Little *v.* Sennett, 7 Iowa, 324; Morrow *v.* Weed, 4 Iowa, 77.
[5] Voorhees *v.* U. S. Bank, 10 Pet. 449, 476, 477.

the oath, if it do not appear whether it was taken or not, and jurisdiction had attached, then the presumption is that the oath was properly taken.[1]

§ 307. But where, by statute or by the settled rulings of the court, it is requisite to the validity of the sale, that from the records and proceedings it shall appear that the requisite oath has been taken, then if from the records and proceedings it does not appear to have been taken, there is in such case no intendment of law to help out the proceedings, but the sale made therein is void and will be so treated when collaterally drawn in question,[2] except such validity as may be given to it by long and uninterrupted possession and by lapse of time.

VIII. Sales Merely Irregular, or in Irregular Proceedings, not Void.

§ 308. A mere irregularity in the proceedings, or in the manner of selling or conducting the sale, if there be no want of jurisdiction in the court, will not avoid a sale of lands in probate by an executor or administrator for payment of a decedent's debts.[3]

§ 309. Nor can the validity of the sale, in a collateral proceeding, be made to depend upon the regularity of the administrator's appointment, if the appointment be mere error as in a wrong county under a law that is only directory.[4] But otherwise if the law inhibit such appointment.[5]

§ 310. If the sale be reported and approved by the court, then it may not be impeached collaterally for any irregularity

---

[1] Voorhees v. U. S. Bank, 10 Pet. 449, 476, 477.

[2] Cooper v. Sunderland, 3 Iowa, 114, 137, 138; Thornton v. Mulquinne 12 Iowa, 549, 554; Babbitt v. Doe, 4 Ind. 355.

[3] Van Syckle v. Richardson, 13 Ill. 171; Freeland v. Dazey, 25 Ill. 294; Madden v. Cooper, 47 Ill. 359, 362; Iverson v. Loberg, 26 Ill. 179; Matilda v. Lockridge, 53 Ill. 503; Ewing v. Higby, 6 Ohio, 472; Grignon's Lessee v. Astor, 2 How. 319; Comstock v. Crawford, 3 Wall. 396; George v. Watson, 19 Texas, 354; Succession of Guerney, 14 La. An. 632; Gregory v. McPherson, 13 Cal. 174, 562.

[4] Wright v. Walbaum, 39 Ill. 554; Schnell v. Chicago, 38 Ill. 382; Cook v. Fry, 2 Mich. 506.

[5] Culls v. Hoskins, 9 Mass. 543.

or insufficiency in the notice given of the sale. If the probate court err in adjudicating the notice to be a sufficient one, when in truth it is not in legal compliance with the law, this error is to be corrected on appeal and cannot be taken advantage of in a collateral proceedings involving title under the sale.[1] In *Morrow v. Weed*,[2] the Supreme Court of Iowa, WOODWARD, Justice, say: "If this were admissible, then every question relating to the sufficiency of a notice and of its service, too, in any of the courts, could be bought up and reviewed in the same manner."

IX. CONFIRMATION—THE DEED—ITS APPROVAL.

§ 311. In some states the practice is to confirm the sale by order in probate of record, and therein direct the execution of the deed.[3] In others the usual course is for the administrator or executor to execute the deed and report the same with the sale for approval; and, thereupon, if acceptable to the court, an order approving the deed is made and is endorsed upon the deed.[4]

§ 312. If the administrator or executor die before carrying the order into effect by a complete sale, his successor should complete the sale and make the deed, or else apply to the court for orders in that respect.[5]

[1] Morrow v. Weed, 4 Iowa, 77; Little v. Sennett, 7 Iowa, 324, 335.
[2] 4 Iowa, 91.
[3] Wells v. Miller, 22 Texas, 302; Dowling v. Duke, 20 Texas, 181; Bradbury v. Reed, 23 Texas, 258; Smith v. Chew, 35 Miss. 153; Hallick v. Guy, 9 Cal. 181, 195; Yerby v. Hill, 16 Texas, 377.
[4] Wade v. Carpenter, 4 Iowa, 361, 366; Morrow v. Weed, 4 Iowa, 77.
[5] Baker v. Bradsby, 23 Ill. 632. This case was in reference to a sale of slaves, but the principle applies with still greater force as to land.

CHAPTER VII.

GUARDIAN'S SALES, AND SALES IN PROCEEDINGS FOR PARTITION.

I. Guardian's Sales.
II. Sales in Proceedings for Partition.

I. Guardian's Sales.

§ 313. In England, the king being sovereign, is by the common law regarded as the universal guardian of all infants or minors.[1] Hence this authority was an attribute of the judiciary, when, as was the case originally, the king held the courts himself in person.

§ 314. It followed that when the judicial power was transmitted from the king in person to the judges by him appointed to hold the courts in his stead, that this attribute of guardianship then devolved upon the courts, whence it eventually centered in the chancellor, whose court is always open. Whether by usurpation as by some jurists contended,[2] or by legitimate means, as alleged by others,[3] is no longer material. Suffice it to say it was there firmly lodged, and the chancery court came to be regarded as guardian of the interests of all minors.[4]

§ 315. This authority as to administrative matters, came to be conferred on others selected and appointed by the chancellor, from time to time, for infants generally, as necessity should require, and as ultimately regulated by act of parliament, chancery, however, retaining and maintaining its supervisory power over both guardians so appointed and over their wards and their interests both moral and pecuniary. This, too, even

[1] Bac. Abt. Vol. 4; Title, Guardian, C.
[2] Co. Lit. 128; note 16.
[3] Fonblanque, Eq. 228, n. *a.*
[4] Bac. Abt. Vol. 4; Title Guardian, C.

(124)

to the extent of superceding the authority of the parent for the interest of the child.[1]

§ 316. Now, such being the powers of the king, the parliament, and the courts under the crown, not only as to England, but as to the colonies also, they legally devolved upon the several sovereign States, legislatures, and courts of the several republican commonwealths established by the American revolution, and as a part of their common inheritance, and also upon the new States, their legislatures, and their courts subsequently established.

§ 317. Although in the American States the administrative powers and duties as to appointment of guardians, their ordinary supervision and accountability, and the administration of the ward's interests and care of his person is conferred and regulated by statutes conforming to the local policies of the several States, yet the uncircumscribed overruling supervisory jurisdiction of the chancellor still exists.[2] This power is to be exercised upon the great principles of equity whenever necessity calls for it for the protection of the infant from all abuse of his rights in property and in person when wielded by the chancellor as a judge of the court of general chancery jurisdiction and by the probate courts of inferior jurisdicton to the extent and in the manner specified and regulated by the legislative enactments of the several States, in each State, according to the *lex loci* thereof.

§ 318. In some of the States it is held that a court of general chancery jurisdiction has full power to decree a sale of a minor's lands when deemed best for his interests.[3] Whilst in some others it is said that though chancery may exercise such a power over the estates of minors that it will not be done to the disposal of a future interest except under extraordinary

---

[1] Bac. Abt.; Title Guardian, C. Whitfield *v.* Hale, 12 Ves. 492. *Ex parte* Warner, 4 Brown, Ch. 101.

[2] 2 Story, Eq. Jur. Sec. 1339, 1340, 1341, 1356; *Ex parte* Crumb. 2 Johns. Ch. 439; Matter of Andrews, 1 Johns. Ch. 99; Allen *v.* Allen, 2 Litt. 97; Aymar *v.* Roff, 3 Johns. Ch. 49.

[3] Williams *v.* Harrington, 11 Ind. 616; Matter of Salisbury, 3 Johns. Ch. 347; Huger *v.* Huger, 3 Des. 18; Stapleton *v.* Longstaff, 3 Des. 22; Williams *v.* Harrington, 11 Ired. 616; *Ex parte* Jewett, 16 Ala. 409.

circumstances, and not in any case for the mere purpose of
increasing the present interest of the adult owner.[1]

§ 319. Again, in others, the converse of this principle is
asserted, and it is held that the general powers of chancery do
not extend to the decreeing a sale of an infant's real estate for
the mere purpose of bettering his pecuniary condition or general interests.[2] Formerly the ruling in Virginia, under the
act of February 18, 1853, was the other way.[3]

§ 320. But whatever the general powers of the chancellor
may be, those of the courts of probate are such only as are
conferred by statute,[4] and must be exercised in conformity to,
and only for the causes allowed by the statutes of the respective States.

§ 321. Yet, if jurisdiction shall have attached such conformity will be inferred, in most cases, after decree and sale;
for although they are courts of limited powers, yet their jurisdiction is general to the extent conferred over the particular
subjects by statute.[5]

§ 322. In some cases it is held that the proceedings by
guardian in probate for a sale of a ward's lands are adversary,
and that there must be notice, or what answers in lieu
thereof.[6] In others it is adjudged that they are *in rem;* that
the action of the court is on the property itself, the proceedings not adversary, and that no notice, or what may answer
instead thereof, is required.[7]

§ 323. But in the latter class of cases, the court of probate

[1] Matter of Jones, 2 Barb. Ch. 22.

[2] Falkner v. Davis, 18 Gratt. 651; Rogers v. Dill, 6 Hill, 415; Baker v.
Lorillard, 4 Comst. 257; Williams' Case, 3 Bland Ch. 186; Pierse v. Trigg,
10 Leigh, 406.

[3] Falkner v. Davis, 18 Gratt. 651.

[4] Wade v. Carpenter, 4 Iowa, 361; Gilmore v. Rogers, 41 Penn. St. 120;
Fitch v. Miller, 20 Cal. 352; Robert v. Casey, 25 Mo. 584; Palmer v. Oakley, 2 Doug. (Mich.) 433.

[5] United States v. Arcdondo, 6 Pet. 709; Iverson v. Loberg, 26 Ill. 179;
Thompson v. Talmie, 2 Pet. 157; Pursley v. Hays, 22 Iowa, 1; Myer v.
Douglass, 47 Ill. 278.

[6] Townsend v. Tallant, 33 Cal. 45.

[7] Mason v. Wait, 4 Scam. 127; Smith v. Race, 27 Ill. 387; Grignon's
Lessee v. Astor, 2 How. 319.

will protect the ward's rights by requiring notice, or by causing a defense to be interposed by a proper guardian *ad litem* if there shall be apparent cause to apprehend that the guardian is abusing his trust.[1] But if, on suggestion as *amicus curia,* it shall appear that there be reason to apprehend an abuse of trust, then the court will appoint a guardian *ad litem.* Otherwise the proceedings to sell a ward's real estate, by his guardian in probate, are not necessarily adversary, as against the ward under ordinary circumstances.[2]

§ 324. In the case of *Smith v. Race,*[3] the court advert to their previous decision in Sturms' case, 25th Illinois 390, wherein they held that the minor heirs should have been made parties to the proceeding or suit of their guardian, and qualify the doctrine there asserted in the following language: "We are aware that the views here expressed are not in accordance with those announced *In re Sturms,* 25 Ill. 390. In that case it was improperly said that the minors were not parties to the original suit, and their interest could not be affected by the sale of their land by the guardian. In that we went too far, according to the case of *Mason v. Wait.*"

In the cases of *Mason v. Wait,* and *Smith v. Race,* the Illinois supreme court go to the full extent of the cases of *Grignon's Lessee v. Astor,* and of *Beauregard v. New Orleans,* on the subject in cases of sales by guardians by proceedings in probate, and hold that as the Illinois statute does not require those in interest to be made parties that the action of the court without regard to parties is within its jurisdiction in such cases and is valid.

§ 325. The court in their discretion might grant the license to sell in the alternative—so as to authorize the sale to be made privately or at public vendue, under the statute of Maine of 1826.[4] But under the statutes of 1840, all sales of lands in that state made by orders of court are to be at public auction.[5]

---

[1] Smith v. Race, 27 Ill. 387; Mason v. Wait, 4 Scam. 127.
[2] Mason v. Wait, 4 Scam. 127; Smith v. Race, 27 Ill. 387.
[3] Smith v. Race, 27 Ill. 386, 392, 393.
[4] *Ex parte* Cousins, 5 Greenl. 240.
[5] Ibid.

§ 326. A deed of warranty executed by a guardian for his
ward's lands, made under decree of the court and sale thereon,
carries only such title as the ward has at the time. Such war
ranty binds the guardian in his individual capacity.[1]

§ 327. To sustain a guardian's sale of his ward's real estate
the authority of the guardian to sell must first be shown, by
production of the decree or license of the court, or such exem
plification thereof as may be proof thereof, before the deed
can be given in evidence. He cannot sell without such
order.[2]

§ 328. A sale and conveyance of the whole interest nominally, of lands, by order in probate on application of the
guardian of one only of several owners, carries title to the
share represented by the ward of such guardian, and to no
more. The proceedings do not affect the interest of the other
owners.[3]

§ 329. The guardian in *socage* has no power to sell his
ward's real estate under order in probate, after the ward attains
the age at which such guardianship terminates by law. A
sale made after the termination of such guardianship is void,
and confers no rights whatever on the purchaser.[4]

§ 330. If the ward after attaining his majority receive the
proceeds of a sale of his real estate made by his guardian
during his minority, under order of court, the same being its
full value, it is an affirmance of the sale, even though the guardian be the purchaser, if received with proper knowledge of
all the circumstances; but such reception of the purchase
money will be construed so as not to prejudice the ward, if it
appear that he acted without due precaution or proper knowledge, or was influenced by threats.[5]

§ 331. The general rule is that a guardian or other person
selling in the relation of trustee cannot purchase at his own

[1] Young v. Lorain, 11 Ill. 624.
[2] Jackson v. Todd, 1 Dutch (N. J.) 121.
[3] Bryan v. Manning, 6 Jones, Law, (N. C.) 334.
[4] Perry's Lessee v. Brainard, 11 Ohio, 442.
[5] Scott v. Freeland, 7 S. & M. 409; Michoud v. Girod, 4 How. 503, 553,
See ante, p. 68, n. 4.

sale. He cannot blend the characters of both seller and buyer so as to unite them in himself.

§ 332. Where neither the law nor the order of sale expressly require a report to be made at the first term after granting the order, but the law being silent on the subject and the order merely requiring a report to the next term of the court, it will be construed to mean the next term after the consumation of the sale. And if by law no confirmation of the sale, or approval thereof, or of the deed, be required, then no such approval or confirmation is necessary to the validity of the sale, especially after great lapse of time. Nor will the failure of the guardian to comply with the order of court in making report of the sale, under such circumstances and law, invalidate the sale, when neither the law or the order of court make its validity dependent on such subsequent act of the guardian. "To hold the title of the purchaser (say the court) dependent upon the return and report of the guardian, is to hold him responsible for a matter over which he has no control. He can look to the order of court and see whether there is authority to sell, and if so, how far that authority is restricted; but when he sees an order, and that the terms upon which the power to sell depends have been complied with, he is not responsible for the subsequent misconduct of the guardian. His title cannot and ought not to be invalidated by matters happening subsequent to its vesting. We might as well require him to see to the application of the purchase money. Undoubtedly where a title cannot be consumated without certain acts being done, and an approval of the court of those acts the case is different. The sales of administrators under the statute are of this character. But no provision is made in the guardian law of 1825 to secure the supervision of the court over the sale; none which looks to an approval by the court, as a preliminary to the purchaser's title."[1]

§ 333. A decree in probate for the sale of a ward's lands to raise a certain amount of money is necessarily to be construed to mean that amount and the costs.[2]

[1] Robert v. Casey, 25 Mo. 584.
[2] Emery v. Vroman, 19 Wis. 689, 700.

9

§ 334. And if a larger sum be raised by such sale than the
decree calls for or allows, and the sale be made in parcels, yet
the illegality will not affect the sale of those parcels that were
sold before the aggregate of the proceeds amounted to an
excess of the sum to be raised.[1]

§ 335. If the lands are sold in different order than that
directed in the license or decree, the defect, if it be one, is
cured by the action of the court in confirming the sale, for, in
the language of the Supreme Court of Wisconsin, "the same
court from which the order emanated had in its discretion the
power to modify it or to dispense with its strict performance
in the particular named. This was done by the order of confirmation."[2]

II. Sales in Proceedings for Partition.

§ 336. Sales of land by order of the court in proceedings
for partition are judicial sales.[3] As such they must be reported
to the court for confirmation, and until confirmed they are of
no effect.[4]

§ 337. On failure of the purchaser to comply with the
terms of the sale, if the land be re-sold by order of the court
and sell for a less price then at first, the original owner or the
commissioners selling may sue for and recover of the first
purchaser the loss on the re-sale.[5]

§ 338. A court of equity may partition part in kind and
sell other parts of lands as may seem for the best interests of
the parties.[6]

§ 339. The purchaser under a sale in partition takes a conclusive title against the parties to the suit,[7] and against their
grantees by conveyance made during the proceedings.[8]

[1] Emery v. Vroman, 19 Wis. 689, 700.
[2] Ibid.
[3] Hutton v. Williams, 35 Ala. 503.
[4] Hutton v. Williams, 35 Ala. 503; Hess v. Voss, 52 Ill. 472.
[5] Hutton v. Williams, 35 Ala. 503.
[6] Haywood v. Judson, 4 Barb. 228.
[7] Gates v. Irick, 2 Rich. 593; Allen v. Gault, 27 Penn. St. 473.
[8] Baird v. Corwin, 17 Penn. St, 462; Michoud v. Girod, 4 How. 503, 559;
Davoue v. Fanning, 2 Johns. Ch. 252.

§ 340. If, whilst proceedings are pending for the partition of lands held in common, a creditor of one of the tenants in common obtain a judgment against his debtor, the creditor so obtaining judgment has no other or better right than has his debtor in the subject matter of the proceeding, and cannot require the sale in partition to be made for cash, so as to meet the cash demands of his judgment.[1] And so in Illinois the lien of a mortgage given by one of the parties to partition proceeding during the pendency of such proceedings, follows the interest when set off of the party giving the mortgage.[2]

§ 341. In Illinois it has been held that in sales in partition under the statute, proof of the notice of sale should be filed and made to appear in the proceedings with a copy of the notice;[3] but, in the same state, in partition sales in the ordinary court of chancery, it is holden that the chancery court need not, as it does not proceed under the statute, conform to the statute in this respect.[4]

§ 342. In sales in proceedings for partition all persons in interest, including lien holders against the property and holders of liens against separate shares or interests, are, in Illinois, required to be made parties, and that too whether the interest be a present and certain or a contingent one. Thus, having before it the parties in interest both as coparceners and creditors, the court will then declare the rights and interest of each of the parties and make such decree as will protect the same. The money arising from the sale should be brought into court and applied by the order of the court where it belongs, and the several liens should be displaced and replaced by their several shares of the funds arising from the sale, and the residue distributed to the proper owners, so as to dispose of the whole matter and give the purchaser a clear title.[5]

§ 343. Decrees of sales in partition should not only ascer-

---

[1] Stern v. Epstin, 14 Rich. Eq. 5; Cradlebaugh v. Pritchett, 8 Ohio St. 646.

[2] Loomis v. Riley, 24 Ill. 307; Manly v. Pettee, 38 Ill. 128, 133

[3] Hess v. Voss, 52 Ill. 473, 479; Tibbs v. Allen, 29 Ill. 535.

[4] Hess v. Voss, 52 Ill. 473, 479.

[5] Kilgour v. Crawford, 51 Ill. 249.

tain and declare the relative rights or interests of the parties and give such judgment as may sustain the same, but should describe the land to be sold and the sale of land not included in the order of sale, although included in the application, is error. If there be minors interested in the suit they must be made parties by process and actual service. The better authority is that appointment of guardian *ad litem* to defend for them without such prior proofs and service is without unauthorized and is error for which a decree will be reversed, as is also the omission to find the several relative interests, and also the selling of lands not described in the decree. For such sale of lands not decreed to be sold and for proceeding without making the minors parties, the sale, it is believed, though affirmed, will be void.[1]

§ 344. In Ohio, sales in proceedings for partition do not carry to the purchaser the growing crops situate upon the premises. The court say: " Sales made in partition are subject to regulations entirely similar to those which govern sales on ordinary execution. The lands must be appraised and cannot be sold for less than two-thirds of their appraised value; and the same considerations which forbid us to hold that the growing crops pass to the purchaser in the one case, forbid it in the other."[2] In *Houts v. Showalter* the court say, BRINKERHOFF, Justice: " When an appraisement is made, it cannot be foreseen when a sale will be effected. It is not for the interest of any party, nor for the public interest, that the land should thenceforth lie waste; then there may have been no crop sown or planted, but when the sale comes to be made there may be growing crops put into the ground in the meantime. If these passed by the sale it would be unjust to the debtor, for they could not have been valued."

§ 345. Thus it is that in Ohio, although in partition sales no interest of a debtor is involved, yet, as the statute of that state requires appraisement in partition sales as in sales on execution, it follows that the same objection arises in the one

---

[1] Hickenbotham v. Blackledge, 54 Ill. 316, 318.

[2] Houts v. Showalter, 10 Ohio St. 124, 127; Cassilly v. Rhodes, 12 Ohio St. 88.

case as in the other to allowing the growing crops to pass by the sale. That is the impracticability of fixing their valuation, whilst without valuation they cannot, with the realty, be sold.[1]

[1] Houts v. Showalter, 10 Ohio St. 124, 127.

CHAPTER VIII.

PURCHASES BY PERSONS CONCERNED IN SELLING.

§ 346. The policy of the law forbids, as conducive to fraud and inimical to fair dealing, the purchase by masters, trustees, executors, administrators, guardians, and all others, at their own sales, as also all agents, public and private, who are concerned in selling, whether such purchase be direct or indirect; and if made, such sales will be set aside on application of the parties interested.[1] When the person selling is willing to give

[1] Lockwood v. Mills, 39 Ill. 602; Sheldon v. Newton, 3 Ohio, St. 494; Torry v. Bank of Orleans, 9 Paige. 649; Kruse v. Steffen, 47 Ill. 112; Michoud v. Girod, 4 How. 503; Wormsley v. Wormsley, 8 Wheat. 421; Davone v. Fanning, 2 Johns. Ch. 252; Church v. Ins. Co. 1 Mason C. C. 345; Remick v. Butterfield, 11 Foster, (N. H.) 70; Shaw v. Swift, 1 Cranch. 565; Reihardson v. Jones, 3 Gill. & J. 163; Ward v. Smith, 3 Sandf. Ch. 592; Dobson v. Racey, 3 Sandf. Ch. 60; Haddix v. Haddix, 5 Litt. 202; Dorsey v. Dorsey, 3 Har. & J. 410; Davis v. Simpson, 5 Har. & J. 147; Base v. Abeel, 1 Paige. 393; DeCaters v. DeChamont, 3 Paige, 178; Purzey v. Senier, 9 Wis. 370; Torry v. The Bank, 9 Paige, 648; Iddings v. Bruen, 4 Sandf. Ch. 223; Field v. Arrowsmith, 3 Humph. (Tenn.) 442; Wilson v. Troup, 2 Cow. 196; McCants v. Bee, 1 McCord, Ch. 389; Britton v. Johnson, 2 Hill, 434; Saltmarsh v. Been, 4 Porter, 283; Miles v. Wheeler, 43 Ill. 123; Harris v. Parker, 41 Ala. 604; Roberts v. Fleming, 53 Ill. 196; Griffin v. Marine Co. 52 Ill. 130; Pewrouneau v. Bleakley, 14 Ill. 15; Terrill v. Anchauer, 14 Ohio, St. 80; Swazey v. Burke, 12 Pet. 11; Robins v. Butler, 24 Ill. 387; Dennis v. McCagg, 32 Ill. 429; Lockwood v. Mills, 39 Ill. 602; Forbs v. Halsey, 26 N. Y. 53; Barrington v. Alexander, 6 Ohio, St. 189; Mitchel v. Dunlap, 10 Ohio, 117; Glass v. Greathouse, 20 Ohio, 503; Rice v. Cleghorn, 21 Ind. 80, In Kruse v. Steffen, the supreme court of Illinois lays down the law of this subject in the following terms: "As a general rule, a person acting in a fiduciary capacity. cannot be permitted to purchase property at his own sale. And in such case it does not matter whether the purchase is in the name of the person conducting the sale, or in the name of another for his use. McConnel v. Gibson, 12 Ill. 128. And in such a sale, even where there is no fraud, the sale will be set aside if the party in interest shall apply in a reasonable time for that purpose. Thorp v. McCullum, 1 Gilm. 627. The fact that the person entrusted by the law to make the sale,

(134)

more for the property than any one else, he should apply to the court for leave to become a purchaser. The court in their discretion may permit it.[1]

§ 347. The supreme court of the United States hold that all such sales are "fraudulent and void and may be so declared."[2] They say: "The general rule stands upon our great moral obligation to refrain from placing ourselves in relations which ordinarily excite a conflict between self interest and integrity. It restrains all agents, public and private." That "it therefore prohibits a party from purchasing on his own account, that which his duty or trust requires him to sell on account of another, and from purchasing on account of another, that which he sells on his own account. In effect he is not allowed to unite the two opposite characters of buyer and seller, because his interests when he is selling or buying on his own account are directly conflicting with those of the person on whose account he buys or sells." That, "he cannot be at the same time vendor and vendee." And, "that no rule

becomes the purchaser whether by direct or indirect means, creates such a presumption of fraud as requires the sale to be vacated if application is made in proper time. * * * * This rule is regarded as firmly established by this court, and it is deemed unnecessary to review authorities or to discuss the reason of the rule." 47 Ill. p. 114, 115. In Lockwood v. Mills, 39 Ill. 602, the same court assert the rule as follows: "The evidence shows that Green was creditor, administrator, auctioneer and purchaser, at the sale, thus having it in his power to strike down the property at his own price, and we see as the result of representing all these relations to the estate, that 960 acres of land were sold for the sum of $1,134. The evidence shows the land embraced in the deed to Lockwood, worth from six to ten dollars per acre. If they were worth eight dollars per acre, that would give $3,840, while they sold but for $600; and if the whole 960 acres were worth the same per acre, their value would be $7,680, and they only brought $1,134. A large compensation for acting as creditor, administrator, crier and purchaser at his own sale. The rule is well established in equity, that the simple fact the purchase by asignees, trustees, commissioners, executors, or administrators at their own sales, renders the sales invalid and it will be set aside by the court." 39 Ill. 608.

[1] Michoud v. Girod, 4 How. 558; Armor v. Cochrane, 66 Penn. St. 308, 311. He should report the bid and apply for leave to give more. Davoue v. Fanning, 2 Johns. Ch. 252, 261.

[2] Michoud v. Girod, 4 How. 503, 553.

is better settled than that a trustee cannot become a purchaser of the trust estate."[1]

§ 348. "An executor or administrator is in equity a trustee for heirs, legatees, and creditors."[2] *Davoue v. Fanning* was the case of an executor for whose wife a purchase was made by one Hedden at public auction *bona fide*, for a fair price, of a part of the estate which Fanning administered, and the prayer of the bill was that the purchase might be set aside and the premises re-sold. The case was examined with special reference to the right of an executor to buy any part of the estate of his testator. And it was affirmed, and we think rightly, that if a trustee or person acting for others, sells the trust estate and becomes himself interested in the purchase, the *cestuis que trust* are entitled, as of course, to have the purchase set aside and the property re-exposed to sale under the direction of the court. And it makes no difference in the application of the rule that a sale was at public auction, *bona fide* and for a fair price, and that the executor did not purchase for himself, but that a third person, by previous arrangement with the executor, became the purchaser to hold in trust for the seperate use and benefit of the wife of the executor who was one of the *cestuis que trust*, and who had an interest in the land under the will of the testator. The inquiry in such case is not whether there was or was not fraud in fact. The purchase is void and will be set aside at the instance of the *cestuis que trust*, and a re-sale ordered on the ground of the temptation to abuse, and of the danger of imposition inaccessible to the eye of the court. We are aware that cases may be found in the reports of some of the chancery courts in the United States, in which it has been held that an executor may purchase, if it be without any property of his testator at open and public sale for a fair price, and that such purchase is only voidable and not void as we hold it to be. But with all due respect for the learned judges who have so decided, we say that an executor is in equity a trustee for the next of kin, legatees and creditors,

---

[1] Michoud v. Girod, 4 How. 555. See also Wormley v. Wormley, 8 Wheat. 421.

[2] Michoud v. Girod, 4 How. 553, 554.

and that we have been unable to find any one well considered decision with other cases, or any one case in the books to sustain the right of an executor to become the purchaser of the property which he represents or any portion of it, though he has done so for a fair price, without fraud, at a public sale."[1]   And again, in the same case, as if to put aside all questions in reference the generalty of the doctrine asserted by it, the court say: "We have thus shown that those purchases are fraudulent and void from having been made *perinterpositum personam*, and if they were not so on that account, that they are void by the rule in equity in the courts of England, and as it prevails in the courts of equity in the United States."[2]

"The rule as expressed embraces every relation in which there may arise a conflict between the duty which the vendor or purchaser owes to the person with whom he is dealing, or on whose account he is acting and his own individual interest." It is the same whether the sale be made with or without the sanction of judicial authority, where the person selling represents that in which others are interested; and releases by those in interest made in ignorance of the circumstances will not bind them.[3]

§ 349. In some of the state courts such purchases are regarded as conveying the legal title in trust for those interested in the estate sold, yet so far void in equity that they will be set aside at the instance of the *certui que trust*, without other cause than the single fact of the purchase being by or for the trustee or person selling.[4]

§ 350. In others it is holden that although thus held in trust and the sale is liable to be set aside as against the purchaser, within a reasonable time, that such sale is valid in favor

---

[1] Michoud *v.* Girod, 4 How. 556, 557.

[2] Ibid.

[3] Michoud *v.* Girod, 4 How. 503, 553, 559; Roberts *v.* Fleming, 53 Ill. 196; Barrington *v.* Alexander, 6 Ohio, St. 189.

[4] Davoue *v.* Fanning, 2 Johns. Ch. 252; Harkrider *v.* Harvey, 3 Ind. 104, 105; Glass *v.* Greathouse, 20 Ohio, 503; Swift *v.* Swift, 1 Ind. 565; Breckenridge *v.* Holland, 2 Blackf. 377; Terrill *v.* Auchaur, 14 Ohio St. 80. In Ohio an appraiser of the property in probate sales is prohibited to bid by statute. Ibid. Barrington *v.* Alexander, 6 Ohio St. 189.

of a *bona fide* purchaser under him before avoidance and without notice of his thus having purchased at his own sale.[1] But if the principle that a grantee is bound by the recitals contained in the title deed of his grantor is applicable to these sales, it is difficult to conceive by what rule of law there may be *bona fide* purchasers, under such circumstances, except where the trust is a secret one.[2]

§ 351. In yet another class of decisions, though the legal title is supposed to pass by the sale and conveyance, and though it is not expressly holden that the title is thus held by the grantee in trust for his *cestui que trust*, yet it is holden that such sales are void in equity at the election of those interested in the property sold, and will, within a reasonable time, on their application, be set aside.[3]

§ 352. And it is further held in some of these cases that if, on a re-sale, the property should not sell for as much as before those interested therein may elect to affirm the first sale and hold the trustee to his bargain.

§ 353. It matters not, so far as the equitable effect is involved, whether the purchase be made directly by and in the name of the trustee or indirectly in the name and through the intervention of another person.[4] In the case of *Miles v. Wheeler* the lands of infant heirs being sold in probate by the administrator were fraudulently purchased for himself through the agency of another person as bidder. The sale was in 1844. The administrator occupied the premises until his death, which occurred in 1859. In 1861 the heirs whose property had thus been fraudulently sold filed their bill in equity for a conveyance of the property and for an account of rents and profits

[1] Wyman *v.* Hooper, 2 Gray, 141; Blood *v.* Hayman, 13 Met. 231; Robbins *v.* Bates, 4 Cush. 106.

[2] Brush *v.* Ware, 15 Pet. 93, 111, 112, 113; Reeder *v.* Barr, 4 Ohio, 458; Willis *v.* Bucher, 2 Binn, 455; Livingstone *v.* Neeley, 10 Johns. 374; Wormley *v.* Wormley, 8 Wheat. 421.

[3] Shaw *v.* Swift, 1 Ind. 565; Remick *v.* Butterfield, 11 Foster (N. H.) 70; Wyman *v.* Hooper, 2 Gray, 141; Jackson *v.* Van Dalfsen, 5 Johns. 44; Blood *v.* Hayman, 13 Met. 231; Hoskins *v.* Wilson, 4 Dev. & Batt. 243; Beeson *v.* Beeson, 9 Barr (Penn.) 279.

[4] Church *v.* Ins. Co. 1 Mason C. C. 341; Miles *v.* Wheeler, 43 Ill. 123.

against the devisees of the deceased administrator or fraudulent purchaser. Notwithstanding the lapse of time which had intervened it was holden that they were entitled to relief.[1]

§ 354. An administrator, who was also one of the heirs, confessed judgment against the estate and suffered the lands to be sold on execution, the purchaser being the attorney of the plaintiff, and openly avowing at the sale that he was buying merely to secure the debt, and afterwards, without making any payment, deeded the land for the amount bid to the administrator in his personal right, receipting the same after making such deed on the execution, was holden not to be a *bona fide* purchaser, and it was also holden that the deed to the administrator from the execution purchaser was not a *bona fide* conveyance as against the other heirs. The Supreme Court of the United States use the following language in disposing of the case: "In making the purchase Ross (the attorney) seems, in effect, to have acted as the agent of the administrator, and it was proper for the jury to inquire whether the transaction was not fraudulent. If the administrator suffered the land to be sold through the agency of Ross with the view of securing the title to himself, to the exclusion of the other heirs of his father, the proceeding was fraudulent and void; and Ross could not be considered a *bona fide* purchaser against the legal and equitable rights of the plaintiffs, he not having paid the purchase money, the deed which he executed to Ormsley (the administrator) is not a *bona fide* conveyance."[2]

§ 355. The two opposite characters of seller and purchaser cannot be united in the same person, unless by the permission of the court first obtained;[3] hence, a trustee, commissioner to sell, executor, administrator, guardian, or other person selling or conducting the sale, are incapable of purchasing at their own sales; sales so made to' themselves are holden by the Supreme Court of the United States to be void. That court

---

[1] Miles *v.* Wheeler, 43 Ill. 123.

[2] Swazey *v.* Burke, 12 Pet. 11. In this case the attorney when he bid in the lands declared his readiness to allow the heirs to redeem, and that the only object of the purchase was to secure the client's debt.

[3] Michoud *v.* Girod, 4 How. 503, 557.

say: " We are aware that cases may be found in which it has been held that an executor may purchase, if it be without fraud, any property of his testator at an open and public sale, for a fair price, and that such purchase is only voidable and not void, as we hold it to be."[1]   That court holds such sale as absolutely void.

§ 356. A sale of real estate situated in Rhode Island, by an executrix, under a license granted by the probate court of New Hampshire, is void, and the deed is inoperative; but confirmation by act of the Rhode Island Legislature renders it valid.[2]

[1] Michoud v. Girod, 4 How. 503, 557.
[2] Wilkinson v. Leland, 2 Pet. 627, 655.

CHAPTER IX.

THE DEED.

I. BY WHOM TO BE MADE.

§ 357. Although the sale, in a popular point of view, is supposed to have been made when the bargain is closed; yet, in a legal sense, the sale is not complete until the deed is delivered.[1] Therefore, it follows that as making of the deed is part of the act of selling, the person appointed to sell is the only one who can make the deed. The sale is not perfected until confirmation thereof and delivery of the deed; and in some cases, as where approval of the deed by the court is also required, then only by the additional act of approval.[2]

§ 358. A contrary doctrine is alleged by Justice CATON,[3] in *Jackson v. Warren*, to exist in Illinois. His Honor treats of the subject as follows: "In England the practice is to keep the biddings open at a master's sale, so that any person may advance on a bid received by the master, which he reports to the court, so, until a final confirmation of the sale, no one can be considered as a purchaser, but a mere bidder; but under

[1] Macy v. Raymond, 9 Pick. 285; Lischey v. Gardner, 3 W. and Sergt. 314; 2 Daniel, Ch. 1474; Rawlings v. Bailey, 15 Ill. 178; Blossom v. R. R. Co. 3 Wall. 207; Child v. Hurst, 2 Swan, 487; Robinson's Appeal, 62 Penn. St. 216; Hays v. Hate, 19 Ala. 367; Koehler v. Ball, 2 Kansas, 160; Vallee v. Fleming, 19 Mo. 454; Williamson v. Berry, 8 How. 496.

[2] Macy v. Raymond, 9 Pick. 285; Rawlings v. Bailey, 15 Ill. 178; Young v. Keogh, 11 Ill. 642; Ayres v. Baumgartner, 15 Ill. 444; Blossom v. R. R. Co. 3 Wall. 205.

[3] 32 Ill. 331.

our practice at such sales, a valid and binding contract of sale
is made when the hammer falls. In the absence of fraud,
mistake, or some illegal practices, the purchaser is entitled to
a deed on the payment of the money." This decision, so far
as relates to the binding effect of the sale at the fall of the
hammer, seems to be in direct conflict with the previous decisions in that State of *Young v. Keogh*, and *Rawlings v. Bailey*,
as also the subsequent decision of *Dills v. Jasper*, and the
Quincy Seminary v. The Same, wherein the same doctrine is
avowed as is laid down by us above.[1]

§ 359. Though the English practice of keeping open the
biddings at a judicial sale for an advanced bid until confirmation, may not, in the States, be the general practice, yet it is

---

Young v. Keogh, 11 Ill. 642; Rawlings v. Bailey, 15 Ill. 178; Dills v.
Jasper, 33 Ill. 262. In the latter case, Justice BECKWITH, delivering the
opinion of the court, says: "A master in chancery, exposing property for
sale, should receive bids for it and report the largest one to court for its
approval. While such is the correct practice, we do not intend to say that
if it is not followed we should hold the sale void. If the order upon which
he acts contains especial directions in regard to requiring a deposit, they
should be followed; but in case no such directions are given, the master
may, in his discretion, require a part or the whole of a bid to be deposited
with him; or he may entirely dispense with such deposit. A bidder
is not allowed to retract his bid after its acceptance by the master,
if it is approved by the court within a reasonable time; but a bid, or
without a deposit, although it is accepted by the master, does not become
an absolute contract until it is approved by the court. The bidder at
such a sale merely agrees to purchase the property upon the terms named
by him if the same are approved by the court; and until the bid is
reported, and the report is confirmed, the sale is incomplete, and the
bidder is under no obligation to complete the purchase. In this country
the master usually requires the amount of the bid to be deposited with
him at the time of its acceptance, or immediately thereafter; and on
failure to do so, the master may reject the bid, and may again expose the
property for sale; or he may report the bid to the court, together with the
failure of the bidder to make a deposit. The master should not take the
responsibility of rejecting a bid after it has been once accepted by him,
where there is danger of loss to the parties in so doing, because he may
render himself liable for it. After the court has approved of the bid, it
may summarily require the bidder to pay the amount thereof, or it may
order the property to be re-sold at the bidder's risk and expense; and if,
upon a re-sale, it does not bring the amount of the bidder's liability, the
court may summarily enforce the payment of the difference."

believed that, as a general rule, an advanced bid, materially increasing the amount, will either be received by the court or else cause a re-sale and re-opening of the biddings to be ordered at any time before final confirmation of the sale.[1]

§ 360. As to the necessity of such confirmation, in some shape or other, there can be no doubt, as a general rule, though the practice may vary in different places; in proceedings in a court of ordinary chancery jurisdiction usually by formal order of confirmation, if not also by an order approving the deed;[2] and in probate and orphan's courts, whose proceedings are directed by statute, but which also, at the same time, in making sales of real estate, exercise a limited chancery jurisdiction in some States by mere approval of the deed, but which in all cases must depend upon the local statutory requirement, if there be such, and if not, then confirmation or approval of sale should appear of record in accordance with the general rule, so as in some shape or other to show the approval or confirmation of the act by the court.

§ 361. Where an administrator obtains a license to sell the real estate of a decedent for payment of debts, and dies before the confirmation of the sale, his successor may go on and complete the transaction, if previous proceedings be regular, without any further order of the court for that purpose, just as in case of any other business of the estate.[3]

§ 362. The license must be considered as inuring to the

---

[1] Norton v. Norton, 2 Brad. (N. Y.) 200; Davis v. Stewart, 4 Texas, 223; Hays' Appeal, 51 Penn. St. 58; Childers v. Hart, 2 Swan, (Tenn.) 487; Wright v. Cantzon, 31 Miss. 514; King v. Masterton, 16 N. Y. 174,

[2] Moore v. Titman, 33 Ill. 358, 367, 369; Shriver v. Lynn, 2 How. 43; Blossom v. R. R. Co. 3 Wall. 207; Vallee v. Fleming, 19 Mo. 454; Webster v. Hill, 3 Sneed, (Tenn.) 333; Henderson v. Herrod, 23 Miss. 424; Walace v. Hale, 19 Ala. 367; Robinson's Appeal, 62 Penn. St. 216; Hays' Appeal, 51 Penn. St. 58; Kohler v. Ball, 2 Kansas 160; Gowan v. Jones, 10 Smede and M. 164; Ayres v. Baumgartner, 15 Ill. 444; Rawlings v. Bailey, 15 Ill. 178; Young v. Dowling, 15 Ill. 481.

[3] Baker v. Bradley, 23 Ill. 632; Gridley v. Philips, 5 Kansas, 349; Peterman v. Watkins, 19 Ga. 153; or in Georgia, the administrator *de bonis non*, may be ordered by the same court granting the license to execute, or complete the sale. Ibid. So, likewise, in Kansas, Gridley v. Philips, 5 Kansas, 349.

administrator, or official capacity, and not to the person of him who fills the place of administrator. If the new administrator has doubts, he can apply to the court for instruction, or to a court of equity for relief; but if to the latter, then the heirs must be made parties. Should the new administrator, (or administrator *de bonis non*) refuse to proceed, then the purchaser may coerce a deed in chancery, if he has in no way lost his rights as such.

§ 363. On a sale of lands of a decedent by the administrator in probate, the deed to the purchaser cannot be executed by the administrator through an agent.[1] It is an act that can only be performed by an administrator.

§ 364. If the rightful administrator be within the probate jurisdictional limits the court can enforce the making of the deed.[2] But if he leave the State, the proper course is to vacate his letters, appoint a successor, and by order in probate cause such successor to execute the proper conveyance to complete the sale. It is not within the jurisdiction of an ordinary chancery jurisdiction to decree a title. The sale must be perfected through the probate court.[3]

§ 365. Where the county court in Virginia was empowered by special act of Assembly to decree a sale of a decedent's lands by the administrator, and decreed accordingly, it was holden that the deed should be by the administor as such, and not as a commissioner.[4]

§ 366. An administrator *pro tem.* cannot execute a deed of conveyance of a decedent's lands without proper order and authority from the court especially allowing him so to do; such deed is inadmissible in evidence and passes nothing.[5]

§ 367. In Mississippi the ruling is, that an administrator *de bonis non* cannot execute a deed of land sold by his predecessor.[6]

[1] Gridley *v.* Philips, 5 Kansas, 349.
[2] Ibid.
[3] Gridley *v.* Philips, 5 Kansas, 349; Baker *v.* Bradley, 23 Ill. 632
[4] Corbell *v.* Zeluff, 12 Gratt, 226.
[5] Robinson *v.* Martel, 11 Texas, 149.
[6] Davis *v.* Brandon, 1 How. (Miss.) 154.

§ 368. A married woman who is a guardian can convey the estate of her ward by deed, under a judicial sale, without being joined by her husband in the deed.[1] In Missouri, a sale and conveyance by one of two administrators is good, the sale being otherwise regular.[2] But the contrary doctrine prevails in California.[3]

II. To Whom to be Made.

§ 369. Ordinarily the conveyance is to be made to the purchaser, if not desired by him to be made to some one else; but in judicial sales, as the whole matter remains under the control of the court until the delivery of the deed,[4] and the purchaser, by his purchase, becomes a party to the proceedings and is, therefore, in court,[5] the court has full power, at his request, to order the deed to be made to another person as grantee in his place on full payment of the purchase money. A deed to such other person, made under such sale and substitution, if otherwise sufficient, will be valid;[6] "without prejudice, however, to any equities, rights, or liens, which may have become vested before such assignment of his bid,"[7] and subject to all equities or liens which, in the meantime, may have vested as against the original purchaser.[8]

§ 370. So, in a sale made by an administrator, made under an order of court, and license to sell real estate of a decedent, the deed may be made to the assignee of the purchaser and will be valid, as to any objection on that account.[9] Likewise in cases of judicial sales generally.[10]

[1] Palmer v. Oakley, 2 Doug. (Mich.) 433.
[2] Vallee v. Fleming, 19 Mo. 454, 464.
[3] Gregory v. McPherson, 13 Cal. 562.
[4] Blossom v. R. R. Co. 3 Wall. 207: Deadrick v. Watkins, 8 Humph. 520; Deadrick v. Smith, 6 Humph. 138; Requa v. Rhela, 2 Paige, 339.
[5] Blossom v. R. R. Co. 3 Wall. 196, 207.
[6] Williams v. Harrington, 11 Ired. 616; Proctor v. Farnum, 5 Paige, 614.
[7] Proctor v. Farnum, 5 Paige, 614.
[8] Ibid.
[9] Ewing v. Higby, 7 Ham. 178.
[10] Voorhees v. The Bank, U. S. 10 Pet. 478, 479.

10

III. When to be Made.

§ 371. So soon as the sale is confirmed by the court and the purchaser has performed on his part the requirements resting on him by the terms of sale as to the purchase money, he then becomes entitled to a deed. The sale, however, in some cases, as for instance sales in probate, is not yet completed until the deed be approved by the court.[1] If the sale be on a credit, then the right of the purchaser to a deed before full payment depends on circumstances and terms of sale.[2]

§ 372. If the order of sale is to remain in force only a limited term, then the deed must be executed and delivered within that time. Otherwise it will be void.[3] But in Michigan there is a contrary ruling.[4]

§ 374. In the case cited of *May v. Raymond*,[5] the ques-

[1] Lischey *v.* Gardner, 3 Watts & Sergt. 314; Morton *v.* Sloan, 11 Humph. 278.

[2] Bains *v.* Morris, 4 Ired. 22.

[3] Mason *v.* Ham, 36 Maine, 573; Macey *v.* Raymond, 9 Pick. 287; Wellman *v.* Lawrence, 15 Mass. 326.

[4] Howard *v.* Moore, 2 Mich. 226.

[5] 9 Pick. 285. *Per Curiam:* A fatal objection to the maintainance of this action arises out of the delay in the sale. The license was to be in force one year. It was not questioned in the argument that if the land had not been put up at vendue within the year the deed would have been ineffectual; but it was said that, as in popular estimation the land was sold within the year, the delivery of the deed after the year expired was sufficient. We think this construction cannot prevail. The object of the Legislature was, that the sale should be concluded and the deed delivered within the year. Otherwise there might be a complete evasion of the statute and the estate be kept open for twenty years. No property passed until the deed was given, and until then, in a legal sense, there was no sale. And though the popular sense may be the true one where the act of the Legislature does not relate to a technical subject, yet it being here the object to limit the time of sales and prevent estates from being kept open longer than is necessary, the legal sense seems to be the proper one to be adopted. It is said, however, that if the land is bid off within the year, but the deed is not given, a bill in equity will lie to enforce a specific performance of the contract, and so it would be absurd to give a different construction of the statute in a writ of entry. Our construction might be incorrect, if a bill in equity would lie after the expiration of the year. But a court of equity would not decree a useless act, a specific performance where the party could not perform. If the statute had said expressly

tion as to when the sale is completed arose incidentally in regard to an administrator's sale. The statute of Massachusetts required the sale to be made within one year from the granting of the order of sale. The deed was delivered after the year had expired. The court held that the power to make it had expired; that the sale was not complete until the delivering of the deed, and that as it was not delivered within the year, the proceedings were void, and that the grantee took nothing under the deed. The statute of Massachusetts has since been altered by the act of 1840 in respect to the time of completing the sale. But the principal in that case adjudged that the sale is only completed by delivery of the deed, is not affected thereby.

IV. Its Recitals and Descriptions.

§ 375. Mere misrecitals in the deed as to the order of sale or previous proceedings will not invalidate the conveyance and title, if enough appears from the whole record, deed, and proceedings to clearly identify the real case and show the true facts and circumstances under which the deed is made.[1]

§ 376. Nor will the misnomer of an executor or executrix, who makes the sale, by describing him or her as administrator or administratrix.[2]

§ 377. In Iowa, the term administrator is, by statute, made to mean as well executor as administrator.[3]

§ 378. The necessity of reciting the order or decree in the deed, depends mainly on the statutes and local practice in the several States. In New York, Illinois, and others of the States,

---

that the deed should be given within the year, a decree of specific performance after the year would be nugatory; and so the case depends on the construction of the statute. Nor is there any need of allowing more than a year for the delivery of the deed If the party who bids off the land demands his deed within the year and it is refused, he has his action at law for damages, and that is sufficient

[1] Thomas v. LaBarron, 8 Met. (Ky.) 355; Shelden v. Wright, 1 Selden (N. Y.) 497; James v. Taylor, 7 Texas, 240; Saltonstall v. Riley, 28 Ala. 164.

[2] Cooper v. Robinson, 2 Cush. 184.

[3] Revision of 1860, Sec. 233.

it is held essential to the validity of the deed.[1] Whilst in
Georgia, Texas, and some others of the States, it is holden
sufficient if the order be referred to and identified.[2] Doubtless
the safer course is to recite the order or decree in the deed at
length and with accuracy. After confirmation it is held that
prior defects as to description are remedied if there be an
accurate description in the sale, order of confirmation, and the
deed.[3]

V. What passes by it.

§ 379. However the proceedings and deed may be as to
regularity and sufficiency in other respects, yet the deed can
only pass the title to such property as is authorized to be sold
by the decree.[4]

§ 380. A sale of a tract of land generally, by the guardian
of one only of two owners, on a decree made in proceedings
in which no reference is made to the other owners or his rights,
and to which proceedings he was not a party, carries to the
purchaser only the title of such guardian's ward and does not
affect the interests of the other owners.[5]

§ 381. The deed, under a mortgage foreclosure and sale,
carries the title and entire interest of both mortgagor and
mortgagee.[6] But not against subsisting equities of those not
made parties to the proceeding.[7]

§ 382. It is a well established principle that in adversary
proceedings, the deed under a judicial sale carries title only as
against parties to the suit, and that "though a purchaser dis-
covering a defective title at a proper time, might be relieved
from his purchase," yet, he cannot "be permitted, whilst holding on to his purchase, to insist upon having his title perfected

[1] Atkins v. Kinnon, 20 Wend. 241; Doe v. Williams, 1 Scam. 323.
[2] Brown v. Bedwine, 16 Ga. 67.
[3] Williams v. Harrington, 11 Ired. 616.
[4] Shriver v. Lynn, 2 How. 43; Neil v. Hughes, 10 G. and J. 7; Ryan v.
Dox. 25 Barb. 440.
[5] Bryan v. Manning, 6 Jones (N. C.) 334.
[6] Carter v. Walker, 2 Ohio St. 339.
[7] Haynes v. Beach, 3 Johns. Ch. 459.

by the application of the proceeds of the sale to the extinguishment of the claims of incumbrances not parties to the suit."[1] Such is the ruling and the language of the Maryland High Court of Chancery in *Duval v. Speed*, 1 Md. Ch. Decis. 235.

§ 383. The widow's dower is not ordinarily affected by an administrator's or guardian's sale in probate, although it appear that the order was made on her application, and no express reservation of dower be made in the sale or deed.[2] In Missouri, however, under the code of 1825, it was otherwise.[3] But if she sell and convey with warranty, she will, by her deed, though made as administrator or as guardian be "completely estopped" from claim of dower.[4]

§ 384. In New Hampshire an administrator of an insolvent estate is invested by the statute with a special and limited estate in the realty. The right to the rents and profits, and to possession until administration be closed or the land be sold by order of court. In *Bergin v McFarland*, in that State, it is holden that a deed of the administrator so imperfect in itself, or in the proceedings under which made, that it will be inoperative to carry the fee as against the heirs, will nevertheless protect the grantee as against the heirs during such time as the estate is not fully administered, for which time the administrator, if no deed were made, would be entitled to the possession, the rents, and the profits.[5]

§ 385. In Pennsylvania it is held that "nothing can be sold (on sales in partition) but the title, which is vested in the parties to the proceedings."[6]

§ 386. A mortgage made by a coparcener, pending proceedings for partition, is overreached by the proceedings in partition, which vest the entire estate in the purchaser at partition sale unencumbered by the mortgage.[7]

---

[1] Duval v. Speed, 1 Md. Ch. Decis. 229, 235; Kholer v. Kholer, 1 Edw. Ch. 577; Darwin v. Hatfield, 4 Sandf. 468; Carter v. Walker, 2 Ohio St. 339.

[2] Jones v. Hallopelter, 10 S. and R. 326; Owens v. Slater, 26 Ala. 547.

[3] Mount v. Vallee, 19 Mo. 621.

[4] McGee v. Mellon, 23 Miss. 585.

[5] Bergin v. McFarland, 6 Foster, (N. H.) 533.

[6] Allen v. Gault, 27 Penn. St. 473.

[7] Sears v. Hyer, 1 Paige, 483

§ 387. Where by law, lands are to be valued before selling, in judicial or execution sales, the growing crops thereon situated do not pass to the purchaser by the sale and deed. The reason given is that the valuation is but of the lands, and that they must sell for a certain proportion of their value or not at all. Thus, in Ohio, where such is the law, requiring lands about to be sold on execution, or in proceedings in partition, it is settled that on a sale and deed in partition of lands in that State, having at the time of sale growing crops thereon such crops do not pass to the purchaser.[1]

§ 388. And so the emblements or growing crops of a tenant in possession of mortgaged premises under the mortgagor do not, upon general principles, pass to the purchasers at a judicial sale on foreclosure of the mortgage. "The annual crops are saved to the tenant under the common rule relating to emblements, because the termination of the lease is uncertain. The elder jurists find abundant reason for the doctrine, in the protection the law owes to agriculture." Such is the rule in reference to a tenant under the mortgagor, *bona fide* such, irrespective of appraisement laws. The courts regard the growing crops as personality.[2]

§ 389. But although (as we have just seen) the emblements do not, as a general rule, pass to the purchaser at judicial (or at execution) sale; and although the sale is not completed until the execution and delivery of the deed:[3]

§ 390. Yet, the occupying tenant or debtor in possession, cannot prolong his occupancy or have the right to gather in the fruits of his labor by putting in a crop, or seeds, after the sale at the biddings and before confirmation and conveyance of the premises, unless the same be put in by consent of the purchaser. In *Parker v. Storts*, involving a judicial sale on mortgage foreclosure, the court say:—"His own unauthorized acts after the sale cannot be allowed to impair the rights of the purchaser, and must be done at his own peril." Such is the

---

[1] House *v.* Showalter, 10 Ohio St. 124. 127; Parker *v.* Storts, 15 Ohio St. 351, 355; Jones *v.* Thomas, 8 Blackf. 428.

[2] 4 Kent, Com. 73; Casselly *v.* Rhodes, 12 Ohio, 88.

[2] Lischey *v.* Gardner, 3 Watts. & Sergt. 314; Erb *v.* Erb, 9 Watts. & Sergt. 147; Parker *v.* Storts, 15 Ohio St. 351.

doctrine holden in *Parker v. Storts*, in Ohio, wherein the court say, in reference to past decisions in that state on the subject, that they are "wholly unaffected by the opinion" in this case of *Parker v. Storts*.[1]

"An irregular or void judicial sale" say the United States supreme court in *Brobst v. Brock*, "made at the instance of the mortgagee, passes to the purchaser all the rights the mortgagee, as such, had."

§ 391. There being no service on the mortgagor in the case above cited, the judgment was holden to be void as to him, and therefore it did not cut off his equity of redemption, nor did the sale. Had the judgment been authorized by service and erroneously entered, yet it would have been valid until reversed or set aside, and a sale under it would have carried the full title of both mortgagor and mortgagee, except the equity of redemption of the mortgagor. But being made at the instance of the mortgagee and purporting to be a sale of the lands and whole interest covered by his mortgage, the mortgagee is estoped to deny that all his rights passed by the sale; and the purchaser having paid the mortgage debt, is subrogated to the mortgagee's rights.[2]

§ 392. In making title under an administrator's sale of lands by virtue of a decree in probate, the appointment or authority of the administrator to act as such must be shown. "The whole record from and including the appointment of the administrator, down to and including the sale of the real estate is but one continuous record; and it must all be considered as before the court and the parties upon application to sell and confirm the sale of the real estate."[3]

§ 393. And where the appointment of the administrator is a void act, so is the sale of real estate that he may make, likewise void and of no effect. This too, notwithstanding a decree authorizing the sale and a subsequent order of confirmation thereof.[4]

[1] Parker v. Storts, 15 Ohio St. 351, 35.

[2] Brobst v. Brock, 10 Wall. 519, 534; Gibert v. Cooley, Walker Ch. 494; Jackson v. Brown, 7 Cow. 13.

[3] Frederick v. Pacquette, 19 Wis. 541; Sitzman v. Pacquette, 13 Wis. 291.

[4] Frederick v. Pacquette, 19 Wis. 541; Sitzman v. Pacquette, 13 Wis. 291.

CHAPTER X.

SETTING ASIDE SALE.

I. THE POWER TO SET ASIDE SALES.

§ 394. Courts of equity and courts exercising equity powers over particular subjects have a "general supervision over their process, and more especially over the particular sales ordered by their decrees and made by their special agents or commissioners," which supervision is effected sometimes by bill or by petition and sometimes by motion,[1] or by the court itself, on

---

[1] Coffey v. Coffey, 16 Ill. 141; Deadrick v. Smith, 6 Humph. 138; King v. Platt, 37 N. Y. 155; Laight v. Pell, 1 Edw. Ch. 577; Yates v. Woodruff, 4 Edw. Ch. 703. In the case of Coffey v. Coffey, SCATES, Justice, delivering the opinion of the court, says: "The only question of any importance in the case is, whether there is such unfairness and fraud in the sale as to warrant the decree setting it aside. Of this we have no doubt. The plaintiff, with his brothers and sisters, had, or pretended to have, a claim of title to one of these tracts, adverse to petitioners. Under these circumstances, if he desired to become a bidder, it was essential to fairness towards petitioner that he should conceal or forbear to assert his adverse claim, whatever consequence might result therefrom to his interest. It is not competent for him to assert his claim to the premises by a public announcement at the biddings, with a threat to litigate it with any purchaser, and then enter into competition in the biddings and purchase at an under value, occasioned by the depreciation his own conduct had produced. If it were essential for the protection of his claims to give notice and make it known at the sale, he thereby disqualified himself to bid or become a purchaser of this adverse title at such sale. He shall not be allowed to depreciate or destroy the value of the land by denying the title, then buy it at a depreciation thus produced, and claim to be a fair pur-

its own motion, as universal guardian of all infants, if the

chaser. Such is proven to have been his conduct in this case. A witness desired to purchase the tract claimed, and would have paid more for it than plaintiff gave had not this claim been made. So he would for the other, to which no claim was made, if he could have purchased with it the piece claimed. Its value depended in part upon its connection with that piece. Another witness, though he had no money to bid, yet desired the land, and actually purchased the same of plaintiff before he bid on it at an advance of some five hundred dollars, on time. These facts show such fraud upon and injury to the rights and interests of defendant as call for correction from the court, in the exercise of a sound legal discretion of its powers of disapproving and setting aside sales under its orders; and we think that discretion properly exercised in this case. The objection taken to the proceedings by motion is not sustainable. The case is essentially different from the case of Day v. Grayham, 1 Gilm. 435. Courts of law have a supervision over the execution of their process, and yet may not, as in that case, properly afford relief by setting aside sales made under it, but leave the party to his bill in equity. Courts of equity have a like general supervision over their process, and more especially over the particular sales ordered by their decrees and made by their special agents or commissioners. So far is this carried under the English practice that the sale, until confirmation by the Chancellor, is treated merely as a bid, and subject to a proposition of advance. 6 Vessey, 513; 8 ibid, 214. We have not adopted the rule to this extent (15 Ill. 447,) but the power, right, and duty of the court to supervise, protect, and preserve the parties from all fraud, unfairness, and imposition, is of universal application here. Ayres v, Baumgartner, 15 Ill. 447; 2 Paige, 99, 339; 3 ibid, 97; 9 ibid, 259; 1 Edw. Ch. 577; 5 Humph. 355; 4 ibid, 372; 2 B. Monroe, 497; 3 Dana, 620; 1 Smede & Marsh, Ch. 522; 23 Miss. 445. And this is well put in Cassamajor v. Stode, 1 Sim. Rev. Sta. 381, (1 Eng. Ch. 382,) upon the ground that the purchaser does, by the act of purchase under a decree, submit himself to the jurisdiction of the court as to all matters connected with that character. This is sometimes done by bill, as in Bacon et al. v. Conn, 1 Smede & Marsh, Ch. 348; by petition, as in Henderson v. Harrodetal, 23 Miss. 451; 2 Paige, 100; 9 ibid, 260; 3 ibid, 94; 15 Ill. 144; and sometimes by motion, 3 Dana, 615; 2 B. Monroe, 408; 5 Humph. 355; 2 Paige, 240; 1 Edw. Ch. 578; 4 ibid, 703. The case before us is a proper one for a motion. The sale by plaintiff to the witness Reynolds, before the bidding, does not present the case of an innocent purchaser who is entitled to be made a party by bill or petition, but is a part of the evidence of the fraudulent conduct of plaintiff in forestalling competition. Decree (setting aside sale) affirmed." Though the English practice of opening the biddings for reception of a higher bid, when offered, does not prevail in Illinois, yet it is by no means unusual in the courts of some others of the states. Childress v. Hurst, 2 Swan (Tenn.) 487; Hay's Appeal, 51 Penn. St. 58; Wright v. Cautzon, 31 Miss. (2 George) 514."

interest of infants demand it.[1] They may reject, set aside, or confirm sales, and order resales, at discretion, as equity and the ends of justice may require.[2]

§ 395. The grounds on which sales are usually sought to be set aside are, inadequacy of price; irregularity; mistake or misapprehension; surprise; frauds; and for reversal of decree of sale. These will be considered in their order.

§ 396. In *Deadrick v. Smith*[3] the Supreme Court of Tennessee hold the following language as to the power of courts over their own judgments, decrees, and sales: "Every court must have an inherent power of enforcing its judgments and decrees; and surely to no tribunal can this power more properly belong than to the chancery court. It has under its control all the sales made by its order until final disposition is made of the cause. It can set aside the sale altogether, or open the biddings, or make any other order that may be necessary for the enforcement of the decree." The court add that the purchaser is a party to the proceedings; must have a final order to make his purchase effectual, and is under the control of the court for enforcement of the purchase against him.

II. For Inadequacy of Price.

§ 397. If there be no fact or circumstance relied on to set a sale aside but inadequacy of price, then the inadequacy must be such as in itself to raise the presumption of fraud, or else the sale will not be disturbed.[4]

§ 398. But if in addition to such inadequacy there be any appearance of unfairness, or any circumstance, accident, or

[1] Lefevre v. Laraway, 22 Barb. 167; 2 Story, Eq. Jur. Sec. 1234.
[2] Deadrick v. Smith, 6 Humph. 138; Stephens v. McGruder, 31 Md. 168; Hay's Appeal, 51 Penn. St. 58; King v. Platt, 37 N. Y. 155.
[3] 6 Humph. 146.
[4] West v. Davis, 4 McLean, 241; Cohen v. Wagner, 6 Gill. 236; Ashby v. Cowell, 1 Busby, Eq. 158; Lefevre v. Laraway, 22 Barb. 167; Strong v. Caton, 1 Wis. 471; Hart v. Blight, 3 Mon. 273; Reed v. Brooks, 3 Litt. 127, Little v. Luntz, 2 Ala. 256; Girt v. Frazier, 2 Litt. 118; Am. Ins. Co. v. Oakly, 9 Paige. 259; Bank of Alexandria v. Taylor, 5 Cranch, C. C. 314, Furgus v. Woodworth, 44 Ill. 374; Trip v. Cook, 26 Wend. 142; Strong v. Caton, 1 Wis. 471.

occurrence in relation to the sale of a character tending to cause such inadequacy, then the sale will be set aside;[1] but inadequacy of price is still the main ground of disturbing the sale,[2] for if the price were full value, or even a passable one, then the objectionable facts or circumstances have worked no evil.

§ 399. In the leading case here cited under this head, his honor Judge McLean holds the following language on the subject of setting aside judicial sales for mere inadequacy of price: "There does not appear to be, in the present case, any irregularity, mistake, or fraud. The only objection urged is, that the property sold for less than its value. We cannot say that this inadequacy is so striking as to authorize the setting aside of the sale.[3]

§ 400. In the case of *Little v. Luntz*,[4] the Supreme Court of Alabama hold the following language on the same subject: "We are therefore of opinion that when a stranger is the purchaser at a mortgage sale, it will not be set aside for mere inadequacy of price, no matter how gross, unless there is some unfair practice at the sale, or unless those interested are surprised without fault or negligence on their part; and in no case of this description after a confirmation, unless fraud can be imputed to the purchaser which was unknown to those interested at the time of confirmation of the sale."

§ 401. It may be accepted as a general rule, that when the cause alleged is fraud, the application to set aside, if after confirmation, then the court must be satisfied that the fraud was unknown to those complaining at the time of confirmation.

§ 402. The prevalence, at the time of sale, of an infectious disease, to such extent as to remove many people, suspend business, and prevent the ordinary probability of a reasonable

---

[1] Cohen v. Wagner, 6 Gill, 236; Gist v. Frazier, 2 Litt. 118; May v. May, 11 Paige, 201; Bank of Alexandria v. Taylor, 5 Cranch, C. C. 314.

[2] Cohen v. Wagner, 6 Gill. 236.

[3] West v. Davis, 4 McLean, 241, 242. See also Trip v. Cook, 26 Wend. 142.

[4] 2 Ala. 260, 261; Am. Ins. v. Oakley, 9 Paige, 259; King v. Masterdon, 16 N. Y. 174.

competition at the sale, will, in connection with inadequacy of price, be cause for setting the sale aside, and for ordering a re-sale.[1]

III. FOR IRREGULARITY

§ 403. A judicial sale is made under the order or decree of the court and by virtue thereof. The person conducting it should be clothed with a copy of the order or decree, duly authenticated, designating the land to be sold. Though sales otherwise properly made, will not be adjudged void for reason of such order not having issued, if such sales are made in conformity to the record of the order;[2] yet if the order or decree be to sell on receiving the order, than a sale on receipt of an informal order which omits the description of the land and was not directed to any one, though not actually void, will be set aside for irregularity on proper application.[3]

§ 404. Insufficiency of description and inadequacy of price combined, will be cause for setting a sale aside.[5]

§ 405. So for irregularity, when made after an appeal is taken and appeal bond filed.[4]

§ 406. Likewise for any misunderstanding resulting in inadequacy of price.[6]

§ 407. So, also, if made by a different master than the one mentioned in the decree.[7]

§ 408. So a mortgage sale will be set aside on bill of review if the mortgagor die during suit and the heirs be not made parties and there also be junior mortgagees who were not parties.[8]

§ 409. And a sale made at an improper time, or under any

---

[1] Littell v. Luntz, 2 Ala. 256.

[2] Rhonemus v. Corwin, 9 Ohio St. 366; Ins. Co. v. Halleck, 6 Wall. 556.

[3] Rhonemus v. Corwin, 9 Ohio St. 366.

[4] Kauffman v. Walker, 9 Md. 229.

[5] Chesapeake Bank v. McClelland, 1 Md. Ch. Decis. 328.

[6] Latrobe v. Hesbert, 3 Md. Ch. Decis. 375.

[7] Yates v. Woodruff, 4 Edw. Ch. 700.

[8] Shriveley v. Jones, 6 B. Mon. 274.

other circumstances than tend to render it inequitable, will be set aside to protect the rights of parties not in fault.[1]

§ 410. But a sale will not ordinarily be set aside, after confirmation and distribution of the proceeds.[2]

§ 411. Likewise a mortgage sale for a price greatly inadequate and much less than the mortgage debt, will be set aside if made without the knowledge of the creditor.[3]

§ 412. A sale made on a different day than the one stated in the notice of sale is void and should be set aside.[4]

§ 413. So if the property be purchased by the person conducting the sale, if so purchased without leave of the court, it is such an irregularity, aside from the question of fraud, as will cause the sale to be set aside.[5]

§ 414. In *Michaud v. Girod*, the Supreme Court of the United States review the whole subject of purchases by trustees and others at their own sales, and hold such to be in all cases void.[6]

§ 415. Under the statute in Illinois, if the petition of the guardian for sale of the ward's lands fail to state the ward's residence, and to make a proper case for decree, a sale made in proceedings thereon, will, for such irregularity, be set aside.[7]

§ 416. So if, for reasons not his fault, a mortgagor fail to attend the sale, and the mortgagee buy in the land at a greatly inadequate price, the sale will be set aside,[8] but not for inadequacy alone.[9]

§ 417. For any negligence or mistake of the officer selling

---

[1] Brown v. Frost, 10 Paige, 243; Collier v. Whipple, 13 Wend. 224; King v. Platt. 39 N. Y. 155.

[2] Stiner's Appeal, 56 Penn. St. 9.

[3] May v. May, 11 Paige, 201.

[4] Miller v. Hull, 4 Denio. 104.

[5] Blood v. Hayman, 13 Met. 231; Man v. McDonald, 10 Humph. 275; Hoskins v. Wilson, 4 Dev. and B. 243; Scott v. Freeland, 7 S. and M. 409; Worthy v. Johnson, 8 Ga. 236; Shaw v. Swift, 1 Ind. 565; Michoud v. Girod, 4 How. 503, 553.

[6] See ante, p. 5 n. 3.

[7] Loyd v. Malone, 23 Ill. 43, 47.

[8] Tripp v. Cook, 26 Wend, 143.

[9] Tripp v. Cook, 26 Wend. 143; Cohen v. Wagner, 6 Gill, 236; Westover v. Davis, 4 McLean, 241, 242.

resulting in an injury to the parties in interest the sale will be set aside.[1]

§ 418. A sale made on application of the administrator alone where the law required the heirs or others to join in such application is irregular and will be set aside, and if allowed to remain, it is void.[2]

§ 419. And a sale of land a second time by the same administrator will be set aside at the personal cost of such administrator.[3]

§ 420. So a sale of lands on a mortgage decree, when the mortgage of a minor's lands was made by his guardian, will be set aside if a full defense be not made by the guardian to test the validity of the mortgage.[4]

IV. For Mistake and Misapprehension.

§ 421. A sale will be set aside for misapprehension caused by a purchaser or others interested in the sale, or by the person conducting it.[5] So likewise if the auctioneer, not hearing a higher bid, strike off the property to a lower bidder.[6] So if the property of infants be sacrificed by the neglect, fraud or misapprehension of their guardian, they will be relieved by setting aside the sale and by a re-sale.[7] The order of re-sale may be made on the court's own motion, as guardian of all infants.[8]

V. For Surprise.

§ 422. Sales of real estate under orders and decrees will be set aside for surprise when an injury or an unfair advantage result therefrom.

[1] Am. Ins. Co. v. Oakley, 9 Paige, 259; King v. Platt, 37 N. Y. 155.
[2] Miller v. Miller, 10 Texas, 319.
[3] Hunt v. Norton, 12 Texas, 285.
[4] Curtis v. Ballagh, 4 Edw. Ch. 635.
[5] Laight v. Pell, 37 N. Y. 577, 578; Lefevre v. Laraway, 22 Barb. 167; Anderson v. Foulk, 2 Har. & G. 346; Strong v. Caton, 1 Wis. 471; Gordon v. Sims, 2 McCord, Ch. 157; Brown v. Gilmor, 8 Md. 322; Veeder v. Fonda, 3 Paige, Ch. 97.
[6] Gordon v. Sims, 2 McCord, Ch. 159; Cohen v. Wagner, 6 Gill. 236.
[7] Lefevre v. Laraway, 22 Barb. 167; Curtis v. Ballagh, 4 Edw. Ch. 635.
[8] Lefevre v. Laraway, 22 Barb. 167.

§ 423. If a complainant in a decree give such assurances of postponement or delay of sale, (though not with intent to deceive) as induces the debtor without other negligence on his part to omit raising means for the present to meet the debt, and a sale be made for a price greatly inadequate, it will be set aside for surprise and a re-sale will be ordered.[1] But not after long or unreasonable delay in making the application, and when other parties have acquired an interest in the property under the sale.[2]

§ 424. But a sale ought not to be set aside and a re-sale ordered for the benefit of those interested in the fund arising from the sale merely to protect them, they being adults, from the consequences of their own negligence or ignorance, when by proper diligence on their part the matter complained of might have been avoided.[3]

VI. For Fraud.

§ 425. It is a principle well settled in law that fraud vitiates all instruments and proceedings, including judgments, orders, and decrees, and sales made thereon or by virtue thereof.[4]

§ 426. If not absolutely void, they will be avoided or set aside at the instance of the injured party if application be made within proper time.[5]

§ 427. Sales, as well judicial as others, will be set aside by the courts where fraud is made to appear, (and in some cases) even after confirmation thereof.[6]

§ 428. If the person conducting a judicial sale purchase at

---

[1] Strong v. Caton, 1 Wis. 471; Williams v. Dale, 3 Johns. Ch. 291; Griffith v. Hadley, 10 Bosw. 587.

[2] Leonard v. Taylor, 12 Mich. 398.

[3] Am. Ins. Co. v. Oakley, 9 Paige, 258, 260, 261.

[4] Hoit v. Holcomb, 3 Foster, (N. H.) 554; Michoud v. Girod, 4 How. 503.

[5] Michoud v. Girod, 4 How. 503; Concord Bank v. Greg. 14 N. H. 331; Davoue v. Fanning, 2 Johns. Ch. 252; Loyd v. Malone, 23 Ill. 43; Neal v. Stone, 20 Mo. 294.

[6] Anderson v. Foulke, 2 Har. & G. 346, 357; Billington v. Forbs. 10 Paige, 487; King v. Platt, 37 N. Y. 155; Garrett v. Moss, 20 Ill. 549; Johnson v Johnson, 40 Ala. 247; May v. May, 11 Paige, 201.

his own sale, it is a fraud for which the sale will be set aside on motion to the same court in which the sale is ordered, if application be made before confirmation; and if after confirmation, then the proceeding to set the sale aside is by petition or bill in chancery.

§ 429.   The rule is the same if the person selling procure the purchase for himself or for his benefit through a third party.   And though some authorities treat such sales as not voidable, by others they are held to be absolutely void.   The latter is the ruling in the Supreme Court of the United States.[5]

§ 430.   A purchase by the attorney of the execution plaintiff at a price greatly inadequate, will be cause for the most vigilant scrutiny, in to every circumstance which might affect the fairness or demonstrate the unfairness of the sale.   Even the purchase by the attorney alone (without such inadequacy,) has been considered good cause for setting aside the sale, as being against "the policy of justice."[6]   In *Bussy v. Hardin*,[7] the court say: (referring to *Howell v. McCreery*, 7 Dana. 389 and 390, and to *Foreman v. Hunt*, 3 Dana. 622;) "it is said, that a sale at which the attorney purchases at a grossly inadequate price, should be considered as *per se*, in the twilight between legal fraud and fairness, and that slight additional facts exhibiting a semblance of unfairness would be sufficient to vitiate the sale or make the purchaser a trustee."   The court adds.   "If there be any ground for such a distinction as we think there is, it rests upon the superior knowledge of the right, and of the subject of sale which the attorney has by reason of his connection with the suit, and upon the presumed influence which he has over the time and manner of the sale and over the person who makes it, by reason of his representing the party for whose interest primarily, the sale is to be made."

---

[5] Michoud r. Girod, 4 How. 503; Davoue v. Fanning, 2 Johns. Ch. 253; Wormsley v. Wormsley, 8 Wheat. 421; Miles v. Wheeler, 43 Ill. 123; Harris r. Parker, 41 Ala. 604; Borasen v. Wells, 4 Green, (N. J.) 87; Swazey v. Burke, 12 Pet. 11.

[6] Busy v. Hardin, 2 B. Mon. 407.

[7] Ibid, 409, 410.

VII. For Reversal of the Decree of Sale.

§ 431. Where the sale is to a third person and *bona fide* purchaser, and has been fully completed by confirmation, conveyance and payment, it will neither be avoided nor will it be set aside by reason of a subsequent reversal of the decree. This rule is so generally recognized as to scarcely require authorities to support it. In the language of the Illinois Supreme Court, "If the court has jurisdiction to render the judgment or to pronounce the decree, that is, if it has jurisdiction over the parties and the subject matter, then upon principles of universal law, acts performed and rights acquired by third persons, under the authority of the judgment or decree, and while it remains in force, must be sustained, notwithstanding a subsequent reversal.[1]

VIII. Re-Sale.

§ 432. A re-sale will ordinarily be ordered when the sale is set aside for fraud, irregularity, mistake, surprise, inadequacy of price, or for such other cause as does not involve a want of jurisdiction or power to sell in the court, if the sale is set aside before confirmation.[2]

§ 433. And in some cases the first purchaser, being in fault, will be holden for the discrepancy in amount between the first and second sale, if the second sale be for a less sum than the first one.[3]

§ 434. In Maryland, under the code or statute, if the sale be partly on a credit and the purchaser fail to meet the deferred

[1] Goudy *v.* Hall, 36 Ill. 319. See also McLagan *v.* Brown, 11 Ill. 523; Young *v.* Loraine, 11 Ill. 637; Iverson *v.* Loberg, 26 Ill. 179; Fitz Gibbon *v.* Lake, 29 Ill. 165; McJilton *v.* Love, 13 Ill. 486: Peak *v.* Shasted, 21 Ill. 137; Grignon's Lessee *v.* Astor, 2 How. 340; McBride *v.* Longworth, 14 Ohio St. 350; Irwin *v.* Jeffers, 3 Ohio St. 389.

[2] Stephens *v.* McGruder, 31 Md. 168; Deadrick *v.* Smith, 6 Humph. 138; King *v.* Platt, 37 N. Y. 155; Hay's Appeal, 51 Penn. St. 58; Lefevre *v.* Laraway, 22 Barb. 167; Am. Ins. Co. *v.* Oakly, 9 Paige, 259; Post *v.* Leet, 8 Paige, 337; Brown *v.* Frost, 10 Paige, 243; Colfey *v.* Coffey, 16 Ill. 141; Roberts *v.* Roberts, 13 Gratt. (Va.) 639.

[3] Mullin *v.* Mullin, 1 Bland. 541; Stephens *v.* McGruder, 31 Md. 168.

11

payments when due, then on application of the master or other
person conducting the sale, the sale may be set aside and a
re-sale ordered at the risk of the first purchaser; or the court,
under its equity powers, (if of general chancery jurisdiction,)
may compel a compliance or specific performance on the part
of the purchaser at its discretion, in view of all the circumstances of the case and as may best subserve, in its opinion,
the interests and rights of the parties.[1] Such, however, is the
general law aside from statute.

§ 435. The making of a judicial sale, in New York, is under
control of the court, and if the parties in interest, creditor and
debtor, cannot agree as to the order in which property shall be
offered for sale, either party may apply to the court for instructions to the referee in that respect.[2]

§ 436. When valuable property is sold by the referee in a
different order from that requested by the debtor, whose property is being sold, and there is reason to believe that selling in
the order requested by the debtor would have resulted in a
benefit, and there are circumstances tending to prevent competition at the sale, a re-sale will be ordered.

§ 437. And so where the inclemency of the weather was
such as to prevent the attendance of bidders, the purchaser
being the only one present and she residing at the place of
sale, it was held that the sale should be set aside, and a re-sale
was ordered.[3]

§ 438. If it become apparent to the court from the face of
the proceedings, or otherwise, that the rights of minors have
been illegally invaded or compromised, the court will, on its
own motion, set aside or decline to confirm the sale, and will
order a re-sale of the property without waiting to be invoked
so to do. It is in such case the duty of the court, in the
exercise of its high powers as guardian of all minors, to pro-

---

[1] Stephens v. McGruder, 31 Md. 168.

[2] King v. Platt, 37 N. Y. 155. In this case the court justly say that,
" Occupying the position of advantage it behooved the plaintiffs to pursue
their remedy with scrupulous care, lest they should inflict an injury on
one who was comparatively powerless." See also to this point Collier v.
Whipple, 13 Wend. 229.

[3] Roberts v. Roberts, 13 Gratt (Va.) 639.

tect the interests of those whom equity makes the special objects of its care;[1] and the purchase of the property by the guardian *ad litem* of an infant owner is a case loudly calling for such interference.[2]

§ 439. The biddings may be opened and a re-sale ordered, at the discretion of the court, on terms, at any time before the confirmation of the sale, in case there be an acceptable advance offered on a greatly inadequate price.[3]

§ 440. The petition to reopen the bidding should state the proposed amount of the advance upon the former bid.[4]

§ 441. Before confirmation an offer of ten per cent. and costs of increase is sometimes deemed sufficient to cause an order of re-sale to be made.[5]

---

[1] Lefevre *v.* Laraway, 22 Barb. 167; Lansing *v.* McPherson, 3 Johns. Ch. 424; Billington *v.* Forbs, 10 Paige, 487.

[2] Lefevre *v.* Laraway, 22 Barb. 161.

[3] Childress *v.* Hurst, 2 Swan (Tenn.) 487; Hay's Appeal, 51 Penn. St. 58; Wright *v.* Cautzon, 31 Miss. 514, 517.

[4] Wright *v.* Cautzon, 31 Miss. 514, 517.

[5] Horton *v.* Horton, 2 Brad. (N. Y.) 200.

CHAPTER XI.

ESTOPPEL—WARRANTY—CAVEAT EMPTOR.

I. ESTOPPEL.
II. WARRANTY.
III. CAVEAT EMPTOR.

I. ESTOPPEL.

§ 442. Sales, as well judicial and on execution, as others, may be so made, or made under such circumstances as will prevent the owner of the property from questioning their validity, though the sales be in other respects defective, or even void. And thus the claimant is subjected to an estoppel. In such cases title is conferred on the purchaser by estoppel.

§ 443. If one so far countenance the sale of his own property as to stand by and see it sold by the sheriff, or other officer, as the property of, and on execution against another, without objecting to the sale, he will be estopped to deny the validity thereof,[1] as against a *bona fide* purchaser.

§ 444. Estoppels not only bind "parties but privies in blood and estate."[2]

§ 445. What estops the ancestor estops the heir, and that which estops the original party estops also those claiming under him, in whatever right they claim.

§ 446. In *Bush v. Cooper*,[3] the United States Supreme Court hold the following language in reference to estoppels which run with the land: "Estoppels which run with the land, and work thereon, are not mere conclusions; they pass estates and constitute titles; they are muniments of title, assuring it

[1] Epley *v.* Witherow, 7 Watts, 163; Carr *v.* Wallace, 7 Watts, 394; Read *v.* Heasley, 2 B. Mon. 254.

[2] Bush *v.* Cooper, 18 How. 85; Baxter *v.* Bradbury, 20 Maine, 260; Carver *v.* Jackson, 4 Pet. 85; Mark *v.* Willard, 13 N. H. 389; White *v.* Patten, 24 Pick. 324.

[3] 18 How. 85.

to the purchaser. Their operation is highly beneficial, tending to produce security of titles."

§ 447. This case was that of a mortgagor, with warranty implied in law, who bought in the premises afterwards on execution sale, based on a judgment lien which was older than the mortgage. The Supreme Court of Louisiana, as also that of the United States, held that he was estopped to sit up his execution deed against the effect of his mortgage, was estopped by his warranty from "denying that he was seized of the particular estate at the time of making" the mortgage. In short, that a mortgagor, or grantor, cannot buy in a superior title and enforce it against those claiming under his own deed of warranty.[1]

§ 448. The recital in a deed, or assertion of ownership, or other fact, upon the strength of which another is induced to commit his interest, or to buy, will estop the person making such recitals or assertions, from denying the truth thereof, or asserting a claim inconsistent therewith.

§ 449. If one entitled to dower in lands of a decedent sell them under proceedings in probate as administrator, and convey by deed of warranty, she is thereby estopped from afterwards claiming dower in the lands so sold and conveyed.[2] Otherwise, however, if she convey without warranty.[3]

§ 450. The obtention of an injunction by a widow and heirs to prevent sales of a decedent's lands on judgments at law until the same can be sold by proceedings in probate, in course of administration, will estop them from objecting that they were not notified of such proceedings in probate afterwards prosecuted for the sale of such lands.[4]

§ 451. A husband and wife being seized of real estate as tenants of the entirety, the husband died leaving a will by which all his real estate was directed to be disposed of by sale, and the proceeds to be applied in a certain way, but not authorizing

[1] Bush v. Cooper, 18 How. 82, 85; Van Rensellear v. Kearney, 11 How. 322; Stewart v. Anderson, 10 Ala.504; Dorsey v. Gassaway, 2 Harr. & J. 411.
[2] McGee v. Mellon, 23 Miss. 585; Maple v. Kussart, 53 Penn. St. 348; Stroble v. Smith, 8 Watts, 208; Heard v. Hall, 16 Pick. 457.
[3] Sipp v. Lawback, 2 Harr. 442; Owens v. Slater, 26 Ala. 547.
[4] Simmons' Estate. 19 Penn. 439.

any one to make the sale. The lands were sold by order of the orphans' court, including that which had been held by the husband and wife as tenants of the entirety. The widow encouraged the purchaser to buy at such sale and herself received part of the purchase money. It was held that although the widow was invested with the ownership in fee as survivor of the husband, that nevertheless she was estopped from setting up title to the property, she having encouraged the purchaser to buy the same as belonging to the estate of the decedent.[1]

§ 452. In ejectment by the purchaser under a mortgage foreclosure, the mortgagor is estopped from denying his own title at the date of the mortgage, and is also estopped from setting up an outstanding title to the premises in a third person. He cannot execute a deed of mortgage on property and then deny his right to that of which he thus assumed to be the owner.[2]

§ 453. A ward is not estopped by the deed of his guardian, though made with warranty. The warranty binds the guardian personally.[3]

§ 454. Nor is a purchaser of lands at a judicial sale made under a void decree estopped to deny the title of those as whose land it is sold.[4]

§ 455. The receipt of a widow or by a ward, after such ward attains to his majority, of their portion of purchase money of

---

[1] Maple v. Kussart and others, 53 Penn. St. 348. In this case the court say: "The proof is that she urged the purchasers to buy that the property might remain in the family, and it was at her request they bought. They paid the purchase money, $6,410, and it was distributed to the widow and heirs." And that, "It is a maxim of common honesty, as well as of law, that a party cannot have the price of land sold and the land itself." * * "If one receive the purchase money of land sold, he affirms the sale, and he cannot claim against it whether it was void, or only voidable; Adlum v. Yard, 1 Rawle. 163; Wilson v. Bigger, 7 W. & S. 162; Crowley v. McConkey, 5 Barr. 168; Stroble v. Smith, 8 Watts, 280; Smith v. Warden, 7 Harris, 424. And the court also held, "That the fact that in sales of this kind, the maxim *caveat suptor* applies, does not avoid the estoppel."

[2] Redman v. Ballamy, 4 Cal. 247; Bush v. Marshall, 6 How. 288; Tarter v. Hall, 2 Cal. 263.

[3] Young v. Lorain, 11 Ill. 624.

[4] Price v. Johnson, 1 Ohio St. 390.

lands sold by an administrator or guardian, under proceedings in probate, will estop them from disputing the validity of the sale, if received with full knowledge of their rights and of all the circumstances, and so likewise does the receipt of the proceeds of such sale vested in other property.[1]

§ 456. If a party request or direct the officer to sell lands as his, and, being present at the sale, do not dissent, he is regarded as assenting, is estopped from denying the title of the purchaser.[2]

§ 457. In *Penn v. Heisey*[3] the court say: "It is a principle, that though in general, estoppels are odious, as preventing a party from stating the truth, yet they are favored when they promote equity. Comyn's Dig. title Estoppel. The application of this principle does not depend, as we understand it, upon any supposed distinction between a void and a voidable sale. If the sale be one or the other, receiving the money or its proceeds in other valuable property with a knowledge of the facts, touches the conscience of the party and therefore establishes the right of the party claiming under the sale, in one case as well as in the other."

II. WARRANTY.

§ 458. It is a well settled principle that in judicial sales there is no warranty.[4] This principle, as a general rule, holds good as to all those sales of real property (they being in character judicial sales) made in equitable proceedings, under the

---

[1] Ellis v. Diddy, 1 Smith, Ind. 354; Stroble v. Smith, 8 Watts, 280; Bohart v. Atkinson, 14 Ohio, 228; Scott v. Freeland, 7 S. & M. 409; Penn v. Heisey, 19 Ill. 295.

[2] Read v. Heasley, 2 B. Mon. 254, 257.

[3] 19 Ill. 295.

[4] The Monte Allegre, 9 Wheat. 616; United States v. Duncan, 4 McLean, 606; Owens v. Thompson, 3 Scam. 502; Lynch v. Baxter, 4 Texas, 431; Williams v. McDonald, 13 Texas 322; Freeman v. Caldwell, 10 Watts. 9; King v. Gunnison, 4 Barr. 171; Fox v. Mensch, 3 Watts. & Sergt. 444; Jennings v. Jenkins, 9 Ala. 285; Rogers v. How, 6 Rich. (S. C.) 361; Breckenridge v. Dawson, 7 Ind. 383; Halleck v. Gray, 9 Cal. 181; Sumner v. Williams, 8 Mass. 162; Bingham v. Maxey, 15 Ill. 295; Evans v. Dendy, 2 Speers. (S. C.) 9.

direction and control of the courts, usually denominated mortgage sales,[1] guardian's, executor's, and administrator's sales,[2]
sales for enforcement of vendors, and statutory liens,[3] and sales
in proceedings for partition.[4] In short, in all sales made under
supervision and control of the courts on decrees in equity or on
decrees made in the exercise of equity powers,[5] there is no warranty; the purchaser takes what he gets.[6] The officer, trustee,
or person executing the deed is the mere "agent or instrument"
of the court;[7] is not liable for defect of title or insufficiency
of the proceedings;[8] nor at all, except for fraud,[9] unless he
conveys with warranty, and then the covenat of warranty binds
him personally and him only.[10] In *The Monte Allegre* more
particularly referred to under the next head this rule is plainly
asserted by the Supreme Court of the United States, and it is
the general doctrine in most if not all of the states, and of the
common law.[11]

III. Caveat Emptor.

§ 459. The rule of *caveat emptor* applies in all its rigor to
judicial sales of real property.[12]

[1] Ante, pp. 22, 24.

[2] Mockbee v. Gardner, 2 Har. & G. 176; Vandever v. Baker, Ib. 126; Lynch
v. Baxter, 4 Texas, 431.

[3] Ohio Life & Trust Co. v. Goodin, 10 Ohio St. 557.

[4] Rogers v. Hoen, 6 Rich. 361; Young v. Loraine, 11 Ill. 624.

[5] United States v. Duncan, 4 McLean, 607.

[6] The Monte Allegre, 9 Wheat. 616.

[7] Mullikin v. Mullikin, 1 Bland, 541; Harrison v. Harrison, 1 Md. Ch.
Decis. 331; Vandever v. Baker, 13 Penn. St. 121, 126.

[8] Mockbee v. Gardner, 2 Har. & G. 176.

[9] Ibid, 175.

[10] Young v. Lorain, 11 Ill. 624; Breckenridge v. Dawson, 7 Ind. 383;
Sumner v. Williams, 8 Mass. 162; Meller v. Boardman, 13 S. & M. 100;
Mockbee v. Mockbee, 2 Har. & G. 175.

[11] The Monte Allegre, 9 Wheat. 616.

[12] The Monte Allegre, 9 Wheat. 616; Lessee of Corwin v. Benham, 2
Ohio (N. S.) 36; Owsley v. Smith, 14 Md. 153; Mason v. Wait, 4 Scam. 127;
Worthington v. McRoberts, 9 Ala. 297; Fox v. Mensch, 3 Watts. & Sergt.
444; Mellen v. Boarman, 13 S. & M. 100; Lynch v. Baxter, 4 Texas, 431;
Bingham v. Maxey, 15 Ill. 295; Vandever v. Baker, 13 Penn. St. 124, 126;
Anderson v. Foulk, 2 Har. & G. 346; Thompson v. Monger, 15 Texas 523;

§ 460. The Supreme Court of the United States hold that "generally in all judicial sales the rule *caveat emptor* must necessarily apply from the nature of the transaction; there being no one to whom recourse can be had for indemnity against any loss which may be sustained. Is there then (they ask) anything peculiar in the powers of a court of admiralty that will authorize its interposition, or justify granting relief to which a party is not entitled by the settled rules of the common law?" They say, "we know of no such principles."[1]

§ 461. Though the case in which this doctrine is thus broadly asserted was a case in admiralty, it will be seen that the decision was avowedly put upon the principles of the common law. The same case is expressly referred to, and the same principle re-asserted by the United States court of claims in the case of *Pucket v. The United States.*[2]

§ 462. In the absence of misconception and of fraud, the buyer must look out for himself. He buys at his own risk, both as to title and as to quality. The rule does not apply however in case there be fraud.[3] And it has been holden in Pennsylvania that the rule applies only to open defects; that as against secret defects in a title, a purchaser will be protected.[4]

Bickley *v.* Biddle, 33 Penn. St. 276; Strouse *v.* Dreman, 41 Mo. 289; Walden *v.* Gridley, 36 Ill. 523. The doctrine is stated in Illinois in the following terms: "Appellant when he purchased at the administrator's sale acquired such title only as was then vested in the heirs of Strain. If it was then subject to the lien of Walker's judgment, he acquired it with that impurity and to preserve his title he must clear it from the incumbrance." Walden *v.* Gridley, 36 Ill. p. 532. Creps *v.* Baird, 3 Ohio St. 277; Corwin *v.* Benham, 2 Ohio St. 36; Miller *v.* Finn, 1 Neb. 255.

[1] The Monte Allegre, 9 Wheat. 616.
[2] 4 Am. L. Reg. 459, 460.
[3] Bingham *v.* Mancey, 15 Ill. 295.
[4] Banks *v.* Ammon, 27 Penn. St. 172.

CHAPTER XII.

COLLATERAL IMPEACHMENT—VOID JUDICIAL SALES—
RETURN OF PURCHASE MONEY.

I. WHEN IMPEACHABLE COLLATERALLY.

§ 463. The principle is well settled, not only in the Supreme Court of the United States, but in the State Courts generally, that if there is no jurisdiction the proceedings are void; they are a nullity and confer no right; are no justification, and will be rejected when collaterally drawn in question.[1]

§ 464. If a court acts without authority its judgments and orders are nullities, and are not voidable only but are absolutely of no effect, and cannot bar a recovery or defense asserted in opposition to them even prior to their reversal.[2]

§ 465. And though the court has jurisdiction, if from any cause the sale or deed be really void, then the objection is good when made in a collateral proceeding.[3]

II. WHEN NOT IMPEACHABLE COLLATERALLY.

§ 466. It is equally well settled in the Supreme Court of the United States that if the subject matter be within the jurisdiction of the court and is brought before them by proper petition, the validity of the proceedings being brought in

---

[1] Thompson v. Tolmie, 2 Pet. 157; Shriver's Lessee v. Lynn, 2 How. 43; Wilkerson v. Leland, 2 Pet. 627; Clark v. Thompson, 47 Ill. 27; Morris v. Hogle, 37 Ill. 150; Swigart v. Harber, 4 Scam. 66.

[2] Thompson v. Tolmie, 2 Pet. 157; Shriver's Lessee v. Lynn, 2 How. 43; Elliott v. Piersol, 1 Pet. 328; Morris v. Hogle, 37 Ill. 150.

[3] Cooper v. Sunderland, 3 Clarke (Iowa) 114; Frazier v. Steenrod, 7 Iowa 346.

question collaterally, they are not void but merely voidable. Errors and irregularities, and all other deficiencies, if any there be, must be reached and corrected by some direct proceeding, either before the same court or in an appellate one, and such too is the general doctrine.[4]

§ 467.   When a court has obtained jurisdiction it is competent to decide every question arising in a cause, and whether decided correctly or incorrectly, the decision until reversed is binding not only in the same, but in every other court.[5]

§ 468.   If the jurisdiction over the subject matter appears on the face of the proceedings in which a sale is made, the errors or mistakes, if any there be, cannot be examined when brought up collaterally.[6]

§ 469.   Where debts have been regularly proven and allowed against the estate of a decedent, and lands sold on proper

[4] Thompson v. Tolmie, 2 Pet. 157; Parker v. Kane, 22 How. 14; Alexander v. Nelson, 42 Ala. 462; Duquindre v. Williams, 31 Ind. 444; Southern Bank v. Humphreys, 47 Ill. 227; Woods v. Lee, 21 La. 505; Covington v. Ingram, 64 N. E. 123; Iversod v. Loberg, 26 Ill. 179. In the case last cited, Iverson v. Loberg, the Supreme Court, Justice CATON, say: "We are obliged to affirm this judgment, much against our inclination. The sale was no doubt a great outrage, and we should as at present advised, not hesitate to reverse the proceeding were it directly before us. But here it comes up collaterally, and we cannot disregard that proceeding unless it was void for want of jurisdiction. We cannot hold that such was the case. The petition stated enough to require the court to act in the premises—to set it in motion, and that was sufficient to give the court jurisdiction, and whatever was done under it was not in the exercise of an usurped power, but of one conferred by law, and although the court may have exercised that power erroneously, its orders and decisions are binding till reversed. If we are to look into any errors in that proceeding, it must be brought before us by writ of error." (26 Ill. 182.)

[5] Elliott v. Piersol, 1 Pet. 328; Parker v. Kane, 22 How. 14; Grignon's Lessee v. Astor, 2 How. 319; Davis v. Helbig, 27 Md. 452; Wright v. Walbaugh, 39 Ill. 554; Iverson v. Loberg, 26 Ill. 179; Fithian v. Monks & Brooks, 43, Mo. 502; Florentine v. Barton, 2 Wall. 210, 216.

[6] Thompson v. Tolmie, 2 Pet. 157; Pursley v. Hays, 22 Iowa 1; United States v. Aredondo, 6 Pet. 709; Grignon's Lessee v. Astor, 2 How. 319; Ex parte Watkins, 3 Pet. 205; Rhode Island v. Massachusetts, 12 Pet. 718; Phil. & Trenton R. R. Co. v. Stimson, 14 Pet. 448; Thomas v. La Barron, 8 Met. 355; Iverson v. Loberg, 26 Ill. 179; Weinen v. Heintz, 17 Ill. 257; Florentine v. Barton, 2 Wall. 210, 216.

application of the administrator to pay the same, as appears
by the record, then parole evidence cannot be received in a
collateral proceeding to show that no debts ever existed against
the estate. If the allowance of the debts and the sale were
brought about by fraud, then the remedy is in a direct proceeding in a court of general equity jurisdiction; but the jurisdiction and record of the probate court cannot be collaterally
impeached.[1]

§ 470. In an action of ejectment involving the effect of an
administrator's deed of lands sold for payment of debts in
probate, the regularity or legality of the administrator's appointment, when the court had jurisdiction, cannot be inquired
into. Whether the appointment be regular or irregular the
person appointed becomes, at least, the administrator *de facto*,
and being such the matter cannot be questioned in a collateral
proceeding.[2]

§ 471. In the case above cited the case of *Cutts v. Hoskins*,
9 Mass., is referred to and regarded as unsatisfactory; but it is
not precisely in point with the question which was raised in
Illinois. The Massachusetts case rested on an appointment by
the probate court of a contrary county to the one in which the
decedent died, an act absolutely prohibited by the Massachusetts statute. Hence the Massachusetts court treated the appointment as simply void, as an act in violation of law and not as
irregularity or mere error.[3]

§ 472. It follows, therefore, that if the court in probate
have jurisdiction properly of the subject matter of the application, by petition properly presented, and of the persons of the

[1] Lamothe v. Leppott, 40 Mo. 142. In this case the court say: "The
record shows that the probate court had full jurisdiction, and the presumption is in favor of its proceedings, and it is not competent to attack
the record by parole in this collateral manner. If the allowances were
procured by fraudulent and false means and pretences, unjustly and to the
injury of the estate and the parties interested, a court of equity, on a
proper showing of the facts, might afford a remedy; but in a proceeding
wholly collateral a party cannot be permitted to introduce oral testimony
to falsify the record, when it plainly appears that the court whose record
is thus sought to be impeached had jurisdiction."
[2] Wright v. Wallbaum, 39 Ill. 554; Riley v. McCord, 24 Mo. 265.
[3] Cutts v. Hoskins, 9 Mass. 543.

parties in interest, if the statute so requires them, the sale, when made and confirmed, may not be impeached in a collateral proceeding, although it may have been made to pay not only a larger amount than was necessary, but also for the payment of claims, some of which were fraudulent in point of fact, and if the purchaser himself be not a party to the fraud; for after conveyance and confirmation the sale can only be assailed by a direct proceeding in chancery by original bill, when complete jurisdiction is obtained by the court making the sale.[1]

§ 473. We do not conceive, however, that these principles, though well settled, can override positive statutory requirements as to things made necessary, or as a pre-requisite, to the validity of judicial sales by the legislation of the several states, but take it to be a general rule that where jurisdiction of the case never actually attached, as for want of notice or other cause, and whereby statute sales are declared void, or may not be made unless certain things appear to have been done, then a deficiency in respect thereto cannot be supplied by intendment or presumptions of law, nor upon the principles of *res judicata*. Yet, when such statutes are merely directory in defining the course to be pursued, then if the court had by law jurisdiction of the subject matter and jurisdiction of the case actually attached by filing a petition, or petition and notice, if notice was required, and such was exercised by the court by adjudication and order or decree, then by intendment of law all questions in regard to such statutory requirements, and as to questions necessary to be adjudicated in arriving at the conclusion attained, are put at rest by the decision and are binding as *res judicata* until reversed for error, or set aside by a direct proceeding; and that in the former class of cases sales are void and will be so treated when collaterally drawn in question;[2] and that in the latter class they are only voidable,

[1] Myer v. McDougal, 47 Ill. 278; Moore v. Niel, 39 Ill. 256. In this case the court hold that it is not required to make valid an administrator's sale in probate that he should report the same to the court; but such is not the current of authorities.

[2] Cooper v. Sunderland, 3 Iowa, 114; Thornton v. Mulquinne, 12 Iowa, 549; Townsend v. Tallant, 33 Cal. 45.

and the remedy to avoid them is by an appeal or else by a direct proceeding to set them aside.[1]

III. Void Judicial Sales.

§ 474. Jurisdiction, as we have seen, being indispensable to the validity of judicial proceedings, it follows that the first great essential to the validity of judicial sales is jurisdiction in the court making the sale. Without this the sale is void.[2]

§ 475. If the court making the order of sale be abolished by law before the final consummation of the sale, then the proceedings end with the court, and a conveyance resting on such circumstances is void.[3] So if the law under which the proceedings are being had is repealed before the order or decree is executed, a sale made afterwards is void.[4]

§ 476. Likewise sales made at a great and unreasonable length of time after making the order or decree, and sales made after the lapse of such time as is by statute allowed for the order to remain in force, are void.[5]

§ 477. So a sale of lands not included in the decree is as to such lands void.[6]

§ 478. And an administrator's sale of lands to raise funds merely to pay costs and expenses is void, though by order of

[1] Morrow v. Weed, 4 Iowa, 77; Little v. Sennett, 7 Iowa, 324; Long v. Burnett, 13 Iowa, 28; Parker v. Kane, 22 How. 14; Voorhees v. Jackson, 10 Pet. 449; Griffin v. Bogart, 18 How. 158; Draper v. Bryson, 17 Mo. 71; Grignon's Lessee v. Astor, 2 How. 242; Miller v. Sherry, 2 Wall. 237; Doe v. Harvey, 3 Ind. 104; Bennett v. Owens, 8 Eng. 177; Saltonstall v. Riley, 28 Ala. 164; Benningfield v. Reed, 8 B. Mon. 102; Field v. Goldsby, 28 Ala. 218; Tomlinson v. McKay, 5 Gill. 256; Boswell v. Sharp, 15 Ohio, 447; Merrill v. Harris, 6 Foster, 142; Jackson v. Robinson, 4 Wend. 440; Cockey v. Cole, 28 Md. 276.

[2] Shriver's Lessee v. Lynn, 2 How. 43; Morris v. Hogle, 37 Ill. 150.

[3] McLaughlin v. Janney, 6 Gratt. 608.

[4] Ludlow v. Wade, 5 Ham. 494; Campau v. Gillett, 1 Mann. (Mich.) 416; Perry v. Clarkson, 16 Ohio, 571; Bank of Hamilton v. Dudley, 2 Pet. 492.

[5] Marr v. Boothby, 19 Maine, 150; Welman v. Lawrence, 15 Mass. 326; Mason v. Ham, 36 Maine, 573.

[6] Shriver's Lessee v. Lynn, 2 How. 43; Ryan v. Dox, 25 Barb. 440.

court.[1] Likewise a sale is void if made on different notice then that ordered in the decree.[2]

§ 479. In Iowa, it is provided by statute that a guardian's sale of a ward's lands under order or decree of court shall "not be avoided on account of any irregularity in the proceedings, provided it shall appear: First—That the guardian was licensed to make the sale by a court of competent jurisdiction. Second—That he gave bond (approved) in case one was required by the court granting the license. Third—That he took the oath prescribed by the statute. Fourth—That he gave notice of the time and place of sale, etc. Fifth—That the premises were sold accordingly at public auction, and are held by one who purchased them in good faith." The Supreme Court of that state construe these provisions to mean that "the sale shall not be avoided for any irregularities, except" in the foregoing particulars, and therefore that it "may be avoided on account of irregularities" in said particulars; that is, if it does not appear that said requirements were complied with.[3] And where it did not appear from the record that the administrator making the sale took the oath so required, the sale was holden to be absolutely void.[4]

§ 480. In the same state where the notice of application for order of sale was for one tract of land and the license to sell, notice of sale, and deed, were of another and different tract, the court held the sale void for want of jurisdiction to grant the license to sell.[5]

§ 481. A sale made in probate without petition or notice, or other means of conferring jurisdiction, though a decree be made on the report of the administrator, is void and parol

[1] Dubois v. McLean, 4 McLean, 486; Summer v. Williams 8 Mass. 200; Sand v. Granger, 12 Barb. 392; Bishop v. Hampton, 15 Ala. 761; Tanner v. Dean, 24 Mo. 16.

[2] Glen v. Wotten, 3 Md. Ch. Decis. 514; Reynolds v. Wilson, 15 Ill. 394.

[3] Cooper v. Sunderland, 3 Clarke (Iowa,) 114, 137, 138; Thornton v. Mulquinne, 12 Iowa, 549, 554.

[4] Ibid.

[5] Frazier v. Steenrod, 7 Clarke, (Iowa,) 339.

evidence may not supply the defect if contradictory to the record.[1]

§ 482. But, although the funds arising from the sale are required to be applied in a particular manner, yet it is not incumbent on a *bona fide* purchaser unless required of him by the statute to see them so applied.[2]

§ 483. A sale made on a void decree in proceedings of foreclosure of a mortgage is absolutely void. In *Harshey v. Blackmarr*,[3] where there was neither actual or constructive service of the original process nor voluntary appearance by defendant, but an unauthorized attorney appeared and answered for the defendant, the court, on application to vacate or relieve from a sale in such proceeding held that the decree of foreclosure was nullity, and that the sale was void.

§ 484. The sale in this case was made on a species of special execution under the statute, but the principle is equally applicable if the sale were on the decree itself. The statutory execution is but a substitute for the decree in the hands of the officer, and describes the property to be sold. In Mississippi it is held that there must be notice of application to all the heirs in an administrator's order of sale, or else the order and sale are void.[4] And so, too, the sale is void if made without the necessary bond.

§ 485. Such, also, is the ruling in Indiana. In *Hawkins v. Hawkins*,[5] the doctrine is fully declared that a sale of real estate by an administrator on an order obtained without notice to the heirs is void, although confirmed by the court. In this case the court say: "It is settled in this state that a sale of real estate by an administrator, without notice to the heirs, though it be ordered and confirmed by the court, is void. Babbitt *v.* Doe, 4 Ind. 355; Doe *v.* Anderson, 5 id. 33; Doe *v.* Bowen, 8

---

[1] Bishop *v.* Hampton, 15 Ala. 761; Thornton *v.* Mulquinne, 12 Iowa, 549.

[2] Cochran *v.* Van Surlay, 20 Wend. 365.

[3] 20 Iowa, 161; and see, Shelton *v.* Tiffin, 6 How. 163. In the latter case the U. S. Supreme Court say, the judgment must be "considered a nullity," and "did not authorize the seizure and sale" of the property.

[4] Hamilton *v.* Lockhart, 41 Miss. 460.

[5] Hawkins *v.* Hawkins, 28 Ind. 66.

id. 197; Gerrard v. Johnson, 12 id. 636; Wort v. Finly, 8 Blackf. 335; Bliss v. Wilson, 4 id. 169."

§ 486. The case cited from 6 Howard, *Shelton v. Tiffany*, in which a judicial sale was declared void, was in reference to a sale made in an adversary proceeding without notice, when on general principles, notice was required. It is parallel, however, with the Indiana cases, cited above, in this, that by statute in Indiana, actual notice is required, in probate proceedings, to sell lands. Such, too, is the ruling in Mississippi. In proceedings in probate, to sell lands, want of notice avoids the sale.[1]

IV. RETURN OF THE PURCHASE MONEY.

§ 487. The better authority seems to be, that one buying at judicial sale, where the principle of *caveat emptor* prevails, is not entitled to relief, (except as for mistake or fraud,) on failure of title to the property purchased, after completion of sale and payment of the purchase money.[2]

§ 488. In Ohio it is held that the purchase money paid upon a void sale of a decedent's lands, constitutes no charge upon the land in the hands of the heirs, nor can it be recovered of the heirs.[3]

§ 489. In Virginia the contrary has been held as to the charge against the land. In *Hardin v. Hudgins*,[4] it was holden that on failure of title the purchaser should be subrogated to the rights of the creditor, and that the purchase money paid by the purchaser became a lien on the land as it was originally a charge thereon. And so in Mississippi.[5]

§ 490. But, in a late case in Virginia, where one purchased land at judicial sale, with knowledge of facts which render the sale inoperative, and whose purchase was confirmed without

---

[1] Gwin v. McCarroll, 1 S. & M. 351; Campbell v. Brown, 6 How. 230.

[2] The Monte Allegre, 9 Whea. 616; Bingham v. Maucey, 15 Ill. 295; and see, Ante. Pt. 1st Chap. 9, No. 4, of this work, where the authorities are referred to more numerously.

[3] Nowler v. Coit, 1 Ham. 519.

[4] 6 Gratt. 320.

[5] Grant v. Loyd, 12 S. & M. 191.

12

objection on his part, it was held that he would not be relieved on the mere ground of failure of title.[1]   Yet, *quere?* If the purchase money is still in the hands of the administrator, and the purchaser has bought without knowledge of the defects, if equity, on failure of title, will not cause the money to be refunded.[2]

§ 491.   In Tennessee it is held that the money may be recovered back before conveyance is made, on discovery of a defect in the title.[3]   And in Mississippi, where the sale proved to be void for want of authority in the administrator to make it, the court allowed that fact in evidence for defendant in an action against for the purchase money to show failure of consideration.[4]   And so in the same state, where an executor's sale was set aside for fraud after payment by the purchaser, the court allowed him a lien for the money on the premises.[5]

§ 492.   And so in Maine, in the case of a void judicial sale, it was held that the purchaser had his action against the guardian for recovery of his money back, the invalidity of the sale being caused by the omission of the guardian to give the bond which was required by the statute before selling.[6]   But in the case cited from Maine, it seems that the deed contained covenants of warranty.   The language of the court is, that "it can be recovered back of the guardian upon his covenants in the deed, or in an action for money had and received by him for their benefit."

[1] Young *v.* Bowyer, 9 Gratt. 336.

[2] Mockbee *v.* Gardner, 2 Harr. & G. 176, 177.   Such is the intimation of Archer, Justice, in the case just cited; but, for as much as it was not made to appear whether the purchase money was still in the administrator's hands or not, the court made no absolute ruling on that point.

[3] Read *v.* Fite, 8 Humph. 328.

[4] Campbell *v.* Brown, 6 How. Miss. 230; Laughman *v.* Thompson, 6 S. & M. 259.

[5] Grant *v.* Lloyd, 12 S. & M. 191.

[6] Williams *v.* Morton, 38 Maine, 47, 51.

PART THIRD.

JUDICIAL SALES OF PERSONAL PROPERTY, CORPORATE FRANCHISES, PROPERTY AND STOCKS.

CHAPTER XIII.

JUDICIAL SALES OF PERSONAL PROPERTY.

I. In Admiralty.
II. At Law.

I. In Admiralty.

§ 494. Judicial sales of personal property occur whenever and in whatever court such property is seized or laid hold of by judicial process and decree *in rem*, and is sold on such decree, without regard to personal judgment against the owner. Sales in admiralty in proceedings *in rem* are strictly such. In the language of the learned Justice, REDFIELD, they "are strictly judicial,[1] and are merely carrying into specific execution a decree of the court *in rem*, which, by universal consent, binds the whole world."[2] If jurisdiction has attached, then by such sale the property passes to the purchaser by operation of law; "all the world are parties," and are bound thereby.[3]

---

[1] Griffith *v.* Fowler, 18 Vt. 390, 394.

[2] Griffith *v.* Fowler, 18 Vt. 390, 394; The Monte Allegre, 9 Wheat. 616; Hight *v.* Steamboat Henrietta, 4 Iowa, 472, 475; Phegley *v.* Tatum, 33 Mo. 461; The Mary, 9 Cranch, 126, Story, Confl. Laws, Secs. 592, 593; The Mary Anne, Ware C. C. 104; Croudson *v.* Leonard, 4 Cranch, 434; Gelson *v.* Hoyt, 3 Wheat. 246, 313; French *v.* Hall, 9 N. H. 137; 3 Kent, Com. 132; Penhallow *v.* Doane, 3 Dall. 86; 2 Bac. Abt. 74; Benedict, Adm. Sec. 364, 434; The Commander-in-Chief, 4 Wall. 52; McCall *v.* Elliott, Dudley (S. C.) 250; Singleton *v.* Herriott, Dudley (S. C.) 254.

[3] Grignon's Lessee *v.* Astor, 2 How. 338; Beauregard *v.* New Orleans, 18 How. 497, 502. 403; Benedict, Adm. Sec. 364, 434.

§ 495.   In admiralty cases purely *in rem* the jurisdiction is exclusively in the courts of the United States.[1]   If the property be within the territorial jurisdiction of the court and there be the proper libel, information, or plaint, to confer jurisdiction of the particular case, and it be actually seized upon the process of the court, then whatever action, decision, or sale, is had in respect to it is binding on all the world, and will be so regarded in every other tribunal and country, unless set aside or reversed by some appellate tribunal competent to review the same.[2]   And though it is holden in many cases of high authority that such validity will not be conferred unless there be notice to the parties interested in the property seized, so that they may defend such interest;[3] yet, in proceedings *in rem*, the notice is served on the thing,[4] and it is questionable, except as to foreign courts, whether the omission, where the proceedings are *in personam* also as well as *in rem*, will amount to more than mere error and cause for reversal of judgment against the same, if jurisdiction over the property has by proper proceedings and seizure actually attached.[5] But for a judgment *in personam*, want of notice is want of validity.

[1] The Belfast, 7 Wall. 624; Brightly Dig. 24; Stratton v. Jarvis, 8 Pet. 11; Mitchell v. Steamboat Magnolia, 45 Mo. 67; Phegley v. Tatum, 33 Mo. 461.

[2] The Siren, 7 Wall. 152; The Propeller Commerce, 1 Black. 581; The Reindeer, 2 Wall. 385, 388, 403; Phegley v. Tatum, 33 Mo. 461; Story, Confl. of Laws, Secs. 592, 593; Croudson v. Leonard, 4 Cranch. 434; Monroe v. Douglass, 4 Sandf. Ch. 180; Whitney v. Walsh. 1 Cush. 29; Grant v. McLachlin, 4 Johns. 34; The Mary Anne, Ware C. C. 104; Holmes v. Remsen, 20 Johns. 229; Barrow v. West, 23 Pick. 270; Peters v. Ins. Co. 3 Sumner C. C. 389; Magoun v. Ins. Co. 1 Story C. C. 157; Williams v. Armroyd, 7 Cranch, 423; Bradstreet v. Ins. Co. 3 Sumner C. C. 600; 2 Greenleaf Ev. Sec. 541.

[3] Bradstreet v. Ins. Co. 3 Sumner C. C. 600; Monroe v. Douglass, 4 Sandf. Ch. 180; Story, Confl. of Laws, Sec. 592.

[4] Benedict Adm. Sec. 365.

[5] Williams v. Armroyd, 7 Cranch, 423, 603; Grignon's Lessee v. Astor, 2 How. 338; Beauregard v. New Orleans, 18 How. 497; Iverson v. Loberg, 26 Ill. 182; Thompson v. Tolmie, 2 Pet. 167; Parker v. Keene, 22 How. 14; U. S. v. Arredondo, 6 Pet. 709; The Globe, 2 Blatch. C. C. 427.

§ 496. Being made by order of the court such sales are not within the statute of frauds.[1]

§ 497. The form of proceedings in courts of admiralty in matters of ordinary admiralty jurisdiction is in conformity to the civil and maritime law; but the powers exercised in dispensing justice and settling rights of property are those of courts of equity; and justice is administered upon equity principles.[2] Therefore in their orders and decrees in proceedings *in rem* the courts act upon the thing or property itself, which is the subject matter of the proceeding;[3] and sales thereon are judicial sales, as is herein before stated, in their strictest sense.

§ 498. The principle is fully settled that the seizure and sale of vessels in cases purely in admiralty, in the courts of admiralty, by proceedings *in rem*, divests all prior liens and claims whatever; and that the holders thereof must look to the fund in court arising from the sale for such rights as the nature of their claims may command, which fund is subject to distribution by the court.[4]

§ 499. In such proceedings and sales against the property itself, the validity of the sales does not depend upon any personal judgment against the owner or master, but the proceeding is purely *in rem*, and of which the United States court have exclusive jurisdiction in admiralty cases. The decree is against the property itself, and all the world are barred by the decree and sale.[5]

§ 500. In *Williams v. Armroyd*,[6] that great jurist, MARSHALL, Chief Justice, holds the following language on the subject of force of sales in admiralty: "It appears to be set-

---

[1] The Monte Allegre, 9 Wheat. 616.

[2] Plummer *v.* Webb, 4 Mason, 380, 387; 1 Kent Com. 354; Delovio *v.* Boit, 2 Gallison, 398; 1 Brightly Dig. 25; 3 Greenleaf, Evid. Sec. 389; Benedict, Adm. Sec. 358.

[3] Benedict, Adm. Sec. 359.

[4] Remnants in Court, Olcott, 382; Bracket *v.* The Hercules, Gilp. 184; Harper *v.* The New Brig, Gilp. 536; The Amelia, 6 Wall. 18.

[5] The Mary Anne, Ware C. C. 104; The Siren, 7 Wall. 152; Williams *v.* Armroyd, 7 Cranch, 423; Benedict, Adm. Sec. 364.

[6] 7 Cranch, 423, 433, 434.

tled in this country that the sentence of a competent court, proceeding *in rem*, is conclusive in respect to thing itself, and operates as an absolute change of the property. By such sentence the right of the former owner is lost, and a complete title given to the person who claims under the decree. No court of co-ordinate jurisdiction can examine the sentence. The question, therefore, respecting its conformity to general municipal law can never arise, for no co-ordinate tribunal is capable of making inquiry." This case involved title under a government sale of vessel and cargo made at St. Martins, by an order of decree of the Governor; and although such decree was repudiated by our government as in violation of international and maritime law, yet as Congress had not gone so far as to declare the sale void and require it to be so treated in our courts, the Supreme Court felt bound, on principles of maritime law, to treat it as of binding force and to recognize the validity of the sale. Upon this branch of the subject the learned judge, in the same case, gives the opinion of the court in the following terms: "The sale was made on the application of the captor, and the possession of the vendee is a continuance of his possession. The capture is made by and for the government, and the condemnation relates back to the capture and affirms its legality." Then again in the same case the court remark that, "If an erroneous judgment binds the property on which it acts, it will not bind that property less because its error is apparent. Of that error advantage can be taken only in a court which is capable of correcting it."[1]

§ 501. In maritime cases, in the United States court, it matters not to the contrary that the sale be made on a species of execution and by the ordinary ministerial officer, the sale is nevertheless a judicial sale. The writ is but a statutory method of executing the decree or judgment of condemnation and order of sale;[2] unlike the ordinary execution it points out the

---

[1] Williams *v.* Armroyd, 7 Cranch, 423, 433, 434.

[2] Conk. Dig. 1st Ed. 388; Act of Congress, March 2, 1799, Sec. 90. In England the sale is by a commissioner of the court. Abbott on Shipping, 162 In the United States courts by the marshal. Ib. 163. Griffith *v.* Fowler, 18 Vt. 390, 394.

property to be sold. No levy is necessary and the proceeds of sale are to be returned into court to be disposed of as that tribunal may direct.[1] The officer is the mere agent of the court to carry its order and authority into effect.[2]

II. At Law.

§ 502. And so proceedings in the state courts for the enforcement of liens and pledges against boats and vessels, and other personal property, not maritime in their nature, are within the ordinary equity powers of chancery courts, whether such liens rest upon express contract or arise by implication of law. To that end such courts, on application by bill or petition, if equity shall require it, will decree a sale of the property to satisfy the debt, and will cause such decree to be carried into effect by the appointment of a commissioner or master to conduct the sale, and he is to produce in court the fund arising therefrom, subject to the final order of the court.[3]

§ 503. Such proceeding being *in rem*, the jurisdiction (unless so enlarged by statute) does not extend to the making of any personal order or decree against the owner of the property in case the fund arising from the sale be insufficient to satisfy the demand.[4]

§ 504. Some of these cases are kindred in their nature to admiralty cases, as for instance proceedings *in rem* against water crafts, under state laws, to enforce liens or else to obtain and enforce liens against such crafts for material and supplies furnished in home ports, which do not come within the admiralty jurisdiction of the United States.

[1] The Phebe, Ware C. C. 354; Andrews *v.* Wall, 3 How. 568, 573; Act of Congress, March 2, 1799, Sec. 90; Conklin Digest, 1st Ed. 388; The Siren, 7 Wall. 152.

[2] Hurst *v.* Stull, 4 Md. Ch. Dec. 391, 393; Inglehart *v.* Armgs., 1 Bland. 527; Mason *v.* Osgood, 64 N. C. 467, 468; Bozza *v.* Rowe, 30 Ill. 198; Armor *v.* Cochran, 66 Penn. St. 308; Coffee *v.* Coffee, 16 Ill. 145; Moore *v.* Shultz, 13 Penn. St. 102; Sowards *v.* Pritchett, 37 Ill. 517.

[3] Black *v.* Brennan, 5 Dana (K). 311, 313; 2 Story Eq. Jur. Sec. 1033; 4 Kent Com. 139; Ambler *v.* Warwick, 1 Leigh. 495, 205, 207, 2 Hilliard on Mortgages, Appendix No. 1, Sec. 38.

[4] Black *v.* Brennan, 5 Dana (Ky.) 311, 312.

§ 505. The effect of such proceedings and sale thereof varies in the several states under the impress of local law. But there are certain principles that run alike through the whole. The vessel must be within the territorial jurisdiction of the court or jurisdiction cannot be obtained; and being so within such jurisdiction, then jurisdiction over the thing actually attaches by corporal seizure thereof under the process of the court, and continues only during such corporal restraint and possession, unless released under some provision of law, as on forthcoming bond or other similar provisions.[1]

§ 506. In such proceedings *in rem* under state laws, it matters not whether the proceedings purport in form, to be at law or in chancery, or in neither one or the other exclusively, as in some modern creations of pleadings. In either case the order of condemnation and sale is made and is executed in the exercise of more or less equity power, and the sale being made by express adjudication of the court pointing out the property to be sold is judicial in its character. The property is already in custody of the court by the original seizure, and judgment of condemnation, and sale. No new levy is necessary; and whether the sale be conducted by the sheriff or by a master, the result is the same. It is the carrying out the order of the court, and not the exercise of any separate authority irrespective of such order and ministerial in character.

§ 507. A *bona fide* purchaser of personal property, at a sale purely judicial, as one made on a seizure, condemnation and order of sale of a water craft in proceedings *in rem*, under the statute for enforcing claims against boats, takes the title to the property in Ohio, free from all ordinary liabilities. The seizure on process creates a lien, and the proceedings perfected by condemnation and sale cuts off all existing claims or mere liabilities which are not in themselves liens entitled to priority.[2] The case last cited was a proceeding under the Ohio statute, which gives the creditor the right to proceed against the owner or master of a water craft, "or the craft itself," and provides for its seizure and detention, and for its subsequent sale on

---

[1] Bradstreet v. Ins. Co. 3 Sumner C. C. 600.

[2] Jones v. Steam Boat Commerce, 14 Ohio, 408.

execution to satisfy the judgment of the court. The Supreme Court of Ohio say: "From the time of this seizure a lien is created, the property is bound and may be sold on execution." The court remark that this construction of the act aids "the vigilant creditor, by allowing to him the same advantage that one secures to himself, by making a levy on personal property." And that "the lien first attaching by virtue of the seizure will be first satisfied, and so on in the order of priority," if the proceeds of sale are more than the amount of the first lien and costs. "The first judicial sale (say the court) then, must pass the entire interest and vest in the purchaser a perfect title."[1]

§ 508. In the case of *Phegley v. Tatum*,[2] cited from Missouri, the Supreme Court of that state recognizing the rule in Admiralty courts of exclusive jurisdiction of maratime liens, and that all the world are bound by their action *in rem* upon such subjects, denies that there is any analogy between such and suits prosecuted in the state courts of that state to enforce liens against boats and vessels under the local statute. The court say, of sales in the regular court of Admiralty: "Such sales are not made for the benefit of every particular creditor, but for the benefit of all persons interested." * * * "The proceeding is entirely *in rem* and all the world are bound by it." Whereas, the benefits of the Missouri statute "are confined to persons in Missouri, or making contracts in Missouri;" and the "effect of a sale under the Missouri law," is to "divest only the liens existing under that law." Therefore, that as sales in Missouri do not affect the liens of strangers resident in Illinois or other states, but as against such persons operate only as would private sales, so, on the other hand, like sales under the statutes of other states are not maintainable in Missouri, as against liens existing under the statute of Missouri. Such too is virtually the ruling in Iowa, in reference to liens arising under the laws of Missouri.

§ 509. Under the Ohio statute the claim against the water craft is not *per se* a lien, nor does the statute make it a lien;

[1] Jones v. Steam Boat Commerce, 14 Ohio, 411, 112.

[2] Phegley v. Tatum, 33 Mo. 461, 466, 467; Hight v. Steam Boat Henrietta, 4 Iowa, 427, 475.

but merely provides a way by which a lien may be obtained. That is by seizure on process in accordance with the provisions of the statute.

§ 510. Whether such seizure and sale will cut off prior liens already existing, is not expressly determined in the case above referred to; but the court declare such sale to be unlike a private sale, wherein the purchaser takes only the interest of the vendor and holds the property as the vendor held it in all purchases where the purchaser had notice of a claim against the same at the time of his private purchase. The claim follows the boat in whomsoever hands the vessel goes, whether by private sale or hire and is capable to be matured by judicial proceedings into a lien against it. But claims that are not so matured are cut off by a seizure and judicial sale, just as a prior attachment over-reaches a subsequent one. In the language of the court: "The judicial sale is the act of the law."[1]

§ 511. This equitable jurisdiction extends only to the enforcement of the lien,[2] and does not authorize any order or decree against the person.

§ 512. In cases of bailment where the lien is for benefits bestowed or labor performed on the property, the expenses of subsequent keeping attach to the liability and become a part of the lien, whenever the party has a right to retain possession as security for his demand. He has " a lien upon the property itself for the re-imbursement of his reasonable expenditures in keeping and providing for it, though he keep it merely for his own security."[3] In the enforcement of the lien judicially by decree and sale, these additional expenditures will be included and satisfied as if part of the original liability, so far as they are reasonable, necessary and just. Or when the property is expensive to keep or is perishable, it may be sold under interlocutory order and the funds be held to answer the final decree.[4]

---

[1] Jones v. Steam Boat Commerce, 14 Ohio, 408, 413; Waverley v. Clements 14 Ohio, 28, 37.

[2] Black v. Brennan, 5 Dana (Ky.) 311, 312; Long Dock Co. v. Mallory, 1 Beasley, 94, 96.

[3] Black v. Brennan, 5 Dana (Ky.) 311, 312.

[4] Black v. Brennan, 5 Dana (Ky.) 313; Long Dock Co. v. Mallory, 1 Beas. 94.

CHAPTER XIV.

JUDICIAL SALES OF CORPORATE FRANCHISES, PROPERTY AND STOCKS.

§ 513. Though the corporate right to operate a rail road and receive the earnings and tolls, may result from a judicial sale and purchase under a decree of foreclosure and sale on a mortgage, yet, by such decree, foreclosure and sale, the corporate existence and franchise of such company will not pass to the purchaser. That is, "The capacity to have perpetual succession under a special name, and in an artificial form, to take and grant property, contract obligations, and sue and be sued by its corporate name, as an individual," are "franchises belonging to the individual stockholders," and will not pass to such purchaser; that although the company "may be divested of its property, together with the franchise of operating and making profit from the use of its road, its corporate existence survives the wreck and endures until the states sees fit to terminate it by a proper proceeding."[1]

§ 514. In the case of *Canal Co. v. Bonham*,[2] the court hold as follows in reference to forced sales of such interests. SERGEANT, Justice: "The spirit of the decision in *Amant v. Alexandria and Pittsburgh Transportation Company*, seems to be that privileges granted to corporations to construct turnpike roads, canals, etc., are conferred with a view to public use and accommodation, and that they cannot voluntarily deprive themselves of the lands and real estate, and franchises which are necessary for that purpose; nor can they be taken from them by execution, and sold by a creditor, because, to permit it, would

[1] Atkinson v. The M. and C. R. R. Co. 15 Ohio, 21, 36; Coe v. Columbus, Piqua and Ind. R. R. Co. 10 Ohio St. 372; Canal Co. v. Bonham, 9 W. & S. 27; Amant v. New Alexandria and Pitts. Transportation Co. 13 S. & R. 210.

[2] Canal Co. v. Bonham, 9 Watts & Sergt. 27, 28.

(187)

tend to defeat the whole object of the charter by taking the improvements out of the hands of the corporation and destroying their use and benefit." * * * * "The remedy for creditors, in such case," say the court, is by sequestration, as was suggested by Chief Justice TILGHMAN, and has since been provided for by statute.

§ 515. And where, as in Ohio, it is by the constitution provided that "the general assembly shall pass no special act conferring corporate powers," it is holden that a special act of assembly declaring that such mortgage sale shall carry the corporate franchise to the purchaser, is unconstitutional and void; and that though the right to operate the road and receive the proceeds thereof would pass thereby, the sale being regular in other respects; that yet, the corporate capacity and existence still remained in the stockholders, and that the attempt by such act of assembly to confer the corporate capacity of the debtor corporation on the purchasers at such judicial sale was tantamount to an attempt to create a corporation by special enactment, and was then inoperative and void. That what the general assembly cannot do directly, it cannot do indirectly. The court say, aside from this act of assembly: "It is certain that the mortgagees, as such, were invested with no corporate capacity, and it is equally certain that a mere purchase at the sale would have invested them with none." So that, without the enactment it could not pass, and that it would not pass by the enactment which in itself was unconstitutional and void.[1]

§ 516. But in Pennsylvania, under somewhat similar conditions, the ruling is the contrary. There, the act of assembly, after conferring power to mortgage the property and franchise, declared that, "in the event of a sale being made of the estate, right, and franchises of said company, under or by virtue of the provisions of any mortgage created under this or any other act, the purchaser or purchasers, their associates and assigns, shall thereupon become a body politic or corporate under the name of the Westchester Direct Railroad Company, and, as such, be entitled to succeed to all the estate, right, and privi-

---

Atkinson v. M. C. R. R. Co. 15 Ohio St. 21, 36, 38.

leges of said company." The court held that a mortgage so made under said act, carried with it the right to have the mortgaged property and franchise sold on nonpayment of the debt according to the terms of the obligation.[1]

§ 517. Where, through the fraudulent acts and procurement of the directors of a railroad company, its franchises, road, and rolling stock were sold at judicial sale, under a mortgage decree for a nominal sum compared with their real value, and thereby the just claims of other creditors were to be cut off and their interests sacrificed, it was held by the Supreme Court of the United States that the purchasers at the mortgage sale, who had in the meantime despoiled the road by taking up and selling the material at great profit, should be "held liable as trustees" to the injured creditors, "for the full value of the property purchased" at the mortgage sale, after deducting therefrom the amount of the judgment at the day of sale paid by them and under which they bought.[2]

§ 518. A judicial sale under a mortgage decree of foreclosure of a railroad and its franchises will not carry title to the mere easement or right of way of the road at places where the damages for the same, though assessed, have not been paid, although the mortgage deed be of subsequent date to the taking and occupancy of the easement. Until paid for, the right to the easement does not vest in the company, and consequently there could be no title in the company to the easement at the date of the mortgage to which the mortgage lien could attach as against the original land owner, or as against his prior right to enforce compensation for his damages for right of way.[3]

§ 519. Although as a general principle in Pennsylvania, the courts will not assume chancery jurisdiction to decree a mortgage foreclosure, or a foreclosure and sale on a mortgage,[4] yet they will do so in cases of insolvency, bankruptcy, or death of

[1] Mendenhall v. The Westchester and Phila. R. R. 36 Penn. St. 145 and 147, n.

[2] Drury v. Cross, 7 Wall. 299.

[3] Western Penn. R. R. v. Johnson, 59 Penn. St, 290.

[4] Bradley v. The Chester Valley R. R. 36 Penn St. 141, 155; Amherst v. The Montour Iron Co. 35 Penn. St. 30.

the mortgagor,[1] and will also "take jurisdiction of a trust created in a mortgage, and will compel trustees to execute whatever powers have been vested in them for the benefit of creditors, even to the sale of the mortgage premises on a proper case made.[2]

§ 520. But that default to pay the interest, merely, on its unmatured mortgage bonds, by a railroad company, does not authorize a decree compelling the trustees in the mortgage to exercise their powers of sale and sell the road and franchises of the company, when their power to sell is in the mortgage based upon the maturity of and default to pay the bonds.[3]

§ 521. In the case of *Mendenhall v. Westchester and Phila-delphia R. R.*,[4] the court say: "We have already indicated the general rule drawn from the civil law, that nothing can be conveyed in mortgage except things which may be sold. This is the reason why a railroad corporation, holding its franchise for public use, although its tolls are for the private benefit of the stockholders, can neither sell nor mortgage its franchises." (That is apart from statutory authority so to do.) "But when the legislature authorized it to execute a mortgage" to secure a debt, such mortgage "carries with it a right to have the mortgaged property and franchise sold on non-payment of the debt, according to the terms of the obligation." And more especially, "where, as in the case before us, the road is unfinished, and there are no tolls or other means of collecting the debts by sequestration."

§ 522. Under the statute in Wisconsin, a railroad company becomes the owner in fee of the real estate taken for right of way, or on which to construct its road; and by the laws of that state the rolling stock of such company is a fixture to such realty, and is a part thereof.

§ 523. Judgments at law are by law, in that state, liens upon the real estate of judgment debtors. Hence it follows that a judgment in that state against a railroad company is a lien

---

[1] Mendenhall v. Westchester and Phila. R. R. 36 Penn. St. 145, n.

[2] Bradley v. The Chester Valley R. R. 36 Penn. St. 141, 155

[3] Ibid.

[4] 36 Penn. St. 145, n.

upon such real estate and fixtures of the company, and that a sale thereof under a decree in chancery, to satisfy such judgment and conveyance made in pursuance thereof, (the sale being confirmed by the court,) carries to the purchaser title to the whole interest of the company, as fully as it existed at the time of the rendition of such judgment.[1]

§ 524. A mortgage sale of the rail road was set aside at the suit of judgment creditors, as fraudulent and void, where the foreclosure was nominally for an amount greatly in excess of the real indebtedness, the notice of sale was of a similar character. The mortgagee acting as auctioneer, and as such bid in the property for certain of the bond holders and directors who had made the mortgage.

The Supreme Court of the United States, NELSON justice, hold the following language in reference to the transaction:

"It needs no authorities to show that such a sale cannot be upheld without sanctioning the grossest fraud and injustice to the mortgagor and its creditors." "The deceptive notice was calculated to destroy all competition among the bidders, and indeed, to exclude from the purchase every one except those engaged in the perpetration of the fraud. The sale therefore must be set aside and the Milwaukee and Minnesota Company be perpetually enjoined from setting up any right or title under it, the mortgage to remain as security for the bonds in the hands of *bona fide* holders for value, and that the judgment creditors the complainants be at liberty to enforce their judgments against the defendants therein, subject to all prior liens or incumbrances."[2]

§ 525. The enforcement of judgments at law against private corporations, and the carrying out the rights of execution purchases on sales of the right to take tolls, where such sales are allowed by statute on execution against such corporations, are fit subjects of equity jurisdiction.

§ 526. Such jurisdiction results from the incompetency of courts of law to afford sufficient or certain relief. The nature

[1] James v. Railroad Co. 6 Wall. 750.
[2] James v. Railroad Co. 6 Wall. 752, 755.

of the interest to be reached, is such, from their intangibility as to preclude the ordinary remedy of corporeal possession which results from execution sales of goods and chattels and of real estate. On such sales of goods and chattels, possession of the property is delivered to the purchaser by the officer selling; and on sales of the realty, the purchaser has his action at law for possession of the property. But on execution sale (if such sales be permissable) of a franchise, a mere easement, or the right to take tolls, no such possibility follows; and a court of law is incompetent to put the purchaser into possession of the fruits of his purchase.[1]

§ 527. In *Covington Draw Bridge Co. v. Shepherd*,[2] the Supreme Court of the United States, CATRON Justice, say of the power of the court of law to meet out a suitable remedy in such cases, that, "One thing however is plainly manifest, that the remedy at law of these execution creditors is exceedingly embarrassed, and we do not see how they can obtain satisfaction of their judgments from this corporation (owning no property but this bridge) unless equity can afford relief."

§ 528. In the case of *The Macon & Western Rail Road Co. v. Parker*, the Supreme Court of Georgia hold the following language in reference to the same subject: "The whole history of equity jurisprudence does not not present a case which made the interposition of its powers not only highly expedient, but so indispensably necessary in adjusting the rights of creditors to an insolvent estate, as this did."[3]

§ 529. In such cases, when there is not tangible property subject to levy and sale belonging to the company, a court of equity will give relief by appointing a receiver to take charge of and manage the corparate property; receive the tolls and income of the corporation from whatever source they may emanate, and account for the same to the court to the end that they be applied to the extinguishment of the judgments and

---

[1] Covington Draw Bridge Co. v. Shepherd, 21 How. 112; Macon & Western R. R. v. Parker, 9 Geo. 378.

[2] 21 How. 124.

[3] Macon & Western R. R. v. Parker, 9 Geo. 393, 394; Covington Draw Bridge Co. v. Shepherd, 21 How. 125.

executions existing against the company, according to their respective rights; first defraying the costs, charges and expenses of the operation and proceedings out of the same.[1] In the case of *The Covington Draw Bridge Co. v. Shepherd*, there were two judgment creditors holding judgments in the circuit court of the United States, for the District of Alabama. The one sold and bought in on execution the right of the corporation to the tolls of the road; but finding his purchase ineffectual as to any more than a nominal satisfaction of the writ, and leaving him no means of obtaining actual payment, he joined with the other judgment creditor in a bill in chancery for the appointment of a receiver to take charge of the franchise and corporate property and operate it in satisfaction of their demands. A decree was accordingly entered granting the relief prayed for; from this decree the case went to the United States Supreme Court, which affirmed the decree of the court below.[2]

§ 530. The corporation and franchise to take toll were created by act of the legislature of Indiana. By the law of said state it is enacted that, "the property, rights, credits, and effects of the defendants are subject to execution."[3] But not the lands until the rents and profits for a term of years are first offered. Under this state of the law "the tolls, under the idea that they were rents and profits of the bridge (say the court) were sold for one year according to the forms of the law. The tolls of the bridge being a franchise and sole right in the corporation, and the bridge a mere easement, the corporation not owning the fee in the land at either bank of the river or under the water, it is difficult to say how an execution could attach to either the franchise or the structure of the bridge as real or personal property. This is a question that this court may well leave to the tribunals of Indiana to decide, on their own laws should it become necessary." The Supreme Court, after reviewing the whole subject, then add in conclusion, that "all that we are called on to decide in this case is,

---

[1] Covington Draw Bridge Co. *v.* Shepherd, 21 How. 112.
[2] Ibid, 125.
[3] 2 Revised Stats. 1852.

13

that the court below had power to cause possession to be taken
of the bridge, to appoint a receiver to collect tolls and pay them
in to court, to the end of discharging the judgments at law,
and our opinion is, that the power to do so exists, and that it
was properly exercised.[1]

[1] Covington Draw Bridge Co. v. Shepherd, 21 How. 124, 125.

PART FOURTH.

EXECUTION SALES OF REAL PROPERTY.

CHAPTER XV

WHAT INTEREST IN LANDS MAY BE SOLD, AND IN WHAT ORDER.

I. How Liable to Sale.

§ 531. Lands were never liable to execution sales at common law. The remedy of the creditor was against the rents and profits. First by the writ of *levari facias,* and subsequently by writ of *elegit.* The latter was given by statute of Westminster, 2–13 Elizabeth.[1]

§ 532. Next came the statute of George II., subjecting lands to execution sale in the American colonies and others. In *Bergin v. McFarland,*[2] the court holds the following language in reference to this statute, BELL, Justice: "By an early British statute, lands in the colonies were subjected equally with personal estate of the debtor to the payment of debts. Stat. 5, George II.; Prov. Stat. of N. H., 1771, p. 233. And by very early statutes both of Massachusetts and of this pro-

---

[1] Gantley's Lessee *v.* Ewing, 3 How. 714; McConnell *v.* Brown, 5 Mon. 480; Erwin *v.* Dundas, 4 How. 58, 77; Bergin *v.* McFarland, 6 Foster (N. H.) 536; 3 Bac. Abt. C. 64; 4 Kent, Com. 429.

[2] 6 Foster (N. H.) 536.

vince, power was conferred upon executors and administrators
to sell the real estate for payment of debts, in case the proper
courts, upon application, should deem the same necessary or
proper."

There were like statutes in Pennsylvania of early date.
Hence the origin of selling lands for debt in the American
colonies and states, a practice continued in most of the states
at the present time varied only in manner and effect by local
regulations. In some, however, the writ of *elegit*, and in
others the remedy by extent, are resorted to. With these latter
remedies we have nothing in this work to do.

§ 533. In some of the states the lands are not only liable
to execution sale, if there be not personal property found, but
the debtor at his option may require their sale on execution in
lieu of the personalty.[1]

§ 534. In others, if there be not personal property found,
then the land is levied on, and the rents and profits are
appraised for a certain term fixed by statute, and for such term
are offered for sale upon the writ. If they do not command
the amount of the debt, then sale is made of the land itself.[2]

§ 535. But the various and diversified statutory regulations
in the several states are too numerous to come within the
scope of our title and purpose, and will, therefore, not be followed out.

§ 536. The more prevalent rule now is, that in those states
where execution sales are made of the realty, every legal interest of the debtor not exempt by statute is subject to levy and
sale, including those that are contingent, in reversion and in
remainder.[3] Also rent charges,[4] and leases.[5] And in some

---

[1] Tuttle *v.* Wilson, 24 Ill. 559; Pitts *v.* McGie, 24 Ill. 610; Cavender *v.*
Smith, 1 Iowa, 306.

[2] Gantley's Lessee *v.* Ewing, 3 How. 707.

[3] Humphreys *v.* Humphreys, 1 Yeates, 427; Wiley *v.* Bridgman, 1 Head,
(Tenn.) 68; Smith *v.* Ingles, 2 Oregon, 43, 45.

[4] Hurst *v.* Lithgrow, 2 Yeates, 25.

[5] Bisby *v.* Hall, 3 Ham. 449; Shelton *v.* Codman, 3 Cush. 318.

of the states, mere equities.[1] But the interest must be in the land itself and not a mere permit to occupy.[2]

§ 537. In Iowa, under the statute, pre-emption rights are holden to be subject to execution sales.[3] And in several of the states an "entry or survey" of lands is such an "inchoate and incomplete legal title," as is subject to execution sale.[4]

§ 538. Likewise are equity of redemption;[5] but not the statutory right to redeem from execution sale.[6] But an interest arising under a resulting trust is liable to execution sale.[7] The purchaser at execution sale has no such interest before expiration of the time allowed for redemption as may be levied and sold.[8]

§ 539. The law is well settled in Louisiana that an execution creditor who would avoid a fraudulent sale of lands made by his debtor, or by a proceedings in probate, must first bring his bill and set aside the sale for the fraud, before he can levy and sell the lands on his execution.

§ 540. The Supreme Court of the United States in disposing of this subject, say: "The judgment creditor is not permitted to treat a conveyance from the defendant in the judgment, made by authentic act, or in pursuance of a judicial sale of the succession by a probate judge, as null and void, and to seize and sell the property which had thus passed to the vendee. The law requires that he shall bring an action to set the alienation aside, and succeed in the same before he can levy his execution. And so firmly settled and fixed is this

[1] Foot v. Cobin, 3 Johns. 216; Kizer v. Sawyer, 4 Kan. 503; Jackson v. Bateman, 2 Wend. 570; Evans v. Wilder, 5 Mo. 313.

[2] West Penn. R. R. Co. v. Johnson, 59 Penn. St. 294; Morrow v. Brenizer, 2 Rawle, 188; Thomas v. Simpson, 3 Barr. 69.

[3] Levy v. Thompson, 4 How. 17.

[4] Landers v. Brant, 10 How. 348; Land v. Hopkins, 7 Ala. 115; Thomas v. Marshall, Hardin, 19.

[5] Waters v. Stewart, 1 Caines Cas. 47; Watkins v. Gregory, 6 Blackf. 113; Hunter v. Hunter, Walker, 194; Phelps v. Butler, 2 Ham. 224; Porter v. Millet, 9 Mass. 101; Taylor v. Cornelius, 60 Penn. St. 187, 195.

[6] Watson v. Reissig, 24 Ill. 281; Merry v. Bostwick, 13 Ill. 398.

[7] Foot v. Colvin, 3 Johns. 216; Jackson v. Bateman, 2 Wend. 270; Evans v. Wilder, 5 Mo. 313, 321.

[8] Den v. Steelman, 5 Halst. 193; Kidder v. Orcutt, 40 Maine, 589.

principle in the jurisprudence of Louisiana, as a rule of property and as administered in the courts of that state, that even if the sale and conveyance by authentic act or in pursuance of a judicial sale are confessedly fraudulent and void, still no title passes to the purchaser under the judgment and execution." That "in effect the sale, if permitted to take place, is null and void, and passes no title." The United States Supreme Court recognize this principle as running through all the books of that state.[1]

§ 541. A claim of land not based upon either right or possession is not an interest in the realty, or subject to execution sale.[2]

§ 542. Lands held in trust by an executor to pay a testator's debts are equitable assets and are not liable to execution sale in proceedings against the heirs or against the executors.[3] The trust must be executed; the proper tribunal will enforce its execution if need be, and will see to the faithful application of the proceeds.

§ 543. Lands held by purchaser of the United States before the issuance of the patent, are subject to execution sale, as also to judgment liens.[4]

§ 544. When the patent issues, the title under the sheriff's sale relates back to the date of the entry, and so does the government patent, and title vests in the execution purchaser by such relation.[5]

§ 545. "There is no rule better founded in law, or reason, or convenience," (says the learned author of Cruise on Real

[1] Ford v. Douglass, 5 How. 143. See also Henry v. Hyde, 5 Martin (N. S.) 633; Yocom v. Bullitt, 6 Martin, 324; Peet v. Morgan, 6 Martin, 137; Childress v. Allen, 3 La. 477; Bennett v. Duvergis, 5 La. 124; Samory v. Hebrard, 17 La. 558.

[2] Hagaman v. Jackson, 1 Wend. 502; Major v. Deer, 4 J. J. Marshall, 585.

[3] Helm v. Dailey, 3 Dana, 185.

[4] Huntingdon v. Grantland, 33 Miss. 453; Landes v. Brant, 10 How. 348, 374; Levi v. Thompson, Morris (Iowa) 235; Cavender v. Smith, 5 Iowa, 157; Rogers v. Brent, 5 Gilm. 573; Jackson v. Williams, 10 Ohio, 69.

[5] Landes v. Brant, 10 How. 348, 372, 373, 374; Cavender v. Smith, 5 Iowa, 157.

Property,) "than this; that all the several parts and ceremonies necessary to complete a conveyance shall be taken together as one act and operate from the substantial part by relation."[1]

II. Dower Lands.

§ 546. The right of dower may not be sold on execution before assignment or possession thereof.[2]

§ 547. But dower lands held by actual possession of the tenant in dower may be levied and sold, and the possessory right will pass, and so will the growing crops, by the sale, if there be no redemption allowed by law.[3]

§ 548. And so the possessory interest of a husband in dower lands already assigned to his wife as the widow of a former husband.[4]

III. Undivided Interest.

§ 549. Neither the interest of husband or wife, where they are tenants of the entirety in lands, can be sold on execution so as to pass away title that may be enforced during their joint lives, or against the survivor after the death of one of them. During their lifetime husband and wife are tenants of the entirety of lands conveyed to the two jointly and each are seized of the whole. On the death of either the entirety remains in the survivor and such survivor becomes the sole owner of the whole estate in the land.[5] So no separate proceeding against one of them, during their joint lives, will by sale affect the title to the property as against the other one as survivor, or as against the two during their joint lives.[6] Neither party to such tenancy can sell or convey their interest, for it is incapable of being separated. The husband and wife being

[1] 5 Cruise, Real Prop. 510, 511.
[2] Nason v. Allen, 5 Greenl. 479; Gooch v. Atkins, 14 Mass. 378; Graham v. Moore, 5 Har. (Del.) 318; Pennington v. Yell, 6 Eng. 212.
[3] Pitts v. Hendrix, 6 Geo. 452.
[4] McConihe v. Sawyer, 12 N. H. 369.
[5] 2 Bl. Com. 182; 4 Kent, Com. 362.
[6] French v. Mehan, 56 Penn. St. 286; McCurdy v. Canning. 64 Penn St. 39.

one,[1] therefore each are seized of the whole; and what one cannot himself sell cannot be sold on execution against him.[2]

§ 550. How far this species of tenancy has been affected by statutory enactment of any of the states, it is not our purpose here to enquire.

IV. EQUITABLE INTEREST.

§ 551. A title merely equitable, without possession, may not be sold, ordinarily, on execution. If subject thereto it is by statutory enactment.[3]

§ 552. But "possession of land, (in the language of SWAN, Justice,) is an estate therein which may ripen into a right of possession and property," and "if a judgment debtor is in possession of land, it may be levied upon and sold."[4]

---

[1] 2 Bl. Com. 182; 4 Kent, 362.

[2] French v. Mehan, 56 Penn. St. 286; Gentry v. Wagstaff, 3 Dev. 270. In French v. Mehan, the court hold that "it is well settled that if an estate in land be given to the husband and wife, or a joint purchase be made by them during coveture, they are not properly joint tenants or tenants in common, for they are but one person in law and cannot take by moieties. They are both seized of the entirety, and though the husband may have the absolute control of the estate during his life, and may convey or mortgage it during that period, neither can alienate any portion thereof without the consent of the other, and the survivor takes the whole. Johnson v. Hart, 6 W. & S. 319; Robb v. Beaver, 8 id. 111; Fairchild v. Chastelleux, 1 Barr, 176; Clark v. Thompson, 2 Jones, 274; Stuckey v. Keefe's Exrs. 2 Casey, 397; Martin v. Jackson, 3 id. 504; Bates v. Seeley, 10 Wright, 248. "If the wife survives the husband she takes the estate discharged of his debts, for the reason that she does not take it under or through him, but by virtue of the paramount grant in the original conveyance. And though the husband's interest may be sold under execution during coveture, (Stoebler v. Knerr, 5 Watt. 181,) yet if his creditors levy upon the estate in his lifetime, and sell it as his property, the wife may recover it on his death in an action of ejectment. Brownson v. Hull, 16 Vt. 309." We may add here that if a sale as against the husband, on execution against him can affect the possession during the joint lives of the husband and wife, it can only be so, upon the principle that during that time her possession is merged in his. French v. Mehan, 56 Penn. St. 288, 289.

[3] Haynes v. Baker, 5 Ohio St. 253; Thomas v. Marshall, Hardin (Ky.) 20; Tyree v. Williams, 3 Bibb. 366; Allen v. Saunders, 2 Bibb. 94; January v. Bradford, 4 Bibb. 566.

[4] Haynes v. Baker, 5 Ohio St. 253; Jackson v. Williams, 10 Ohio, 69.

§ 553. In Indiana, by statute, lands fraudulently conveyed away by a judgment debtor are subject to execution sale, without first being uncovered in equity from the fraud.

§ 554. And so lands holden in trust for another may be levied and sold for the debt of the person for whose benefit they are held.[1]

§ 555. In Iowa, by statute, equitable interests in the realty are liable to execution sale, and judgments are liens thereon.[2] In the case here cited the court say: "The question involves no principle not heretofore settled by this court. First—It has been held that the interest of the judgment debtor in real estate is vendible upon execution, and the judgment itself operates as a lien thereon. Harrison v. Kramer et al., 3 Iowa, 543; Blain v. Stewart, 2 Iowa, 378." And in Harrison v. Kramer et al., the Supreme Court of Iowa hold that "a judgment is a lien upon the real estate of the defendant, and by real estate is meant all right thereto and interest therein, equitable as well as legal."[3]

V. The Homestead.

§ 556. Though judgments at law are ordinarily a lien on the lands of judgment debtors, yet they are not so as to the lands occupied as a homestead; and if the homestead be abandoned by sale, conveyance, and delivery of possession by the debtor whilst a judgment exists against him, the lien thereof does not attach to the premises, but the grantee takes a clean title to the same so far as regards the judgment, and an execution sale thereof under the judgment is void.[4]

---

[1] Tevis v. Doe, 3 Ind. 129, 131.

[2] Crosby v. Elkader Lodge, 16 Iowa, 399, 405; Harrison v. Kramer, 3 Iowa, 543; Blain v. Stewart, 2 Iowa, 378.

[3] Harrison v. Kramer, 3 Iowa, 543, 561. The title, when perfected by patent, to lands sold on execution when the estate was but inchoate, inures to the benefit of the execution purchaser, and by relation invests him with the fee. Cavender v. Smith, 5 Iowa. 157.

[4] Morris v. Ward, 5 Kan. 239; Lamb v. Shays, 14 Iowa, 567; Cummins v. Long, 16 Iowa, 41; Revalk v. Kraemer, 8 Cal. 66; Wiggins v. Chance, 44 Ill. 175; Green v. Marks, 25 Ill. 221; Fishback v. Lane, 36 Ill. 437; Bliss v. Clark, 39 Ill. 590.

§ 557. The same doctrine is held in Iowa. The lien being the creature of the statute, it can only apply where the statute applies it. The law giving the lien and the law granting the homestead are to be construed together.[1] A judgment lien can only be co-extensive with the right to enforce it.[2]

§ 557. In the case cited from 5th Kansas, the subject is discussed by Judge VALENTINE with equal ability, and the same conclusion is arrived at as by the Supreme Court of

[1] Lamb v. Shays, 14 Iowa, 567; Cummins v. Long, 16 Iowa, 41.

[2] Scriba v. Dean, Marshall, Justice, 1 Brock. 166; Bank of U. S. v. Winston, 2 Brock. 252; Shrew v. Jones, 2 McLean, 78; Lamb v. Shays, 14 Iowa, 567; Bliss v. Clark. 39 Ill. 590. The learned court in Iowa, BALDWIN, Justice, dispose of this subject in the following forcible language: "The section in relation to the liens of judgments of the Supreme and District Courts, and the one giving to the owner of the homestead the exemption, were passed by the Legislature at the same time; the one giving to the judgment creditor a lien on the lands of the defendant, and the other denying him the right to enforce it so far as the homestead is concerned. The right of the judgment to seize or to enforce his judgment by selling the lands of the debtor exists only by force of the statute, and is regulated altogether by its provisions. The lien of a judgment upon lands in this state being conferred by statute, it can only have such force as is given thereby, and it can only attach and become effective in the manner, at the time, and upon the conditions and limitations imposed by the statute itself. A lien without the power to enforce it carries with it no advantage to the owner thereof. It cannot be enforced as against the homestead, because it is exempt from judicial sale. It is inoperative and cannot be otherwise as long as the homestead is used as a home. Construing the two sections together, having been passed at the same time by the Legislature, we think that it could not have been designed that the lien should ever attach upon property that was declared exempt from judicial sale. This exemption exists only so long as the homestead is occupied and used as a home. The moment it ceases to be used as such, the lien attaches, the same as it attaches against property acquired by the judgment debtor after the judgment is rendered, and the priority of liens can be determined in the same manner. If, therefore, this lien does not attach so as to be effective against the owner, how can it affect the rights of a purchaser of the homestead property? The right of exemption continues until the sale and delivery of the deed to the vendee, and the lien cannot attach until after sale and delivery, nor until after it ceases to be occupied by the owner. Prior to this the vendee's rights become absolute." Lamb v. Shays, 14 Iowa, 569, 570.

Iowa.[1] The same is substantially the ruling in Illinois. It is there holden that neither judgment nor levy will operate as a lien upon the homestead. That temporary abandonment of the same, with intent to reoccupy it as homestead, though rented out in the interim, will not subject it to lien, of judgment, levy, or to sale. That a grantee of the owner holds against a prior judgment which would have been a lien on the land but for the homestead law; and that if sold on execution, the sale, on application, will be set aside.[2] But that whether

[1] In this case the court hold the following principles and language: "It is claimed that the judgment lien remains simply dormant during the time that the land is occupied as a homestead, and that as soon as it is transferred and ceases to be occupied as a homestead, the lien attaches and becomes effective. Now suppose the husband, in whom the title is vested, dies. The title to the property is immediately, by law, transferred from him to his widow and children, and he ceases to occupy the property as a homestead, will the judgment lien then attach and take the homestead away from the widow and children? And suppose the whole family die, except those children born after the judgment was rendered, can those children hold the property as a homestead? If they can, then where is the certainty of a judgment lien ever attaching to a homestead and becoming effective? And as long as the lien is not effective it is practically no lien at all. In the case at bar, several days before the land was abandoned as a homestead, and, therefore, several days before the judgment lien could have any practical existence the land was conveyed to Morris. Then when did this lien attach and become effective? Upon the whole we decide the questions in this case as follows: 1. A mortgage of the homestead, executed by the husband alone, is void. 2. A judgment rendered against the husband alone is not a lien on the homestead. 3. Neither is such a mortgage, nor such a judgment any incumbrance on land owned by the husband and occupied by himself and family as a homestead. 4. Such land may be sold and conveyed by the husband and wife jointly, and the purchaser will take the title free and clear from all incumbrances, notwithstanding said mortgage and judgment. 5. After said sale and conveyance, and after the land has been abandoned as a homestead, if an execution issue on said judgment, and the land be sold under said execution, the sale is void. 6. After said sale and conveyance, and abandonment, if a decree of foreclosure be entered on said mortgage against the husband, in a suit in which the wife is not a party, the decree is void so far as it affects and is no evidence of anything as against her." Morris v. Ward, 5 Kan. 247, 248, 249.

[2] Green v. Marks, 25 Ill. 221; Stevenson v. Marony, 29 Ill. 534; Fishback v. Lane, 36 Ill. 437; Bliss v. Clark, 39 Ill. 590; Wiggins v. Chance, 54 Ill. 175; Cipperly v. Rhodes, 53 Ill. 346. In Wiggins v. Chance, 54 Ill. 175,

set aside or not, such sale is absolutely void, and not even a permanent abandonment of such homestead subsequent to such void sale can render the sale valid which was invalid before.[1]

§ 558. On an abandonment of the homestead, there being several judgments against the owner, the first levy made thereon will take priority. There being no lien of either judgment on the premises while they continue to be a homestead, a release of the homestead privilege in favor of the plaintiff in execution of a junior judgment and a levy of his execution

the opinion of the court is given as follows: "The evidence shows that this land was a part of appellee's homestead when the levy and sale were made, and the whole property was worth less than $1,000, and there is no pretence that the homestead right was waived or released in the mode prescribed by the law. In the case of Green v. Marks, 25 Ill. 221, it was held that the law exempted the homestead of the debtor from levy and sale on execution, and they created no lien on the homestead while the debtor was in a position to claim the benefits of the land. In the case of Stevenson v. Marony, 29 Ill. 534, it was held that when the homestead is sold and the debtor is in a position to claim the benefit of the act, he may have the levy and sale set aside. And in the case of Fishback v. Lane, 36 Ill. 437, it was held that the grantee of the debtor held the land as against a prior judgment, which would have been a lien had it not been for the homestead law, and that case was based upon the prior case of Bliss v. Clark, but not reported until the 39 Ill. 590, and upon Green v. Marks, supra. It is manifest, from those cases, that there was no lien created on this homestead by issuing the execution, the levy, or the sale, and that the sale was void and passed no title to Garrison. He or appellee could have applied to the court and had the levy and sale set aside, as nothing was acquired thereby. It is urged that appellee, subsequently to the sale, abandoned the premises by removing from them for some months and by leasing the place. He swears he only left to earn money to pay his debts, intending to return and continue it as his home, which he did, and nothing is found in the record to rebut this evidence. But even admitting that he did not intend to return, how is the case changed? If the levy created no lien, and the sale transferred no title, how could appellee's subsequent abandonment render this void sale valid? How could it impart vigor to the sale and conveyance by the sheriff, which was unauthorized and conferred no title? We are at a loss to perceive how appellee's position could be thus changed. Failing to perceive that appellant had shown any defense, we must hold the court below acted correctly in rendering the judgment, and it must be affirmed."

[1] Wiggins v. Chance, 54 Ill. 175, and cases there cited.

then in the sheriff's hands will take precedence over the senior judgment and the levy of an execution subsequently issued thereon and levied on the same land.[1]

VI.   In What Order to be Sold.

§ 559. When a part of the lands subject to a judgment lien are sold by the judgment debtor after the lien has attached, yet if a sufficiency thereof still remains to realize the judgment, the creditor must in equity make his levy and sale of the part so remaining; and if the part so remaining unsold be not sufficient to discharge the whole amount, yet the creditor must exhaust the same before proceeding against the part so sold by the debtor; and so likewise he must exhaust any other property of the debtor, provided it does not interfere with intervening equities or rights of other creditors.[2]

§ 560. By some authorities, if lands subject to judgment lien be sold by the judgment debtor to several different purchasers, in parcels, and at different dates, after the lien of the judgment has attached, so as to leave no remaining unsold part thereof sufficient to satisfy the judgment then in equity, after exhausting what remains, the judgment creditor may be compelled to resort to those parcels last disposed of, in their several orders of conveyance, on which to levy his debt. That is to say, the parcel last sold is first to be exhausted; then the next; and so on in order until the debt is satisfied, or the parcels be all exhausted. So in like manner as to mortgage liens.[3] They

---

[1] Bliss v. Clark, 39 Ill. 590,

[2] Clowes v. Dickenson, 5 Johns. Ch. 235; and same case, 9 Cow. 405; Hurd v. Eaton, 28 Ill. 122; Bates v. Ruddick, 3 Iowa, 423; Massie v. Wilson, 16 Iowa, 391; Barney v. Myers, 28 Iowa, 427.

[3] Clowes v. Dickenson, 5 Johns. Ch. 235; Stuyvesant v. Hall, 2 Barb. Ch. 151; Wisconsin v. Titus, 17 Wis. 241; Ins. Co. v. Miller, 1 Barb. Ch. 353; Marshall v. Moore, 36 Ill. 321; Mason v. Payne, 1 Walker, Ch. 459; Carey v. Fulsom, 14 Ohio, 365; Schriver v. Teller, 9 Paige, 173; Rathbone v. Clark, 9 Paige Ch. 648; LaFarge Ins. Co. v. Bell, 22 Barb. 54; Ogden v. Gidden, 9 Wis. 46; Aiken v. Bruen, 21 Ind. 137; Gill v. Lyon, 1 Johns. Ch. 446. See also Maine, S. C. and others. In Clowes v. Dickenson, 5 Johns. Ch. 235, by the Chancellor: "If there be a judgment against a person owning at the time three acres of land, and he sells one acre to A., the two remaining acres are first chargeable, in equity, with the payment of the judg-

are to be sold in the inverse order of their sale by the execution debtor.

§ 561. By others it is held, however, that whilst the rule is recognized that on sale of a part only of the lands subject to the lien, by the judgment debtor, the execution creditor in enforcing his judgment lien is in equity bound to exhaust the remaining portion still belonging to his debtor before proceeding against the part that has been sold; yet that if the whole be sold in different parcels and at different dates, instead of the creditor having to sell the parcels in the inverse order of their sale by the debtor, he may coerce an equal *pro rata* contribution out of each, in proportion to the value thereof respectively.[1] The former we conceive to be the better ruling. Yet each must be regarded as law within the jurisdiction of the tribunals making these diverse rulings.

§ 562. If there be senior and junior judgment liens in favor of different creditors against the same premises of a judgment debtor, and the junior judgment creditor execute and sell a portion of the lands so subject to the judgment liens, then a *bona fide* purchaser under the execution sale of the junior creditor, will, in equity, have a right to turn the senior judgment creditor over to the remaining part of the lands of the

---

ment debt, as we have already seen, whether the land be in the hands of the debtor himself or his heirs. If he sells another acre to B., the remaining acre is then chargeable, in the first instance, with the debt as against B. as well as against A., because when B. purchased he took his land chargeable with the debt in the hands of the debtor in preference to the land already sold to A. In this respect we may say of him, as is said of the heir, he sits in the seat of his grantor, and must take the land with all its equitable burdens; it cannot be in the power of the debtor, by the act of assigning or selling his remaining land, to throw the burden of the judgment, or a ratable part of it back upon A. * * * * The case is not analogous to a rent charge, which grows out of the land itself, and where every purchaser of distinct parcels of a tract of land charged with the rent takes it with such a proportionate part of the charge." But in cases of mortgages and judgment liens "the charge on the land (says the learned Chancellor) is only by way of security."

[1] Bates v. Ruddick, 2 Iowa, 423; Massie v. Wilson, 16 Iowa, 391; Barney v. Myers, 28 Iowa, 472; Parkman v. Welsh, 19 Pick. 241; Job v. O'Brien, 2 Humph. 34; Dickenson v. Thompson, 8 B. Mon. 321; Green v. Ranage, 18 Ohio, 428.

debtor, for satisfaction of his judgment, either in the whole, or as far as the same will go, before such senior judgment creditor can come upon the part so sold under the junior judgment.[1]

§ 563. In *United States v. Duncan*,[2] the court, DRUMMOND, Justice, say: "The doctrine that where a man owns different parcels of land and transfers some of them, himself also retaining some, all the parcels being subject before the transfer to a general incumbrance made by him, the part which he still retains shall be applied to the payment or discharge of that general incumbrance, rather than that which he has transferred, is founded on the plainest principles of equity. It would be manifestly unjust that those persons to whom he had made transfers should be compelled to pay off the incumbrance when he held land which would satisfy it."

---

[1] Wise *v.* Shepherd, 13 Ill. 41; Hurd *v.* Eaton, 28 Ill. 122; Marshall *v.* Moore, 36 Ill. 321. The reason of the rule for selling by inverse order is, that when a part only is sold by the debtor, then, in equity, the unsold remainder as between him and his grantee becomes primarily liable for the debt, and if subsequently sold, the purchaser takes it liable to this charge, for if the prior conveyance be of record so as to confer notice thereof, then the second purchaser takes no better right than his vendor had. Mason *v.* Payne, Walker, Ch. 459.

[2] 4 McLean, 624.

CHAPTER XVI.

THE WRIT—THE LEVY—AND NOTICE OF SALE.

I. The Writ of Execution.

§ 564. If a judgment be valid, an execution issued thereon cannot be impeached collaterally. It is good until superseded or set aside.[1] But if the judgment be void, an execution thereon is void also,[2] and may be so treated however brought in question.

§ 565. An execution issued on a dormant judgment is fraudulent as against a subsequent *bona fide* purchaser, who buys while the judgment is dormant.[3] A writ of *venditioni exponas*, directing a sheriff to sell lands specifically described as condemned by judgment in attachment proceedings, is not invalidated by a division of the county after the teste of the writ and before the day of sale, although the lands to be sold be situated in the new county formed by such division; but the sheriff may go on and sell, and the sale will, in that respect, be valid.[4]

§ 566. An execution and sale thereon issued against two defendants, after the death of one of them, are void and no title passes by the sale. The judgment should be revived as to the deceased defendant. The plaintiff cannot proceed otherwise without the aid of a statute. Execution cannot go against the survivor alone, nor can it go against the survivor and the

---

[1] 3 Bac. Abt. Execution, A.; Stewart *v.* Stoker, 13 Sergt. & R. 199; Durham *v.* Heaton, 28 Ill. 264.

[2] 3 Bac. Abt. Execution, A.; Abbe *v.* Ward, 8 Mass. 79.

[3] Ball *v.* Shell, 21 Wend. 222; Kellogg *v.* Griffin, 17 Johns. 274.

[4] Tyrell *v.* Roundtree, 7 Pet. 464.

dead defendant jointly. The proper course is to revive the judgment.[1]

§ 567. But in the state of Mississippi, (under the code,) it is held that where judgment is against two or more defendants, and one dies, execution may go against the survivor or survivors; and that the writ will be good against the survivor or survivors, although it omit to mention the death of the co-defendant who is dead.[2]

§ 568. In Tennessee, if plaintiff die before execution issues, the judgment must be revived, as is the general rule, by *scire facias*. If, however, execution be issued, or bears teste, prior to his death, the writ may be levied and enforced by sale, with the same effect as if the plaintiff were still living.[3]

§ 569. It is held in Illinois that although it is the more proper practice where a judgment creditor dies before execution issues, to "recite" in the execution "the fact of the recovery of the judgment, the death of the defendant," and to also state that notice of the judgment has been given to the administrator of the deceased; and thereupon command the sheriff to levy the lands of the decedent which he owned at the time of his death, yet an execution issued against the defendant in the ordinary way will be substantially good.[4]

§ 570. The execution must conform substantially to the judgment. A want thereof will avoid the sale.[5]

§ 571. Execution against a party for costs created by himself, there being no judgment against him, is void, and so is any sale made by virtue thereof.[6]

§ 572. If there be not substantial correspondence between the execution and the judgment, a sale made on such execution may be impeached in a collateral proceeding.[7] But a

---

[1] Erwin *v.* Dundas, 4 How. 59.

[2] Wade *v.* Watt, 41 Miss. 248.

[3] Gregory *v.* Thadwell, 3 Cold. (Tenn.) 390.

[4] Wright *v.* Walbaum, 39 Ill. 554, 563.

[5] Commonwealth *v.* Fisher, 2 J. J. Marsh. 137; Crittenden *v.* Leitensdorfer, 35 Mo. 239.

[6] Washington *v.* Irving, Mart. & Yerg. 45.

[7] Rider *v.* Alexander, 1 Chip. 274; Butler *v.* Haynes, 3 N. H. 21.

14

mere clerical variance will not be cause for such collateral impeachment.[1]

§ 573. By statute, in Indiana, process of execution is required to be sealed with the seal of the court, and it is there held that an execution for a foreclosure decree not so sealed, is invalid, and that a sale thereon by the sheriff is void and his deed will not confer title on the purchaser at such sale.[2]

§ 574. Though an execution cannot issue against a party that is dead without revival,[3] yet if there be several persons plaintiff in a judgment and one dies, it is held, in Massachusetts, that it may still issue in the joint names of the plaintiffs.[4]

§ 575. Where there are several judgments against the same debtor and none of the judgments are liens, then the first execution which is levied takes priority.[5]

II. The Levy.

§ 576. The levy cannot be made after the return day of the writ.[6]

§ 577. The levy must describe the land levied upon with sufficient certainty to enable it to be identified without other evidence.[7] Therefore, where all the calls in a levy are properly answered, and yet the description is such that the land levied on could not therefrom be identified or certainly found, the levy is void for uncertainty. It should be such that a sheriff could know what to put a party in possession of.[8] And so a levy of "all the unsold land in a forty thousand acre tract."[9] Likewise

---

[1] Butler v. Haynes, 3 N. H. 21.

[2] Ins. Co. v. Halleck, 6 Wall. 556.

[3] Hildreth v. Thompson, 16 Mass. 191.

[4] Hamilton v. Lyman, 9 Mass. 14; Bowdoin v. Jordan, 9 Mass. 160.

[5] Lathrop v. Brown, 23 Iowa, 40.

[6] 3 Bac. Abt. Execution, 734; Caines v. Clarke, 1 Bibb. 608; Barnard v. Stevens, 2 Ark. 429.

[7] Huddlestone v. Garrett, 3 Humph. 629; Proud v. Pullum, 3 Yerg. 388; Shields v. Bates, 5 J. J. Marsh. 13; Williamson v. Perkins, 1 Harr. & J. 449; Summers v. Moore, 2 McLean, 59.

[8] Chadbourne v. Mason, 48 Maine, 389, 393; Gault v. Woodbridge, 4 McLean, 329.

[9] Huddlestone v. Garrett, 3 Humph. 629.

a levy of five hundred acres to be taken off the most northerly side of a widow's dower lands, without other identity of the lands, is void.[1]

§ 578. Though a levy must ordinarily describe the land with such certainty as will enable an officer to find and identify it, yet a levy in that respect defective may be cured and rendered valid by the more perfect and sufficiently correct description contained in the appraisement, where the proceeding is under an appraisement law;[2] and so likewise a defective levy, as to the description of the land, is cured by a correct description in the sheriff's deed.[3]

§ 579. If several judgment creditors have judgments of equal date, and whose judgments are in law all liens on the real estate of the same defendant, the one that levies thereon first obtains priority.[4]

§ 580. And though the proper course is, after levy of a *fieri facias* on lands, and return thereof without sale, to sue out a writ of *vendi. exponas* against the property levied on, yet the plaintiff will not lose the lien of his levy if instead thereof he causes to be issued an alias *fi. fa.* and sells the property thereon.

§ 581. The latter course, though irregular, is not a waiver of the previous levy.[5] For the alias *fi. fa.* by relation reaches back to the levy of the original writ and preserves its lien so as to bind the property and prevent priority of another levy made in the interim upon the same property, if the subsequent or alias *fi. fa.* has issued in due time.[6]

§ 582. Where, by law, the officer holding an execution is required to first exhaust the property, real and personal, of a principal debtor, before proceeding against that of a security of such debtor, for stay of execution, it is held that if by reason of the principal's death, or incumbrance of his prop-

[1] Shield *v.* Bates, 5 J. J. Marsh. 13; Gault *v.* Woodbridge, 4 McLean, 329.

[2] Summers *v.* Moore, 2 McLean, 59.

[3] Hopping *v.* Burnam, 2 G. Green, 39; Summers *v.* Moore, 2 McLean, 59.

[4] Rockhill *v.* Hanna, 15 How. 189, 195, 196, 197; Adams *v.* Dyer, 8 Johns. 347, 350; Waterman *v.* Haskin, 11 Johns. 228; Halstead *v.* Haskin, ib.

[5] Bouton *v.* Lord, 10 Ohio St. 454.

[6] Brasfield *v.* Whitaker, 4 Hawks, 309.

erty, it cannot be immediately reached by the execution, the amount of the writ may, in such case, be made out of the property of the surety. The creditor is not bound to remove the obstacles that prevent a levy of the principal's property.[1]

§ 583. Property placed by a court of competent jurisdiction in the hands of a receiver, whether rightfully or wrongfully so placed, is in legal custody, and is not subject to execution. "To permit it to be levied and sold," say the Supreme Court of Pennsylvania, "would at once raise a conflict of jurisdiction."[2]

§ 584. In Minnesota, it is held that where a judgment is a lien upon real property, no formal levy of an execution emanating from such judgment is necessary to be made on such property as preliminary to execution sale thereof; and that the provision of the statute of that state which declares that "until a levy property is not affected by the execution," applies to a levy upon personal property only.[3]

§ 585. That court hold also that where a levy is required the sheriff is not bound to return the particular facts constituting the levy; that the general return that he "levied upon" property, is sufficient, and cannot be disputed except in a proceeding directly against the officer or his sureties for a false return.[4]

§ 586. A levy grossly excessive will be deemed fraudulent, and a sale thereon will be set aside; and where on such levy a sale of lands *en masse* is made, without its appearing that the land was first offered in less parcels, the inference will not arise that such was the course pursued by the officer, but rather the reverse thereof.[5]

§ 587. A levy of property of the value of eight hundred dollars for a claim of twenty-one dollars is grossly excessive

---

Cheatham *v.* Brien, 3 Head. (Tenn.) 552.

[2] Robinson *v.* Atlantic & G. W. R. R. Co. 66 Penn. St. 160, 162; 2 Story, Eq. Jur. Sec. 833.

[3] Tullies *v.* Brawley, 3 Minn. 277; Folsom *v.* Carli, 5 Minn. 333, 337.

[4] Tullies *v.* Brawley, 3 Minn. 277; Rhorer *v.* Terrill. 4 Minn. 407; Folsom *v.* Carli, 5 Minn. 333.

[5] Cook *v.* Jenkins, 30 Iowa, 452.

and oppressive. In the language of the court, in *Cook v. Jenkins,*[1] it is "a fraud in fact upon defendant," and "we know of no principles of equity that will sustain proceedings which work such gross injustice and oppression, except in cases where innocent parties claim rights under them."

III. The Notice of Sale, and Return.

§ 588. "The purchaser depends on the judgment, the levy, and the deed. All other questions are between the parties to the judgment and the officer selling."[2]

§ 589. It matters not then, as respects the rights of a *bona fide* purchaser at sheriff's sale, whether there be a legal notice of the sale,[3] or a return of the officer selling.[4] And though the purchaser relies on the judgment execution, the levy and the deed, yet when the purchaser at sheriff's sale shows an authorized execution and deed, a correct levy and notice is presumed. A judgment, execution, and deed from the sheriff are sufficient to support the title of a purchaser, without proof of a levy, though the return be incorrect, or there be no return.[5] The purchaser is not bound to see that the sheriff makes a return.[6]

§ 590. If after levy and notice of sale on one writ of execution another writ be received by the officer against the same defendant, he can only sell, if no further notice be given, on

---

[1] 30 Iowa, 454.

[2] Wheaton *v.* Sexton, 4 Wheat. 503; Brooks *v.* Rooney, 11 Geo. 423; Sullivan *v.* Hearndon, 11 Geo. 294; Philips *v.* Coffee, 17 Ill. 154.

[3] Lawrence *v.* Speed, 2 Bibb. 401; Whittaker *v.* Sumner, 7 Pick. 551; Wheaton *v.* Sexton, 4 Wheat. 503, 506; McIntire *v.* Durham, 7 Ired, 151; Maddox *v.* Sullivan, 2 Rich. Eq. 4; Natchez *v.* Minor, 10 S. & M. 246; Kilby *v.* Haggin, 3 J. J. Marsh. 208; Brooks *v.* Rooney, 11 Geo. 423; Draper *v.* Bryson, 17 Mo. 71; Philips *v.* Coffee, 17 Ill. 154.

[4] Wheaton *v.* Sexton, 4 Wheat. 503; Hopping *v.* Burnam, 2 G. Green, 39, 44; Brooks *v.* Rooney, 11 Geo. 425; Webber *v.* Cox, 6 Mon. 110; State *v.* Salyers, 19 Ind. 432; Philips *v.* Coffee, 17 Ill. 154.

[5] Brooks *v.* Rooney, 11 Geo. 423; Hopping *v.* Burnam, 2 G. Green, 39, 44; Evans *v.* Davis, 3 B. Mon. 344; McIntire *v.* Durham, 7 Ired, 151; Jackson *v.* Young, 5 Cow. 259; Brooks *v.* Rooney, 11 Geo. 423; Philips *v.* Coffee, 17 Ill. 154.

[6] State *v.* Salyers, 19 Ind. 432.

the first writ. The certificate of such sale should refer to but
the one writ, and however the proceeds of sale may be applied,
yet the whole amount thereof must be mentioned as the consideration in the certificate of sale, and in the deed when
given.[1]

§ 591. The purchaser will not be prejudiced by omission
of the officer to return and file a certificate of sale, under the
statute. The requirement is only directory.[2]

---

[1] Mascraft v. VanAntwerp, 3 Cow. 334.

[2] Jackson v. Young, 5 Cow. 269, 270. By the statute, in New York, the
certificate of the sheriff's sale is required to be filed in the clerk's office
by the sheriff. In the case here cited it was claimed that omission to file
the certificate voided the sale; but the court held the statute to be directory only.

CHAPTER XVII.

THE SALE.

I. By whom to be Made.

§ 592. If the direction of the writ is simply to the sheriff
or officer as such, then it may be executed by himself or by his
deputy; but if directed to the officer by his personal name, as
well as by his title, then he must execute it himself in person.[1]
In the case cited from 2d Washington, the court say: "This
is a writ directed to the sheriff, which means as well the deputy
as the high sheriff. It is a writ, and all writs may be executed
by a deputy sheriff. It is not a judicial act; it is not a case
excepted from the general authority given to deputy sheriffs,
and, therefore, I can see no reason why he may not execute the
inquisition."[2]

§ 593. In the same case the court lay down the general rule
to be, in the absence of statutory regulation to the contrary,
that where the "process" is directed to the sheriff generally,
and not by his name, if the high sheriff be not required by
the command of the writ to go in person, he may act by

---

[1] 8 Bac. Abt., Undersheriff, 676; Wroe v. Harris, 2 Wash. C. C. 126; Tillotson v. Cheatham, 2 Johns. 63.

[2] Wroe v. Harris, 2 Wash. C. C. 126, 127; Tillotson v. Cheatham, 2
Johns. 63.

deputy.[1]   The term "process" used by the court is a comprehensive term, broad enough to cover cases of executions generally.   The execution of an *elegit* is referred to by the court as within the powers of the deputy, which, as to the exercise of power, very nearly corresponds with the act of selling on execution, where the latter practice prevails.

§ 594.   A sheriff cannot sell on an execution in which he is plaintiff, nor in his own behalf, where he has purchased the benefit of the writ.[2]

§ 595.   Under the act of Congress of 1789, it is held by the United States Supreme Court that a United States marshal may proceed to sell lands on execution after his removal from office if the writ was in his hands at the time of his removal, and that the sale will be valid, if in other respects unexceptionable.   The writ, in the particular case referred to, was a *venditioni exponas* and was in the possession of the officer at the time of his removal.

§ 596.   The act referred to reads, in this respect as follows: "Every marshal or his deputy, when removed from office, or when the term for which the marshal is appointed shall expire, shall have power notwithstanding to execute all such precepts as may be in their hands, respectively, at the time of such removal or expiration of office," etc., and it is held by the United States Supreme Court, in the same case, that the act of May 7th, 1800, does not repeal the clause in that of 1798, above recited; that in respect to the same subject it is merely cumulative in the remedy afforded.[3]

§ 597.   The case of *Miner v. Cassat*[4] was an action of ejectment involving the validity of the marshal's sale in the case previously cited of *Doolittle v. Bryan*, as to the power of the marshal to complete execution of a writ in his hands after removal from office.   The state court of Ohio, conforming its

[1] Wroe v. Harris, 2 Wash. C. C. 126, 127, 128; Tillotson v. Cheatham, 2 Johns. 63.

[2] Riner v. Stacey, 8 Humph. 288; Chambers v. Thomas, 3 A. K. Marsh. 536; May v. Waters, 1 McCord, 470.

[3] Irwin v. Brian, 14 How. 563; Minor v. Cassat, 2 Ohio St. 198.

[4] 2 Ohio St. 198.

decision to that of the United States Supreme Court, sustained the power of the ex-marshal to sell, and held the title under the marshal's sale valid in the action of ejectment. The Supreme Court of Ohio affirmed the decision of the court below, thereby holding the ruling of the United States Supreme Court on the subject conclusive.

§ 598. By the constitution of our respective state and federal judiciaries, the United States Court is the proper and controling tribunal to decide upon the effect of the enforcement of its own process. Hence its decision was rightly deferred to by the state court.

II. How to be Made.

§ 599. Execution sales are to be made at public auction;[1] for money in hand,[2] and to the highest unconditional bidder.[3] They must be made by the officer himself or by his general deputy, as we have seen under the last preceding head.

§ 600. When the land is divided into several separate parcels, though of one and the same tract, the several tracts cannot be sold together as in a body, but must be sold separately with suitable identity of the several lots. If sold in the aggregate, the court, on motion, will set the sale aside. "Sales in mass of real estate held in parcels are not to be countenanced or tolerated."[4]

§ 601, And so, if the tract be an entirety, it is the duty of

---

[1] 3 Bouvier, 581.

[2] Noy, Max. Ch. 42; Mumford v. Armstrong, 4 Cow. 553; Griffin v. Thompson, 2 How. 244; Swope v. Adery, 5 Ind. 213; Williamson v. Berry, 8 How. 544; Hushmacher v. Harris, 2 Wright, 498; Bigley v. Risher, 63 Penn. St. 152; Sauer v. Steinbaeur, 14 Wis. 70.

[3] Swope v. Adery, 5 Ind. 213.

[4] Jackson v. Newton, 18 Johns. 355; McLaughlin v. Scott, 1 Bin. 61; Wheeler v. Kennedy, 1 Ala. 292; Adams v. Kiser, 7 Dana, 208; Garrett v. Moss, 20 Ill. 549; Tyler v. Wilkinson, 7 Ind. 450; Phelps v. Conover, 25 Ill. 309; Meeker v. Evans, 25 Ill. 322; Piel v. Brayer, 30 Ind. 332; Winters v. Buford, 6 Coldw. 328. In Indiana, selling in parcels is required by statute, and is alike applicable to mortgage sales or sales on execution. 30 Ind. 332.

the officer to sell in parcels, if susceptible of division, unless the sale of the whole is necessary to satisfy the writ.[1]

§ 602. Though it is the duty of the officer to sell property in the exercise of a fair discretion and to the best advantage, so as to make the debt demanded by the execution without unnecessary sacrifice of the debtor's property;[2] yet, having levied on lands which were then but one body, but which after levy and before sale are divided by the debtor into several lots, the sheriff is "not bound upon," say the court, "to sell the lots separately," according to such subdivision. He may exercise in respect thereto an honest discretion.[3]

§ 603. In New York it is held that where premises are owned by several execution defendants in the same execution, their separate interest may be sold together at once, unless some one of them, being entitled to redeem from the sale, require the separate interests to be sold separately. If so required it must be so sold, under the New York statute.[4]

§ 604. In *Hewson v. Deygert*[5] it is held by the Supreme Court of New York that, "The proper course, both on sales of real and personal property (on execution,) is to sell only so much of the property charged as will probably satisfy the execution, and which can conveniently and reasonably be sold separately. A party who sells under a power is not bound to sell at once all the property bound by the power, and in many cases it would be an act of great oppression." It was also held in the same case that if he sells the whole to satisfy a part of the charge upon it, that he cannot sell it again or a second time to satisfy newly matured and growing installments, unless it be redeemed by the execution debtor.

§ 605. To avoid exhausting the lien by one sale only, the sale should be of only so much of the property as is requisite

---

[1] Kinny v. Noble, 51 Ill. 112, 121; Berry v. Griffeth, 2 Harr. & Gill. 337; Hewson v. Daygert, 8 Johns. 333; Winters v. Buford, 6 Coldw. 328.

[2] Kiser v. Ruddick, 8 Blackf. 382, 383; McLean Bank v. Flagg, 31 Ill. 290; Phelps v. Cowen, 25 Ill. 309.

[3] Kiser v. Ruddick, 8 Blackf. 382, 383.

[4] Nielson v. Nielson, 5 Barb. 565.

[5] 8 Johns. 333, 335; Davis v. Abbott, 3 Ind. 137; Wheeler v. Kenedy, 1 Ala. 292; Meeker v. Evans, 25 Ill. 322; Day v. Graham, 1 Gilm. 435.

to satisfy the amount due. But the court will not interfere by injunction to prevent a second sale. The party having title has his remedy, if injured, and no execution sale of the realty will affect the title if the lands be not subject to sale on execution.[1]

§ 606. In some of the states it is held that if more be sold on execution than will satisfy the writ, that the sale is void.[2] But if the excess be very small and results from a mere mistake in calculation, or other unintentional circumstance, the sale will not be set aside.[3]

§ 607. No bid may be received but what is unconditional; the officer himself, and not the bidders, is to fix the terms of sale.[4]

§ 608. The officer selling has power to adjourn the sale and to sell on the day to which it is adjourned. On the subject of adjournment he has a sound discretion, which must be exercised fairly, and as to his judgment is best for all the parties concerned.[5]

§ 609. The case of *Wolf v. Van Metre*[6] involved the validity of an adjournment made by the attorney of the execution plaintiff. The sheriff levied an execution on land, and gave notice of sale, but from some cause did not attend at the time and place of intended sale. Foreseeing his non-attend-

[1] Hewson v. Deygert, 8 Johns. 333, 335.

[2] Patterson v. Carneal, 3 A. K. Marsh, 618; Pepper v. Commonwealth, 6 Mon. 30; Davidson v. McMurtry, 3 J. J. Marsh, 63; Carlisle v. Carlisle, 7 J. J. Marsh, 625; Stover v. Boswell, 3 Dana, 235; Addison v. Crow, 5 Dana, 277; Adams v. Kiser, 7 Dana, 209; Isaacs v. Gearhart, 12 B. Mon. 231; Gearhart v. Thorp, 9 B. Mon. 35.

[3] Southard v. Pope, 9 B. Mon. 263; Adams v. Kiser, 7 Dana, 208; Morrison v. Bruce, 9 Dana, 216.

[4] Swope v. Ardery, 5 Ind. 215; Chapman v. Harwood, 8 Blackf. 82.

[5] Swortzell v. Martin, 16 Iowa, 519; Kelly v. Green, 63 Penn. St. 299; Phelps v. Conover, 25 Ill. 309; Tinkom v. Purdy, 5 Johns. 346. But see to the contrary Patten v. Stewart, 26 Ind. 395. This adjournment, however, was made after the sale was enjoined. When the injunction was removed notice anew became necessary. In Louisiana, however, the power to adjourn is denied by the settled doctrine in the courts of that state. Montgomery v. Barrows, 19 La. Ann. 169. Nor can plaintiff's attorney adjourn the sale by authority of the officer. Wolf v. Van Metre, 27 Iowa, 348.

[6] 27 Iowa, 348.

ance he authorized the attorney of the execution plaintiff to
adjourn the sale. The return showed that the sale was adjourned by such attorney for want of bidders. It was adjourned
for two days; sale was then made under the adjournment by
the sheriff. The Supreme Court of Iowa, BECK, Justice, held
the sale to be invalid. That court say: "To permit the sheriff
to authorize the attorney of either party to discharge the duty
for him, would open a wide door to fraud and abuse." And
that it was "a gross irregularity for the sheriff to entrust his
business with the plaintiff's attorney."

§ 610. Executions are to be enforced and satisfied in their
order of priority. In Indiana it is held that when different
writs enforceable under different laws are holden by the officer
at one and the same time against the same defendant, each
shall be enforced according to its legal effect and in order of
priority.

§ 611. The Supreme Court of Indiana, in *Harrison v.
Sipp*, say: "Where a sheriff has several executions in his
hands, governed by different laws as to the terms upon which
the property levied upon is required to be sold, it is evident
that he cannot possibly comply, at a single sale, with the
requisitions of each execution. If the property is divisible,
however, he may sell under each a sufficient portion for its
satisfaction. It would seem that in such case the obvious
course, and the only one by which the law can be complied
with is to commence with the execution in his hands first to
be satisfied and sell enough under the law of the contract by
which it is governed to make the sum demanded by it, and
then to sell under the others, in their order, in the same way,
until all are satisfied, or the property is exhausted. But when
the property is not susceptible of a division this cannot be
done." In the latter case, the same court hold, that "the
sheriff should ordinarily proceed to sell first upon the execution upon the oldest judgment, or for the payment of the debt
first to be satisfied out of the proceeds. He would thus comply with the law as far as it would be in his power to do so,
and the least injury would be likely to result to the rights of
the various parties." And the court further hold that if the

property be appraisable under the elder execution or older lien, then sale under the appraisement law as for the whole where the property is indivisible is legal if made in proper conformity to such law of appraisement. But if not so made, that the sale will be set aside.[1]

§ 612. It is not in itself an objection to a bid at a sheriff's sale of lands on execution that it is made by letter, provided there be no unfairness about it, and it be publicly cried as bids usually are. If there be no advance on a bid so offered, the officer will be justified in selling on it, as he would be in selling on a bid orally made, all other circumstances being the same. "But the creditor has a right to insist on all the forms." If however the bid be not publicly cried at the appointed place of sale, but be received and privately noted in the house, instead of at the door of the place appointed, or there be other evidences of collusion or unfairness, the sale will be set aside.[2] And if in such case the return on the execution be of a sale to the person so bidding, and the certificate of purchase be given to and in the name of another and different person, the certificate will be inoperative and void. In the language of the Supreme Court of Illinois, "there must be entire conformity in all these proceedings, in the return, the certificate, and the deed, and if they do not possess it they will be invalid. *Davis v. Mc Vickers*, 11 Ill. R. 320." And that issuing the certificate to a different person than the supposed purchaser was a void act under Chap. 57, Sec. 12, R. S., 1845.[3]

§ 613. It is uniformly holden in Illinois that where lands or lots which could be divided and sold in parcels are sold in a mass, such sale is irregular and is subject to be set aside.[4]

§ 614. The case of *Greenup v. Stoker*[5] is adjudged to be

---

[1] 8 Blackf. 455. See also Bronson *v.* Kinsey, 1 How. 311.

[2] Dickerman *v.* Burgess, 20 Ill. 266. In this case the court say: "We do not mean to be understood as objecting to receiving a bid by letter, but the officer must cry the bid, and if there be no advance on it he would be justified in selling at the bid."

[3] Dickerman *v.* Burgess, 20 Ill. 280; Davis *v.* McVickers, 11 Ill. 320.

[4] Phelps *v.* Conover, 25 Ill. 313; Day *v.* Grayham, 1 Gilm. 435, and 4 Gilm. 338; Ross *v.* Weed, 5 Gilm. 171; Stewart *v.* Gay, 5 Gilm. 442.

[5] 12 Ill. 24.

no exception to the rule, for that in that case the sale was of but a single quarter section, and it was not made to appear that it could have been advantageously divided, or that any subdivision of it would have satisfied the writ.[1]

§ 615. When there is a body of land levied on which is composed of several contiguous tracts, each tract is to be offered separately, the officer using his best judgment as to subdividing into lots; failing thus to sell, he is to add the subdivisions together, one by one, and offering them thus unitedly; and if not sold in this manner, then the whole may be sold together, on a reasonable bid, the particulars of which is to be reported in the officer's return.[2]

§ 616. So, when the lands are situated in different townships and ranges, or the tracts are otherwise disconnected, they are to be offered severally and separately, each one in like manner as above—first in smaller subdivisions as forties, and then in larger as eighties, and finally each tract separately as a whole, if not disposed of in parcels, and if there is a reasonable bid, the same that is each tract, to be sold in a body in this manner, and so on in like manner each tract, until the sum required be raised. The creditor may insist on a sale, and if sold under value, the debtor finds relief in the redemption laws.[3]

§ 617. In Minnesota the statutory provision requiring land to be sold in parcels, on execution sale, is held to be merely directory, and a sale in the aggregate being otherwise unobjectionable is valid. The injured party is left to his remedy against the officer selling.[4]

§ 618. In Wisconsin the sale in such case is voidable and may be set aside at the option of those in interest.[5]

§ 619. In California, a sale in mass was holden valid, though the general ruling there is to the contrary. There were several adjoining parcels sold together. The sheriff and purchaser

[1] Phelps v. Conover, 25 Ill. 313.
[2] Ibid.
[3] Ibid.
[4] Tillman v. Jackson, 1 Minn. 183.
[5] Raymond v. Pauli, 21 Wis. 531, 534; Bunker v. Rand, 19 Wis. 258

being ignorant of the subdivisions at the time of sale, and the conduct of the defendant being such as tended to mislead the officers; he having surrendered the land to the sheriff without informing him there existed any subdivisions, and the sale was made according to the description which he furnished.[1] But, *quere*, if it would not be set aside, if sold below value, on the application of other creditors, in case the debtor has no other property?

§ 620. The ruling in Indiana, as to place of sale by a United States marshall, is that under the state statute adopted by the federal court, such sales are to be made in the county where the land lie which are sold.[2] These two decisions are by the respective state courts of those states wherein the questions arose in collateral proceedings.

§ 621. In Tennessee the rule is, in selling lands on execution, that the sale be made, when practicable, in parcels, so as not only to obtain the required sum for the smallest amount of property, but also to the better enable the judgment debtor to redeem when the price of each lot is thus separately fixed. If sale be made in violation of the above principles, it is voidable, though not void, and will be set aside by the court on the proper application of those interested, including the holders of other unsatisfied judgments against the same judgment debtor.[3]

§ 622. If different parcels be sold *en masse*, the delivery of the deed to the purchaser, on application of the execution debtor may be arrested by injunction; but on terms that he pay off the execution and costs with interest.[4]

§ 623. Sales may be made on several executions at once.

[1] Smith *v.* Randall, 6 Cal. 47. The court lay down the general rule as follows, TERRY, Justice: "As a general rule the sales in mass, of land consisting of separate lots are not tolerated or countenanced in courts of justice. But this rule should not be extended so as to allow a debtor, by misleading the officer with a false description, or by withholding information to invalidate a sale under execution, made in good faith, in the entire absence of fraud." (6 Cal. 51.)
[2] Jenners *v.* Doe, 9 Ind. 461.
[3] Winters *v.* Burford, 6 Coldw. (Tenn.) 328.
[4] Ballance *v.* Loomis, 22 Ill. 82.

"It can do no harm (say the court) as the sheriff sells so much as will satisfy all." If the amount bid for the whole is more than will satisfy all the writs, then, little by little the quantity of land may be redeemed by proper bidding. Therefore the officer can combine the writs and do equal justice to all the parties in interest. He can afterward apply the proceeds as the law may require. So if part of the sale is for cash and part on credit, some of the writs being on judgments and some on replevin bonds, it only requires that the terms and proportion of cash and credit respectively be made known to the bidders.[1]

§ 624. In Indiana it is provided by statute, that "if the estate shall consist of several lots, tracts, and parcels, each shall be offered separately; and no more of any real estate shall be offered for sale than shall be necessary to satisfy the execution, unless the same shall not be susceptible of division."

§ 625. The supreme court of that state hold that it is well settled that if the sheriff, in violation of such statute, offer and sell several distinct tracts or parcels of land in one body, the sale is void; and that the provisions of the statute apply as well to sales on foreclosure of mortgages as to sales on ordinary execution.[2]

§ 626. And when the sheriff's return and record showed that more than one parcel were sold as an entirety, the sale was holden void in the hands of a third party claiming under the execution purchaser, who was also plaintiff in execution.[3]

§ 627. If the land consist of several tracts or parcels, it is the imperative duty of the sheriff (say the court) under said statute to offer the parcels separately; and if but a single tract or body, and is susceptible of division without injury, and the sale of the whole is not required to satisfy the execution, he is to divide it, and offer at one time only so much of it as may be necessary to satisfy the judgment, interest and costs.[4]

---

[1] Locke v. Coleman, 4 Mon. 317; Southard v. Pope, 913 Mon. 263.

[2] Piel v. Brayer, 30 Ind. 332, 339; Sherry v. Nick of the Woods, 1 Ind. 575; Reed v. Diven, 7 Ind. 189; Banks v. Bales, 16 Ind. 423; Tuler v. Wilkinson, 27 Ind. 450.

[3] Piel v. Brayer, 30 Ind. 332, 339.

[4] Piel v. Brayer. 30 Ind. 332.

§ 628. Under that statute it is also held that to enable the court to carry out its requirements, the court should, in mortgage foreclosures for interests or installments only, and other installments are not yet due, first ascertain if the property can be sold in parcels, without injury, so as to enable it to determine on the proper decree to render in the case. In case the whole is due, then the proper order is to sell the premises, or so much thereof as may be necessary to pay the debt and costs.[1]

§ 629. When judgments are liens upon real estate, such liens confer no manner of right or interest on the judgment creditors in or to the land, but merely the prior right to make out of the land the debt secured by the judgments.[2]

§ 630. Subject to this right of the creditors the judgment debtor may sell and convey his land. If sold and conveyed in parcels to different persons, and at different dates, during the life of the judgment liens and executions sales thereof be afterwards made to satisfy such judgments, the lands are to be levied and sold in the inverse order of their sale and conveyance by the debtor.[3] Upon the same principle, if part only of the lands be sold by the judgment debtor, then the remaining part is the first to be sold to satisfy judgment liens.[4]

§ 631. If a regular and sufficient deed of lands be made and delivered, but afterwards before resort thereof be voluntarily destroyed by the parties, it nevertheless confers the legal title on the grantee; and if no reconveyance be made, then a judgment subsequently rendered against the grantee becomes a lien on the land, and execution sale and deed thereon will convey the title to the purchaser at the execution sale.[5]

[1] Piel v. Brayer, 30 Ind. 340; Harris v. Makepeace, 13 Ind. 569; Smith v. Pierse, 15 Ind. 210; Benton v. Wood, 17 Ind. 260.

[2] Gilman v. Brown, 1 Mason, C. C. 221.

[3] Stuyvesant v. Hall, 2 Barb. Ch. 151, 155; Ins. Co. v. Milner, 1 Barb. Ch. 353; Marshall v. Moore, 36 Illinois, 321; Mason v. Payne, 1 Walker Ch. 459; Snyder v. Stafford, 11 Paige, 71; Relfe v. Bibb, 43 Ala. 519.

[4] Clowes v. Dickinson, 5 Johns. Ch. 235; Clowes v. Dickinson, 9 Cow 405; Hurd v. Eaton, 28 Ill. 122.

[5] Parshall v. Shirts, 54 Barb. (N. Y.) 99.

15

§ 632. It has been held that by the mutual consent of plaintiff and defendant, an execution sale may be made on a credit instead of for cash in hand. That it will be none the less the sale of the officer, or execution sale, in its nature and effect: and that therefore the failure of title to the property purchased at such sale will be no defense to an action on a note given for the purchase money.[1]

§ 633. Nor is such ruling at all at variance with the doctrine that the purchaser may recover (in equity) from the execution debtor, on it transpiring that the debtor did not own the property sold, for here the note is to the sheriff or to plaintiff in execution.

§ 634. If the notice be to sell on one execution only, and the officer has additional ones against the same defendant at the time of the sale, he cannot, without other notice of sale as such additional executions, state the additional executions in his certificate of sale or in his deed. It is as to such other writs, if such course be taken, a virtual selling without notice.

§ 635. The return, certificate, and sale should be based upon the writ, under which the notice is given; and the amount sold for is to be correctly stated therein, so those entitled to redeem may know the amount to be paid.[2] The fund raised will then be subject to the order of the court as to its application on the several writs.[3]

§ 636. Though an officer holding an execution against several co-defendants will be bound, as in other cases, to first proceed against the personal property, yet he is not compelled to first exhaust the personal effects of each one of the defendants before proceeding to sell the lands of either; but it is his duty to first exhaust the personalty of each one of such defendants, whose land he undertakes to levy and sell before so proceeding against the land.[4]

§ 637. If the return and other evidences of sale of several lots of land sold on execution are silent as to the manner of

---

[1] Killgore v. Pedew, 1 Strobt, 18.
[2] Mascroft v. Van Antwerp, 3 Cow. 334.
[3] Wiley v. Bridgman, 1 Head, 68.
[4] Faris v. Banton, 6 J. J. Marsh. 235.

selling them, then the presumption is that the officer did his duty and sold them severally.[1]

III. WHO MAY NOT BUY.

§ 638. "No man can serve two masters." He who acts for others will not be permitted to act in the same matter for himself. He who sells for others, or on their account, cannot buy for himself. The two relations of seller and buyer cannot exist at one and the same time in one and the same person in reference to the same subject matter. The principle is the same whether the sale be made in proceedings at law or in equity. Such sales are void.[2]

§ 639. It has been held, however, that by consent of the execution debtor the officer selling may buy.[3] But certainly not, if to the prejudice of other creditors.

IV. SALES IRREGULAR OR UNDER IRREGULAR PROCESS, OR JUDGMENTS.

§ 640. Mere irregularities will not avoid an execution sale. fairly made, to a *bona fide* purchaser. To render it void there must be wanting some one of the substantials which are indispensable to a valid sale.[4]

[1] Love v. Cherry, 24 Iowa, 210.

[2] McConnell v. Gibson, 12 Ill. 128; McLeod v. McCall, 3 Jones (N. C.) 87; Michoud v. Girod, 4 How. 503; Remick v. Butterfield, 11 Foster (N. H.) 70; Wormsly v. Wormsly, 8 Wheat. 421; Harris v. Parker, 41 Ala. 604; Rice v. Cleghorn, 20 Ind. 80; Haddix v. Haddix, 5 Litt. 202: Wilson v. Troup, 2 Cow. 196; Cruse v. Steffen, 47 Ill. 112, and *ante* chap. xi.

[3] Lazarus v. Bryson, 3 Bin. 54.

[4] Allen v. Parish, 3 Ham. (Ohio) 187; Hopping v. Burnam, 2 G. Greene, 39; Jackson v. Roosevelt, 13 Johns. 97; Jackson v. Delancy, 13 Johns. 537: Woodcock v. Bennett, 1 Cow. 711; Jackson v. Bartlett, 8 Johns. 361; Landes v. Brant. 10 How. 371; Childs v. McChesney, 20 Iowa, 431; Herrick v. Graves, 16 Wis. 157; Simpson v. Simpson, 64 N. C. 427; Cunningham v. Felkner, 26 Iowa, 117; Hubbard v. Barnes, 29 Iowa, 239; Durham v. Heaton, 28 Ill. 264; Maurier v. Cook, 16 Wis. 465; Hinds v. Scott, 11 Penn. St. 19: Wheat v. Sexton, 4 Wheat. 503; Cavender v. Smith, 1 Iowa, 306; Lovel v. Powell, 5 Ala. 58; Ware v. Cradford, 2 Ala. 676; Stow v. Steele, 45 Ill. 328; Kinney v. Knoeble, 47 Ill. 417; Armstrong v. Jackson, 1 Blackf. 210; Anderson v. Clark, 2 Swan. (Tenn.) 156; Dunn v. Merriweather, 1 A.

§ 641. About what are the requisites to a valid sale on execution, as a general principle, there is some diversity of authorities. Some of the rulings are, that the party setting up an execution sale must show a valid judgment; valid writ of execution; a levy and deed; and that all else, when these are shown, is between the parties to the execution and the officer selling.[1] Whilst in other cases it is holden that merely a valid judgment, and valid writ of execution, need be shown; and that if it does not appear whether there was a levy, and nothing to the contrary appears, the presumption is that the officer did his duty; and, therefore, where levies are holden to be necessary, the presumption of law arises that the officer did his duty, and that a proper levy has been made;[2] but if no levy or return was really made, or notice of sale given, it would

K. Marsh. 158; Philips v. Coffee, 17 Ill. 154; Hubbard v. Barnes, 29 Iowa, 239; Bunton v. Emerson, 4 G. Greene, 397; Williard v. Whipple, 40 Vt. 219; Butterfield v. Walsh, 21 Iowa, 97; Stein v. Chambliss, 18 Iowa, 474.

[1] Wheat v. Sexton, 4 Wheat. 503; Landes v. Brant, 10 How. 371; Landes v. Perkins, 12 Mo. 254; Allen v. Parish, 3 Ham. (Ohio) 187; Taylor v. Thompson, 5 Pet. 369; Butterfield v. Walsh, 21 Iowa, 97, 101; Stein v. Chambliss, 18 Iowa, 474, 476, 477; Remington v. Linthicum, 14 Pet. 84; Sumner v. Moore, 2 McLean, 59; Thompson v. Philips, Bald. C. C. 246; Shepherd v. Rowe, 14 Wend. 600; Griffith v. Bogart, 18 How. 158, 164; Kinney v. Knoeble, 47 Ill. 417; Crane v. Hardy, 1 Mann (Mich.) 56.

[2] Carpenter v. Doe, 2 Ind. 465, 467; Smith v. Hill, 22 Barb. 656; Mercer v. Doe, 6 Ind. 80; Webster v. Smith, 6 Mon. 110; Lawrence v. Speed, 2 Bibb, 401; Draper v. Bryson, 17 Mo. 71; McFadden v. Worthington, 45 Ill. 362, 366; Dunn v. Merriweather, 1 A. K. Marsh. 158; Martin v. McCargo, 5 Litt. 293; Smith v. Mormon, 1 Mon. 154; Riggs v. Dooley, 17 B. Mon. 239; Wilson v. McGee, 2 A. K. Marsh. 602; Cox v. Joiner, 4 Bibb. 94; Furguson v. Miles, 3 Gilm. 358; Cooper v. Gilbraith, 3 Wash. C. C. 546; Bowen v. Bell, 20 Johns. 338; Whatley v. Newsome, 10 Geo. 74. In Whatley v. Newsome, 10 Geo. 76, the court say, LUMPKIN, Justice: "Where a party relies on sheriff's title, it is only necessary to produce the execution, with the sale under it, and the deed made in pursuance thereto, and prove either title in the defendant or possession subsequent to the rendition of the judgment." And 3 Wash. C. C. lays down the rule that the claimant under a sheriff's deed " need not show any other title than a judgment, execution, and sheriff's deed." In Cooper v. Galbraith, 3 Wash. C. C. 550, the rule is laid down by WASHINGTON, Justice, that "the purchaser under an execution, in an ejectment against the defendant in the execution, or one claiming under him, need not show any other title than a judgment execution and a sheriff's deed."

not affect an *bona fide* purchaser. Such are the general rulings on the subject,[1] while yet another class of cases hold that when the judgment on which the execution issues is in law a lien upon the land to be sold, then no levy whatever is necessary; and that as a consequence arising therefrom, the production of a valid judgment, execution, and a sheriff's deed purporting to have been made on a sale under such execution, is all that is required.[2]

§ 642. In the case first cited, the court, BRONSON, Justice, cite *Catlin v. Jackson*, 8 John. 546. But on reference to that case it is seen that the necessity of a levy was not therein involved, and that a levy was in reality made, and a return thereof setting it out at large. The real objection was that the officer did not, on levying, take corporeal possession of the land which the court held was not only unnecessary, but was impracticable. That it was unlike a levy on personal property wherein the possession accompanies the levy; a special property is vested in the officer: and he is ordinarily requested to exercise over the property actual possession or control. In *Catlin v. Jackson*, the court say that the first question "is as to the effect of the sheriff's seizure." * * * * That, "In several essentials the effect of the execution must be different from a *fi fa.* levied on personal estate only. The delivery of the *fi fa.* gives no new rights to the plaintiff, and vests no new interests. The general lien is created by the judgment, and execution is merely to give that lien effect; not by vesting a possessory right to the land affected by it in the plaintiff, but by designating it for conversion into money by the operation of the *fi fa.* and the act of the sheriff by virtue of it. It is not so as to personal property. That is bound from the delivery of the *fi fa.* to the sheriff. When he seizes he may remove it for safe keeping, and this not only to give effect to the seizure, but for his own security. * * * * None of these reasons apply to real estate. It is not necessary that the

[1] Draper v. Bryson, 17 Mo. 70; Brooks v. Rooney, 11 Geo. 423; Smith v. Hill, 22 Barb. 656.
[2] Wood v. Colvin, 5 Hill, (N. Y.) 228; Tullis v. Brawley, 3 Minn. 277; Folsom v. Carli, 5 Minn. 333, 337.

sheriff should possess himself of it for safe keeping."[1] Then this case, so far from involving the necessity of a levy, shows that a levy was really made on the land; that a return was made setting out the levy at large; and that a *venditioni exponas* then issued, on which the land was sold. The real point was, not whether a levy is necessary, but whether the levy which was made had the effect, before sale, to take away the debtor's right of entry on the land. The court held that it did not, because unlike a levy of personalty, the possession of the lands is not by the levy changed. We have given thus much of the opinion in that case to show that it does not bear out the subsequent ruling in *Wood v. Colvin* as to there being no necessity of a levy when the judgment is a lien upon the land to be sold. Nor does the case of *Greene v. Burke*, referred to in *Wood v. Colvin*, come up to the point. This case was in replevin and there was no necessity to consider levies on land; yet the learned judge, (Justice Cowen) refers to the subject, and intimates an opinion that such levies are unnecessary inasmuch as unlike a levy on personal property, they neither satisfy the judgment to any extent nor vest an interest in the officer in the land.[2]

§ 643. The same principle, however, is fully asserted in Minnesota. It is there holden in as broad terms as in *Wood v. Colvin*, that in executing writs of execution issued on judgments which are liens upon the lands to be sold, no levy is necessary.[3]

§ 644. So, where in attachment proceedings, there is a judgment identifying the levy of the attachment, the date thereof, and land attached, and ordering the land by description to be sold on writ of *venditioni exponas*, or on special execution, then no levy of the writ of execution, or of *venditioni exponas* is required. The attachment levy and order of sale stand in stead of a subsequent levy of the execution, and the sale will relate back to and carry title from the date of the levy of the attachment. In such case the judgment itself is sufficient, and

[1] Colvin v. Wood, 5 Hill, 228.
[2] Greene v. Burke, 23 Wend. 490, 498.
[3] Tullis v. Brawley, 3 Minn. 277: Folsom v. Carli, 5 Minn. 333, 337.

indeed the best evidence of the attachment levy and of the date thereof, which are therein fixed by judicial finding. The reason why no levy is then required of the writ of execution is that the original attachment levy and the judgment seize the land, and the only office of the writ of special execution, or of *venditioni exponas* is to bring about a sale.

§ 645. If, however, only an ordinary judgment be taken, and only an ordinary writ of execution issue, then a levy may be necessary, as in such case the chain of the attachment lien is broken of record; to fix that lien in any future controversy, (if it can be done at all) the execution purchaser must rely on the writ of attachment and levy thereof, if possibly to be found in the files of office under the modern practice where complete records are not usually made. If found, however, would they cut off the rights of an innocent intervening purchaser, without knowledge, and who buys of the execution debtor between the date of the attachment levy and the date of the judgment? We submit that in such case a *bona fide* purchaser would not be charged with notice of the attachment levy and lien thereof after the writ had served its functions and had become dormant in the mere files of office.

§ 646. Although no interest is vested in the officer or in the plaintiff by the levy of an execution on lands: that is, no interest in the property; yet a lien attaches, if none existed before, in behalf of the plaintiff by virtue of the levy, and a right in consequence thereof to make his debt thereof as of priority to and proceeding of another subsequent thereto.

§ 647. It is urged, as we have seen, that because a levy on lands, unlike one on personalty, vests no property in the officer, that therefore no levy need be made, where there is execution on a judgment which in law is a lien; but suppose the judgment lien expire before sale, though after advertisement of sale, under such circumstances, what then becomes of the plaintiff's lien? What protection has he, as against an intervening *bona fide* purchase, made without notice, or even with notice of the intended sale? It is well settled that if a levy on lands be made during the execution debtor's lifetime that a

sale may be made after his death.[1]   But how so if the levy is
unnecessary, or if a levy has no effect?   Although a levy on
the realty, unlike one on personal property, vests not a property in the officer, yet we conceive that it affects such a lien
upon and so seizes the title as not only to place the same
beyond the power of the debtor to sell as against the judgment
lien, but as also to give priority over subsequent levies.

§ 648. This very point was decided in *Bank of Missouri
v. Wells*,[2] where the judgment lien expired after levy and
before sale of the land by the sheriff.   The court held that the
previous levy preserved the lien of the judgment until the
writ was fully executed.

§ 649. When the sale, as in *Wood v. Colvin*, is made upon
a writ of *venditioni exponas*, no levy of that writ is necessary,
for, if it follows a *fi. fa.*, the levy has already been made by
the latter; and if it is ordered as an original, then it describes
the land that is therein ordered to be sold.   Such writ, however, usually follows a *fi. fa.* on which a levy has been made,
but no sale; the *vendi* then goes to complete the work, by
order of the court.   It directs the land previously levied on to
be sold.   The sale, when made, relates back to date of the levy
on the *fi. fa.*, and if the proper relation thereto has been kept
up on the record and in the latter writ, carries title from that
date; and the order for issuing the writ of *venditioni exponas*
shuts out all collateral inquiry as to the regularity of the prior
writ of *fi. fa.* and of the levy and return thereof.[3]

§ 650. In *Smith v. Hill*[4] it is expressly ruled that a levy

<hr/>

[1] Wheaton v. Sexton, 4 Wheat. 503.

[2] 12 Mo. 361. In this case the Supreme Court of Missouri dispose of the
question in the following terms: "The lien of the judgment under which
the defendant deduces his title was prior to that of the plaintiff, and long
before the expiration of the prior lien an execution was sued out and
delivered to the sheriff, the effect of which was to continue that lien until
the execution of the writ, although the time had elapsed during which
the lien of a judgment continued." * * * * "Then the prior levy
of the executioner under the junior judgment, although the lien of that
had not expired, did not divest the priority of the older judgment."

[3] Weir v. Clayton, 19 Ala. 132.

[4] 22 Barb. 656, 660.

is presumed in law, when an execution sale, that is in other respects sufficient in law, is shown. In that respect the court hold the following language: "It is said there is no proof of levy. The presumption is that the sheriff did his duty, and levied before the sale."

§ 651. In *Mercer v. Doe*[1] the court say: "The levy, sale, and return of the writ were sufficiently shown by the sheriff's deed; but whether the land was sold with or without appraisement, does not appear in the record. * * * * It is true when the law requires a sheriff to appraise property taken on execution a sale without appraisement would be a nullity; but in the absence of any proof on the subject, he will be presumed in that respect to have done his duty."

§ 652. In *Carpenter v. Doe*[2] the action was ejectment involving title to land under a sheriff's sale. The court held that the execution purchaser was only bound to show a judgment, execution, sale, and deed. In that case the court lay down the rule as follows: "It is a general rule that a purchaser at sheriff's sale is bound only to show the judgment of a competent court, an execution warranted by the judgment, and a sale and deed under it."

§ 653. As to the showing of a sale, we submit that the deed itself is sufficient evidence thereof in the first place.

§ 654. Allowing the doctrine that ordinarily it is necessary only to show a judgment execution and sheriff's deed purporting to have been made in pursuance of a sale thereon to be the better ruling, still it does not follow that the ruling in the leading case of *Wheaton v. Sexton*, 4 Wheat. 503, was incorrect, for in that case the sale was made after the death of the defendant in execution, and it became therefore necessary to show a levy to bring the case within the power of the officer to sell, to do which he had no power as against a dead defendant, unless the levy was made before the death occurred. In cases then of that class a levy becomes important as fixing the power of the officer to proceed. The want of it then is not a mere irregularity, but a question of power. The one is

---

[1] Mercer *v.* Doe, 6 Ind. 80, 81; Carpenter *v.* Doe, 2 Ind. 465.
[2] 2 Ind. 465, 467.

cured by presumption of law when judgment, execution, and sale is made; the other, like jurisdiction in an inferior court, is not inferred. The letter of the case of *Wheaton v. Sexton* seems to have been subsequently followed in some cases wherein the sales were against living defendants, and which were not in fact within the spirit or the reason of the case thus recognized as a precedent without any controversy raising the question of distinction.

§ 655. Upon the whole we conceive it to be the duty of the officer, in all cases, in executing a writ of *fieri facias*, to levy, whether the property be real or personal; and that if the sale be subsequent to the death of the execution defendant, a levy must not only be shown, but must have been made prior to the defendant's death, or else the sale cannot, without more, be sustained, whatever the effect might be, of lapse of time coupled with possession. That in all other cases arising under such writ of *fieri facias*, whilst it is in like manner the duty of the officer to levy, the omission so to do, or to advertise the sale, or to make a return, will not affect a *bona fide* purchaser, if the sale be in all other respects sufficient and fair, even if it be made to appear thereafter in a collateral proceeding that such irregularities occurred; and that in case it is not made to appear either the one way or the other, then by presumption of law the officer did his duty, and the court will hold that the requirements of the law in these particulars were complied with.

§ 656. An execution issued after a year and a day from the rendition of the judgment, "the time limited" within which an execution must issue, and at the end of which the judgment becomes dormant, is holden to be valid, though there be no revival of the judgment. Such process is only voidable and not void. It is a justification until set aside, and a sale thereon in other respects proper will be sustained as against the execution debtor. He cannot stand by and suffer the sale to be consummated and afterwards be allowed to question its validity in a collateral proceeding.[7]

---

[7] Summers *v.* Moore, 2 McLean, 59; Armstrong *v.* Jackson, 1 Blackf. 310; Childs *v.* McChesney, 20 Iowa, 431; Willard *v.* Whipple, 40 Vt. 219.

§ 657. In the case of *Childs v. McChesney*, in reference to irregular execution sales, the court, after noticing the fact that the Iowa state raises a presumption in favor of regularity where the contrary does not appear, go on and lay down the rule of law on general principles, that a mere irregularity in the proceedings, writ or sale, will not render the sale void, and such is the prevailing doctrine of the books. In *Wheaton v. Sexton*, Supreme Court United States, the court lay down the rule that "the purchaser depends on the judgment, the levy, and the deed." "All other questions are between the parties to the judgment and the marshall."[1]

§ 658. But if a sale be made in a manner inhibited by the statute, and such irregularity is made to appear upon the face of the proceedings, under and by virtue of which the purchase at sheriff's sale makes title the presumption of regularity and that the officer has conformed to his duty is, by such showing to the contrary overcome and will not avail the execution purchaser.[2] The rule of *caveat emptor* will then apply.

§ 659. But a clerical error merely will not vitiate a sheriff's deed;[3] especially when offered in an equitable proceeding.

§ 660. Statutes requiring levies to be made of personal property, before proceeding to levying real estate, are ordinarly directory only, and a non compliance therewith will not render a sale of lands invalid.[4]

§ 661. And the omission of the sheriff to inquire, in selling, if any one will pay the debt and costs for a less quantity of land than that covered by the best bid, though an irregularity will not vitiate the sale.[5] If the sale be on two executions, one of which is void and the other valid, the title of the pur-

---

[1] Childs v. McChesney, 20 Iowa, 431. Wheaton v. Sexton, 4 Wheat. 503; Philips v. Dana, 3 Scam. 558; Wood v. Colvin, 5 Hill, 231; Jackson v. Rosevelt, 13 Johns. 97; Cavender v. Smith, 1 Iowa, 306; Cox v. Joiner, 4 Bibb, 94; Averill v. Wilson, 4 Barb. 180.

[2] Piel v. Brayer, 30 Ind. 332; and see Stewart v. Houston, 25 Ark. 311, as bearing on the same principle.

[3] Stow v. Steel, 45 Ill. 328.

[4] Cavender v. Smith, 1 Iowa, 306; Hayden v. Dunlap, 3 Bibb, 216; Beeler v. Bullett, 3 Marsh. 281.

[5] Floyd v. McKinney, 10 B. Mon. 89.

chaser will be sustained.[1]   The contrary is holden in Indiana.[2]

§ 662. A sale, on an *alias* writ, when the process should be a *venditioni exponas* is not void.[3] Nor will a variance in the amount sold for and the amount named in the deed avoid the title.[4]

§ 663. Where a judgment bore date on the 12th day of the month and the execution described the judgment as rendered on the 13th day of the month, and a sale was made under the execution by the sheriff, it was holden that such discrepancy did not avoid the sale.[5]

§ 664. Upon the principle that in law the whole term of the court is as one day, the exact date of the judgment may well be immaterial if the term is sufficiently apparent.

§ 665. Nor will the variance of a small sum between the real amount of the judgment and the amount stated in the execution render a sale void if the execution otherwise identifies the judgment.[6]

§ 666. The irregularity of selling lands situate in a county other than the one from which the execution emanates, without first filing a transcript of the judgment in the county where the lands are, as required by statute, will not avoid the execution sale as between the execution debtor and purchaser who buys with notice. The object of the statute is to impart notice of the sale and to afford the judgment creditor the means of making his judgment a lien. But the statute is merely directory, and therefore a levy before the debtor has sold away the land gives the lien and a sale thereon gives title as against all persons buying with actual notice of the sales. Where actual notice exists, the implied notice from the record contemplated by the statute becomes unnecessary. Its necessity is superceded.[7]

[1] Herrick *r*, Graves, 16 Wis. 157.
[2] Brown *v.* McKay, 16 Ind. 484.
[3] Stein *v.* Chambless, 18 Iowa, 474; Simpson *v.* Simpson, 64 N. C. 427.
[4] Herrick *v.* Graves, 16 Wis. 157.
[5] Stewart *v.* Severance, 43 Mo. 322.
[6] Cunningham *v.* Felkner, 26 Iowa, 117.
[7] Hubbard *v.* Barnes, 29 Iowa, 239; and Chap. XVIII. Collateral Impeachment. Revision of Iowa, Secs. 3248, 3249, 4105, 4107.

SALES MADE AFTER THE DEATH OF THE EXECUTION DEFENDANT.

§ 667. At common law no execution could legally issue on a judgment after the death of either of the parties, plaintiff or defendant, until the judgment was, by *scire facias* revived in favor of or against the administrator or executor of the deceased party, plaintiff or defendant, as the case might be, except where otherwise provided by statute. Such is the general law yet of the several states where the common law prevails. But as to the effect of execution and sale thereon where the execution thus issued without revival, after the death of a party, there is a difference of opinion. In some of the states they are holden to be absolutely void, in others only voidable.[1] The weight of authority is that they are void.[2] Yet each of the different rulings are paramount authority in the respective states wherein they are made. In some of the states the practice of revival still exists; in others statutory innovations

[1] Doe *v.* Hamilton, 23 Miss. 496; Butler *v.* Haynes, 3 N. H. 21; Speer *v.* Sample, 4 Watts, 367; Lucas *v.* Doe, 4 Ala. 679; Abbercrombe *v.* Hall, 6 Ala. 657; Woodcock *v.* Bennett, 1 Cow. 711.

[2] Stymets *v.* Brooks, 10 Wend. 297; Hildreth *v.* Thompson, 16 Mass. 191; Massie *v.* Long, 2 Ham. 287; State *v.* Pool, 6 Ired, 288; Gwyn *v.* Latimar, 4 Yer. 22; Abbercrombie *v.* Hall, 6 Ala. 657; Webber *v.* Kenny, 1 A. K. Marshall, 345; The State *v.* Michaels, 8 Blackf. 436; Erwin *v.* Dundas, 4 How. 58; Brown *v.* Parker, 15 Illinois, 307. Speaking of common law proceedings, in Brown *v.* Parker, the court say, the weight of authority is that "proceedings upon an execution sued out after the death of one of the parties without first reviving the judgment for or against the proper representative, are absolutely void, whether their validity be drawn in question directly or collaterally." That "judicial proceedings cannot be carried on in the name of a dead man. There is as much necessity for a plaintiff as a defendant. The proceedings in either case are as much arrested by the death of one as of the other." (Brown *v.* Parker, 15 Ill. p. 310.) In Erwin's Lessee *v.* Dundas, the Supreme Court of the United States sum up the law of this subject in the following terms: "Upon the whole, without pursuing the examination further, we are satisfied that, according to the settled principles of the common law, and which are founded upon the most cogent and satisfactory grounds, the execution having issued and bearing teste in this case after death of one of the defendants, the execution was irregular and void, and the sale and conveyance of the real estate of the deceased under it to the plaintiff was a nullity."

have been made. Again, where innovations are made, the practice of revival, and the statutory remedy, are sometimes, if not always concurrent, so that either may be pursued, and omission to pursue one or the other will result in the same consequences, to an execution and proceedings thereon without, as if sued out at common law without revival. All will be void or voidable according to the rulings above referred to in the different states.

§ 668. By statute, in Illinois, execution may issue after the death of the judgment debtor against the lands and tenements of the decedent without first reviving the judgment against the administrator or heirs, provided the plaintiff first give the executor or administrator of such deceased debtor three months' notice in writing of the existence of such judgment. If execution issue and sale be made without first giving such notice, it is holden that the purchaser at such sale takes nothing, and the sale is void, so that no title passes under the deed of the sheriff. And if a notice be given, but describing the date of the judgment as of a different year than the date of the one on which execution really issues, the result will be no better; if sale be made no title will pass by the deed,[1] although it may have been intended to give notice of the judgment on which the writ really issued, as was probably the intention in the case above cited. And a sale made on execution issued on a dormant judgment, after the death of the judgment debtor, and without revival by *scire facias*, is void, and will not confer any rights as against the heir.

§ 669. The statute of Illinois allowing writs of execution to issue on judgments after the death of the judgment debtor, does not authorize their issuance on dormant judgments.

§ 670. When judgment liens have become dormant by running seven years, they must then be revived by *scire facias* before execution can legally issue. Nor, under said statute, can execution issue in a like case, or even if the judgment be not dormant, after the death of the plaintiff, without the appointment of an administrator of such plaintiff, and record-

---

[1] Picket *v.* Hartsock, 15 Ill. 279.

ing the appointment in the court where the judgment is. And in either case, if the lien has expired by the intervention of seven years, from the date of the judgment, then, although execution has been issued within a year and a day, the judgment must be revived from its dormant state before execution can legally go.[1]

§ 671. If the judgment plaintiff die before execution issues, then, by the statute of Illinois, the personal representative of the decedent may have execution in his own name, by recording in the court where the judgment is the letters of administration or testamentary of such personal representative, (or may revive the judgment in his own favor by *scire facias*, and thus have execution;) but if, on the death of the plaintiff, the executor or administrator take out execution without so recording his letters in the court where the judgment exists, or first making himself a party to the judgment, such execution, if neither the one or other of these previous steps be taken, will be void, and all the proceedings and any sale under it will likewise be void, and no rights will inure therefrom.[2]

§ 672. But in case the execution issue and be levied during the lifetime of the parties, then the officer in charge thereof may proceed to sell notwithstanding the death of a party, and it will, at most, amount merely to an irregularity, but will not render the sale invalid.[3]

§ 673. And though, by statute, in Iowa, the presumption is in favor of sheriff's sales, by reason whereof the silence of the sheriff's deed as to whether the sale was made on an *alias fi. fa.*, or on a *venditioni exponas*, would be presumed to have been made on the latter; yet the Iowa courts hold that on gen-

---

[1] Scammon v. Swartwout, 25 Ill. 326. If the judgment debtor be dead, the *scire facias* must make the heirs a party and give them a day in court, after the lien has expired, as the title has then vested in them. Ib., and Turney v. Young, 22 Ill. 253.

[2] Brown v. Parker, 15 Ill. 307.

[3] Sumner v. Moore, 2 McLean, 59; Wolf v. Heath, 7 Blackf. 154; Sprott v. Reid, 3 G. Greene, 489; Speer v. Semple, 4 Watts, 367; Butler v. Haynes, 3 N. H. 21; Butterfield v. Walsh, 21 Iowa, 97; Gamble v. Woods, 53 Penn. St. 158, 160; Wheaton v. Sexton, 4 Wheat. 503.

eral principles an irregularity in selling on *alias* instead of on a *venditioni exponas*, will not vitiate the sale.[1]

§ 674. And where a levy of a *fi. fa.* is made during the life of the execution defendant, the Supreme Court of the United States have holden that writ of *venditioni exponas* may issue after defendant's death, to complete the sale.[2]

§ 675. And so, where sale on execution under the valuation law fails for want of a bid to the amount by law required, and the execution, after levy and such effort and failure to sell, is returned, if in the meantime the defendant in execution dies, a writ of *venditioni exponas* may legally issue without revival by *scire facias*, notwithstanding the death of the defendant, and a sale thereon will be legal and valid. Such sale will confer on the purchaser the same rights in reference to the date of the lien as if it were made on the original writ and levy.[3]

VI. Sales when there is a Valuation Law.

§ 676. As respects valuation of the property, execution is to be made in accordance with the law in force at the date of the contract on which the judgment is rendered; and if the contract be made under a valuation law, then the sale on execution should conform to its provisions, although the law be repealed, before execution or even before judgment.[4]

§ 677. In such case no bid, when the property has been appraised, should be received of a less sum than the relative amount of the appraised value required by the statute; and a

---

[1] Childs v. McChesney, 20 Iowa, 431; Butterfield v. Walsh, 21 Iowa, 97.

[2] Taylor v. Miller, 13 How. 287; Bleeker v. Bond, 4 Wash. C. C. 6.

[3] Taylor v. Miller, 13 How. 287. This was a case brought up from Mississippi, where the doctrine prevails in the state courts that such a sale is not absolutely void, but is only voidable in some direct proceeding, cannot be assailed successfully in a collateral proceeding. Smith & Montgomery v. Winston, 2 How. (Miss.) 601; Drake v. Collins, 5 How. (Miss.) 253; Harrington v. O'Riley, 9 S. & M. 216.

[4] Rew v. Wood, 3 McLean, 575; Coviell v. Ham, 4 G. Greene, 455; Burton v. Emerson, 4 G. Greene, 393; McCracken v. Haywood, 2 How. 608; Hobson v. Doe, 4 Blackf. 487; Lane v. Fox, 8 Blackf. 58; Harrison v. Shipp, 8 Blackf. 455; Law v. Smith, 4 Ind. 56; Tevis v. Doe, 3 Ind. 129; Kenzie v. Bronson, 1 How. 311; Rawley v. Hooker, 21 Ind. 144; McCracken v. Hayward, 2 How. 813; Collier v. Stonbaugh, 6 How. 21.

sale for a less sum is void.[1] To make a valid appraisement all the appraisers must ordinarily agree.[2]

§ 678. And so, in Iowa, it is held in like manner that an execution plaintiff buying in satisfaction of his own writ, at sheriff's sale made without appraisement, is chargeable with notice of the irregularity and takes nothing by his purchase. So likewise if the assignee of the judgment buy under like circumstances. The court decline to say what the effect in Iowa would be if the purchase was by a third party, as the question did not arise in the case before them; but held the purchase by the beneficiary of the writ as void.[3]

§ 679. So in *Sprott v. Reid,* and other cases, in Iowa, it had been previously held that whoever were the purchasers, such sales, without valuation, were void; that the want of valuation went to the power of the officer.[4]

§ 680. As to the result of execution sales made in disregard of a valuation or appraisement law, the authorities are by no means uniform, some holding that such sales are void,[5] whilst by others, though regarded as irregular, they are held to pass the title to the purchaser, as only voidable and as not open to collateral inquiry.[6]

§ 681. We regard that as the true rule which is laid down in a parallel case, *Gantley's Lessee v. Ewing,*[7] by the Supreme Court of the United States, that if the law be merely directory as to the duty of the officer, then the sale and deed, without appraisement, will carry the title; but if the law contains an inhibition to sell without conforming to its requirements, then sales in disregard thereof are void. A sale on execution to

---

[1] Harrison v. Rapp, 2 Blackf. 1; Tyler v. Wilkinson, 27 Ind. 450.

[2] Evans v. Landon, 1 Gilm. 307.

[3] Maples v. Nelson, 31 Iowa, 322; Sprott v. Reid, 3 G. Greene, 497.

[4] Sprott v. Reid, 3 G. Greene, 497; Coriell v. Ham, 4 G. Greene, 455; Burton v. Emerson, 4 G. Greene, 393.

[5] Doe v. Holman, 1 Smith (Ind.) 58; Evans v. Ashley, 22 Ind. 15; Tyler v. Wilkinson, 27 Ind. 450.

[6] Shafer v. Bolander, 4 G. Greene, 201; Butterfield v. Walsh, 21 Iowa, 101.

[7] 3 How. 707, 716, 717.

satisfy pecuniary fines due to the state are not subject to valuation laws.[1]

§ 682. An appraisement law in force in a state at the time of making a contract in such state, enters into and becomes a part of the contract, and execution sale thereon in such state must be in conformity thereto.[2] But in case of a contract made in a state other than that wherein the judgment is rendered thereon, then the sale is not to be in conformity to the appraisement law of the state where the contract was made, but in accordance with the law of the state where the judgment is rendered, as it exists at the date of the judgment.[3]

§ 683. If one becomes replevin bail for another, in a judgment when and where there is no law requiring appraisement of property to be sold under such judgment, and the debt is realized out of the bail, then no appraisement is necessary in selling the land of the principal on execution in favor of the bail to reimburse to the bail the amount paid by him if the sale be in the same state.[4]

§ 684. If judgment be rendered as an entirety on debts due by two distinct notes, one of which was executed under a valuation or appraisement law, and the other not, and land of the judgment debtor be sold without appraisement, and without the debtor's consent, upon a general execution issued on such judgment, and a conveyance be made accordingly, it is held in Indiana that the grantee of the sheriff takes no title.[5]

§ 685. The mere omission of the sheriff in his return to show that the property was appraised is not conclusive; that fact is open to proof *aliunde:*[6] moreover valuation will be presumed if nothing appears in regard to it.[7]

§ 686. Where it does not appear under what law the con-

---

[1] Walshe v. Ringer, 2 Ohio, 327.

[2] Law v. Smith, 4 Ind. 56; Doe v. Collins, 1 Smith, (Ind.) 58.

[3] Hutchins v. Barnett, 19 Ind. 15; Doe v. Collins, 1 Carter, (Ind.) 24; Doe v. Collins, 1 Smith, (Ind.) 58; Shaffer v. Bolander, 4 G. Greene, 201; Story, Conf. of Laws, Sec. 556.

[4] Tevis v. Doe, 3 Ind. 129.

[5] Babcock v. Doe, 8 Ind. 110.

[6] Thurston v. Barnes, 10 Ind. 289.

[7] Evans v. Ashby, 22 Ind. 15.

tract was made on which the judgment is rendered, then the appraisement law in force at time and place of the rendition of the judgment must control.[1]

§ 687. In Indiana a valid levy of an attachment upon real estate is a lien from the date of the levy, both in its own behalf and in behalf of other creditors subsequently attaching and thus come in to participate in the proceeds. Such lien overreaches the lien of judgments of subsequent date, rendered in proceedings instituted on ordinary process of summons.

§ 688. When such attachments are prosecuted to judgment, and several executions issue thereon, some of which are subject to the valuation law and others not, and none of them have priority of another, then as the sale must necessarily be made on all the writs together, it may be made without valuation, and will, when so made, be valid.[2]

§ 689. When, under the valuation law, a sale of real estate on execution fails for want of a bid, to the amount required on valuation by the statute, by reason whereof the writ is returned on a *venditioni exponas* issues and sale is made thereon, such sale relates back to the original levy and is but a continuation of the proceedings on the original writ. It saves the lien as an *alias* would have saved it and is a valid sale.

§ 690. If, in the meantime, the defendant die between the time of the levy of the *fieri facias* and the issuing of the writ of *venditioni exponas*, the latter may legally issue, notwithstanding his death, and a sale thereon is valid, and carries with it all the rights as to lien acquired by the original levy of the *fieri facias* or by the judgment. No revival by *fieri facias* is necessary.[3]

§ 691. And where in Indiana, the execution debtor assented to a sale being made in disregard of the valuation law, upon a writ of execution which came within the terms of the law,

---

[1] Indiana R. Way Co. v. Bradley, 15 Ind. 23; where by statute the rents and profits are first required to be appraised and offered, a sale in disregard thereof is void; ib. and Davis v. Campbell, 12 Ind. 192.

[2] Shirk v. Wilson 13 Ind. 129.

[3] Taylor v. Miller, 13 How. 287. This case came up from Mississippi, where it is holden as has been seen, that in case of levy before a defendant's death, sale thereafter may be made without reviewing the judgment.

and which required valuation of the property about to be sold, the courts of that state held that such defendant "could not be heard to say that the sale was void for want of appraisement." In such case the court say: "The maxim, 'that to which a person assents is not esteemed in law to be an injury' is applicable here." The sale thus made by consent, without the property being appraised, was sustained by the court, as to that particular point as valid and good in law.[1]

§ 692. The disqualification of one of the appraisers of lands about to be sold on execution, as that he is not a householder, where the statute requires holders as appraisers, does not in Iowa avoid an execution sale.[2] Though the contrary is the ruling in some others of the states.[3]

§ 693. In Iowa the policy of the law is to uphold and maintain execution sales; and the statute of Iowa does not require the qualification of appraisers to be embodied or shown in the sheriff's return. These, the court say, "rest *in pais*." And if the validity of a sheriff's sale is made to depend upon the qualification and selection of the appraisers, the purchaser holds his title continually at the hazard of having it defeated by parole testimony.[4]

§ 694. By act of Congress of March the second, 1793, it was enacted that wherever by the laws of any state it was then required that goods taken in execution should be appraised, so in like manner there should be an appraisement when taken in execution on executions from the United States courts; and that in case the appraisers, on being summoned by the marshal, fail to attend, then the marshal should sell without appraisement.[5] This provision was in effect extended to all the states then in existence, by the act of May 19th, 1828, which latter act gave the United States courts power to adopt, from time to time, the forms and process of the several states wherein they were holden, and this act was extended to all the

---

[1] Stockwell *v.* Byrne, 22 Ind. 6.
[2] Hill *v.* Baker, 31 Iowa, 302.
[3] Eddy *v.* Knapp, 2 Mass. 154; Whitman *v.* Tyler, 8 Mass. 284.
[4] Hill *v.* Baker, 31 Iowa, 302, 306.
[5] Brightley's Digest, 268. Sec. 2.

states then in existence by act of Congress of the first of August, 1842.[1] So that wherever the state processes have been adopted by such acts, or subsequent acts of Congress, or by orders of court made in pursuance thereof, the appraisement laws of the several states in force at such adoption are applicable to process from the United States courts.

, § 695. The state law of the former is the law and guide of the United States courts in the several states in ascertaining the rights of litigants in the subject matter of litigation before them up to the time of judgment; but not the law of practice and process before or after judgment unless adopted by act of Congress or by some order or rule of court.

§ 696. The remedy after judgment as to proceedings on execution conforms to the state laws in similar cases, if such laws are adopted, and not otherwise.[2] But it is holden that the adoption of the process and "proceedings thereupon," is also an adoption of the incidents attached thereto, as to valuation and exemption laws; provided they be not unconstitutional, whether the law of such incidents be expressly adopted or not.[3]

§ 697. In *Amis v. Smith*,[4] the United States Supreme Court, McKINLEY, Justice, hold the following language: "We think this section of the act of 1828 (referring to the third section) adopted the forthcoming bond in Mississippi as a part of the final process of that state at the passage of the act. And we understand by the phrase 'final process' all the writs of execution then in use in the state courts of Mississippi which were properly applicable to the courts of the United States; and we understand the phrase 'the proceedings thereupon,' to mean the exercise of all the duties of the ministerial officers of the state, prescribed by the laws of the state, for the purpose of obtaining the fruits of judgments. And among these

[1] Brightley's Digest, 239, Sec. 6; Catherwood *v.* Gapete, 2 Curt. C. C. 94; U. S. *v.* Knight, 14 Pet. 301.

[2] Wayman *v.* Southard, 10 Wheat. 1; U. S. Bank *v.* Halstead, 10 Wheat. 51; Amis *v.* Smith, 16 Pet. 309, 313.

[3] United States *v.* Knight, 14 Pet. 301, S. C., 3 Sumner, 358; Amis *v.* Smith, 16 Pet. 309, 313; Wayman *v.* Southard, 10 Wheat. 1.

[4] Amis *v.* Smith, 16 Pet. 309, 313.

duties is to be found one prescribed to the sheriff directing him to restore personal property levied on by him to the defendant, upon his executing a forthcoming bond, according to law, and the further duty to return it to the court forfeited, if the defendant fail to deliver the property on the day of sale, according to the condition of the bond. These are certainly proceedings upon an execution, and, therefore, the forthcoming bond must be regarded as part of the final process." So likewise proceedings under appraisement laws and laws exempting certain property from sale, when adopted, present parallel cases with the above.

VII. SALES AT WHICH THE EXECUTION CREDITOR IS PURCHASER.

§ 698. In some of the states it is held that when the execution plaintiff is the purchaser, he is chargeable with all irregularities and omissions, and with full notice of all things militating against the validity of the sale. In contemplation of law he is not, where there are irregularities, a *bona fide* purchaser. He pays nothing.[1] If the sale be not valid he may be reinstated to his rights on his judgment. In the case cited from 2 Ind. the irregularity was the selling without obtaining half the appraised value required by the appraisement law. How far this irregularity would have effected a stranger buying at the sale, the court say they pass over as not within the case; but hold the purchase of the execution creditor void for such cause in an action at law.

§ 699. By statute, in Indiana, if the execution creditor is the purchaser of the land at sheriff's sale on execution, and the judgment under which the sale is made be afterwards reversed, the sale is voided thereby;[2] and likewise if it be

---

[1] Harrison v. Doe, 2 Blackf. 1; Simonds v. Catlin, 2 Caines, 61; Hayden v. Dunlap, 3 Bibb, 261; Stephens v. Dennison, 1 Oregon, 19; McLean Co. Bank v. Flagg, 31 Ill. 290; Keeling v. Heard, 3 Head. (Tenn.) 592; Piel v. Brayer, 30 Ind. 332; Twogood v. Franklin, 27 Iowa, 239. The same rule applies with equal force if the purchase is made by the attorney of the plaintiff. Ib. But see *ante* ch. iv., pp. 59, 60, and also Wood v. Morehouse, 1 Lans. (N. Y.) 405, wherein every execution purchaser, including the plaintiff, is declared a *bona fide* purchaser.

[2] Hutchens v. Doe, 3 Ind. 528; Doe v. Crocker, 2 Carter (Ind.) 575.

reversed only in part, as for costs, where the sale was for the costs as well as for the debt.[1] And so it is held, in Wisconsin.[2] And on the other hand, the ruling, when he takes nothing, is in his favor. In Illinois it is held, upon general principles, that if the execution creditor purchase land at sale on his execution by a description so indefinite that he takes nothing by the purchase, that, on application, the sale will be set aside and satisfaction vacated, and a new execution will be awarded.[3]

§ 700. In other and numerous cases it is held that the plaintiff, as execution purchaser, is protected as a purchaser *bona fide*. In these cases, both in law and in equity, the execution plaintiff, as a general rule, when a purchaser at sheriff's sale in discharge of his own debt is protected to the same extent as third persons or strangers to the suit.[4]

§ 701. The courts hold that, "unless the equities of the adverse claimant are so strong and persuasive as to prevent the application of the rule, which indisputably obtains as to third persons," the purchaser will be protected. Such is the language of the court in *Butterfield v. Walsh*, 21 Iowa, 99.

§ 702. In the case cited from 21st Iowa the court say further: "Defendant had not even a deed. But if he had and failed to record it, and plaintiff have no notice of it, then in the absence of equities such as we have referred to, it would have had no validity against him, and his title would prevail. And certainly defendant can occupy no better position, holding an equitable claim without any paper evidence of it, and without notice thereof to plaintiff."[5]

§ 703. We have given the text of this case thus fully to show that the ruling of court is fully up to the point that the execution plaintiff, when a purchaser, is protected to the full extent, if the proceedings are regular, as is a third person or stranger.

---

[1] Hutchens *v.* Doe, 3 Ind. 528.

[2] Corwith *v.* State Bank, 18 Wis. 560.

[3] Hughes *v.* Streeter, 24 Ill. 647.

[4] Butterfield *v.* Walsh, 21 Iowa, 99; Wood *v.* Chapin, 3 Kan. 509; Evans *v.* McGlasson, 18 Iowa, 150.

[5] Butterfield *v.* Walsh, 21 Iowa, 98, 99; Wood *v.* Morehouse, 1 Lans. (N. Y.) 405.

§ 704. But it is also held in Iowa, however, that an execution plaintiff who buys at sheriff's sale on the execution in his favor, after an appeal is taken from the judgment on which his execution emanates, and with a knowledge of such an appeal, although no supercedeas bond be filed, is not a *bona fide* purchaser.[1] That if the judgment be reversed on such appeal, his title as executioner purchaser fails. And that it is equally invalid in the hands of his grantee, who buys after the reversal of the judgment. That such purchaser or his grantee do not come within the provision of the Iowa Revision, which declares that "property acquired by a *bona fide* purchaser, under a judgment subsequently reversed, shall not be affected by such reversal."[2]

VIII. Sales Made After the Return Day of the Execution.

§ 705. If the levy be made before the return day of the writ, the officer may sell afterwards on the same writ without a renewal of process.[3]

§ 706. It is immaterial to the purchaser as to the validity of the sale, whether the sale be made before or after the return day; or at what time the return is made; or whether the return be correct or incorrect; or whether any return be made at all, if the writ really be levied before the return day mentioned therein.[4] "It is not the return of the officer that gives title to the purchase, but the sale," say the court in *Remington v. Linthicum.*[5]

---

[1] Twogood v. Franklin, 27 Iowa, 239.

[2] Revision of 1860, Sec. 3541,

[3] Remington v. Linthicum, 14 Pet. 84, 92; Wheaton v. Sexton, 4 Wheat. 503; Barnard v. Stevens, 2 Ark. 420; Childs v. McChesney, 20 Iowa, 341; Stewart v. Severance, 43 Mo. 322; Stein v. Chambliss, 18 Iowa, 474; Philips v. Dana, 3 Scam. 558; Wood v. Colvin, 5 Hill, 231.

[4] Remington v. Linthicum, 14 Pet. 84, 92; Wheaton v. Sexton, 4 Wheat. 503; Stewart v. Severance, 43 Mo. 322; Barney v. Patterson, 6 Har. & J. 204.

[5] 14 Pet. 84, 92.

IX. SALES TO THIRD PERSONS, BONA FIDE PURCHASERS.

§ 707. Whether a *bona fide* purchaser at execution sale, he being a third person and not the execution plaintiff, and buying without notice, will take the estate free from unrecorded deed and prior equities, the same as an ordinary purchaser for value by private contract without notice, is a question upon which there is some conflict of authorities. But the later and better doctrine is that the execution purchaser takes the property against all such claims of which he has no notice.[1]

§ 708. The general rule has been extended further, and the prevailing doctrine is, as has been seen, that the sale is equally valid, as in favor of a purchase by the execution creditor.[2]

X. VOID EXECUTION SALES.

§ 709. If the court from which the writ emanates has not jurisdiction of the subject matter of the judgment then the execution sale is void. The purchaser takes no title. Having none himself, he is therefore incompetent to confer title by transfer to another.[3]

§ 710. So a sale made on process issued on a void judgment,[4]

[1] Butterfield v. Walsh, 21 Iowa, 97, 99; Parker v. Pierce, 16 Iowa, 227, 233; Lead. Cas. Eq. pt. 1, p. 75; Waldo v. Russell, 5 Mo. 387; Jackson v. Chamberlain, 8 Wend. 620; Den v. Rickman, 1 Green, 43; Ins. Co. v. Ledyard, 8 Ala. 866; Orth v. Jennings, 8 Blackf. 420; Heister v. Fortner, 2 Binney, 40; Killam v. Janson, 5 Harris, 467; Wood v. Chapin, 3 Kern, 509.

[2] See *ante*, chapt. iv., pp. 60, 62, and Wood v. Morehouse, 1 Lans. (N. Y.) 405.

[3] Abby v. Ward, 8 Mass. 79.

[4] Abby v. Ward, 8 Mass. 79; Webster v. Reid, 11 How. 437; Wright v. Boone, 2 G. Greene, 457; Harshey v. Blackmarr, 20 Iowa, 161. In the case last cited, Harshey v. Blackmarr, 20 Iowa, 161, the validity of an execution sale under a special foreclosure of a mortgage was involved. In the foreclosure proceedings under which the sale on execution was made, there was neither actual nor constructive service on nor voluntary appearance of the defendant debtor; but an unauthorized and insolvent attorney entered an appearance in his behalf. In a proceeding to vacate the sale the court held that the judgment being void, the sale was a nullity and conferred no title. So in Webster v. Reid, 11 How. 437, the Supreme Court of the United States say: "These suits were not a proceeding *in rem* against the land, but were *in personam* against the owners of it. Whether

from whatever cause the judgment be void, the sale is also void. So also if the sale be made on a forged execution.[1] Or on an execution otherwise valid but enjoined.[2] Or on an original execution issued after defendant's death, the judgment not having been revived.[3]

§ 711. But though a sale of lands upon a void execution is void, when made on it alone, yet if at the same time the sale be made on one or more writs that are valid, the officer selling on the several writs together, the title of the purchaser will be sustained.[4] Otherwise in Indiana.[5]

§ 712. In Missouri, a sale of lands on an execution which had been amended and altered by the clerk, after it had been issued and delivered to the sheriff, was held to be void where the execution plaintiff was the purchaser.[6] But, *quere?* if the sale would have been void if made to a stranger to the execution without notice to him of such alteration.[7]

§ 713. A levy of "all the unsold land" in a given tract is void for uncertainty of description, and a sale under such levy is likewise void, and confers no title or rights upon purchaser.[8]

§ 714. The identity of lands sold on execution must be shown to a reasonable certainty.[9]

they all resided within the territory or not, does not appear, nor is it a matter of any importance. No person is required to answer in a suit on whom process has not been served, or whose property has not been attached. In this case there was no personal notice, nor an attachment or other proceeding against the land until after the judgments. The judgments, therefore, are nullities, and did not authorize the executions on which the land was sold."

[1] Silver v. Coffee, 20 Texas, 4.
[2] Morris v. Bradford & Walker, 19 Geo. 527.
[3] Scammon v. Swartwout, Ill. 326; Erwin v. Dundas, 4 How. 58; Carter v. Read, 5 Ham. 221; Lieper v. Thompson, 60 Penn. St. 177; Sample v. Barr, 1 Casey, 457.
[4] Herrick v. Graves, 16 Wis. 157.
[5] Brown v. McKay, 16 Ind. 484; Hutchins v. Doe, 3 Ind. 528; Clark v. Watson, 2 Ind. 400; Harrison v. Sip, 8, Blackf. 455.
[6] Trigg v. Ross, 35 Mo. 165.
[7] Trigg v. Ross, 35 Mo. 165.
[8] Huddleston v. Garrett, 3 Humph. 629.
[9] Pound v. Pullen, 3 Yerg. 323; Clemens v. Reynolds, 34 Mo. 579; Hart v. Rector 7 Mo. 531.

§ 715. The unassigned right of dower is not the subject of execution sale; and if it were, the sale of a given number of acres to be taken off of a certain side of the dower land, prospectively to be assigned, is void for uncertainty. It has no identity until set off, and the subsequent assignment of dower cannot make that valid which was invalid at the time the sale was made.[1]

§ 716. A levy and sale of land on execution described only as a "tract containing" a certain number of acres, more or less, being a part of a tract granted to a certain person in such levy, sale, and deed named, is void for uncertainty, and so is a deed by the officer made thereon. For, though as between individuals in a private transaction it might possibly pass an interest capable of being ascertained or reduced to a certainty by a judicial proceeding, yet as such aid is not usually given to deeds on execution sales, the sale is void for uncertainty.[2]

§ 717. If judgment be against an infant defendant, and the execution issue against the estate of the next friend of such infant, and sale be made thereon, the sale is void and the purchaser takes nothing.[3]

§ 718. A levy and sale made after the official term of the officer expires, and when his official power has ceased, or after his removal from office, is simply void.[4] But otherwise if the writ be levied by him before his office ceases in either manner above named, and only the sale be made after the termination of his office.[5]

§ 719. By act of Congress it is provided that when a United States marshal goes out of office, a new writ of execution issues to his successor, who is to proceed as the former marshal would have proceeded in law if he had remained in office, and thus complete the levy and sale.[6] The case of *Wheaton v.*

[1] Shields *v.* Batts, 5 J. J. Marsh, 13.
[2] Clemen *v.* Reynolds, 34 Mo. 579.
[3] Wilson *v.* McGee, 2 A. K. Marsh, 600.
[4] Bank of Tennessee *v.* Beaty, 3 Sneed, 305.
[5] Larned *v.* Allen, 13 Mass. 295; Wheaton *v.* Sexton, 4 Wheat. 503; Furguson *v.* Lee, 9 Wend. 258, 260.
[6] Stewart *v.* Hamilton, 4 McLean, 534.

Sexton originated in that part of the District of Columbia which formerly belonged to Maryland.

§ 720. The writ of execution being the only authority of the officer to sell, it follows that if the writ is satisfied or is based on a satisfied judgment he has no power to sell, and that if a sale be made after such satisfaction it will be void.[1]

§ 721. But a sale to a *bona fide* purchaser will not be void by reason of the writ or judgment being only in part satisfied, where no evidence of such part satisfied accompanies the writ and none was apparent on the record of the judgment.[2] In case of part satisfaction, if the land be sold for the whole original amount of the judgment, and the execution plaintiff be the purchaser, then on bill filed in equity to set aside the sale, after possession and improvements by the purchaser, equity will compel a reconveyance of a proportionate part of the land to the execution debtor.[3] But in *Knight v. Applegate*,[4] where a large portion of the judgment was satisfied on the judgment record, and the clerk issued execution for the whole amount of the judgment without noting the credit on the writ or otherwise giving the sheriff notice thereof, by reason of which the sheriff raised the whole amount by sale of land, the court held that the sale was void. There was in reality no judgment to sustain the execution. The two amounts were different, whereas they should correspond. The true amount of the judgment at the time of issuing execution was the unpaid balance thereof, and that amount only of the original judgment the execution should have commanded the officer to make.

§ 722. As to the effect of an execution sale to a *bona fide* purchaser, when the judgment was fully satisfied previously to the issuing of the writ, and the purchaser buys ignorant of such satisfaction, and nothing appears of record as notice

---

[1] Hunter *v.* Stephenson, 1 Hill, (S. C.) 415; Weston *v.* Clarke, 37 Mo. 568; Chiles *v.* Bernard, 3 Dana, 96; States *v.* Salyers, 19 Ind. 432; Lavalle *v.* Rowley, 17 Ind. 36.

[2] Walker *v.* McKnight, 15 B. Mon. 467, 476, 477.

[3] Ibid. 467.

[4] 3 Mon. 388.

thereof, the authorities are variant, but the better opinion seems to be that such sale is void and confers no title on the purchaser.

§ 723. The sale held invalid in *King v. Goodwin*, 16 Mass., was one in which the creditor first caused the arrest, impressment and voluntary discharge of his judgment debtor; then finding land on which to levy, issued a *pluries* execution, on which the land was extended. Upon trial of the right under the extent, the court held that the voluntary discharge of the debtor was a satisfaction of the judgment; that the *pluries* writ afterwards issued thereon was therefore void, and that no right or title passed by the extent.[1]

§ 724. The same principle should apply, it would seem, to a sale as to an extent, made upon a satisfied judgment. If not good to pass a title for a term of years it ought not be good to pass the fee.

§ 725. In *Wood v. Colvin*, in New York, it was held that a purchaser at sheriff's sale, under a satisfied judgment, buying with knowledge, acquired no title as against a purchaser under a junior unsatisfied judgment, and that his assignee or vendee occupied no better position. That if satisfied the power to sell ceased; such, too, it is believed, is the general rule; for who buys under a power buys at his own risk.[2]

§ 726. And in *Swan v. Saddlemire*,[3] Justice SUTHERLAND says: "I am strongly inclined to the opinion that an execution issued upon a judgment which has been paid and satisfied, is to be considered absolutely void, and not voidable, and that the purchaser under such execution would acquire no title. It is a general rule that a purchaser under a power purchases at his peril. If there was no subsisting power or authority to sell, no title is acquired. But I abstain from a definitive

---

[1] King v. Goodwin, 16 Mass. 63.

[2] Wood v. Colvin, 2 Hill, (N. Y.) 566; Sherman v. Boyce, 15 Johns. 443; Jackson v. Anderson, 4 Wend. 447; Lewis v. Palmer, 6 Wend. 367; McGinty 6. Herrick, 5 Wend. 240; Swan v. Saddlemire, 8 Wend. 676, 681; Nielsen v. Nielsen, 3 Barb. 565; King v. Goodwin, 16 Mass. 63; Monchat r. Brown, 3 Rich. 117.

[3] 8 Wend. 676, 681.

opinion upon this point because I do not deem it necessary to the decision of this motion, and it may hereafter directly arise between other parties connected with this transaction."

§ 727. Again in *Wood v. Colvin*,[1] the court say: "If a purchaser can acquire a title under a satisfied judgment, it must be on the ground that there has been some fault on the part of the judgment debtor. If he stands by without taking any measures to arrest the sale, and without giving notice of the payment, and suffers a purchaser in good faith to part with his money, he may be estopped from afterwards alledging the payment to defeat the title of the purchaser."

§ 728. But such would not be the case if the purchaser himself knew the judgment was satisfied at the time of the purchase; having full notice thereof, the debtor would not be in fault by omitting to tell him what he already knew.[2]

§ 729. In Illinois it is held that a sale made on a day prior to the day of sale designated by the notice, is absolutely void, not only as to the purchaser, but also as to his grantee with notice; and moreover, that if the plaintiff be the purchaser he is chargable with notice of such irregularity.[3]

§ 730. In Missouri, it is held that a levy and execution sale of a tract of land as an entirety, by its original description, after it was subdivided into lots, streets and alleys, and sales of lots made to other parties, was void and conferred no title on the purchaser.[4]

§ 731. In Kentucky it is well settled by repeated decisions that if the sheriff sell on execution a material quantity of land more than is required to satisfy the writ when the land is susceptible of division, he exceeds his authority and the sale is void.[5]

<hr/>

[1] 2 Hill, 566, 568.

[2] Wood v. Colvin, 2 Hill, 566, 568; Myers v. Cochran, 29 Ind. 256. In the case last cited, Myers v. Cochran, the purchaser, who had made payment, refused repayment, with a knowledge that the judgment was satisfied, and he took nothing by his purchase.

[3] King v. Cushman, 41 Ill. 31.

[4] Henry v. Mitchell, 32 Mo. 512.

[5] Stover v. Boswell, 3 Dana, 232; Patterson v. Corneal, 3 A. K. Marsh. 618; Davidson v. McMintry, 2 J. J. Marsh. 68; Morris v. Bruce, 9 Dana, 211; Adams v. Kiser, 7 Dana, 208; Shropshire v. Pullen, 3 Bush. (Ky.) 512.

§ 732. And so, if the writ calls for one sum and the judgment for another and different one, a sale on such writ is void unless the difference is so small as to come within the principle "*diminumus non curat lex;*" and the transfer of the property to a *bona fide* purchaser, by the purchaser under the execution will not alter the case.[1]

§ 733. So an execution sale of real estate based on a proceeding *in rem* by attachment levied on real estate of a non-resident owner, was held to be void where it appeared from the record that there was no personal service nor newspaper publication, or mailing of notice and petition to defendant as required by statute, and no evidence appeared of defendant's residence being unknown, or that it could not be ascertained.[2]

§ 734. The statute in Illinois allows execution to issue against the lands of a decedent, on a judgment rendered in his life time, by first giving a certain notice to the executor or administrator; the Supreme Court of the United States, as also the Supreme Court of Illinois, hold that such statutory remedy is cumulative, and does not prevent a resort to the common law remedy of *scire facias* to revive the judgment. But that an execution issued without either such notice or revival by *scire facias* against lands of a decedent is a nullity, and all proceedings under it are void.[3]

§ 735. Such judgment, on the death of the defendant, (says Justice SWAYNE,) "survives only for the preservation of its lien, and as a basis of future action." It has no practical vitality for enforcement by the mere issuance of an execution. The notice provided by the statute, or else its alternative process of revival by writ of *scire facias* must be resorted to, and is indispensable to give the judgment such vitality as will sustain an execution and sale thereon.[4]

§ 736. In a proceeding bringing in question the title of a

[1] Hastings v. Johnson, 1 Nev. 613.
[2] Hudson v. Tibbetts, 16 Iowa, 97; Broghill v. Lash, 3 G. Greene, 357; McGaher v. Carr, 6 Iowa, 331.
[3] Ransom v. Williams, 2 Wall. (U. S.) 313; Picket v. Hartsock, 15 Ill. 279; Brown v. Parker, ib. 307; Finch v. Martin, 19 ib. 111.
[4] Ransom v. Williams, 2 Wall. 313; Picket v. Hartsock, 15 Ill. 279; Brown v. Parker, ib. 307; Finch v. Martin, 19 ib. 111.

purchase under sheriff's sale, made on execution issued after the death of the execution debtor, the burthen of proof rests upon the purchaser at sheriff's sale, to show that the notice was given in compliance with the statute, or else a revival as at common law, by *scire facias*.[1]

§ 737. Where two parcels of land are included in one and the same mortgage, a separate execution sale of the right of redemption of one tract only, on execution against the mortgagor, is inoperative and void. It passes nothing to the purchaser. (There is no rule by which redemption can be made of the one tract alone; and the execution purchaser has no claim to redeem the other tract which is not included in his purchase.)[2]

§ 738. If an order of sale on execution issued to an officer be without a seal, when by the law of the land a seal is required, it is invalid, and a sale of lands made in virtue thereof is void; the purchaser takes nothing.[3] So, in Indiana, a

[1] Ranson *v.* Williams, 2 Wall. 313.

[2] Webster *v.* Foster, 15 Gray (Mass.,) 31; Johnson *v.* Stevens, 7 Cush. 435.

[3] Ins. Co. *v.* Halleck, 6 Wall. 556. This case arose under the local code of Indiana, which provides that the execution is in all cases the remedy on a money judgment, and shall be sealed with the seal of the court. "In courts which pursue the chancery practice in foreclosing mortgages unaffected by statutory provisions, the sale is made by a commissioner appointed by the court. This is usually one of the standing master commissioners of the court, or, for reasons shown, some special commissioner that purpose. In neither case does any process, or order, under the court, issue to the commissioner. He may, if he thinks proper, procure a copy of the decree and order appointing him commissioner, or if the party who wishes the decree executed thinks proper in this mode to demand of him to proceed, he may furnish him with a copy. But it is believed that the decree itself is the authority on which the commissioner acts, and if he proceeds in conformity to the decree, the sale will be valid, although no copy has been placed in the hands of the commissioner. In the courts of Indiana, the distinction between common law and chancery proceedings is abolished, and under their code of civil procedure but one form of action, called a civil action, is known. This code provides, § 407, that 'when a judgment requires the payment of money, or the delivery of real or personal property, the same may be enforced by execution.' § 409 says: 'The execution must issue in the name of the state and be directed to the sheriff of the county, sealed with the seal and tested by the clerk of the court.' § 635, which relates to the proceedings to foreclose a mort-

sheriff's sale of several parcels of land, all together *in solido*, not having first offered each separately, is absolutely void.[1]

§ 739. Where the mode and form of proceedings in the highest courts of common law of a state are adopted as the practice in the United States courts of any district, a United States marshal's sale on execution, in such district, made otherwise than in accordance with such common law practice of said state courts, is invalid and will not confer title on the purchaser. A departure in such case from the local law and practice requiring an appraisement of the property to be sold, and inhibiting sale for less than a named proportion of the appraised value, avoids the sale.[2]

§ 740. A judgment *in personam* without jurisdiction of the person of defendant, is a void judgment, and an execution sale thereon is also void. He who redeems from such sale as a judgment creditor takes nothing by his redemption; and an

gage, we give *verbatim:* 'A copy of the order of sale and judgment shall be issued and certified by the clerk, under the seal of the court, to the sheriff, who shall thereupon proceed to sell the mortgaged premises, or so much thereof as may be necessary to satisfy the judgment, interest and costs, as upon execution; and if any part of the judgment, interest, and cost, remain unsatisfied, the sheriff shall forthwith proceed to levy the residue of the other property of the defendant.' Though the order of sale here described may not come under the name of any of the recognized common law writs of execution, as *capias, fieri facias*, or others, yet it comes clearly within the function and supplies the purpose of an execution—that is a process issuing a court to enforce its judgment. The statute recognizes it as such, and requires that it shall issue under the seal of the court. The sheriff to whom it is directed is required to proceed 'as upon execution.' If the debt is not satisfied by the sale of the property specifically mentioned in the order, it then operates as a *fieri facias*, under which the sheriff is directed to levy the residue of any other property of the defendant. It is, therefore, to all intents and purposes an execution, and the statute expressly requires that it must issue under the seal of the court. Without the seal it is void. We cannot distinguish it from any other writ or process in this particular. It is equally clear that under the Indiana statute the sheriff could not sell without this order, certified under the seal of the court, and placed in his hands. This is his authority, and if it is for any reason void, his acts purporting to be done under it are also void."

[1] Tyler *v.* Wilkinson, 27 Ind. 450.

[2] Smith *v.* Cockrill, 6 Wall. (U. S.) 756.

17

execution sale of the premises made under the statute of Illinois, at the instance of the redemptioner and in pursuance of such redemption, is also void, and will be so regarded even in collateral proceedings.[1]

§ 741. If a sale be merely irregular, or on irregular process it is voidable only; but if made without authority, it is void.

§ 742. In *St. Bartholomew's Church v. Wood*[2] the rule laid down in Pennsylvania is declared to be "that a sheriff's sale on a *fi. fa.* without a waiver of inquisition is void as wanting authority, and is not confirmed by the acknowledgment of the deed, or the distribution of the proceeds of sale." And as to mere irregularities, the court add, in this case, that " the acknowledgment of the sheriff's deed cures irregularities on the process or proceedings, but not a want of authority to sell." But this acknowledgment is not to be understood to be the mere acknowledgment *in pais* of the officer. In Pennsylvania it is an act in court, and its reception is a judicial act.[3] Hence, in *McAffee v. Harris*[4] the court say: " After acknowledgment of the sheriff's deed in open court the title of the sheriff's vendee cannot be effected by mere irregularities, however gross; nothing but fraud in the sale, or want of authority to sell, can defeat the title."

§ 743. This mode of taking the acknowledgment of a sheriff's deed in open court in Pennsylvania operates as confirmation of the sale, so as to assimulate such sales in that state, and in that respect, to a certain extent, to judicial sales, as has elsewhere been stated; but while such is the case, it does not seem to give validity to a sale made without authority of law, which otherwise would be void. Nor would it in a judicial sale.[5]

---

[1] Johnson *v.* Baker, 38 Ill. 98.

[2] 61 Penn. St. 96, 103. See also David *v.* Lent, 8 Watts, 422; Wolf *v.* Payne, 11 Casey, 97; McLaughlin *v.* Shields, 2 Jones, 289; Shoemaker *v.* Ballard, 3 Harris, 91; McAffee *v.* Harris, 1 Casey, 102; Shields *v.* Miltenberger, 2 Harris, 78.

[3] Thompson *v.* Philips, 1 Bald. C. C. 272.

[4] 1 Casey, 102; St. Bartholomew's Ch. *v,* Wood, 61 Penn. St. 96, 103.

[5] Shriver *v.* Lynn, 2 How. 43, 59, 60; 2 Bouvier, 415; *ante* chap. 3, Thompson *v.* Philips, 1 Bald. C. C. 216, 272.

§ 744. A judgment *in personam*, on service by publication and no personal service of process whatever, is void, when rendered by default, there being no appearance of the defendant; and whenever on such judgment an ordinary writ of *fieri facias* issues and property is sold thereon, the sale is void, and the execution purchaser takes nothing thereby. Such a proceeding is not "due process of law." Instead of a general judgment *in personam* the creditor should proceed by attachment so as to obtain jurisdiction over the property, and should take judgment against the property specifically and an order of sale thereof. A sheriff's sale and deed on the judgment *in personam* is of no effect and may be impeached in a collateral proceeding.[1]

§ 745. A purchase at an execution sale, made with intent to defraud, hinder, or delay the creditors of the execution debtor, is fraudulent and void as against all *bona fide* creditors, or other execution purchasers of such debtor.[2]

§ 746. The execution and judgment must correspond as to the character of the parties. A recovery of judgment by one in his character of administrator will not support an execution in his favor describing him only in his individual character, without the addition of administrator. The writ will be void, and so whether the judgment and writ be against or in favor of an administrator. The execution, in either case, must correspond with the judgment as to the names and character of the parties.[3]

§ 747. So, a sale of a given quantity of land out of a specified tract, without identity or description of the land sold, is void.[4]

§ 748. As well at common law as by the statute, a sale, in Indiana, of lands of a decedent cannot be made upon an execution which is issued on a judgment rendered against the

---

[1] Abbott *v.* Shepherd, 44 Mo. 233; Smith *v.* McCutchen, 38 Mo. 415; Lattimer *v.* Union Pacific R. R. Co., 43 Mo. 105.

[2] Duncan *v.* Forsythe, 3 Dana, 229.

[3] Palmer *v.* Palmer, 2 Conn. 462.

[4] Peck *v.* Mallams, 10 N. Y., 509; Clemens *v.* Rannels, 34 Mo. 579.

executor; and if the semblance of it be carried out, it will confer no title. It will be void.[1]

§ 749. And so a sale of lands made on an execution and judgment against two defendants, one of which is dead, is void, if the execution bear *teste* of a date subsequent to the death of one of them.[2]

§ 750. "If a bidder make representations to deter other bidders and is successful in deterring them, his purchase is fraudulent and void,"[3] and will be set aside.

---

[1] Doe v. Woody, 4 McLean, 75.

[2] Erwin v. Dundas, 4 How. 58.

[3] Vantrees v. Hyatt, 5 Ind. 487; Hogg v. Wilkins, 1 Grant Cas. (Penn.) 67; Bunts v. Cole, 7 Blackf. 265.

CHAPTER XVIII.

THE DEED.

I. By Whom to be Made.

§ 751. The deed can only be executed by the officer himself, or by his general deputy, and whether by the one or by the other, it must, in either case, be in the name of the principal officer, and as his act.[1]

§ 752. A special deputy cannot execute the deed; nor can a deputy execute the deed in his own name.[2]

§ 753. By statute in most of those states in which lands are sold on execution, instead of being extended, the deed may be made by the successor of the officer who sells, when such officer has, after the sale, ceased from any cause to exercise the functions of the office before executing a deed for the lands sold; and, even without such a statute, the court, in a proper case, will order the successor of the officer selling to execute the deed.[3] But in California the rule seems to be established that

---

[1] Jackson v. Bush, 10 Johns. 223; Tillotson v. Cheatham, 2 Johns. 63; Haines v. Linsey, 4 Ham. 88; Jackson v. Randall, 18 Johns. 7, 8; Glasgow v. Smith, 1 Overt. 144; Carr v. Hunt, 14 Iowa, 206; Young v. Smith, 10 B. Mon. 293, Iowa, 206; Keller v. Blanchard, 21 La. Ann. 38.

[2] Anderson v. Brown, 9 Ham. 151; Lewis v. Thompson, 3 Cal. 266.

[3] Fowble v. Rayburg, 4 Ham. 45; Woods v. Lane, 2 S. & R. 53; Prescott v. Everts, 4 Wis. 314; Conger v. Converse, 9 Iowa, 556; Thurston v. Boyd, 25 Miss. 598; Fretwell v. Mooraow, 7 Geo. 264; McElmurry v. Ardis, 3 Strobh. 212; People v. Boring, 8 Cal. 406; Philips v. Jamison, 14 B. Mon. 579.

the individual officer selling shall execute the deed, even if his term of office has subsequently expired, and in case of his death, then by a master appointed by court.[1] In Ohio, Pennsylvania, and some others of the states, the practice is to confirm the sales in court;[2] and it has been holden where this practice prevails that without confirmation sales on execution are invalid.[3]

§ 754. In the leading case here cited, the court held that a "deed executed by the deputy sheriff, in the name and on the behalf of his principal was a good execution of the deed." That a "sale, and the consummation of that sale by deed, are acts which the sheriff may do by deputy." That "the law does not require them to be done by the sheriff in person."[4] This doctrine holds good to the present day.

§ 755. In Missouri the law requires sheriff's deed for property sold on execution to be acknowledged before the clerk of the court, by the sheriff; a certificate of such acknowledgment to be endorsed by the clerk on the deed under the seal of the court, and a correct entry to be made of record by the clerk, describing the conveyance and the names of the parties to the suit in which the judgment was rendered on which the execution emanated.

§ 756. It is held by the supreme court of that state, that this provision of the statute is merely director so far as to the entry of record. That a purchaser having no control over the clerk cannot be prejudiced by the omission, or by the irregularity of the entry, and that the deed will be good if the proper endorsement is made thereon, although the entry of record be substantially defective.[5]

§ 757. The deed must contain apt words of conveyance and grant, and though no particular form is required, it must substantially purport to grant and convey the premises to the purchaser in consideration of the contract of sale and payment

[1] Anthony v. Wessell, 9 Cal. 103; People v. Boring, 8 Cal. 406.
[2] Curtis v. Norton, 1 Ham. 278.
[3] Curtis v. Norton, 1 Ham. 378.
[4] Jackson v. Bush, 10 Johns. 223. The same ruling had been previously made in Tillotson v. Cheatham, 2 Johns. 63.
[5] Scruggs v. Scruggs, 41 Mo. 242.

of the purchase money. In the language of the court, in
Johnson v. Bantock, "it must appear from the language
employed that it was the intention to convey the title, and the
language must purport to have that effect."[1]

§ 758. We may also add that it must purport to be act of
the officer in his official capacity, and not merely the individual
act of the man or person filling the office.

§ 759. However sufficient it may be to show that a purchase had been made at execution, and however sufficient as a
mere certificate of purchase on which to base a deed, yet, unless
it purport to transfer the land, and convey the title, it will not
be sufficient as a deed. In the case cited from Illinois, the
instrument, (a copy of which is given in the subjoined note,)
instead of purporting to be a deed, really negatives such idea
by the words, "are *entitled* to a deed for the premises so
sold."[2]

[1] Johnson v. Bantock, 38 Ill. 111.

[2] See Johnson v. Bantock, the instrument there relied on as the
deed, was in words and figures as follows: "Know all men by these
presents: That I have this day sold to Olof Johnson and Samuel
Remington the following described tract of land, to wit: The south-
east quarter of the north-east quarter of Section No. 29, in township
No. 14, north of Range four, east of the fourth principal meridian, in the
county of Henry, in the state of Illinois. The above described land being
the same that was to Joshua Johnson on execution in favor of B. F. Johnson, and against John J. Hall and Robert Duncan, on the 24th day of July,
1858, for the sum of $195.42, and redeemed on the 24th day of October,
1859, by Olof Johnson and Samuel Remington, who were judgment
creditors of the said John J. Hall and Robert Duncan, by paying to me
good and lawful money for said Joshua Johnson, the sum of $218.69, it
being the full amount of said judgment and interest up to that date and
no more, and I have advertised and offered the same for sale at public
auction this 14th day of December, 1859, according to law; and the said
Olof Johnson and Samuel Remington, by force of the statute in such case
made and provided, were considered as having bid the sum of $219.88, it
being the amount of said redemption money so paid by Olof Johnson and
Samuel Remington and interest thereon from the day of such redemption
up to the present time, and no more, and there being no bid greater than
said amount offered, the said lands were struck off and sold to said Olof
Johnson and Samuel Remington, judgment creditors as aforesaid, at the
said amount of redemption money and interest; and the said Olof Johnson and Samuel Remington are entitled to a deed for the premises so sold,

§760. In some states the officer who sells may execute the deed after his term expires.[1] This, too, though his successor may have entered on the duties of his office.[2]

§ 761. The certificate of sale and the deed should refer to or recite the writ on which the sale is made, and no other, although several writs be in the hands of the officer. But the full amount sold for should be stated.

§ 762. The disposition of the money is matter for statement in the return.

§ 763. The deed is good as between the purchaser and execution defendant, if made officially by the officer, although the certificate of acknowledgment be defective as to the official character of the person acknowledging it and refer to him only by his personal name.[3] And so it is good if made to the assignee of the purchaser, stated to be such in the deed by the officer.[4]

II. To whom to be Made.

§ 764. The sheriff's deed may be made to the purchaser, or to his assigns.[5] Or, in case of the death of the purchaser, to his devisee,[6] or legal heirs,[7] as the case may be.

§ 765. The purchaser can assign his bid, and a deed from

to have and to hold the said described premises, with all the appurtenances thereunto belonging to the said Olof Johnson and Samuel Remington, their heirs and assigns forever.

"Witness my hand and seal this 14th day of December, 1859.

{ SEAL. }   [Duly acknowledged as a deed.]

"PURNELL H. SMITH.
"Sheriff of Henry County, Illinois."

This instrument the court, that as a deed it "is not sufficient." 38 Ill. 111.

[1] Lemon v. Craddock, Litt. Sel. Cas. 251.
[2] People v. Boring, 8 Cal. 406; Anthony v. Wessell, 9 Cal. 103.
[3] In the matter of Smith, 4 Nev. 254.
[4] McClure v. Englehart, 17 Ill. 47; In the matter of Smith, 4 Nev. 254.
[5] Blount v. Davis, 2 Dev. 19; Small v. Hodgen, 1 Litt. 16; In the matter of Smith, 4 Nev. 254; McClure v. Englehart, 17 Ill. 47; Frizzle v. Veach, 1 Dana, 211.
[6] Summers v. Palmer, 10 Rich. 38; McElmurry v. Ardis, 3 Strobh. 212.
[7] Swink v. Thompson, 31 Mo. 336.

the sheriff to the assignee will be valid.[1] So, the purchaser may assign the sheriff's certificate of purchase where the practice is to give certificates, and the deed may be made to the assignee thereof.[2]

§ 766. But a recital of such assignment in the sheriff's deed is only *prima facie* evidence thereof, it being the act of a third person and not of the sheriff.[3]

§ 767. And though the transfer or assignment of the sheriff's certificate be so defective that a deed to the assignee could not be coerced from the officer, yet if he execute a deed in pursuance thereof to the assignee, the deed will be good.[4] The assignee of the certificate under the sheriff's sale is, in law, the assignee of the original party defendant to the execution.[5] It may be enforced in equity.[6]

§ 768. A sheriff's deed to two persons for land sold to one of them as nominal purchaser, if in all other respects sufficient, will pass the title to both the grantees in common.[7]

III. When to be Made.

§ 769. If by law there is no redemption, then it follows that the deed is due on payment of the purchase money, (and confirmation, if the latter is required.) Payment is to be made at once. The deed is then to be delivered within a reasonable time; that is, so soon as it can conveniently be made.

§ 770. But if there be redemption, then the ordinary and most general practice is to give the buyer a certificate of sale showing his right to a deed at the end of the redemption term, if the land be not redeemed.[8]

[1] Matthews v. Clifton, 13 S. & M. 330; Elcringer v. Moriarty, 10 Iowa, 78; Brooks v. Ratcliff, 11 Ired, 321; Carter v. Spencer, 7 Ired, 14.

[2] McClure v. Englehart, 17 Ill. 47; Summers v. Palmer, 10 Rich. 38; Elcringer v. Moriarty, 10 Iowa, 78; In the matter of Smith, 4 Nev. 254.

[3] Stafford v. Williams, 12 Barb. 240.

[4] McClure v. Englehart, 17 Ill. 47; U. S. Bank v. Voorhees, 1 McLean, 221; In the matter of Smith, 4 Nev. 254.

[5] McCready v. Brisbane, 1 N. & M. 104; Brooks v. Ratcliff, 11 Ired, 321; In the matter of Smith, 4 Nev. 254.

[6] Whipple v. Farrar, 3 Mich. (Gibbs) 436.

[7] Frizzle v. Veach, 1 Dana, 211.

[8] 4 Kent, Com. 431.

§ 771. Where the law calls for such practice, a deed made before the term of redemption expires is void.[1]

§ 772. In Tennessee, however, it is holden that the sheriff may make the deed at once, although there be redemption, and that the purchaser is in the meantime entitled to possession, but must account for rents and profits if the premises are redeemed.[2]

§ 773. But if confirmation is by law required, as is the case in some of the states, then the deed cannot be made under any circumstances until the sale is confirmed, nor can the certificate.[3] In such cases the sale is *quasi* a judicial one.

§ 774. If the plaintiff be the purchaser, he need only pay the costs and fees which are going to others than himself, and may discharge the purchase money by receipting the same on the execution. He is not bound to pay it to the officer unless there be other liens or conflicting claims as to priority.[4]

§ 775. Though the deed be dated anterior to the time at which the right of redemption expires, yet if not delivered until that time, it will be valid. The delivery is the true date, and if the contrary be not shown it is presumed to have been delivered at the proper time.[5]

§ 776. The officer cannot pass the title without actual receipt of the purchase money, as by charging himself with the amount bid.[6]

IV. WHAT PASSES BY IT.

§ 777. Not only the land itself passes by the deed, if valid, but also such covenants of title as run with the land by ordinary conveyance, also pass to the purchaser by the sheriff's deed on execution sale.[7] He gets the whole interest and estate of the

---

[1] Gorham *v.* Wing, 10 Mich. 486; Gross *v.* Fowler, 21 Cal. 392; Bernal *v.* Gliem. 33 Cal. 668.

[2] Burk *v.* Bank of Tennessee, 3 Head. 686.

[3] McBain *v.* McBain, 15 Ohio St. 337.

[4] Fowler *v.* Pearce, 2 Eng. 28.

[5] Warfield *v.* Woodward, 4 G. Greene, 386.

[6] State *v.* Lawson, 11 Ark. 114.

[7] Rawle, Covenants of Title, 344; Laport *v.* Todd, 3 Vroom (N. J.) 124.

execution debtor in the premises, including covenants of title,
if any.[1] If the land be redeemed by the debtor, he is thereby
re-invested with the covenants of title.[2] It is to the interest
of the debtor that the covenants of title should pass. They
enhance the value and are presumed to increase the price at
the sale. Were they not to pass they would become of no
value to the execution debtor, he having no longer any estate
in the land.

§ 778. There is some diversity of opinion as to whether
growing crops will pass to the purchaser at execution sale.
Where lands are sold subject to redemption the question cannot well arise, for the title remaining, as also the possession,
in the defendant during the time allowed to redeem usually
affords to the execution debtor the opportunity of securing his
growing crop, if any there be.

§ 779. In Indiana, where lands are to be appraised and
must bring a certain proportionate part of their appraised
value, when sold on execution, and there being no redemption
from such sales, the question necessarily arises as to the growing crops, and the ruling is that they pass with the land to
the execution purchaser.[3] But, in Ohio, under statutory
regulations nearly similar to those of Indiana in that respect,
it is held that growing crops, inasmuch as they are not
appraised with the land, do not pass with the land by the
execution sale.[4]

§ 780. In Massachusetts it is held that the execution purchaser, if he makes peaceable entry into possession, becomes
entitled to growing crops.[5]

§ 781. The sheriff's deed on execution sale made to satisfy
one or more installments of a judgment debt, discharges the
lien of the subsequent installments and invests the purchaser
with the whole estate. He is presumed to have paid, as the

[1] Rawle, Covenants of Title, 369, 370; White v. Whitney, 3 Met. 81;
Laport v. Todd, 3 Vroom (N. J.) 124.
[2] Rawle, Covenants of Title, 370, 371, n.; White v. Whitney, 3 Met. 81.
[3] Jones v. Thomas, 8 Blackf. 428.
[4] Cassaly v. Rhodes; Houts v. Showalter, 10 Ohio St. 126.
[5] Nichols v. Dewey, 4 Allen, 386.

highest bidder, the full value of the land, and is entitled to hold it clear of the judgment.[1]

§ 782. It was formerly held in Pennsylvania that the sheriff's deed, if there were no express understanding to the contrary, cut off all liens;[2] though in the case cited this is alleged to be a rule of all courts, yet we deem it to have been so only in Pennsylvania, and there it was by statute.[3]

§ 783. To remedy this judicial anomoly, after the case of *Williams v. Norris*, the Pennsylvania act of April, 1830, relative to execution sales, was passed, and the rule in that state now is that such sales are subject to superior liens, except such as the law entitles to participate in the proceeds of sale.[4]

§ 784. These latter, however, are not cut off by the sale, technically speaking, but are to be satisfied in their order of seniority out of the fund arising from the sale.[5]

§ 785. The deed on execution sale of mortgaged premises, on a judgment at law and execution sale, for the mortgage debt, carries only the mortgagor's equity of redemption, and is subject to the mortgage for the rest of the mortgage debt, if sold only for a part.[6]

§ 786. Where judgments are liens the deed of the sheriff relates back to the date of the judgment and carries title from that date against all claims and liens junior thereto.[7]

§ 787. Mere remarks of persons at the sale, not given as notice, will not charge the purchaser.[8] The title passes only by the deed.[9] Until then and the end of the term of redemption the right of the purchaser is held in abeyance, and if there be redemption, may be discharged by payment of the redemption money.[10]

---

[1] Hewson *v.* Dygert, 8 Johns. 333.
[2] Williams *v.* Norris, 2 Rawle, 56; Zeigler's Appeal, 35 Penn. St. 173.
[3] Johnson *v.* Crawley, 25 Geo. 316; Hunter *v.* Watson, 12 Cal. 363.
[4] Helfrich *v.* Weaver, 61 Penn. St. 385.
[5] Ibid.
[6] Jackson *v.* Hall, 10 Johns. 481.
[7] McCormick *v.* McMurtrie, 4 Watts, 192; Martin *v.* Martin, 7 Md. 368.
[8] Ticke *v.* Ersick, 2 Rawle, 166.
[9] Catlin *v.* Jackson, 8 Johns. 520; Anthony *v.* Wessel, 9 Cal. 103.
[10] Vaughn *v.* Eli, 4 Barb. 159; Smith *v.* Colvin, 17 Barb. 157.

§ 788. Though the levy and sale be junior, yet they pass the title if on a senior judgment, as against a senior levy and sale on a junior judgment where judgments are liens.[1]

§ 789. Though the execution sale and deed of the mortgagor's equity of redemption passes the remaining right of the mortgagor,[2] yet if the judgment be not a lien, and before execution the mortgagor convey away his remaining right, or equity of redemption, to a *bona fide* purchaser, then by execution sale thereof against the mortgagor nothing passes, for there was no longer anything to sell.[3]

§ 790. So if the sale purport to be of merely the equity of redemption from a mortgage, and the mortgage is already redeemed, then nothing passes by the sale and sheriff's deed, for nothing remained to sell.[4]

§ 791. If the purchaser takes nothing by his deed, owing to the debtor's having no title, he cannot recover back his money from the creditor, but may, in equity, of the debtor, as the amount went to pay his debt.[5]

§ 792. If the description of the land is such as to not identify it, then the deed is void, and the purchaser takes nothing.[6]

§ 793. The sheriff's deed will not pass the right to a house on the land which another person has a right to take away, if the purchaser buy with knowledge of such right; nor will he be entitled to damages for its removal.[7]

§ 794. Where a vendor sells land on a credit, retaining the legal title until payment, then takes judgment against his vendee for the purchase money, and causes the same land to be levied and sold generally on execution under such judgment, the purchaser at sheriff's sale takes the full legal and equitable title to the land, (unless it be subject to right of

[1] Marshall v. McLean, 3 G. Greene, 363; Rankin v. Scott, 12 Wheat. 177.
[2] Dougherty v. Linthicum, 8 Dana, 194.
[3] Ibid.
[4] Ibid.
[5] Dunn v. Frazier, 8 Blackf. 432.
[6] Mason v. White, 11 Barb. 173; Glenn v. Malony, 4 Iowa, 314; Bosworth c. Farenholtz, 3 Iowa, 84.
[7] Coleman v. Lewis, 27 Penn. St. 291.

redemption) leaving no interest whatever, equitable or legal, in either the original vendor or his vendee.[1]

§ 795. There is a forcible illustration of this principle in the case of *The Pittsburgh and Steubenville Railroad Co. v. Jones,* above cited, in which the court say: "The vendors by proceeding to sell the land under execution issued thereon, elected to sell the legal as well as the Company's equitable estate, and the sale upon the judgment for the purchase money was a virtual recision of the contract."[2] In this case the court add, as a conclusion, that, "the sheriff's vendees, therefore, took the whole estate in the land—the Company's equitable interest under the judgment and execution upon which the sale was made, and the vendor's legal title in virtue of their implied agreement to sell the whole estate which they had agreed to convey to the company. As the sheriff's sale divested the Company's entire equitable estate, it follows that it no longer had any right or interest in the land whatever."[3] And so if a mortgage creditor take judgment at law for the mortgage debt or a part thereof, and cause execution to issue thereon, and the mortgaged premises to be levied and sold, generally, and without stating that the sale is subject to the remainder of the debt and mortgage lien, the execution purchaser takes the whole title both of the mortgagor and the mortgagee, and acquires the property free of the residue of the mortgage debt and free of the mortgage lien.[4]

§ 796. A lien creditor having thus elected to enforce his claim, or a part thereof at law, by taking judgment and causing the land subject to the lien to be sold generally, and without reservation, or as still subject to the lien, and as the property of the debtor, will be, by the principle of estoppel, prevented thereafter from denying that the complete title was in the

---

[1] Pittsburgh and Steubenville Railroad Co. v. Jones, 59 Penn. St. 433, 436, 437.

[2] Pittsburgh and Steubenville Railroad Co. v. Jones, 59 Penn. St. 436-7; Love v. Jones, 4 Watts, 465; Horbach v. Riley, 7 Barr. 81; Bradley v. O'Donnell, 32 Penn. St., 281.

[3] Pittsburgh and Steubenville R. R. Co. v. Jones, 59 Penn. St. 436, 437; Freeby v. Tupper, 15 Ohio, 467.

[4] Fosdick v. Risk, 15 Ohio, 84.

execution defendant at the time of the sale, and estopped from again subjecting to sale for any unsatisfied portion of his claim.[1]

§ 797. But if the vendor, who still retains the legal title, take judgment for the unpaid purchase money, and execute and sell the mere equitable right of the vendee in the premises, the sale will not be void, though the more regular way is to sell the land itself.[2]

§ 798. In Iowa the vendor of real estate, "when part or all of the purchase money remains unpaid after the day fixed for payment whether time is or is not of the essence of the contract, may (by statute) file his petition asking the court to require the purchaser to perform his contract or to foreclose and sell his interest in the property, and the vendee in such proceeding is to be treated as to foreclosure as a mortgagee.[3] And the vendor may have a decree for rescission of the contract, or for a sale of the premises to satisfy the unpaid purchase money and costs of suit. The same right will follow the note given for the purchase money in to the hands of an assignee or endorsee, if transferred with the understanding that the assignee should be subrogated to the benefit of the lien.[4]

§ 799. Where land is sold on execution, subject to a vendor's lien, the purchaser under the execution sale stands in the shoes of the judgment debtor, except that the judgment debtor has a right to redeem from the execution sale. If he fail to do so within the time allowed for redemption by law, then the purchaser may receive the deed of the sheriff and redeem from the lien of the vendor, and thus obtain complete title to the land, free alike from the claims of the original vendor and of the execution debtor.[5]

[1] Simond's Estate, 19 Penn. St. 439; McGee v. Mellon, 23 Miss. 585; Mahoney v. Horan, 53 Barb. 29; Freeby v. Tupper, 15 Ohio, 467; Fosdick v. Risk, 15 Ohio, 84; Pitts. and Steu. R. R. Co. v. Jones, 59 Penn. St. 436; Love v. Jones, 4 Watts, 465; Horbach v. Riley, 7 Barr, 81.

[2] Gaston v. White, 46 Mo. 486.

[4] Revision of 1860, Secs. 3671, 3672; Blair v. Marsh, 8 Iowa, 144; Pierson v. David, 1 Iowa, 84; Page v. Cole, 6 Iowa, 154.

[4] Blair v. Marsh, 8 Iowa, 144.

[5] Bondurant v. Owens, 4 Bush. (Ky.) 662.

§ 800. When husband and wife are seized of lands as tenants of the entirety, a purchaser of the husband's interest therein, under execution at sheriff's sale, cannot, in the state of Pennsylvania, maintain ejectment on his purchase for any part of the property. In the language of the court, such purchaser "does not acquire, during the wife's life, any right to the possession, either jointly with her or to her entire exclusion."[1] The husband and wife as tenants of the entirety are mutually seized of the whole; neither can alienate their interest without the consent of the other.[2] And though the decision in *McCurdy v. Canning* is mainly put upon the Pennsylvania statute of April 11, 1848, yet, to our mind, the same result must follow if the statute be left out of the question. What one cannot sell himself cannot, on execution, be legally sold for his debts.[3] But this case, which so fully illustrates this

[1] McCurdy v. Canning, 64 Penn. St. 39; French v. Mehan, 56 Penn. St. 286.

[2] 2 Bl. Com. 182; 4 Kent, Com. 362.

[3] Gentry v. Wagstaff, 3 Dev. 270; French v. Mehan, 56 Penn. St. 286. THAYER, Judge: "This was an action of ejectment. The defendants, Robert Canning and Eliza, his wife, held under a conveyance in fee made to them during their coverture, and the question is whether the plaintiffs, who were purchasers at sheriff's sale of the husband's interest, can recover possession of any part of the property by this action. If an estate in lands be given to the husband and wife, or a joint purchase be made by them during coverture, they are not properly joint tenants, nor tenants in common, for they are but one person in law, and cannot take by moities, but both are seized of the entirety, *per tout et non per my.* The consequence of which is, that neither the husband or wife can dispose of any part without the assent of the other, but the whole must remain to the survivor. 2 Bl. Com. 182. So long ago as Doe v. Prarratt, 5 T. R. 652, Lord KENYON remarked: 'It has been settled for ages that where a devise is to the husband and wife they take by entireties and not by moities, and the husband alone cannot, by his own conveyance, without joining his wife, divest the estate of the wife.' This species of tenancy arises from the unity of husband and wife, and it applies to an estate in fee for life or for years. The same words of conveyance which would make two other persons joint tenants will make the husband and wife tenants of the entirety. Joint tenants are each seized of the whole and not of undivided moities. Of such an estate MONTAGUE, C. J., says, in Plowden, 58: 'The husband has the entire use and the wife has the entire use, for there are no moities between husband and wife.' The attainder of the husband does not affect the wife's estate. 1 Inst. 187, *a.* Nor can the husband forfeit on

interesting subject, is of sufficient importance to warrant the giving of the opinion of the learned judge at length.

§ 801. The inability of either party to convey without the other joining, has reference to the whole and to each one's moiety of the whole, for each are seized of the whole, which seizin continues in the survivor on the death of either, leaving such survivor the sole owner of the whole fee. Hence a purchase of the separate interest of either vests no right in the purchaser enforceable during the joint lives of the husband and wife, and of course not against the survivor of the execution defend-

alien so as to sever the tenancy, 'because,' as CRUISE says, 'the whole of it belongs to his wife as well as to him.' Tit. 18, ch. 1. Nor is such an estate affected by the statutes of partition. 4 Kent's Com. 363; Thornton v. Thornton, 3 Rand. R. 179. The act of 31st March, 1812, which destroyed survivorship between joint tenants in Pennsylvania, does not apply to entireties held by husband and wife. Robb v. Beaver, 8 W. & S. 111. So that this estate remains as at common law, excepting in so far as it may have been affected by the act of 11th April, 1848, commonly called the Married Woman's Act. It would seem to have followed, at common law, from the unity of husband and wife, and the subjection of the latter to the former, that the husband had the control of the estate during his life and might convey or mortgage it during that period. This is conceded by KENNEDY, J., in Fairchild v. Chastellux, 1 Barr. 181, and decided in Barber v. Harris, 15 Wend. 615; Jackson v. McConnell, 19 id. 175. If the husband might convey or mortgage it for the period of his own life, it would seem to follow necessarily that it might be taken in execution and sold by the sheriff for the same period, and that a purchaser of such an interest would be entitled to recover the possession during the life of the husband by an action of ejectment. But just here the act of 11th April, 1848, interposes an insuperable bar to such a result, declaring that 'every species and description of property, of whatever name or kind, which may accrue to any married woman during coverture, by will, descent, deed of conveyance, or otherwise, shall be owned, used, and enjoyed by such married woman as her own separate property, and shall not be subject to levy and execution for the debts or liabilities of her husband, nor shall such property be sold, conveyed, mortgaged, or transferred, or in any manner incumbered by her husband without her written consent first had and obtained, and duly acknowledged, etc.' The case, therefore, stands thus: Here is a married woman who is neither a joint tenant or tenant in common with the husband, but who is seized of the whole estate, and with him entitled to possession of the whole. If a purchaser of the husband's interest may be put into possession with her, what follows? This: 1st. You have destroyed her estate and turned her entirety into a joint tenancy or tenancy in common. 2d. You have deprived her altogether of

18

ant, whose interest may have sold on execution, as such interest ceases at his death and becomes sole in the survivor.

§ 802.   An easement incident to a mill and to the ground on which the mill is situated, for the supply of water to the mill, is in connection with the mill and premises a subject of judgment lien and of execution sale.   The lien of the judgment covers the land or premises, which, being the principal thing, draws to it all its incidents as appurtenant thereto. They, together, constitute one whole.   They pass together and cannot be separately sold without destruction to a great extent

the possession, because it is not in the nature of things that she can enjoy actual possession with a stranger as she did with her husband. 3d. You have taken away her property without her consent and destroyed her rights, which were protected by the act of April 11th, 1848. She was entitled to possession of the whole with her husband. You propose to give possession of the whole with a stranger, a possession which she cannot, and which he probably would not, enjoy. If it should be answered that the property may be rented, and a moiety of the rents and profits may be paid to her, that is only to say that you may deprive her of her estate and give her another of inferior value, a substitution which you have no right to propose. The words of the act of 1848 are of so comprehensive a character, and its purpose to protect every possible interest of the wife is so plain, that we cannot, by any possible construction consistent with the object of the Legislature and the language which they have used, except this interest from its protection. These considerations lead us to the conclusion that one who, without the consent of the wife, purchases the husband's interest in real estate in which both husband and wife are seized of the entirety, and to the possession of the whole of which she is entitled equally with him, does not acquire, during the wife's life, any right to the possession, either jointly with her or to her entire exclusion. Practically these two propositions are not alternatives, but the same, for we can as easily marry her to a stranger as marry her possession to his without destroying her estate. The case of Stoehler v. Knerr, Watts, 181, is not in conflict with these views. The point to be determined here did not arise in that case, which was decided twelve years before the passage of the Married Woman's Act. In that case the husband and wife did not hold by entireties. There was an absolute conveyance in fee simple to the husband, coupled with a contemporaneous agreement, the intent of which was to control the conveyance and to give the estate jointly to the daughter of the donor and her husband in special tail, but it failed for want of apt words to accomplish the result, and it was held that the whole estate was in the husband for life, and that his freehold was a legitimate subject of execution. Judgment for the defendant on the point reserved." McCurdy v. Canning, 64 Penn.

of the lien security of the creditor, and at the same time sacrificing the property of the debtor. They are rightfully sold together, and together will pass to the purchaser, without particular reference to the easement, and under the general description of the premises by metes and bounds.[1]

V. Its Recitals.

§ 803. The deed of the sheriff need not recite the execution or other proceedings. It is sufficient that they be referred to and identified; and then if inaccurately, such inaccuracy will not vitiate the deed. The variance is immaterial so long as the origin of the deed is clearly traceable to a proper source. Such irregularity can work no injury to the parties concerned.[2]

§ 804. The recitals of the deed are ordinarily *prima facie* true, so far as relate to the steps taken by the officer, and as to the authority to levy and sell.[3]

§ 805. It has been held that in their absence, proof of notice of sale must be made to enable the purchaser to enforce the deed.[4] But the general rule is to the contrary.[5]

§ 806. In some states the recitals in the sheriff's deed are evidence by statute.[6] But if the judgment be not referred to in the recitals, then to enforce the deed the existence of the judgment must be made to appear by other evidence.[7]

[1] Morgan v. Mason, 20 Ohio, 401.

[2] Humphry v. Beeson, 1 G. Greene, 199, 214; Perkins v. Dibble, 10 Ohio, 433; Armstrong v. McCoy, 8 Ham. 128; Huggins v. Ketchum, 4 Dev. and Batt. 414; Cherry v. Woodlard, 1 Ired. 438; Driver v. Spence, 1 Ala. 540; Jackson v. Jones, 9 Cow. 182; Sneed v. Reardon, 1 A. K. Marsh, 217; Jackson v. Streeter, 5 Cow. 529; Welsh v. Joy, 13 Pick. 477; Craig v. Vance, 1 Overt. 209; Jackson v. Pratt, 10 Johns. 381; McGuire v. Kouns, 7 Monr. 386; Read v. Heasley, 9 Dana. 324; Wing v. Burgess, 13 Maine, 111; Philips v. Coffee, 17 Ill. 154; Jackson v. Roberts, 7 Wend. 83; Harrison v. Maxwell, 2 N. & M. 347; Hines v. Scott, 11 Penn. St. 19; Loomis v. Riley, 24 Ill. 307; Buchanan v. Tracy 45 Mo. 437.

[3] Orsborne v. Tunis, 1 Dutch. 633, 662; Hardin v. Cheek, 3 Jones. Law. (N. C.) 135; Kelly v. Green, 53 Penn. St. 302.

[4] Orsborne v. Tunis, 1 Dutch. 633, 662.

[5] Perkins v. Dibble, 10 Ohio, 433.

[6] Jourdan v. Bradshaw, 17 Ark. 106.

[7] Jourdan v. Bradshaw, 17 Ark. 106; Bettison v. Budd, 17 Ark. 546.

§ 807. In California the recitals in the deed are not evidence of their own truth as against strangers to the proceedings claiming adversely thereto.[1]

§ 808. In Illinois a misrecital of the name of the judgment plaintiff, as *John* H., for *Jacob* H., is fatal to the deed without more; but is holden to be open to remedy by other proof, showing the variance to be matter of mistake.[2]

VI. Its Relation.

§ 809. Where by law the judgment is a lien on the land, the deed, on execution sale has relation back to the time of the judgment, so as to avoid, as against the execution purchaser, all intermediate liens and alienations.[3]

§ 810. Where the judgment is not a lien, and there has been no attachment of the property sold on execution the deed relates back only to the levy,[4] or to the test;[5] or, as in some of the states, to the delivery of the execution to the officer,[6] as may be regulated by the local authority of the several states wherein there is not a judgment lien. The rulings in several of these, as will be seen by the above references are variant. But if the proceedings were by attachment, then the relation will be to the date of the attachment and levy, in some cases from delivery to the officer.[7]

§ 811. In Illinois there is a statute requiring a certificate of levy to be filed in the recorder's office in the county where the lands levied on lie whenever levy is made by the sheriff of an execution emenating from a different county, and making

[1] Donahue v. McNulty, 24 Cal. 411.

[2] Johnson v. Adleman, 35 Ill. 265.

[3] Bac. Abt. Execution, 725; McCormack v. McMurtrie, 4 Watts, 192; Smith v. Allen, 1 Blackf. 22; Riddle v. Bryan, 5 Ohio, 48,55; Kirk v. Vonberg, 34 Ill. 440, 448.

[4] Reichart v. McClure, 23 Ill. 516; McClure v. Englehard, 17 Ill. 47.

[5] Winstead v. Winstead, 1 Hayw. 243; McLain v. Upchurch, 2 Morph. 353; Gilky v. Dickenson. 2 Hawks, 341; Lewis v. Smith, 2 S. & R. 157.

[6] Savage v. Best, 3 How. 111; Bank U.S. v. Tyler, 4 Pet. 366, 383; Million v. Riley, 1 Dana, 360.

[7] Shirk v. Wilson, 13 Ind. 129; Cockney v. Milne, 16 Md. 200; McMillan v. Parsons, 7 Jones, Law. (N. C.) 163.

such certificate where filed notice of such levy to all subsequent purchasers, and declaring that before such certificate is so filed the levy shall be of no effect as to subsequent creditors and *bona fide* purchasers. But if such certificate be filed, then a sheriff's deed on execution sale under such levy bears relation as to title to the date on which such certificate is filed.[1]

VII. PRIORITY.

§ 812. In *Rankin v. Scott*, the Supreme Court of the United States, (MARSHALL, Justice,) say: "The principle is believed to be universal that a prior lien gives a prior claim, which is entitled to prior satisfaction out of the subject it binds, unless the lien be intrinsically defective, or be displaced by some act of the party holding it which shall postpone him in a court of law or equity to a subsequent claim."

§ 813. Therefore it follows from this, as was holden in that case, that a junior sheriff's sale and deed on an execution from a senior judgment, where judgments are liens, gives title to the purchaser against a senior execution sale and deed, on a junior judgment.[2]

§ 814. The rule is not only "universal," but is as old as the law of liens itself, and is inseparately an essential part of it. Priority is the very essence of the lien, and is its primary object.

§ 815. It is holden by many authorities, that where the plaintiff in execution becomes the purchaser, he will not be protected against an unrecorded deed from the debtor for the same land older than his lien, as for want of notice of such deed, for that he has parted with no money, but merely receipted the writ. Whereas, as is alleged, to place himself in the position of *bona fide* purchaser he must have actually made payment.[3] But even the ground of this reasoning is untrue

[1] McClure v. Englehart, 17 Ill. 47.

[2] Rankin v. Scott, 12 Wheat. 177; Kirk v. Vonberg, 34 Ill. 440; Rogers v. Dickey, 1 Gilm. 636; Marshall v. McLean, 3 G. Greene, 363.

[3] Williams v. Hollinsworth, 1 Strob. Eq. 103; Freeman v. Hill, 1 Dev. & Batt. Eq. 389; Polk v. Gallant, ib. 395; Rutherford v. Greed, 3 Ired. E. 1222; Freeman v. Mebane, 2 Jones Eq. 44.

in part, for he must at all events pay money in discharge of costs and charges of sale.

§ 816. Under the statute of Iowa, declaring that "no instrument affecting real estate is of any validity against subsequent purchasers for a valuable consideration without notice, unless recorded in the office of the recorder of deeds of the county in which the land lies,"[1] it is holden that a *bona fide* purchaser at sheriff's sale of lands takes the property discharged in law, of all equities arising under a unrecorded deed of which he had no notice; and that a judgment creditor who buys in good faith at such a sale, is a *bona fide* purchaser in that respect, and so is made other of the states.[2] Not so, however, if the purchase in some with notice of the deed.[3]

§ 817. Though there is a conflict in the rulings on this subject, more especially in reference to registry acts in some of the states, yet the weight of authority is that third persons, *bona fide* purchasers at sheriff's sale, who have paid the purchase money without notice of an unrecorded deed, or equity, will be protected against the same.[4] Latterly, decisions have gone far towards extending the same rule to purchases by execution plaintiffs. In *Walker v. Elston*, the supreme court of Iowa adjudge the same protection at law to such purchasers as to third persons, and say, "the only question presented by the foregoing facts is, whether a judgment creditor purchasing at sheriff's sale takes, as in this case the lot of ground dis-

---

[1] Revision of 1860, sec 2220.

[2] Walker v. Elston, 21 Iowa, 529; Butterfield v. Walsh, 21 Iowa, 97; Vance v. Bergen, 16 Iowa, 555; Evans v. McGlosson, 18 Iowa, 150; Bounton v. Winslow, 37 Penn. St. 315.

[3] Hoy v. Allen, 27 Iowa, 208.

[4] Leading Cas. in Eq. Pt. 1, 75; Jackson v. Chamberlain, 8 Wend. 620. Parker v. Pierce, 16 Iowa, 243; Waldo v. Russell, 5 Mo. 387; Deun v. Rickman, 1 Green, 43; Scribner v. Lockwood, 9 Ohio, 184; Ins. Co. v. Ledyard, 8 Ala. 866; Orth v. Jennings, 8 Blackf. 420; Mann's. Appeal, 1 Barr. 24: Heister v. Foster, 2 Bin. 40; Woods v. Chapin, 3 Kern. 509; Williams v. Janson, 5 Harris, 467; Walker v. Elston, 21 Iowa, 529; Butterfield v. Welch, 21 Iowa, 97; Vanice v. Berger, 16 Iowa, 555; Evan v. Glasson, 18 Iowa. 150; Norton v. Williams, 9 Iowa, 529; Massey v. Westcott, 40 Ill. 160; Fosdick v. Barr, 3 Ohio St. 471; Stewart v. Freeman, 22 Penn. St. 120; Goup v. Gartier, 35 Penn. St. 130; McFadden v. Worthington, 45 Ill. 368.

charged of all equities arising under an unrecorded deed of which he had no notice actual or constructive at the time of the purchase. We have several times held that he did, and would be protected as an ordinary *bona fide* purchaser under section 2220 of the revision."[1]

§ 818. But the mere *lien*[2] of a judgment will not in itself, before sale, override a prior unrecorded deed of conveyance or mortgage, so as to confer title on an execution purchaser, who afterwards buys under it with notice thereof, actual or constructive.[3] If the deed or mortgage be recorded before sale the purchaser will be legally affected with notice.[4]

§ 819. Where a judgment is rendered against a mortgage debtor subsequent to the date of the mortgage deed, and such mortgage deed is regularly executed and recorded prior to execution sale upon the judgment, a purchaser at the execution sale takes nothing but the debtor's mere right of redemption from the mortgage; and such, too, is the general rule, though the mortgage deed be not recorded; *provided* the purchaser at the execution sale *has notice* of the mortgage.[5]

[1] Walker v. Elston, 21 Iowa, 531; Massey v. Westcott, 40 Ill. 160; Evans v. McGlasson, 18 Iowa, 151.

[2] For a lien is not an *interest in* the property. It is merely a right to make the money out of it; until enforced by sale and deed no control exists over the property in the owner of the judgment lien. Conrad v. Atlantic Ins. Co. 1 Pet. 448; Miller v. Sherry, 2 Wall. 244.

[3] As is said by THOMPSON, Justice, in Grenemeyer v. Southern Mutual Insurance Company: "A judgment is not a general and not a specific lien. If there be personal property of the debtor it is to be satisfied out of that. If there be not, then it is a lien on all his real estate without discrimination, and hence the plaintiff is not interested in the property as property, but only in his *lien*. The judgment creditor has neither *jus in re* nor *ad rem*, as regards the defendant's property. He has a *lien*, and the law gives a right to satisfaction out of the property, and that is all." (62 Penn. St. 342.) See, also, Conrad v. Atlantic Ins. Co. 1 Pet. 384; Kemper v. Bavey, 5 McLean, 507; Schaffer v. Cadwallader, 12 Casey, 126; Thelusson v. Smith, 2 Wheat. 396.

[4] Chipman v. Coats, 26 Iowa; Valintine v. Havener, 20 Mo. 133, 288; Norton v. Williams, 9 Iowa, 528; Parker v. Pierse, 16 Iowa, 227; Bell v. Evans, 10 Iowa, 353; Welton v. Tizzard, 15 Iowa, 495; Evans v. McGlasson, 18 Iowa, 151; Hoy v. Allen, 27 Iowa, 208; Potter v. McDowell, 43 Mo. 93; Thomas v. Kennedy, 24 Iowa, 397.

[5] Hubble v. Vaughn, 42 Mo. 138.

§ 820. But if there be nothing of record to show a prior mortgage or other conveyance by the judgment debtor older than the judgment at the time of execution sale and payment of the purchase money, and the purchaser is without notice of such prior mortgage or deed, then the purchase under sheriff sale prevails against such prior conveyance.[1]

§ 821. In Ohio, however, under the statute of Feb. 22, 1831, which gives force, as between the mortgagee and third persons, to mortgages only from the time they are recorded, it is holden that a purchaser under execution sales, though buying with knowledge of an older unrecorded mortgage, and though he be the plaintiff in execution, takes a title to the land that overrides the lien of an unrecorded mortgage or assignment to secure a *bona fide* debt; and this, too, where the judgment was junior in date to the assignment or mortgage deed.

§ 822. The Ohio courts hold "that such unrecorded instruments are good and effectual between the parties, but entirely nugatory as to third parties, both at law and in equity, until they are recorded." The same ruling exists in Ohio as between two mortgages where one is recorded and the other not. The first of record has priority.[2]

---

[1] Massey v. Westcott, 40 Illinois, 160. In this case, involving a purchase by judgment creditor, the supreme court of Illinois say: "Under our statutes a purchaser and a judgment creditor having a lien, stand upon the same equity, and this has been so held ever since the act of 1833, and the case of Martin v. Dryden, 1 Gilm. 216. The same remark applies to another point made by appellant's counsel, to wit: That the lien of a judgment attaches only to whatever interest in the land the judgment debtor may, in fact, have, and does not take precedence of a prior purchaser claiming under an unrecorded deed. This has been so held in some of the states, but under our act of 1833, *it is the settled law of this state* that a judgment lien attaches to whatever interest in real estate the records disclose in the judgment debtor, in the absence of actual notice from other sources." Massey v. Westcott, 40 Ill. 163.

[2] Fosdick v. Barr, 3 Ohio St. 471, 575; Holloday v. The Franklin Bank, 16 Ohio, 533; White v. Denman, 16 Ohio, 59; Jackson v. Luce, 14 Ohio, 514; Mayham v. Coombs, 14 Ohio, 428; Stancel v. Roberts, 13 Ohio, 148. Before the recording act of 1831, the recording of mortgages was placed on the same footing as absolute deeds; hence the rulings were different. Fosdick v. Barr, above cited; White v. Denman, 1 Ohio St. 110; Stancel v Roberts, 13 Ohio, 148.

§ 823. In Ohio the rights of an execution purchaser at sheriff's sale, bear relation by statute as against a dormant or unrecorded equity to the date of the sheriff's sale, and the deed, when executed, confers title as against all such equities from the date of the sale and not from its own date; therefore, where such equity is unknown to the purchaser at the time of the execution sale, his deed from the sheriff, though of subsequent date, will override such equity, although notice thereof be imparted to the purchaser after the day of sale and before the delivery of the deed to him by the sheriff. The court say: "The deed executed at a subsequent date has relation back to that date, and is as effectual as if then made."[1]

§ 824. An execution purchaser who has not paid the purchase money is not a *bona fide* purchaser.[2]

§ 825. But when the purchase money is paid, the sale will confer a prior equity over an assignment of the land to a creditor to secure a prior debt, though the assignment be anterior in date to the judgment.[3]

§ 826. As between executions emanating from several lien judgments of even date, the writ first levied is holden to obtain priority.[4] So, as a sequence, if the judgments be not liens.[5]

§ 827. When an execution purchaser buys land subject to a mortgage debt, and afterwards sells and conveys the same to a grantee, who takes with knowledge of the mortgage and who retains out of the purchase money a sum sufficient to discharge the mortgage, with a view to meet the same and protect himself against it by paying it off, he is thereby estopped to deny that the execution sale was made subject to the mortgage debt.[6]

§ 828. And in the same state a *bona fide* purchaser at

[1] Oviatt v. Brown, 14 Ohio, 285.
[2] Swazey v. Burke, 12 Pet. 11.
[3] Fosdick v. Barr, 3 Ohio St. 471; Stewart v. Freeman, 22 Penn. St. 120.
[4] Rockhill v. Hanna, 15 How. 189; Adams v. Dyer, 8 Johns. 350; Waterman v. Haskins, 11 Johns. 228; Bruce v. Vogle, 38 Mo. 100.
[5] Lathrop v. Brown, 23 Iowa, 40.
Crooks v. Douglass, 56 Penn. St. 51.

sheriff's sale, on a junior judgment, will take priority over the lien of an older judgment marked of record "satisfied," although not satisfied in point of fact. The record, as to the subsequent execution purchaser, is verity.[1]

§ 829. If two mortgages be given for the purchase money of lands in one of the same transaction, and of one date, both being recorded on the same day and within the time required by law, their equities are equal and their liens are cotemporaneous; no priority is gained by either over the other. A sheriff's sale of the whole property on either extinguishes the other.[2]

§ 830. But if one of the mortgages, though expressed to be for a part of the purchase money, be in reality the fruits of a different transaction, then it will become secondary to the other in point of priority, and a sheriff's sale in foreclosure of the same will not divest or extinguish the other.

§ 831. A sheriff's deed for lands on execution sales, in Pennsylvania, comes within the registry acts, and is overreached by a deed for the same lands executed by the debtor in Ohio, according to the laws of Pennsylvania, and recorded in the latter state within the time allowed for recording foreign deeds, although the judgment under which the sale by the sheriff was made was rendered before the recording of the deed made in Ohio, and although the sheriff's deed was recorded within the time allowed by the laws of Pennsylvania for recording domestic deeds.

§ 832. The deed of the debtor made in Ohio prior to the rendition of the judgment in Pennsylvania left no interest in the land in the debtor to which the judgment lien could attach.[3] The estate had passed out of the judgment debtor

[1] Coyne v. Souther, 61 Penn. St. 455, 458.
[2] Duncan v. American Life Ins. Co. 52 Penn. St. 253, 256. In the case above cited from 52 Penn. St. the court hold this language: "And the doctrine is unquestionably true that if purchase money be secured by two mortgages, and both are recorded on the same day, and within sixty days of their date, their liens are contemporaneous, and no priority of one over the other can be predicated; and, of course, a sheriff's sale on either divests the other."
[3] Hultz v. Hackley, 63 Penn. St. 142, 144. The court, in this case, say:

to his grantee by deed, and this deed being recorded in due time was not fraudulent as to the execution purchaser.

VIII. Registration.

§ 833. Sheriff's deeds, on execution sales, are within the provisions of recording acts.[1] The purchaser is bound by and entitled to claim all the provisions thereof.[2] Therefore, in those states where priority in recording gives priority of title, an execution purchaser who first records his deed, within the law, gains thereby the same preference as if the deed was from the debtor himself.[3]

§ 834. Such purchaser is no more chargeable by a deed

"As it (the deed made in Ohio) was made and delivered before the recovery of the plaintiff's judgment, it vested in the grantee a valid and absolute title to the lot, which was not affected by the judgment, for, at the time of its recovery, the grantor had no interest in the premises to which its lien could attach, and consequently no title passed to the plaintiff under the sheriff's sale. It still remains in the grantee unless he has lost it, as contended, by his laches in not recording his deed within the time allowed by law, in order to render it valid and operative against the plaintiff. As a sheriff's vendee is a purchaser for a valuable consideration within the meaning of the recording acts, he is protected by them. If, therefore, the defendant failed to record his deed in proper time, it must be adjudged fraudulent and void against the subsequent deed of the sheriff under which the plaintiff claims, and which was registered in the prothonotary's office before the defendant's deed was recorded. If the defendant's deed had been executed and acknowledged within the state, then under the provisions of the first section of the recording act of 18th March, 1775, it would have been his duty to record it within six months after its execution, and the omission would have rendered it fraudulent and void as against the plaintiff. But as we have seen his deed was executed and acknowledged in Ohio, and if it is governed by the second section of the act, he had twelve months within which to record it before incurring the penalty of having it adjudged fraudulent and void against a subsequent purchaser whose deed might be first recorded."

[1] Hoosier v. Hall, 2 Carter, 556; 3 Bouvier, 58, n.; Massey v. Thompson, 2 N. & M. 347; Jackson v. Terry, 13 Johns. 471; Lessee of Wallace v. Lawrence, 1 Wash. C. C. R. 503; Walker & Elston v. Green, 21 Iowa, 529, Hultz v. Hackly, 63 Penn. St. 142, 144; Jackson v. Post, 15 Wend. 588.

[2] Hoosier v. Hall, 2 Carter, 556; Potter v. McDowell, 43 Mo. 93; Massey v. Wescott, 40 Ill. 160; Goup v. Gartier, 35 Penn. St. 130.

[3] Ellis v. Smith, 10 Geo. 253; Jackson v. Post, 15 Wend. 588; Jackson v. Chamberlain, 8 Wend. 620; Jackson v. Terry, 13 Johns. 471.

imperfectly recorded than he would be if the deed were not recorded at all.[1]

§ 835. By the laws of Iowa, § 1947 of the Revision, a purchaser at execution sale is required to record his deed within twenty days after the expiration of the time allowed for redemption. The failure to do so, however, will not postpone the deed to the benefit of a junior purchaser who buys with notice of the deed. In *Harrison v. Kramer*,[2] the Supreme Court, WRIGHT, Justice, say: " However much this section might operate to protect a *bona fide* purchaser without notice, who might take title after the twenty days therein named, it certainly cannot protect one who purchased with actual notice of the rights of the purchaser under the execution, or one who purchases with a fraudulent intention to defeat the execution purchaser's title." This statute was not designed to protect fraud, nor as a penalty against a failure to record, but to protect the innocent. A purchaser with notice of prior right in another is not innocent in that respect.

IX. COLLATERAL IMPEACHMENT.

§ 836. A sheriff's deed on execution sale, to a *bona fide* purchaser, if regular in itself, cannot be impeached collaterally in a collateral proceeding for mere error or irregularity in the proceedings, judgment, execution, or return, or for want of a return, if there be a valid judgment and execution.[3] Nor for

---

[1] Goup v. Gartier, 85 Penn. St. 130.

[2] Harrison v. Kramer, 3 Iowa, 543.

[3] Landes v. Brant, 10 How. 371; Landes v. Perkins, 12 Mo. 254; Jackson v. Bartlett, 8 Johns. 361; Jackson v. Rosevelt, 13 Johns. 97; Ware v. Bradford, 2 Ala. 676; Love v. Powell, 5 Ala. 58; Hubert v. McCullum, 6 Ala. 221; Cockerell v. Wynn, 12 S. & M. 117; Davis v. Wornack, 8 B. Mon. 383; Huluph v. Beeson, 1 Iowa, (Green,) 199; Draper v. Bryson, 17 Mo. (2 Bennett,) 261; Thompson v. Philips, 1 Bald. C. C. 246; Ashby v. Abney, 1 Hill, (S. C.) 380; Dew v. Wright, 1 Pet. C. C. 64; Wood v. Colvin, 5 Hill, 231; Hines v. Scott, 11 Penn. St. 19; Maurior v. Coon, 16 Wis. 465; Bowen v. Bell, 20 Johns. 338; Lessee of Wilson v. McVeagh, 2 Yates, 86; Wilson & Gibbs v. Corine, 2 Johns. 280; Vance v. Readdon, 2 N. & M. 299; Morrison v. Dent, 1 Mo. 246; Dew v. Despeaux, 7 Halst. 182; Dew v. Farley, 7 Halst. 326; Dew v. Moore, 7 Halst. 331; Weyand v. Tipton, 5 Sergt. & R. 332; Clark v. Lockwood, 21 Cal. 220; Hendrickson v. R. R. Co. 34 Mo. 188;

the reason that the appraisers, where the sale is under the appraisement law, acted without seeing the land.[1] Nor by parole evidence that the execution on which the sale was made was withdrawn, or that the levy had been abandoned before the sale.[2] Nor for the execution having issued out of season, or for any fault of the sheriff in not following the statute, if the court has jurisdiction of the case from which the execution emanated.[3] Nor by failure of the sheriff to advertise, if the purchaser be a *bona fide* one.[4]

§ 837. In *Hubbard v. Barnes,* 29th Iowa, the court held that a sale of lands situate in one county, on an execution issued on a judgment in a different county, was valid as between the execution plaintiff and debtor, as also against a subsequent purchaser under the execution debtor with notice thereof, although a transcript of the judgment had not been filed as is by the statute provided, (Secs. 3248, 3249,) in the county where the lands were situate previous to the levy and sale. The court held that though the judgment could not become a lien on such lands without the filing of the transcript, and though the judgment and sale together would not be noted without such transcript which would be implied in law; that nevertheless actual notice of such judgment, execution and sale to a subsequent purchaser under the execution debtor serves in that respect in the stead of such filing of a transcript,

Cox v. Joiner, 4 Bibb. 94; Furguson v. Miles, 3 Gilm. 358; Sexton v. Wheaton, 4 Wheat. 503; Durham v. Eaton, 28 Ill. 264; Jackson v. Roosevelt, 13 Johns. 97; Lovell v. Powell, 5 Ala. 58; Ware v. Bradford, 2 Ala. 676; Stow v. Steele, 45 Ill. 328; Kinney v. Knoeble, 47 Ill. 417; Armstrong v. Jackson, 1 Blackf. 210; Hinds v. Scott, 11 Penn. St. 1; Anderson v. Clarke, 2 Swan, (Penn.) 156; Dunn v. Merriweather, 1 Marsh. 158; Martin v. McCargo, 5 Litt. 293; Smith v. Morrison, 1 Mon. 154; Riggs v. Dooley, 7 B. Mon. 239; Wilson v. McGee, 2 Marsh. 602; Childs v. McChesney, 20 Iowa, 431; Willard v. Whipple, 40 Vt. 219; Philips v. Coffee, 17 Ill. 154; Bunton v. Emerson, 4 G. Greene, 397.

[1] Jackson v. Vanderheyden, 17 Johns. 167.
[2] Jackson v. Vanderheyden, 17 Johns. 167.
[3] Armstrong v. Jackson, 1 Blackf. 210; Thompson v. Tolmie, 2 Pet. 157; Henry v. Ferguson, 1 Bailey, 512; Barkley v. Screven, 1 N. & M. 408, Hubbard v. Barnes, 29 Iowa, 289.
[4] Lawrence v. Speed, 2 Bibb. 101.

and renders the execution sale valid.[1] Of said section 3249 the court say: BECK, Justice, its provisions "are directory only, and compliance therewith is not necessary to authorize the service of an execution in a county other than the one where the judgment was rendered." That if there be not such compliance, then there will be "no record notice of the levy and sale," and "neither will a judgment be a lien upon lands" situate in such other county; that although "in such case the law will raise no presumption of notice of sale," yet "actual notice" "will supply the want of record notice, or, rather, the existence of actual notice, the very end aimed at by the statutory provisions above quoted will supercede the necessity of the record;" and that the deed on the sheriff's sale "will be held valid as to all having actual notice thereof."[2]

§ 838. In New Jersey it is held that evidence may not be received to invalidate an execution sale by showing satisfaction of the judgment.[3] Nor will omission to endorse the writ repleviable, nor omission of the notice of sale to defendant required by the statute render the sale invalid.[4]

§ 839. In Mississippi the ruling is that issuing execution and selling after the death of defendant is merely an irregularity and does not affect the sale when brought up collaterally.[5]

§ 840. Though the deed may be made to a person other than the purchaser, at the purchaser's request, and will in that respect be valid;[6] yet, if so made without authority to one not entitled to have it, such fact may be shown according to the ruling in South Carolina, and will avoid the deed.[7]

§ 841. But the evidence of the officer who made it is not allowable to alter, vary, or contradict the deed itself, or the legal effect thereof.[8]

---

[1] Hubbard v. Barnes, 29 Iowa, 239, 242.

[2] Hubbard v. Barnes, 29 Iowa, 242.

[3] Nichols v. Disner, 5 Dutch, (N. J.) 293.

[4] Elinger v. Moriaty, 10 Iowa, 78.

[5] Harper v. Hill, 35 Miss. 63; but see to the contrary, Erwin v. Dundas, 4 How. 58.

[6] Landrum v. Hatcher, 11 Rich. Law. (S. C.) 54.

[7] Ib.

[8] Donahue v. McNulty, 24 Cal. 411.

§ 842. And though not impeachable collaterally for mere error or irregularity in the proceedings and judgment, if there be a valid judgment and execution, yet where a seal is required to deeds, and the instrument or deed is not sealed it will be void.[1]

X. ESTOPPEL.

§ 843. The defendant in execution is estopped by the sheriff's deed to deny title in himself at date of sale to the lands sold. So from date of levy if the judgment be not a lien; and from the date of the judgment where judgments are liens; and he cannot set up an outstanding title to avoid the sheriff's sale.[2]

§ 844. This disability cannot be evaded by going out of possession after the sale and re-entering under color of an alleged better title any more than if the deed be made by himself.[3]

§ 845. In the case cited from 3 Washington C. C. the court, WASHINGTON, Justice, state the rule in terms as follows: "The cases cited by the plaintiff's counsel are full to the point, that the purchaser under an execution in an ejectment against the defendant in the execution, or one claiming under him, need not show any other title than a judgment, execution and sheriff's deed; and that the defendant will not be permitted to controvert such title by showing it to be defective, or by setting up a better outstanding in a third person."[4]

§ 846. But this rule will not apply in a case of a bare claim to sell without foundation where the execution debtor has neither title nor possession, and does not direct the levy and sale of it as his property.[5]

§ 847. Nor is the execution debtor estopped to deny title in himself in lands sold under a *void* execution, although he direct the sale; for such execution and sale being both void

[1] Moore v. Detchmandry, 11 Mo, 431; Morsan v. Branham, 27 Mo. 351.

[2] Cooper v. Galbraith, 3 Wash. C. C. 550; O'Neal v. Duncan, 4 McCord, 246.

[3] Cooper v. Galbraith, 3 Wash. C. C. 550; Jackson v. Bush. 10 Johns. 223.

[4] Cooper v. Galbraith, 3 Wash. C. C. 550.

[5] Hagaman v. Jackson, 1 Wend. 502.

there is no authority for the sale to impart validity to the estoppel.[1]

§ 848. As against a purchaser at execution sale, the debtor is estopped to deny his ownership of that which he directs the officer to levy and sell. So also so, as to those claiming under such purchaser.[2] This doctrine is asserted in *Major v. Deer*, by the supreme court of Kentucky in the following terms: " When the land is sold at the instance, or with the assent, express or presumed, of the defendant, as he is benefited by it, he should be bound by it, as his own voluntary act; and therefore should not be permitted to deny that the purchaser acquired any title."[3]

§ 849. Though ordinarily the statute of frauds will cut off a parole authority to sell real estate, yet when there is legal power to sell and convey without it, then such parole expression of a preference as to the property to be sold will be valid.

[1] Gogeyan v. Ditto, 2 Met. (Ky.) 433.
[2] Read v. Heasley, 2 B. Mon. 254.
[3] Major v. Deer, 4 J. J. Marsh. 585; Read v. Heasley, 2 B. Mon. 254.

CHAPTER XIX.

SETTING SALE ASIDE.

I. POWER OF THE COURT TO SET SALE ASIDE.

§ 850. The court upon whose judgment the execution issues has full power to set aside an execution sale whenever the ends of justice and fair dealing require it, and to order a re-sale, or award execution anew, at discretion.[1]

§ 851. This principle is aptly illustrated, in few words, in *McLean County Bank v. Flagg*,[2] by the Supreme Court of Illinois: "The power over its own process is possessed by all courts. Such power is a species of equitable jurisdiction that is inherent in courts of law as well as those of equity. This court has repeatedly held, as between the purchaser and the original parties to the suit, that a court of law will not hesitate to exercise the power of setting a sale aside on account of fraud or irregularity."

§ 852. The application to set a sale aside should ordinarily be made first by motion to the same court from whence the process of execution issued;[3] and must be made within a reasonable time, unless there be circumstances to excuse delay.[4]

§ 853. It has been held that (if made by motion) it should

---

[1] Draine v. Smelser, 15 Ala. 423; Reed v. Diven, 7 Ind. 189; Nelson v. Bowen, 23 Mo. 13; Cummings' Appeal, 23 Penn. St. 509; Jones v. R. R. Co. 32 N. H. 544; Davis v. Campbell, 12 Ind. 192; Hayden v. Dunlap, 3 Bibb. 216.

[2] 31 Ill. 295.

[3] Prather v. Hill, 36 Ill. 402.

[4] Prather v. Hill, 36 Ill. 402; Stewart v. Marshall, 4 G. Greene (Iowa) 75.

be made within the time allowed by law for redemption;[1] but at all events it should be before the intervention of intermediate rights of third persons,[2] and we may add before barred by lapse of time.

II. FOR INADEQUACY OF PRICE.

§ 854. Ordinarily, inadequacy of price is not alone sufficient cause for setting aside an execution which is in other respects unexceptionable, and when the sale is made to a *bona fide* purchaser.[3]

§ 855. But when the inadequacy is such as to amount to a badge of fraud, or together with other circumstances is such as to shock the moral sense, and particularly when surrounded by indications of hardship and unfairness, the sale will be set aside.[4]

§ 856. And when the price sold for is greatly inadequate, and the notice of sale is indifferently given, or set up at a great distance from the place of sale, or there are other circumstances tending to show that an opportunity was not given for proper competition of bidders, the sale will be set aside.[5]

[1] Raymond v. Pauli, 21 Wis. 531; Stewart v. Marshall, 4 G. Greene, (Iowa) 75.

[2] Prather v. Hill, 36 Ill. 402.

[3] Duncan v. Saunders, 50 Ill. 475; Boyd v. Ellis, 11 Iowa, 97; Coleman v. Bank of Hamburg, 2 Strobh. Eq. 285; Reed v. Brooks, 3 Litt. 127; Wallace v. Berger, 25 Iowa, 456; King v. Tharp, 26 Iowa, 283; Mixer v. Sibley, 53 Ill. 61; Comstock v. Purple, 49 Ill. 158; McMullen v. Gable 47 Ill. 67; Am. Ins. Co. v. Oakley, 9 Paige, 259; Hannibal and St. Joe R. R. Co. v. Brown, 43 Mo. 294.

[4] Boyd v. Ellis, 11 Iowa, 97; Howell v. Baker, 4 Johns. Ch. 119, 120; Gist v. Frazier & Stewart, 2 Litt. 121; Blight v. Tobin, 7 Mon. 616; King v. Tharp, 26 Iowa, 283; Hannibal and St. Joe R. R. Co. v. Brown, 43 Mo. 294; San Francisco v. Pickley, 21 Cal. 56.

[5] Nesbitt v. Dallam, 7 Gill. & J. 494; Swope v. Ardery, 5 Ind. 213, 215; Griffith v. Hadley, 10 Bosw. 587; Hannibal and St. Joe R. R. Co. v. Brown, 43 Mo. 294; Ringold v. Patterson, 15 Ark. 209. In Hannibal and St. Joe R. R. Co. v. Brown, the Supreme Court of Missouri lay down the rule as follows: "It may be stated as a general proposition that inadequacy of consideration is not of itself a distinct principle of relief in equity. Nevertheless, where the transaction discloses such unconscionableness as shocks the moral sense and outrages the conscience, courts will interfere

§ 857. So, when the price sold for is inadequate and the purchaser concealed knowledge which would tend to influence others to bid a greater sum, the sale will be set aside.[1]

§ 858. Likewise, if the plaintiff in execution bid in the property by an oversight for less than his debt, and is willing to bid the full amount thereof, the sale will be set aside, and a re-sale will be ordered on his application.[2]

§ 859. Where at an execution sale there was confusion in bidding by reason of conflicting writs of execution and liens, and also from conditional and unconditional bids being made by one and the same person, having a tendency to confuse and disconcert the officer, and the property sold for a very inadequate sum compared to its real value, the court held that the sale should be set aside.[3] The officer "can receive only an unconditional cash bid." Those accompanied with a condition should not be heeded.[4]

§ 860. If a purchaser at sheriff's sale succeed, by false statements or suggestions, in deterring others from bidding and thereby obtain the property for an inadequate price, the sale will be set aside[5] and a re-sale ordered.

§ 861. But one claiming an interest in lands under an executory contract of sale which is fraudulent as against the creditors of the party thus undertaking to sell, cannot complain that the lands were sold on execution against his intended grantor for an inadequate price as a reason for setting aside the execution sale; nor can the fraudulent claimant of such spurious incipient right set it up against the prior legal title of the execution purchaser procured by means untainted with

to promote the ends of justice and defeat the machinations of fraud. The very fact that upwards of eleven thousand acres of valuable land in one of the best counties in the state was levied on to satisfy an execution of less than one hundred and fifty dollars, is suggestive of the most flagrant abuse of legal process."

[1] Hutchinson v. Moses, 1 Browne, 187.
[2] Ontario Bank v. Lansing, 2 Wend. 260.
[3] Swope v. Ardery, 5 Ind. 213.
[4] Ibid.
[5] Vantrees v. Hyatt, 5 Ind. 487; Bouts v. Cole, 7 Blackf. 265; Bethel v. Sharp, 25 Ill. 173.

fraud. Such fraudulent claim is invalid as against the rights of a *bona fide* purchaser under the execution.[1] For the pretended owner of it the law affords no remedy or day in court. Were it untainted with actual fraud it would still be invalid for want of consideration, as against the *bona fide* creditors of the maker of it.

III. For Misconduct of the Officer Selling.

§ 862. A court has full power over its officers and their acts in making execution sales, so far as to correct all wrongs and abuses, errors and irregularities, mistakes, omissions, and frauds; and whenever it is satisfied that a sale made under its process is affected with fraud, irregularity, or error, to the injury of either party in interest, or that the officer selling is guilty of any wrong, irregularity, or breach of duty, to the injury of the parties in interest, or of either, or of any one of them, the court, on proper application, will set the sale aside and order a re-sale.[2]

§ 863. Though it is the duty of the officer to sell in parcels, or a less parcel than the whole tract, where a less quantity will subserve the purpose of satisfying the execution, yet the subdivision must be discreetly made with a view to the interests of all concerned. Therefore, for an officer to sell a central portion of a tract of land to his own son-in-law, and so taken out of the tract as to greatly impair the value of the residue, and so as to cut off all direct communication between the remaining parcels, is an abuse of the process of the court; such an abuse is the more aggravated if the land be sold for a sum greatly below its true value, and the court will set aside such a

---

[1] Daniel *v.* McHenry, 4 Burk, (Ky.) 277.

[2] Hamilton *v.* Burch, 28 Ind. 233; Lashley *v.* Cassell, 23 Ind. 600; Drain *v.* Smelser, 15 Ala. 423; White Crow *v.* White Wing, 3 Kan. 276; Bentz *v.* Hines, 3 Kan. 390. In Hamilton *v.* Bush, the court say: "Where there is any departure from duty on the part of the sheriff, which may prove injurious to the rights of the execution defendant, in the sale of the property, and the consideration paid is greatly inadequate, the sale will be set aside."

sale, both for the improper conduct of the officer and for inadequacy of price.[1]

IV. For Mistake, Irregularity, and Fraud.

§ 864. A sheriff's sale of land on execution will be set aside for irregularity, fraud, or mistake, or for a willful disregard of the law, as to the manner of selling, whereby an injury results to either party in interest, or to third persons interested *bona fide* in the subject matter of the sale. Such is the general tenor of the authorities on the subject.[2]

§ 865. Thus, the sale on execution of " specific farms and lots of land together," (says Spencer, Justice,) or "sales in mass of real estate held in parcels, are not to be countenanced or tolerated." They are oppressive and unnecessary, even if there be no actual frauds, and will on motion be set aside.[3]

§ 866. So, likewise, if by law the execution plaintiff has the right of election as to what property shall be levied, or the order in which it shall be taken, and is not allowed to exercise that right, the levy in such cases, will be set aside,[4] and so would the sale if made.

§ 867. And so if the sheriff raise by execution sale a greater amount of money than by the writ he is commanded to make, with costs, and the land sold was susceptible of subdivision so as to sell a less quantity and raise the amount only of money required, the sale will be set aside, unless the separation and

[1] Hamilton v. Burch, 28 Ind. 233; Lashley v. Cassell, 23 Ind. 600.
[2] Cattell v. Gilbert, 23 Ind. 614; Vantrees v. Hyatt, 5 Ind. 487; Mobile Cotton Press Co. v. Moore, 9 Port. 679; Myers v. Saunders, 7 Dana, 506; Dougherty v. Linthicum, 8 Dana, 194; Rector v. Hart, 8 Mo. 448; Bay v. Gilleland, 1 Cow. 220; Hayden v. Dunlap, 3 Bibb, 216; Hutchins v. Moses, 1 Browne, 187; Wiggins v. Chance, 54 Ill. 175; Stewart v. Nelson, 25 Mo. 309; Abby v. Dewey, 25 Penn. St. 416; Niel v. Hone, 20 Mo. 296; Hooten v. Himkle, 20 Mo. 290; Stewart v. Severance, 43 Mo. 322; Reed v. Carter, 3 Blackf. 376; Bethel v. Sharp, 25 Ill. 173.
[3] Jackson v. Newton, 18 Johns. 355; Boyd v. Ellis, 11 Iowa, 97; Bradford v. Limpus, 13 Iowa, 424; Patton v. Stewart, 19 Ind. 233; City of San Francisco v. Pirley, 21 Cal. 56; Griffith v. Hadley, 10 Bosw. 587.
[4] Evans v. Langdon, 1 Gilm. 307; Wiggins v. Chance, 54 Ill. 175; Stevenson v. Marony, 29 Ill. 534.

sale of a smaller quantity would have tended to impair the value of the different parts when so separated.[1]

§ 868. The sheriff's deed will not be set aside for being executed by the sheriff's deputy. In *Carr v. Hunt*, the Iowa Supreme Court hold on this subject the following language: "That the sheriff's deed was executed by the deputy of the sheriff is no cause for setting it aside at the instance of the defendant in execution. And then if the deed was set aside the judgment or decree and sale would remain. If the sale was valid, to set aside the deed would accomplish no practical good."

§ 869. The principal, or high sheriff, may execute the deed by his deputy; that is, the deputy may perform the manual act of making it; but it must purport to be the act and deed of the principal by his deputy, and not the act of the deputy. It must be done in the name of the principal officer.[2]

§ 870. If lands consisting of several parcels be levied and sold in the aggregate, the sale will be set aside.[3] This, too, notwithstanding they bring an adequate price, for such manner of selling puts impediments in the way of redemption, as the judgment debtor will be compelled to redeem the whole or none. Moreover, although the price sold for may appear adequate, yet the debtor is entitled to have the property bring all it will command, and *non constat;* but that if offered in parcels the aggregate amount of the sale would have been greater than when sold as a whole.

§ 871. And the court will interfere, if necessary, by injunction to prevent the delivery of the deed by the sheriff where different parcels of land are so sold in the aggregate.[4]

§ 872. If the plaintiff in execution be the purchaser and it turns out that defendant had no interest in the land, so that by the sale plaintiff took nothing, the sale will be set aside and satisfaction of the judgment will be cancelled.[5]

---

[1] Carlisle v. Carlisle, 7 J. J. Marsh. 625.

[2] Carr v. Hunt, 14 Iowa, 206.

[3] Jackson v. Roosevelt, 18 Johns. 255; Piel v. Brayer, 30 Ind. 332; Winters v. Burford, 6 Coldw. (Tenn.) 326; Catlett v. Gilbert, 23 Ind. 614.

[4] Ballance v. Loomis, 22 Ill. 82.

[5] Riter v. Henshaw, 7 Clarke (Iowa) 97; Watson v. Reissig, 24 Ill. 281.

§ 872. The execution sale of lands at a greatly inadequate price, and in mass, by description of the original tract, which had been subdivided into city lots and platted as such on the official map, was set aside as irregular for not having been sold or offered in parcels, as also for inadequacy of price.[1]

§ 873. But in some of the states it is held that, to justify the setting aside a sale for being sold in mass instead of in parcels, it should be made apparent, to the satisfaction of the court, that a materially larger sum would have resulted from the sale if sold in parcels, or else that the sale of less than the whole tract would have brought enough to satisfy the writ.[2]

§ 874. If one, by means of promises of favor, prevents others from bidding for lands at an execution sale, and thereby obtain them himself at an under value, he will not be permitted thus to enrich himself at the expense of others against all the principles of equity and moral propriety. Such a sale will be set aside if a proper application, in proper time, be made.[3]

§ 875. And so, where property was bid in at execution sale at a price greatly above its true value, under the impression and belief of the purchaser and of the officer selling, induced by the defendant in execution that the land covered a factory of considerable value, when, in fact, the premises sold consisted of merely a garden spot of trivial value, the sale was set aside.[4]

§ 876. A charge on land by will for the payment of a decedent's debts, is in effect a devise of the land for the payments of the debts, and is a trust which chancery will take hold of and see that it is equitably applied. The land being thus a subject of trust, which is cognizable in equity only, is not liable to levy and sale on execution under a common law judgment, and, therefore, one creditor of the decedent cannot take advantage of other creditors and absorb the fund by taking judgment against the heirs, but must come into equity for a just

---

[1] City of San Francisco v. Pixley, 21 Cal. 56.
[2] Wallace v. Berger, 25 Iowa, 456; Cunningham v. Felker, 26 Iowa, 117.
[3] Mills v. Rogers, 2 Litt. 217.
[4] Mulks v. Allen, 12 Wend. 253; Ontario Bank v. Lansing, 2 Wend. 260.

and ratable distribution, and if he undertakes to proceed against the heirs by levy and sale, on a judgment against them, the administrator may maintain before the chancellor a motion to quash or set aside the sale.[1] Equality is equity, and one creditor cannot by superior diligence appropriate a trust fund for creditors generally to his own benefit.

§ 877. If a sheriff's sale be regular and fair when made no subsequent fraud or irregularity in anything regarding it will affect its validity or cause it to be set aside. The cause must have existed at the time of the sale.[2]

§ 878. A sale will be deemed fraudulent and will be set aside in Illinois for being made of lands in a distant county from defendant's residence, without his knowledge and under circumstances rendering it improbable that he may learn of it, more especially when, at the same time, there is ample property of defendant liable to sale on execution in the county wherein defendant resides. Such a procedure is indicative of fraud and will not be upheld if application be made in proper time and manner to set the sale aside.[3]

§ 879. Where there is such misdescription of the premises that the purchaser can take nothing by his purchase, the sale will be set aside on application of the purchaser.[4]

§ 880. So where the defendant in execution has no interest in the premises sold, and is not in possession, so that the buyer takes nothing, the court will, under certain circumstances, set aside the sale.[5]

§ 881. Though a bid may be received, if fairly made, and publicly cried at the time and place of sale, notwithstanding it is made by letter; yet if it be not publicly announced, but be received and privately noted in the house, instead of at the door of the place of sale, with publicity, or if there be any other indications of unfairness, the sale will be set aside.[6]

[1] Helm v. Darby, 3 Dana, 185.
[2] McCollum v. Hubbert, 13 Ala. 289.
[3] Hamilton v. Quinby, 46 Ill. 90.
[4] McPherson v. Foster, 4 Wash. C. C. 45; Hughes v. Streeter, 24 Ill. 647.
[5] Rockwell v. Allen, 3 McLean, 357.
[6] Dickinson v. Burge, 20 Ill. 266

§ 882. In *Davis v. Campbell*, which was a direct proceeding to set aside a sale of lands on execution, the Supreme Court of Indiana hold, that where the statute inhibits the sale of the lands in fee, until the rents and profits be first offered for a term of years without finding bidders, that a sale of the fee of the realty in the first instance, without first offering the rents and profits, is erroneous and will be set aside. And that where the statute declares the realty is not to be sold without appraisement, and a sale is made in disregard thereof, that such sale is unauthorized and will be set aside. And so if the statute give the debtor the right to select the property to be levied and sold, and the right is denied him, and a sale made in disregard of it, such sale also will be set aside. The court in that case make no decision, they say as to whether the sale would or would not have been held void collaterally, but remark that " a sale will be set aside as erroneous in a direct proceeding for that purpose, when it would not be held void in a collateral suit."[1]

§ 883. Where a sheriff's sale of land was made under three writs of execution, the senior one of which being the first, if valid, to be satisfied, was void, such sale was held invalid and was ordered to be set aside.[2]

§ 884. And so two writs of execution, being at the same time in the hands of an officer for levy and sale against one and the same execution debtor, the senior one of which writs was subject to the valuation of appraisement law, and the other not, a sale made thereon, not in accordance with the valuation law, was held irregular and was set aside.[3] Such were the rulings in the Supreme Court of Indiana.

§ 885. But in Wisconsin it is held that an execution sale on two writs, one of which is void and the other valid, will confer title under the valid writ.[4]

§ 886. Where the execution plaintiff is purchaser at sheriff's

[1] 12 Ind. 192.

[2] Brown v. McKay, 16 Ind. 484; Hutchins v. Doe, 3 Ind. 528; Clark v. Watson, 2 Ind. 400.

[3] Harmon v. Stipp, 8 Blackf. 455.

[4] Herrick v. Graves, 16 Wis. 167.

sale, by a description so defective that nothing passes by the sale, the purchaser "has an equitable right to have the levy and sale set aside and an execution awarded, by which he can have the benefit of his judgment." But it must be done by the court. The clerk has no power, being a ministerial officer, to set aside a levy or sale, or to vacate an entry of satisfaction. These are judicial acts, and require the exercise of a judicial power equal to that which rendered the judgment.[1]

§ 887. If a sheriff omit to give the proper notice of an execution sale, and a person cognizant of that fact induce the officer to sell without notice by giving him a bond of indemnity, and then becomes the purchaser, such conduct of the sheriff is illegal, and the purchaser being *particeps criminis* to it, the sale is illegal, erroneous, and void for fraud, and will be set aside.[2]

§ 888. The endorser of a mortgage note has such an interest as will entitle him to prosecute proceedings to set aside the judicial sale of the mortgaged premises, and more especially so if the mortgagor or payor of the note be insolvent. Consequently, where the whole amount of the mortgage debt was estimated by the appraiser, in appraising the lands, as resting on the lands so appraised, when other lands were also liable therefor, and thereby diminishing its appraised value, and the land was then sold in bulk, without an effort to sell it in separate parcels, it was holden that for these irregularities such endorser was entitled to have the sale set aside for his own protection as such endorser.[3]

§ 889. The statute of Iowa, (Revision of 1860, sec. 3318,) requiring notice of levy of a writ of execution on lands to be given to the defendant in the writ, applies as well to special executions in mortgage foreclosures as to ordinary executions of a general character.[4]

§ 890. And where a levy and sale is made under such special execution of lands in actual possession of the execution debtor,

[1] Hughes v. Streeter, 24 Ill. 647.
[2] Haydon v. Dunlap, 3 Bibb. 216.
[3] Whitney v. Armstrong, 32 Iowa, 9.
[4] Fleming v. Maddox, 30 Iowa, 239.

without giving him the notice required by the statute, the court will, on proper application, made in due time, set the sale aside; if by motion under the statute the application is to be made "at the same, or the next term thereafter."[1] But doubtless the sale would be set aside for the same cause on petition at any time, before the rights of innocent persons intervene, and within a reasonable time. The remedy by motion is not exclusive.

§ 891. And so, when an attachment, or execution levy, is so grossly excessive as to raise the presumption of unfairness, and as to amount to oppression, and valuable lands are sold on execution in a body, for a sum greatly below their real value, the sale, where rights of innocent persons have not attached, will be set aside; and especially where the attorney of the plaintiff is the execution purchaser.

§ 892. And in such case, in answer to the objection of selling *en masse*, it will not be inferred that the officer first offered a smaller portion of the land without obtaining a bid; but the inference will be rather that of misconduct on his part in that respect. The Supreme Court of Iowa, BECK, Justice, in this respect, hold the following language: "It cannot be presumed that the proceeding upon the execution, beginning in the violation of law and duty, and resulting in injustice and oppression, was made valid by obedience to the law in its intermediate steps."[2]

§ 893. In Wisconsin it is holden that sale of real property as a whole tract, when by statute it is directed to be sold in parcels, though not void, is voidable at the discretion of the aggrieved party, and on application therefor; but that such application, unless prevented by mistake, fraud, or other legal excuse, must be made within the time allowed by law for redemption from the sale. And that a subsequent mortgagee cannot apply to set the sale aside, but must seek his equitable right by action to redeem.[3]

§ 894. The courts will sometimes interfere by injunction

[1] Fleming v. Maddox, 30 Iowa, 239.
[2] Cook v. Jenkins, 30 Iowa, 152.
[3] Raymond v. Pauli, 21 Wis. 531; Griswold v. Stoughton, 2 Oregon, 61.

to prevent delivery of a deed, when different parcels of land have been sold in mass, at a price greatly under value; but the relief will be afforded on the principle of doing equity, when equity is asked, and therefore the judgment debtor asking the injunction will be required to pay off the judgment when the injunction is made perpetual.[1]

§ 895. In the case of *Ballance v. Loomis*, here cited, the plaintiffs in execution were the purchasers at sheriff's sale, hence the requirement in the decree that payment be made of the judgment.

§ 896. An execution sale of land and deed thereon, though as to the description of the land so uncertain as to render it inoperative or void at law, in an action of right, will not be set aside or treated as void in a proceeding in chancery in the course of which it is made to appear that the very lands intended to be levied and sold were levied, sold and conveyed, and that though the irregularity in that respect is against the execution purchaser, yet the equity of the case is on his side and in favor of sustaining the sale and conveyance.[2] In the case here cited from 30 Iowa, the court say, MILLER, Justice: "The appellants insist, that the sheriff's deed is void for uncertainty in the description. This objection would perhaps be good if defendants were suing at law in ejectment. But plaintiffs are asking a court of equity to quiet the title to this land in them, and the defendants aver facts which in equity make it their property. These facts the demurrer confesses. The plaintiffs admit that this very same land was levied on under the execution issued upon the judgment of the Wapello district court, in favor of the State Bank of Indiana, against Charles F. Harrow; that this very same land was sold by the sheriff to Hall & Wilson; but they (the plaintiffs) endeavor to avoid the effect of this by pointing out a defect in the description of the land thus sold in the sheriff's deed, and in equity, to take advantage of such defective description. There is no

---

[1] Ballance v. Loomis, 22 Ill. 82.

[2] Hackworth v. Zollars, 30 Iowa, 435, 438; Glenn v. Malona, 4 Iowa, 314, 320; Dygert v. Pletts, 25 Wend. 402; Lamb v. Buckmelier, 24 N. Y. 620.

equitable principle upon which they can be permitted to do this."[1]

§ 897. Equity will not avoid a sale for mere irregularity, nor for uncertainty of description, rendered sufficiently certain in the very proceedings by which it is sought to be set aside. It is not the office of the chancellor to relieve upon grounds merely technical.

V. For Reversal of Judgment.

§ 898. It is a principle well settled, that where, at an execution sale, the plaintiff in execution, or owner, or beneficiary of the judgment, becomes the purchaser, and the judgment be afterwards reversed, that the sale will on motion or on any other proper and timely application be set aside. That the defendant will be entitled to be placed in the same position which he occupied before the rendition of the judgment, and to have restitution of whatever he has lost by the sale, provided the same, or the title thereto, has not passed out of such purchaser to a *bona fide* purchaser, or in some manner become subject to some right, equity or lien *bona fide* acquired by an innocent person.[2]

§ 899. And the same principle applies and will be enforced where the purchase at the execution sale is made by the agent of the plaintiff or beneficiary of the judgment, or by his or their attorney in charge of and prosecuting the proceedings, or by any other person for or in privity of interest with the plaintiff or beneficiary of the judgment, so long as the property remains clear of *bona fide* rights of innocent third persons.[3]

§ 900. But the contrary is the rule when the purchaser at the sheriff's sale is an innocent third person, and is a *bona*

---

[1] Hackworth *v.* Zollars, 30 Iowa, 433, 438.

[2] Gott *v.* Powell, 41 Mo. 416; Corwith *v.* State Bank, 15 Wis. 289; McBain *v.* McBain, 15 Ohio St. 337; Hannibal & St. Joe R. R. Co. *v.* Brown, 43 Mo. 294; Milton *v.* Love, 13 Ill. 486; Dater *v.* Troy, etc. Co. 2 Hill, 629; Winston *v.* Ortley, 25 Miss. 456; Hubble *v.* Broadwell, 8 Ohio, 120, 127.

[3] Hannibal & St. Joe R. R. Co. *v.* Brown, 3 Mo. 294; Gott *v.* Powell, 41 Mo. 416.

fide purchaser, who has paid the purchase money before obtaining knowledge of the reversal of the judgment.[1]

§ 901. In the case of *Goodwin v. Mix*[2] the Supreme Court of Illinois hold the following language in regard to the effect of a judgment and sale to a *bona fide* purchaser: "The complainant's counsel make a point here, that the judgments confessed by the Woodworths in favor of Fridley were irregular, and they are attacked on that ground. It is sufficient to say, an objection of this character cannot be sustained in this suit. Until reversed for irregularity they can be enforced, and if reversed, a *bona fide* purchaser under them would be protected." And such is the general doctrine. In such case the defendant in the judgment, whose property is thus taken from him, must look for his remedy over against the plaintiff who may have received the proceeds of it. The innocent purchaser is not to bear the loss.

VI. RETURN OF THE PURCHASE MONEY.

§ 902. A purchaser of lands at sheriff's sale has no claim on the plaintiff in execution for return of the purchase money, where the sale is void or the execution debtor had no interest in the property sold; and he cannot maintain a suit either in law or equity against such plaintiff for the same.[3]

§ 903. Nor can he recover for the same, at law, against the execution debtor; but he may in equity.[4]

§ 904. Such purchaser has no right, however, to be subrogated into the place and rights of the execution plaintiff, so as to thus assume the character of a judgment debtor; for by the

---

[1] Stimson v. Ross, 51 Me. 556; Guitteau v. Wiseley, 47 Ill. 433; McLean v. Brown, 11 Ill. 519; Clark v. Pinney, 6 Cow. 297; Hubbell v. Broadwell, 8 Ohio, 120; Goodwin v. Mix, 38 Ill. 115; Voorhees v. The Bank, 10 Pet. 449.

[2] 38 Ill. 116.

[3] Dunn v. Frazier, 8 Blackf. 432; Julian v. Beal, 26 Ind. 220; Hawkins v. Miller, 26 Ind. 173.

[4] Dunn v. Frazier, 8 Blackf. 432; Hawkins v. Miller, 26 Ind. 173; McGee v. Ellis, 4 Litt. 244; Muir v. Craig, 3 Blackf. 293; Preston v. Harrison, 9 Ind. 1; Pennington v. Clifton, 10 Ind. 172; Richmond v. Marston, 15 Ind. 134; Julian v. Beal, 26 Ind. 220.

application of the purchase money paid by him, the judgment is extinguished to the extent of the amount so paid.[1]

§ 905. But where the execution plaintiff is himself the purchaser, and the sale passes no title, the sale being void, or the property not being subject to sale on execution for plaintiff's demand, it is proper for the court to set aside the sale; vacate satisfaction of the judgment if satisfaction is entered, and allow execution anew on the judgment. So also where the property, though belonging to the defendant at one time, had ceased to be his by reason of a previous sale under a mortgage which had priority over the plaintiff's judgment.[2]

[1] Laws v. Thompson, 4 Jones, Law, (N. C.) 104; Richmond v. Marston, 15 Ind. 134.

[2] Watson v. Reissig, 24 Ill. 281; Henry v. Keys, 5 Sneed, 488; Riter v. Henshaw, 7 Clark, 97; Mason v. Thomas, 24 Ill. 285; Lansing v. Quackenbush, 5 Cow. 38; Tudor v. Taylor, 26 Vt. 444; Adams v. Smith, 5 Cow. 280; Ontario Bank v. Lansing, 2 Wend. 260.

CHAPTER XX.

REDEMPTION.

I. THE RIGHT OF REDEMPTION.

§ 906. The right in law to redeem lands from execution sale exists only when given by statute; and the existence of this right in each particular case depends upon the state of the law in that respect at the time and place of creating the liability on which the judgment and execution were obtained.

§ 907. If by law the right exists at the time when, and place where, the liability is incurred, then the right remains within the same state, wherever therein the sale be made; but if the right does not exist when and where the liability is incurred, then there is no redemption from the sale made at such place, although in the meantime a redemption law be there passed.[1]

§ 908. If, however, the liability which is the foundation of the judgment and execution be created in one state, and the judgment and sale be in another, then the right to redeem from the sale will be regulated and controlled by the law of the *forum*, or state in which the judgment is rendered, as it is at the date of the judgment;[2] by analogy to the ruling of the

---

[1] Howard v. Bugbee, 24 How. 461; Field v. Dorris, 1 Sneed (Tenn.) 548; Malony v. Fortune, 14 Iowa, 417; Rosier v. Hale, 10 Iowa, 440; Bronson v. Kinsey, 1 How. 311.

[2] Hutchens v. Barrett, 19 Ind. 15; Doe v. Collins, 1 Carter (Ind.) 24; Doe v. Collins, 1 Smith (Ind.) 58.

courts in relation to valuation laws or the law of appraisement in execution and other forced sales.[1]

§ 909. Generally, where the right of redemption from execution sales exists, in favor of the execution debtor, it is also given by statute, if not exercised by him, to judgment and mortgage creditors of such debtor, under certain limitations and restrictions.

§ 910. The right to redeem lands from execution sale may be created also by agreement of the parties independent of the statutory right to redeem;[2] and will be enforced.

§ 911. The legal right of redemption, and the terms thereof, are as diversified, perhaps, in the different states as the states are numerous. Of the particulars of these it is not our purpose to treat; they will be found by reference to the ever-changing statutory enactments.

§ 912. But the rulings of the several courts on the subject, of a general character, are, in like manner as decisions on other subjects, a sort of common law and guide to the courts and profession as far as applicable to cases arising, and are therefore attempted to be given. In Illinois the right of redemption is extended by statute to sales made on decrees of foreclosure of mortgages in like manner as from sales under ordinary process of execution,[3] and a decree of foreclosure in that state ordering a sale without redemption is erroneous, and will be reversed.[4]

§ 913. A judgment debtor may redeem any one of several separate parcels of land, sold at the same time, but separately, to one and the same purchaser, and under one and the same execution. Not to allow separate redemption (say the court) "would be a prodigious hard case."[5]

§ 914. As a means of enabling debtors to exercise this

---

[1] Howard v. Bugbee, 24 How. 461.

[2] Wallace v. Wilson, 34 Miss. (5 George) 357; Southard v. Pope, 9 B. Monroe, 261; Miller v. Lewis, 4 Comst. 553; Lillard v. Casey, 2 Bibb, 459.

[3] Farrell v. Palmer, 50 Ill. 274.

[4] Ibid. In this case, the court, speaking of the Illinois statute, say: "This section was intended to and does prohibit sales of mortgaged lands, under a decree of foreclosure, without redemption. It then follows, that the decree was erroneous in ordering a sale without redemption."

[5] Robertson v. Dennis, 20 Ill. 313.

20

right of redeeming separate parcels separately, we find here
an additional reason, wherever lands are subject by statute to
redemption, for requiring sales of separate and distinct parcels
to be made on separate bids. Otherwise there would be no
standard of values by which any one tract could be separately
redeemed, and the debtor would be subjected to the oppression
of redeeming the whole number of tracts together, and in case
of inability so to do, lose the whole. The same reason applies
as an additional objection to selling real and personal property
collectively, together. The one being redeemable and the
other not, the separate values relatively bid for each, could not
be ascertained.

II. By the Execution Debtor.

§ 915. A purchase at execution sale, under a written agreement for redemption, is not a waiver or a merger of the
statutory right to redeem. And though the redemption be
limited both by statute and by the agreement to one year, yet
the transaction amounts in equity to a mortgage, and the execution debtor will be allowed in equity a reasonable time in
which to redeem, irrespective of the one year's time stipulated
for in the agreement.[1]

§ 916. And such a promise of redemption made at time
of bidding as influences others not to bid, or causes the debtor
to lessen his efforts to otherwise protect his interests, will be
enforced in equity, though the time limited be longer than the
statutory time of redemption.[2]

§ 917. To consummate the redemption in such case the ten
per cent. allowed by law can only be exacted up to the end of the
time allowed by law in which to redeem, and six per cent. per
annum afterwards.[3] And the time allowed by law for redemption may be extended by parole, without interfering with the
statute of frauds.[4]

[1] Wallace v. Wilson, 34 Miss. 357; Southard v. Pope, 9 B. Monroe, 264.
[2] Lillard v. Casey, 2 Bibb, 459.
[3] Southard v. Pope, 9 B. Mon. 267.
[4] Griffin v. Coffey, 9 B. Mon. 453.

§ 918. By receiving a part of the redemption money, the purchaser is precluded from treating the sale as absolute after expiration of the time of redemption.[1]

§ 919. The execution debtor may redeem without paying off other liens of the execution purchaser in Minnesota.[2]

§ 920. But a contrary rule is held in California.[3] And during the time allowed for redemption, the purchaser in California should pay the taxes; therefore a purchase at tax sale, by himself, for such taxes, will avail him nothing.[4]

§ 921. So, the judgment debtor may redeem, (and so may his grantee,) though he has conveyed away his right to the land. He may do so to protect his conveyance, and so may his grantee to protect his purchase.[5]

§ 922. The right of the debtor to redeem is not affected by selling the land a second time, either by the same plaintiff or by another; and if the same plaintiff, having a junior judgment, sell it again, then a judgment debtor redeeming from the first sale has priority of right.[6]

§ 923. If an execution sale be unknown to the execution debtor, and fraudulent means be used, or resorted to for the purpose of preventing the fact from coming to his knowledge, and the proper evidences and records of such sale be not made out within the usual time of redemption, the aggrieved party may, by bill in chancery filed within a reasonable time in a court of general chancery jurisdiction, enforce redemption. In such case, twelve months after the discovery of the fraud, has been deemed a reasonable time by analogy to the statute of limitations of redemption, and this, too, against the assignee of the sheriff's certificate who took with notice.[7]

---

[1] Southard v. Pope, 9 B. Mon. 264.
[2] Warren v. Fish, 7 Minn. 432.
[3] Vandyke v. Herman, 3 Cal. 295.
[4] Kelly v. Abbott, 13 Cal. 609.
[5] Harvey v. Spalding, 16 Iowa, 397.
[6] Merry v. Bostwick, 13 Ill. 398.
[7] Briscoe v. York, 53 Ill. 484. In this case, Justice BREESE, after reviewing the facts and statements of the bill, and admitted by demurrer, disposes of the case in the following terms: "It is clear that he (defendant,) purchased the certificate with notice of the rights of complainant, and

III. By Judgment Creditors.

§ 924. The right of judgment creditors to redeem lands of their debtors from execution sales, when given by law, applies alike to creditors whose judgments are rendered before or after the sale.[1]

§ 925. When the redemption is made by a judgment creditor after the death of the debtor in execution, it thereby becomes the estate of the deceased debtor, and the title vests in heirs subject, as other lands, to judgment debts. The remedy of the redeeming creditor is to sell on his judgment, and the amount paid for redemption goes to his credit on his bid if the purchase is made by him; and if by another, he is re-imbursed out of the proceeds of sale,[2] for the amount as part of his demand.

§ 926. "The land is stricken off to him by legal intendment," say the court. But the redeeming creditor cannot issue execution on his judgment and sell, without proper proceedings first taken against the heirs. On a mere revival of the judgment against the administrator, no lien or right attaches to levy and sell the land on a *fieri facias*. Such revival of judgment against the administrator without notice to the heirs was holden to be error in *Turney v. Gates*, and was reversed.[3] And a judgment so revived and execution sale thereon are void and confer no title on the purchaser.[4]

§ 927. If a judgment creditor purchase the certificate of sale while the time is yet running for redemption, he will be entitled to the redemption money as assignee, in case any other creditor redeems. And if the creditor so redeeming redeems on a judgment which is junior to the judgment of such assignee,

must be affected with all the equities existing against the original purchaser. It seems to us the bare statement of the case is the strongest argument which can be made in support of complainant's right to redeem from the sale, at least within twelve months after the papers evidencing the sale were actually made out."

[1] Couthway v. Berghaus, 25 Ala. 393.
[2] Turney v. Young, 22 Ill. 253; Keeling v. Head, 3 Head. (Tenn.) 592.
[3] Turney v. Gates, 12 Ill. 141; Turney v. Young, 22 Ill 253.
[4] Turney v. Young, 22 Ill. 253.

such junior creditor must also pay the amount of the assignee's judgment.[1] The assignee of a judgment creditor has the same right to redeem as the judgment creditor had.[2]

§ 928. If the debtor sell his equity of redemption, and the purchaser fail to redeem, a creditor under a junior judgment may redeem after twelve, and within fifteen months, in Illinois.[3]

§ 929. If two parcels of land be sold as a whole, on execution sale, and the plaintiff in a junior execution redeems, and then causes the parcels to be levied and sold separately on his junior writ, bidding them in on his judgment for a sum less than what he paid for redemption, he will be regarded in law as having abandoned his rights under the redemption, and as selling independent thereof.[4]

§ 930. Redemption of lands sold at a master's judicial sale, cannot be made by payment to such master where by law the payment is to be to the sheriff. It is inoperative; and moreover the sheriff cannot ratify the act of the master in receiving the money and give validity to the intended redemption.[5]

IV. REDEMPTION BY MORTGAGE CREDITOR.

§ 931. In California, though a mortgagee lose his priority by failing to record his mortgage, yet he may redeem under the statute from execution sale, as a creditor; but if he fails to do so, he will have no relief in equity.[6] In Iowa, a junior mortgagee, who is not made defendant to the senior mortgagee's suit of foreclosure, is not confined, in redeeming, to the statutory remedy but may redeem as at common law, or foreclose his mortgage, making the purchaser under the senior foreclosure a defendant and tendering the amount of his purchase money.[6]

[6] Wilson v. Conklin, 22 Iowa, 452.

[7] Sweezey v. Chandler, 11 Ill. 445.

[8] McLogan v. Brown, 11 Ill. 519.

[9] Olliver v. Croswell, 42 Ill. 41.

[1] Littler v. People, 43 Ill. 188.

[2] Smith v. Randall, 6 Cal. 47.

[3] Anson v. Anson, 20 Iowa, 55; Bates v. Ruddick, 2 Iowa, 523; Ten Eyck v. Cassad 15 Iowa, 524; Veach v. Schaup, 3 Iowa, 194; Heimstreet

§ 932. If, in case of such sale under the proceedings in foreclosure of the senior mortgagee, the purchaser enter into and enjoy the benefit of the mortgaged premises prior to foreclosure by the junior mortgagee, who has had no notice as a party, then the purchaser under the first mortgage will be accountable for rents and profits and waste; but in accounting will be entitled to interest on the mortgage debt, upon the principle of equitable subrogation.[1]

§ 933. Where a case exists for such accounting, the junior mortgagee will not be held to a strict tender or bringing into court the necessary redemption money on filing his bill.[2]

§ 934. It is believed to be sufficient if, in such case, a readiness to redeem be averred whenever the amount required shall be ascertained by the court. More especially so when the right to redeem is resisted.[3]

§ 935. But under the code of Iowa of 1851, which gave no redemption from mortgage sales, it was holden that mortgage creditors and other lien holders who had been made parties, could not redeem lands sold under decree of foreclosure after sale to satisfy the mortgage decree. They had already had their day in court.[4]

§ 936. Partial redemption is not allowable. Who redeems must redeem the whole interest sold. A purchaser of a part thereof cannot redeem such part without paying the whole amount and redeeming the whole, unless such part was sepa-

---

v. Winnie, 10 Iowa, 480; Knowles v. Rablin 20 Iowa, 101. But, quere? If the junior mortgagee ought to be subjected to redeem also, as against the costs of such proceeding of the first mortgagor, to which he was not made a party, which costs might have been avoided, after service, by redemption of the junior mortgagee if he had been made a party to the proceedings.

[1] Anson v. Anson, 20 Iowa, 60; Ten Eyck v. Cassad, 15 Iowa, 524; Benedict v. Gilman, 4 Paige, 58; Bradley v. Snyder, 14 Ill. 267; 1 Washb. Real Prop. 565, 568, 631; Goodman v. White, 26 Conn. 317; Thompson v. Chandler, 7 Me. (Greenlf.) 377.

[2] Laverty v. Hall, 19 Iowa, 526.

[3] Laverty v. Hall, 19 Iowa, 526; Stap v. Phelps, 7 Dana, (Ky.) 296; Haywood v. Munger, 14 Iowa, 517; Rutherford v. Haven, 11 Iowa, 587.

[4] Cramer v. Redman, 9 Iowa, 114.

rately sold, and then he can. Nor can redemption be made as for an undivided share.[1]

§ 937. If redemption is of the mortgagee as purchaser, the party redeeming must not only pay the amount bid with interest, but if the bid is less than the decree he must also pay off the decree; he cannot redeem, in such case, by simply paying the amount of the purchase money and interest.[2] "Who claims equity must do equity."

V. How and When to be Made.

§ 938. Redemption can only be made in that which is by law a legal tender, in money. The officer is not bound to receive anything else as bank bills, checks, or orders for money. In some cases it is holden that redemption cannot be effected by the act of his receiving such substitutes for money, although by its acceptance he renders himself liable for money.[3]

§ 939. But in others it is holden that if such instruments be accepted by him and actually converted into money, so that the money is ready for the holder of the certificate of purchase, it will be a valid redemption.[4]

§ 940. The time of redemption is to be calculated by excluding the first day and including the last, or day of making payment.[5]

§ 941. It being a statutory right the time in which it is to be exercised in the different states will depend on the statutory provisions in that respect. As a general rule it may be made

[1] Street v. Beal, 16 Iowa, 68; Knowles v. Rablin 20 Iowa, 101; Massie v. Wilson, 16 Iowa, 390, 396, 397; Taylor v. Porter, 3 Mass. 355; Gibson v. Creshore, 5 Pick. 146; Smith v. Kelly, 27 Me. 237; Johnson v. Candage, 31 Me. 28.

[2] Knowles v. Rablin, 20 Iowa, 101, 104; Johnson v. Harmon, 19 Iowa, 58; White v. Hampton, 13 Iowa, 259.

[3] Dougherty v. Hughes, 3 G. Greene, 92; Thorne v. San Francisco, 4 Cal. 127; People v. Baker, 20 Wend. 602.

[4] Webb v. Watson, 18 Iowa, 537; Hall v. Fisher, 9 Barb. Sup. Ct. 17.

[5] Tuecher v. Hiatte, 23 Iowa, 529; Bigelow v. Wilson, 1 Pick. 485; Simms v. Hampton, 1 S. & R. 411; Gillespie v. White, 16 Johns. 117; Rand v. Rand, 3 N. H. 267; Windser v. China, 4 Greenl. 298

"at any time before the close of the last day allowed by law for that purpose," or of any day within the time allowed by law for redemption. "Business hours are not in this respect regarded."[1]

§ 942. Redemption by an unauthorized person, assuming to act as agent, will be valid if ratified or approved by the principal.[2]

§ 943. In redeeming, strict compliance with the statute is necessary,[3] unless such compliance be waived.[4]

§ 944. In *Hughes v. Feeter*[5] the Supreme Court of Iowa lay down the rule "that the statutory right to redeem property from execution sale within one year, cannot be extended by any act of the party claiming that right, such as a suit to redeem, or the like, without more. Such, too, is the general doctrine.

§ 945. But where the property, as in the case of *Hughes v. Feeter*, brought but a small proportion of its value, and where that value depended on a protracted suit, calculated to prevent a sale at a fair price, if redeemed and sold again during its pendency, and where suit was commenced in good faith before redemption expired to taste the *bona fides* of the sale, the court enlarged the time of redemption after the expiration of the statutory period.[6]

§ 946. From an execution sale of several tracts of land separately made on the same writ, the owner may redeem either of them separately, whether they be bought by one or by several different persons.[7]

§ 947. If the redemption is made of the sheriff by a judgment creditor, it has been held in Illinois that the payment should be accompanied by an execution delivered to the officer on the judgment of such redeeming creditor.[8]

---

[1] *Ex parte* Bank of Monroe, 7 Hill, 177; Tuecher *v.* Hiatte, 23 Iowa, 529.

[2] Tuecher *v.* Hiatte, 23 Iowa, 529; Blackw. Tax Titles, 501, 504, 505.

[3] *Ex parte*, Bank of Monroe, 7 Hill, 177; Hail *v.* Thomas, 27 Barb. (N. Y.) 55; Silliman *v.* Wing, 7 Hill, 159.

[4] Bank of Vergennes *v.* Warren, 7 Hill, 91

[5] Hughes *v.* Feeter, 23 Iowa, 547.

[6] Ibid.

[7] Robertson *v.* Dennis, 20 Ill. 313.

[8] Stone *v.* Gardner, 20 Ill. 304.

§ 948. It is also held in Illinois that the money may be paid to the sheriff or to the purchaser.[1]

§ 949. From a purchase by the trustee of a *feme covert,* the redemption, in Alabama, is made by payment to such trustee and not to the *cestui que* trust.[2] Otherwise if the trustee is non-resident.[3]

§ 950. The receipt by the sheriff of depreciated paper as money from the purchaser, affords no ground for the owner or others to redeem by paying like currency, or its value, in par money. He must pay the full amount in good money.[4]

§ 951. If the purchaser pays off a prior lien on the premises the amount must be reimbursed to him by adding the same with interest to the redemption money.[5]

§ 952. Oversight, neglect, or mere ignorance of the law is not such excuse for omitting to redeem as will call for relief in equity.[6]

§ 953. It is held in New York (MORGAN, Justice, dissenting,) that under the statute of 1847, requiring redemptions from execution sales of lands on the last day of the fifteen months allowed by law in which to redeem, to be made at the sheriff's office, that redemption at the dwelling house of that officer, between nine and ten o'clock in the night of that day, the party redeeming have failed to find the officer during the day at the sheriff's office, is illegal and void, for non-conformity to the letter of the act requiring the redemption to take place at the sheriff's office when the conflicting claimants to redeem might respectively redeem from each other. The court hold that to make the redemption valid, the statute must be strictly conformed to.[7]

---

[1] Stone *v.* Gardner, 20 Ill. 304; Robertson *v.* Dennis, 20 Ill. 313.

[2] Barringer *v.* Burke, 21 Ala. 765.

[3] Couthy *v.* Berghans, 25 Ill. 393.

[4] Schofield *v.* Bessenden, 15 Ill. 78.

[5] Couthway *v.* Bergans, 25 Ala. 393.

[6] Campau *v.* Godfrey, 18 Mich. 27.

[7] Gilchrist *v.* Comfort, 34 N. Y. 235. In this case the court say: "As the law now exists a redemption by a creditor on the last day of the fifteen months, to be valid and effectual, must be made at the sheriff's office. The statute is plain and peremptory in this respect and cannot be dis-

§ 954. We are not to understand that the objection on
which the case of *Gilchrist v. Comfort* turned was that the
redemption was made in the night time; for in that there is
nothing objectionable in itself. Business hours in reference to
redemption are not regarded in law.[1] But it was objectionable, under the circumstances, in like manner as was the place
of redeeming, inasmuch as it put difficulties, if not impossi-
bilities, in the way of such other judgment creditors who,
under the statute, had a right in like manner and at the same
time to redeem of the creditor first redeeming, and so on in
turn from one to another so long as there remained judgment
creditors willing to redeem, or to bid at what is aptly termed
an "auction among the creditors of the land." The real point
of objection was that the redemption was not made at the office
of the sheriff instead of at his house. Its being in the night
time gave weight to the objection in a moral point of view, in
so much as it tended to prevent simultaneous redemptions by
other creditors.

VI. Effect of Redemption.

§ 955. The effect of redemption from execution sale, by the
execution debtor or his assigns or grantee, is merely to terminate the sale and restore the property to its original condition.
It confers no new right. If the sale was made for a part only
of the judgment debt, the land becomes by such redemption
again liable for the residue of the judgment. And so likewise
it becomes thereby liable to sale on any other intervening or
subsisting judgment lien older in date than the transfer or
assignment made by the judgment debtor, to the same extent
as if the judgment debtor had not disposed of his right to
redeem, or his interest in the estate.[2]

obeyed or disregarded. It is an express and positive requirement, and
must be strictly followed, or nothing is accomplished." See *Ex parte,*
Bank of Monroe, 7 Hill, 177; Hall v. Thomas, 27 Barb. 55.

[1] *Ex parte*, Bank of Monroe, 7 Hill, 777; Tuecher v. Hiatie, 23 Iowa, 529.

[2] Stien v. Chambless, 18 Iowa, 474; Crosby v. Elkader Lodge, 16 Iowa,
399; Curtis v. Millard, 14 Iowa, 128; Warren v. Fish, 7 Minn. 432; Hays
v. Thode, 18 Iowa, 51, 52; Titus v. Lewis, 3 Barb. 70.

§ 956. In *Stein v. Chambless*[1] the court say: "The purchase by Chambless of Banford's right to redeem the property from the sale to Dougherty, and to Lemp and Sells, conferred upon him no other or better right than Banford himself possessed, and the legal effect of a redemption by him is the same as if Banford himself had redeemed, leaving the property subject to be taken in satisfaction of any subsisting lien or judgment thereon."

§ 957. The same court, in *Crosby v. Elkader Lodge*,[2] hold the following language: "If the debtor or his grantee redeem land which has been sold in part satisfaction of a subsisting judgment, the property at once becomes liable to satisfy the unpaid balance of the execution from the moment of such redemption."

§ 958. Still earlier, in *Curtis v. Millard*,[3] the same court review the whole subject and assert the rule to be that if during the interval between the sale on execution and delivery of the sheriff's deed to the purchaser other judgments be rendered against the debtor, where judgments are liens, that they attach as liens against the execution debtor's interest in the premises so sold, and that if there be redemption from such sale, the land is liable to sale on execution to satisfy such subsequent judgments. "That the legal estate of the judgment debtor is not divested by the sale of his land under execution until after expiration of the time for redemption and the title has vested in the purchaser by deed from the sheriff." It therefore follows that judgments rendered within that time attach as liens to the premises, subject to be defeated by failure to redeem and by execution and delivery of the sheriff's deed.

§ 959. In the same case *Curtis v. Millard*, the doctrine is broadly asserted by the court that "the purchaser of lands sold on execution acquires by his purchase no more than a lien upon the lands for the amount of his bid, and interest during the time allowed for redemption. He acquires no right or estate upon which he could maintain ejectment, or which could be

[1] 18 Iowa, 475, 476.
[2] 16 Iowa, 405.
[3] 14 Iowa, 129, 130.

levied upon and sold for his debts;" that it is simply an inchoate and conditional right to an estate, "liable to be defeated at any time within one year by the payment of the purchase money and interest." That is, by redemption.[1]

§ 960. A judgment creditor, or other creditor, in redeeming, is substituted to the execution purchaser's rights. He acquires no new or better rights than the right of those from whom he redeems. Therefore, if the purchase is made under a void execution, or an execution issued on a judgment which has been paid, or where the execution itself has been satisfied, then the purchaser at the execution sale having obtained nothing by his purchase, nothing inures to the party redeeming, by virtue of the redemption.[2] Thus it follows, that a creditor redeeming from a void execution sale takes nothing, and a subsequent execution sale, in his own behalf, in pursuance of such redemption, under the Illinois statute, is also void.[3]

§ 961. From sales made in a loyal state during the war of rebellion, of lands belonging to a citizen and resident of a state in rebellion, where no negligence in redeeming attaches to the judgment debtor, the debtor or his representatives will in equity, by analogy to the statute of limitations, be allowed one year in which to file their bill to redeem, after the obstacles caused by the war have ceased; and where, in such case, the sheriff's deed has intervened, the proper course is to apply by bill to the court of ordinary chancery jurisdiction for relief. If in the meantime the judgment debtor dies, redemption may be thus effected by a bill on the part of his heirs, but upon terms. Not, however, as to such portion of the lands as may have passed by conveyance to innocent purchasers.[4]

[1] 14 Iowa, 190.

[2] Keeling v. Heard, 3 Head (Tenn.) 592.

[3] Johnson v. Baker, 38 Ill. 98. Of such sales the Supreme Court say: "They are both void, because they fail to conform to and are in violation of the statute. And it follows, as the judgment is utterly void, that such a sale under it would be equally; and being void, it is not such a judgment as the statute contemplated, as the basis of a sale from which a junior judgment creditor might redeem."

[4] Mixer v. Sibley, 53 Ill. 61; Hanger v. Abbott, 6 Wall. 532; Stiles v. Easley 51 Ill. 275.

PART FIFTH.

EXECUTION SALES OF PERSONAL PROPERTY.

CHAPTER XXI.

I. THE WRIT.
II. ITS LIEN.
III. WHAT MAY BE SOLD.

I. THE WRIT.

§ 962. The writ of *fieri facias* is the process on which execution sales of personal property were made at common law.[1]

§ 963. It is a common law writ, and is directed to the sheriff of the county, by his official title, commanding him, that of the goods and chattels of the defendant, to be found in his bailwick, that is in his county, he levy and cause to be made a sum of money mentioned in the writ, and to have the same before the court on the return day of the writ.[2]

§ 964. In olden time, in England, when the monarch held the court in person, the command of the writ was to have the money in court, before the king.

§ 965. Sales of personal property, in the American States, to satisfy judgments at law, are usually made on this writ, or one closely assimilated to it, and which, in some states, also run against the lands and tenements of the execution debtor, either absolutely or as an alternative, in case sufficient goods and chattels be not found whereof to satisfy the writ.

§ 966. Whatever the form of the writ may be, it must *substantially* conform to the judgment upon which it issues. If it does not it will, on motion, be quashed.[3]

---

[1] 3 Bac. Abt. "Execution," 193; 3 Black. Com. 417; 2 Tidd's Prac. 913, 917
[2] 2 Tidd's Prac. 913; 3 Black. Com. 417.
[3] Reese v. Burts, 39 Geo. 565.

(317)

§ 967. A slight variance, however, will not vitiate the writ, though it may be subject to be quashed therefor before sale thereon; but if it be not quashed, and sale is made thereon, the sale will be valid, if possession of the property be delivered to the purchaser.[1]

§ 968. If property be not found on which to levy the *fieri facias*, or its kindred writ as modified by statute, within the lifetime of the writ, then, on return thereof, the proper course is to sue out an *alias fieri facias*, and so on in succession, as a like necessity occurs, a *pluries*, and *alias pluries;* but if there be a levy effected, and from any cause not affecting the validity of the writ or levy, the writ be returned without sale of the property levied, then an order for the issuing of a writ of *venditioni exponas* is to be obtained, and the latter writ thereupon issues to the officer commanding him to *sell* the property so levied on the former writ of *fieri facias* and remaining unsold. This writ of *venditioni exponas* confers no new or additional authority on the officer, but commands and compels him to do that which he was before authorized and commanded, by the writ of *fieri facias*, to do.[2]

§ 969. In Alabama, and some other of the States, if execution issue during defendant's lifetime, and be not executed, then an *alias*, or *pluries*, as the case may be, may issue after his death, whereon personal effects may be levied and sold, (but not the realty without revival of the judgment,) the lien of the first writ having attached to such personalty during defendant's life time.[3] If the judgment, however, be against two or more defendants, and one die, execution cannot go as against the realty without revival of *scire facias*, but may as to the personalty of the survivors.[4]

§ 970. The writ, under all circumstances, must correspond to the judgment substantially; and if one defendant be dead, it must nevertheless run as against them all, but can only be executed against the personal property of the survivor or sur-

[1] Williams v. Brown, 28 Iowa, 247; Hunt v. Loucks, 38 Cal. 372.

[2] Johnson v. Lynch, 3 Bibb. 345.

[3] Erwin v. Dundas, 4 How. 58.

[4] Erwin v. Dundas, 4 How. 58; Hildreth v. Thompson, 16 Mass. 193.

vivors. Some times, however, on suggestion, the death of one of the defendants of record, the writ will be ordered against the survivor or survivors alone.[1]

§ 971. The alteration of an execution in any manner whatever, after it has passed out of the hands of the clerk, destroys its vitality and renders it void. All proceedings thereon are in like manner void. The alteration of process will not be tolerated by the law, or courts, under any circumstances.[2]

§ 972. In the case here cited, WALKER, Justice, lays down the rule as follows, and no doubt correctly: "If the execution were altered in a material part, it would thereby become void. Courts can never per.nit such alterations of their process, thereby endangering the rights of parties as effectually as any other species of forgery." If wrong, it should be returned, that by leave it can be amended, or a legal writ issue.

II. Its Lien.

§ 973. At common law, this writ of *fieri facias* bore relation to its date, usually called the teste;[3] and bound the goods and chattels of the defendant from that time, or such thereof as were subject to levy, by which means it became a lien from its date.[4]

§ 974. But this relation is taken away in England by statute, and with it the lien, so far as to purchases intermediate between the *teste* of the writ and the time of its actual delivery to the sheriff; and is made to commence only on such delivery as against such purchaser, so as to save intervening *bona fide* sales; the lien still remained, however, against the goods in

---

[1] Erwin *v.* Dundas, 4 How. 58, 79; Johnson *v.* Adair, 3 Bibb. 334. In the case last cited, although the writ was quashed, yet it was for other cause than issuing after the death of one defendant. The objection, on this point was in effect overruled,

[2] White *v.* Jones, 38 Ill. 159, 164.

[3] 1 Black. 179; Erwin *v.* Dundas, 4 How. 58; Dodge *v.* Mack, 22 Ill. 95,

[4] 2 Tidd's Prac. 914; 3 Bouv. 573, 574; Archb. Civil Plds. title, "Execution," 1 Hay. (N. C.) 396; Erwin *v.* Dundas, 4 How. 58, 73; Dodge *v.* Mack, 22 Ill. 95.

the hands of the debtor himself, and overreaches other writs subsequently issued and levied.[3]

§ 975. In some of the American States, as in England, at common law, this lien of the writ of execution, in the hands of the sheriff, attaches to the goods and chattels of the defendant in the bailwick, or county, from the teste of the writ.[4]

§ 976. In others the lien attaches only by the levy;[5] while in yet another class, the statute of 29th, Charles the Second, is either followed or is substantially re-enacted. In this latter class the lien attaches as against the debtor, by delivery of the writ to the proper officer for service, but subject to *bona fide* purchases made before levy.[6]

---

[3] Stat 29, Car. II. 2 Tidd's Prac. 914, 915; Erwin *v.* Dundas, 4 How. 58; Woodward *v.* Hill, 3 McCord, 241.

[4] Harding *v.* Spivey, 8 Ired, 63; Union Bank *v.* McClung, 9 Humph. 91; Barnes *v.* Haynes, 1 Swan, 304; Erwin *v.* Dundas, 4 How. 58, 75.

[5] Reeves *v.* Sebem, 16 Iowa, 234; Field *v.* Milburn, 9 Mo. 492; Gilkey *v.* Dickson, 2 Hawks, 341.

[6] Ray *v.* Birdseye, 5 Denio. 619, 624; Johnson *v.* McLean, 7 Blackf. 510; Marshall *v.* Cunningham, 13 Ill. 20; Furlong *v.* Edwards, 3 Md. 99; Tabb *v.* Harris, 4 Bibb, 31; McMahon *v.* Green, 12 Ala. 71; Newel *v.* Sibley, Dodge, Adm'r *v.* Mack, 22 Ill. 93, 95. On this subject we avail ourselves of the learned opinion of the Iowa Supreme Court, by DILLON, Justice, in Reeves & Co. *v.* Seborn, from which we make the following extract: "The defendant now claims that the execution, though not levied, was a lien upon the goods and chattels of the debtor. We are aware of no decision in this state fixing the *time* when the goods of an execution defendant are bound, whether from the teste of the writ or from its delivery to the officer, or from actual levy only. This subject is now settled by statute, which provides that execution shall bind only from the time of levy. (Laws 1862, p. 231.) This act was not in force at the date of the transaction now in question, and hence it becomes necessary to state what the law was before the act was passed. At common law the writ of *fi. fa.* bound the chattels of the defendants from its teste. 3 Bouv. Inst. 573, 574, Arch. Civil Pl. title, 'Execution,' 1 Hay. (N. C.) 396; 2 Id. 57; 2 Hawkes, 232; 3 Id. 296. As this had the unjust effect to overreach and defeat sales made even before the writ was delivered to the sheriff, it was remedied by the statute of 29 Charles II. which made the writ binding from the time of its delivery to the sheriff to be executed. We have very few if any decisions as to what the common law in this country is, because the subject is, in most of the states, regulated by express statute. Thus, in New York, the statute of 29 Charles is re-enacted, expressly. Ray *v.* Birdseye, 5 Denio, 624; see, also, 12 Johns. 403. So in Indiana, 7 Blackf. 501; 4 Id. 496; 4 Ind. 255. So in Illinois, 13 Ill. 20; 22 Id. 93. So in Ken-

§ 977. The lien of the original execution is kept alive by issuing of an *alias*, or *pluries*, or other subsequent writ resting on the original, in proper time, and will cut off process issued during the intervening period between the time of issuing such subsequent writ and the issuance of its original.[1]

§ 978. In Kentucky the death of the defendant in execution abates the writ and no further proceedings can be had thereon; but it does not discharge the lien of the levy, if there be a levy, and equity will enforce the same.[2]

§ 979. It is held in Illinois that the death of the defendant after the teste of the execution and before it comes to the hands of the officer, destroys its vitality, and that no valid levy can be made thereon;[3] but it is there holden also, that the lien of the writ is fixed by delivery to the officer, and that, therefore, if defendant die after the writ comes to the officer's hands, that such officer may go on and execute the writ by levy and sale.[4]

tucky, 1 Litt. St. 540; 4 Bibb, 31; 2 J. J. Marsh, 421. So in Florida, 4 Flor. 126; and Maryland, 3 Md. 99; and Alabama, 12 Ala. 71; Id. 247; 18 Id. 387. In Missouri, as between two officers the first levy holds, though the writ was delivered last. Field *v.* Milburn, 9 Mo. 492. In California and Ohio, by statute, the lien is from the levy only. In North Carolina, where the common law, as a body, is adopted, the lien is from the teste, (8 Ire. 63, and cases supra,) and Tennessee follows North Carolina, (9 Humph. 91; 1 Swan, 301.) In the absence of statute, we must conclude that the execution is a lien, either from its teste, as at common law, or only from actual levy. We do not feel bound to adopt the unreasonable and unjust rule of the ancient common law, so unjust, indeed, that it had to be remedied by statute. It does not accord with the policy of our laws, nor harmonize with the decisions on kindred subjects. The whole current of judicial decisions, in this state has ever, and we think most wisely, been against secret constructive liens, especially when these are set up against purchasers. Barney *v.* McCarty, 15 Iowa; Same *v.* Little, Id.; and Cummings *v.* Long, Id.; Jones *v.* Peasley, 3 Green, 52; Gimble *v.* Ackley, 12 Iowa, 27. And we are not mistaken in saying that the professional sentiment in this state has always been that executions were not liens on chattels until actual levy. This was the opinion of the court below, and in this respect there is no error." (Reeves & Co. *v.* Seborn,) 16 Iowa, 236, 237.

[1] Brasfield *v.* Whittaker, 4 Hawks, 309.

[2] Holeman *v.* Holeman, 2 Bush. (Ky.) 514; Wagner *v.* McCoy, 2 Bibb, 198.

[3] The People *v.* Bradley, 17 Ill. 485.

[4] Dodge *v.* Mack, 22 Ill. 93, 96.

III. What may be Sold.

§ 980. On the writ of *fieri facias*, at common law, in
England, everything that is chattel belonging by legal title to
the defendant, except necessary wearing apparel, was liable to
be levied and sold; also, leases or terms for years, which are
chattels real; likewise growing grain, which went to the
executor as personalty; and all such fixtures as might be
removed by the tenant, if the tenant was the defendant in
execution.[1]

§ 981. But such things as belonged to the freehold and
descended to the heir, as furnaces, growing apple trees, and
other things attached to the soil, or tenement, could not be
seized and sold on execution.[2] Neither could judgments,
accounts, bonds, bank notes, and other choses in action;[3] nor
goods which were mortgaged or pawned for debt;[4] nor goods
distrained, or demised for years, or goods seized and holden on
a prior execution;[5] nor fixtures of a house which was the freehold of the execution defendant.[6]

§ 982. Property in the hands of a receiver appointed by a
court is not the subject of execution levy or sale. It is in the
custody of the law. Nor is it subject to an attachment or
other interfering process. If a party has rights as against it,
application should be made to the court, which controls both
receiver and property, for the allowance or adjustment of such
rights.[7]

§ 983. In the case cited above from Iowa, the Supreme
Court of that state, Cole, Justice, say: "The property levied
upon by the appellants was, at the time of their levy, in the
hands of a receiver appointed by the court. It was, therefore,

[1] 2 Tidd's Prac. 917; 3 Bac. Abt. "Execution," 698.
[2] 2 Tidd's Prac. 917; Craddock v. Riddlesbarger, 2 Dana, 206.
[3] 2 Tidd's Prac. 917; McGee v. Cherry, 6 Geo. 550; Taylor v. Gillean, 23
Texas, 508; Rhodes v. Megonegal, 2 Barr, 39; Ingals v. Lord, 1 Cow. 240;
McCloud v. Hubbard, 2 Blackf. 361; Orsborn v. Cloud, 23 Iowa, 104.
[4] 2 Tidd's Prac. 917; 3 Bac. Abt. "Execution," 689; Johnson v. Crawford,
6 Blackf. 377.
[5] 2 Tidd's Prac. 917.
[6] 3 Bac. Abt. "Execution," 705; Winn v. Ingilby, 5 B. & A. 625.
[7] Martin v. Davis, 21 Iowa, 535; Drake, Attachts. Secs. 492, 501.

in the custody of the law and not properly or legally liable to seizure by an officer under an execution."

§ 984. In most of the several states, as a general rule, all movables, including bank notes and money not expressly exempt by statute, are subject to levy and, except money, to sale on execution.[1] Money, when levied, is applied on the writ by the officer.

§ 985. In some states choses in action and debts due to the defendant,[2] shares of stocks in joint stock companies and in corporation,[3] may be levied and sold, as also the mortgagee's right to personal property mortgaged to him, after forfeiture by non-payment when due;[4] but not the interest of the mortgagor after such forfeiture.[5] But if the interest be for a fixed time, then it is liable to levy and sale.[6] Also growing grain and other crops of annual planting can be levied and sold as at common law in some of the states, it is said, and the officer and others entering to levy, sell, or buy, will not be trespassers.[7] But whether the term "annual productions," used by jurists when treating of this principle, extends legitimately to such crops as grow in the ground, is by no means clear to

---

[1] Handy v. Dobbins, 12 Johns. 220; Homes v. Duncaster, 12 Johns. 395.

[2] Collier v. Stanbrough, 6 How. 14.

[3] Stamford Bank v. Ferris, 17 Conn. 259.

[4] Ferguson v. Lee, 9 Wend. 258.

[5] Lamb v. Johnson, 10 Cush. (Mass.) 126. (Unless he have an interest for a fixed time such interest may be levied and sold. See Rindskoff v. Lyman, 16 Iowa, 260.) Marsh v. Lawrence, 4 Cow. 467; Otis v. Wood, 3 Wend. 500; Campbell v. Leonard, 11 Iowa, 489.

[6] Hull v. Carnly, 1 Kern, 501; Mattison v. Bancus, 1 Comst. 295; Rindskoff v. Lyman, 16 Iowa, 260, 269, 270. In this case, Dillon, Justice, said: "The effect of such a sale is the same as if made by the mortgagor in the ordinary way. It does not defeat the mortgage, or destroy, or in any manner impair the legal rights of the mortgagee. It gives the purchaser the right to take possession of and use the property until the day of payment, or until the stipulated time expires; and it gives such purchaser the further right, by transferring to him the equity of redemption, to pay off the mortgage debt, thereby extinguishing the lien of the mortgage, and thus making his title absolute."

[7] Whipple v. Foote, 2 Johns. 418; Hartwell v. Bissell, 17 Johns. 128; Pennablow v. Dwight, 7 Mass. 34; McKinney v. Lampley, 31 Ala. 526; Parham v. Thompson, 2 J. J. Marsh. 150; Pierce v. Roche, 40 Ill. 292.

our mind, for they cannot be gathered without digging up and disturbing the land, which, to our mind, cannot be legally done in virtue of any sale of a mere personalty. In others of the states, crops may only be levied and sold, when standing on the ground, after they have ripened or matured.[1]

§ 986. In *Craddock v. Riddlesbarger*,[2] the Supreme Court of Kentucky, Chief Justice ROBERTSON, hold the following language on this subject: "Although such annual productions, or fruits, of the earth as clover, timothy, spontaneous grasses, apples, pears, peaches, cherries, etc., are considered as incidents to the land in which they are nourished, and are, therefore, not personal; nevertheless, everything produced from the earth by annual planting, cultivation, and labor, and which is, therefore, denominated for the sake of contradistinction, *fructus industriæ*, is deemed personal, and may be sold." And the purchaser, by the same authority, has right of ingress and egress to cultivate, preserve, and remove the same, but acquires no interest in the land itself than such as is for the time being necessarily incident to his right to such growing *fructus.*

§ 987. The interest of one of several tenants in common in personal property may be levied and sold on execution for the debt of such one. The officer in levying takes possession of the whole and delivers the whole to the purchaser,[3] for each one of such common owners may take possession of the whole, as their interests cannot be separated; and so may the officer, who represents, in that respect, the execution debtor. The interest of the debtor, however, alone passes to the purchaser, and not the whole interest in the entire property.[4] The execution purchaser holds the other interests for his co-owners. If after levy of such common interest, and before sale, the execution debtor buy one or more of the other interests in the prop-

---

[1] Shannon v. Jones, 12 Ired, 206.

[2] 2 Dana, (Ky.) 206; Parham v. Thompson, 2 J. J. Marsh. 159.

[3] Birdseye v. Ray, 4 Hill, 158; Hayden v. Binney, 7 Gray, (Mass.) 416; Neary v. Cahill, 20 Ill. 214; White v. Jones, 38 Ill. 159; James v. Stratton, 32 Ill. 202.

[4] Neary v. Cahill, 20 Ill. 159.

erty, the officer, without further notice, may sell the entire interest of the debtor, including the rights so acquired by his purchase.

§ 988. In New York, the sheriff may levy and sell the interest of one partner in goods of a co-partnership, upon a judgment and execution against one only of the firm, recovered against him for his own individual debt. And if an attachment of the firm goods of a co-partnership be made as against non-residents, and afterwards be vacated as to one or more of the partners who are residents, such attachment is not in itself an appropriation of all the goods so originally attached to the payment of the attachment debt. Under execution emanating from such proceedings the officer can sell the interest only of the non-resident partners as to whom the writ of attachment and levy were kept alive.[1]

§ 989. A merely equitable interest in personal property, unaccompanied with possession, cannot be levied and sold at common law; and such, too, is the rule in Missouri.[2] It can neither be handled nor seen, and is incapable of delivery. If subject to sale it is only so by statute. But before forfeiture, the interest of a mortgagor in mortgaged personal property may be levied and sold if he still retains possession of the property. The purchaser takes subject to, and may redeem the mortgage.[3]

§ 990. In levying and selling shares of stock, where liable by statute, it is the shares, or interests, and not the certificates, that are acted on and sold, and a description by the numbers of the several shares, and by the owner's name, is sufficient.[4]

§ 991. Manuscripts secured by copyright, or which are the subjects of copyright, are liable to levy and sale on execution against the owner.[5] But the officer levying can neither legally

[1] Berry v. Kelly, 4 Rob (N. Y.) 106.
[2] Yeldell v. Stemmons, 15 Mo. 443; Sexton v. Monks, 16 Mo. 156; Boyce v. Smith, 16 Mo. 317.
[3] Cotton v. Marsh, 3 Wis. 221; Merritt v. Niles, 25 Ill. 282; Schrader v. Wolfln, 21 Ind. 238.
[4] Stamford Bank v. Ferris, 17 Conn. 259.
[5] Banker v. Caldwell, 3 Minn. 89.

use them, nor make, sell, or publish copies of them. If he does either, he is liable to an action for so doing.[1]

§ 992. In Iowa it is held that the right of redemption in land from a trust deed is the subject of judgment lien, and that after sale by the trustee, the surplus fund, if any, represents the subject of the judgment lien, and that the lien of the judgment is subrogated to this surplus fund, and may be enforced in equity against the same in the hands of such trustee; or may be levied and seized on execution, and process of garnishee.[2] But a judgment is not liable, in Iowa, to execution levy and sale.[3]

§ 993. Iron safes and planing-mills, when not attached to the realty in such manner "as to indicate that it is designed to be permanent," are regarded as personal property subject to execution;[4] and though owned and used by a railroad company, have been holden not to be exempt from execution as property appurtenant to the franchise, or as connected with the freehold; so, likewise, fuel, office furniture, stationery, material for lights, and other detached property of the corporate company, are regarded in Illinois as subject to execution in proceedings against the company.[5]

§ 994. Under the statute of Kentucky subjecting lands to execution sale it is holden in that state that only such lands are so liable to be sold as the debtor himself might dispose of by sale and conveyance. That the language of the statute being "of the lands, tenements and hereditaments in possession, reversion, or remainder," the debt should be levied, and that the deed should "be effectual for passing to the purchaser all the estate and interest which the debtor had and might lawfully part with in the lands," and as, by the then existing laws of Kentucky, lands adversely holden could not be sold or conveyed by the owner whilst thus out of possession, so the

[1] Banker v. Caldwell, 3 Minn. 94.

[2] Cook v. Dillon, 9 Iowa, 407, 412.

[3] Orsborn v. Cloud, 23 Iowa, 104. It can only be reached by garnishee against the judgment debtor.

[4] Titus v. Mabee, 25 Ill. 257, 260.

[5] Hunt v. Bullock, 23 Ill. 320; Palmer v. Forbs, 23 Ill. 302.

power to sell on execution was limited to such lands as the debtor himself might voluntarily sell and convey, and that lands adversely holden against a defendant in execution could not during such adverse possession be subjected to execution sale.[1]

§ 995. It is moreover held, in the same case, in Kentucky, that a subsequent act of assembly, enlarging the powers of owners to make sales of lands so as to cover lands holden adversely, did not authorize their sale under execution whilst such adverse possession continued; that while thus adversely occupied, the lands did not come within the description given in the statute of those which were to be subject to execution sale; that though the debtor might now sell and pass the title thereto, yet they were not his "in possession, reversion or remainder," and therefore not liable under the act subjecting lands to execution and sale for debt.[2]

§ 996. Nor can the officer legally sell the lands of an execution defendant for his fees only, after the judgment as to principal is satisfied. He must look to the plaintiff for his costs.[3]

---

[2] McConnell v. Brown, 5 Mon. 481; Griffith v. Huston, 7 J.J. Marsh. 388; Myers v. Sanders, 7 Dana, 510.

[3] McConnell v. Brown, 5 Mon. 482.

[4] Jackson v. Anderson, 4 Wend. 474.

CHAPTER XXII.

THE LEVY.

I. When to be Made.

§ 997. Unless made at a time prohibited by law, a levy will doubtless be valid at any time within the life of the execution.

§ 998. Though ordinarily it should be made, when practicable, within reasonable hours and not at dead of night, to the annoyance of the debtor, yet there are emergencies which justify the making of it whenever practicable.[1] But it must be made during the lifetime of defendant[2] and of the writ.[3]

§ 999. Returnable to next term means the first day of such term. A levy made after the judicial end of that day, and sale thereon, are unwarrantable as on a levy made too late.[4]

§ 1000. For such illegal levy and sale,[5] or even for the levy alone, trespass lies against the officer.[6]

§ 1001. If sale be made, however, and the proceeds applied to the debt, such fact goes in evidence in diminution of damages.[7]

---

[1] 3 Bac. Abt. "Execution," 734; State v. Thackham, 1 Bay, 358.

[2] Arnold v. Fuller, 1 Ohio, 458, 463; Cartney v. Reed, 5 Ohio, 221.

[3] Devoe v. Elliott, 2 Caine, 243; Vail v. Lewis, 4 Johns. 450; Gaines v. Clark, 1 Bibb, 608.

[4] Prescott v. Wright, 6 Mass. 23.

[5] Ibid.

[6] Ibid.

[7] Ibid.

II. How to be Made.

§ 1002. "A mere paper levy" is void.[1] The officer should take actual possession;[2] but removal of the goods is not absolutely necessary;[3] yet there must be actual control and view of the property, with power of removal.[4]

§ 1003. The property may then be placed in the care of a third party;[5] but at the risk of the officer.[6] Such control must be exercised as if done without the writ, would amount to trespass.[7]

[1] Cary v. Bright, 58 Penn. St. 84. In this case the court say: "A mere paper levy is no levy at all, and a sale under it is a nullity. * * * A man might have his bed sold from under him by that means without his knowing it." Duncan's Appeal, 37 Penn. St. 500.

[2] Westewelt v. Pinckney, 14 Wend. 123; Levi v. Shockley, 29 Geo. 710; Banks v. Evans, 10 S. & M. 35; Brown v. Lane, 19 Texas, 203; Leach v. Pine, 41 Ill. 66; Beckman v. Lansing, 3 Wend. 446; Logsdon v. Spivey, 54 Ill. 104.

[3] Very v. Watkins, 23 How. 469, 474; Bullitt v. Winston, 1 Mumf. 269; Moss v. Moore, 3 Hill, (S. C.) 276; Pugh v. Callaway, 10 Ohio, (N. S.) 488; Logsdon v. Spivey, 54 Ill. 104.

[4] Ray v. Harcourt, 19 Wend. 495; Haggerty v. Wilber, 16 Johns. 287; Van Wyck v. Pine, 2 Hill, 666; Duncan's Appeal, 37 Penn. St. 500; Cawthorn v. McCraw, 9 Ala. 519; Mintuan v. Striker, 1 Edm. (N. Y.) Sel. Cas. 356; Carey v. Bright, 58 Penn. St. 70; Logsdon v. Spivey, 54 Ill. 104. In Carey v. Bright the court hold the following language as to the levy: "In this case the question was only whether, as to part of the goods alleged to have been sold, there ever had been a legal levy. A mere paper levy is no levy at all, and a sale under it is a nullity as to subsequent execution creditors and purchasers. Lowry v. Coulter, 9 Barr, 349. A man might have his bed sold from under him by that means without his knowing it. There was here a considerable amount of personal property levied on, but the sheriff added to the inventory 'all other personal property in, about, and connected with said colliery,' and without having ever gone down into the mines or seen the property, he sold under that description, and left the whole in the possession of the defendants in the execution, from whom the landlord afterwards purchased it."

[5] Very v. Watkins, 23 How. 469, 474; Bullitt v. Winston, 1 Mumf. 269.

[6] Logsdon v. Spivey, 54 Ill. 104; Bullitt v. Winston, 1 Mumf. 269; Clever v. Applegate, 2 South. (N. J.) 479; Moss v. Moore, 3 Hill, (S. C.) 276; Smith v. Hughes, 24 Ill. 270.

[7] Westewelt v. Pinckney, 14 Wend. 123; Havely v. Lowry, 30 Ill. 446; Davidson v. Walden, 31 Ill. 120; McBurnie v. Overstreet, 8 B. Mon. 303; Carey v. Bright, 58 Penn. St. 70; Allen v. McCalla, 25 Iowa, 464; Minor v. Herriford, 25 Ill. 344; Roth v. Wells, 29 N. Y. 471; Duncan's Appeal, 37 Penn. St. 500.

§ 1004. A description of the goods and the facts constituting the levy should be endorsed on the writ, under signature of the officer.[1] A reasonable time therefor, and for removal, if the goods which are to be removed, is allowed by law.[2]

§ 1005. A levy of goods within from the outside of a locked up house is invalid, although one or more articles found outside are actually seized. It is only valid as to the articles seized.[3]

§ 1006. Though the officer cannot release the levy[4] and take other property, yet he may levy other if the defendant, by any means, prevent the sale of the property first levied on.[5] So, to render an additional levy valid, it must appear that the first had become in some manner unavailable.[6]

§ 1007. A levy and sale of a certain number of bricks in a kiln, will be valid if they are in the power of the officer to deliver the same; and the buyer may, by direction of the officer, open the kiln and take them away;[7] but not by selecting the same; only in the usual manner.

§ 1008. If from any circumstance actual possession cannot be taken, and a levy on mere view is relied on, then the officer should call indifferent persons to witness his open assertion of the levy.[8]

§ 1009. The writ first received must be first levied. A postponement of the first, if by plaintiff's order, gives right to priority of levy to the second.[9]

§ 1010. If both are received at once, then they should be levied together, and of the proceeds of sale take share and share alike until either be satisfied; then the balance until satisfaction, goes to the other writ.[10]

---

[1] Haggerty v. Wilber, 16 Johns. 287; Davidson v. Welden, 31 Ill. 120.
[2] Woods v. Van Arsdale, 3 Rawle, 401.
[3] Haggerty v. Wilber, 16 Johns. 287.
[4] Smith v. Hughes, 24 Ill. 270.
[5] Ibid.
[6] Ibid.
[7] Hill v. Harris, 10 B. Mon. 120.
[8] Moore v. Fitz, 15 Ind. 43.
[9] Deposit Bank v. Berry, 2 Bush, (Ky.) 236.
[10] Campbell v. Roger, 1 Cow. 215.

III. Its Effect.

§ 1011. A proper levy to an amount sufficient to satisfy the writ satisfies the judgment *sub modo*.[1] Unlike a levy on the realty, it vests in the officer levying a special property in the thing taken.

§ 1012. But if without fault of the officer or plaintiff the levy becomes unavailing, then it is not a satisfaction of the judgment.[2]

§ 1013. The levy of personalty vests a special property in the officer[3] which will be respected and maintained even in different jurisdiction, as against the execution debtor, or a wrong-doer.[4]

§ 1014. In such case, the expenses of regaining the property will be reimbursed to the officer, with reasonable compensation for his services.[5]

IV. When Void, or Discharged.

§ 1015. A levy made after return day is void.[6] So if made after death of the debtor.[7] So, also, if the property be not subject to the writ, as if holden in valid trust for the payment of other debts of the execution debtor.[8]

§ 1016. A levy may be lost by unreasonable delay to sell,[9] and when so discharged by delay its seniority cannot be reinstated.[10]

[1] Ford v. Skinner, 4 Ohio, 378; Corning v. Hoover, 4 McLean, 133; Smith r. Hughes, 24 Ill. 270; Trenary r. Cheever, 48 Ill. 28; Cass v. Littleton, 3 Ohio, 223; Green r. Burke, 23 Wend. 490.

[2] Curtis v. Root, 28 Ill. 367, 377; Smith v. Hughes, 24 Ill. 270; Green v. Burke, 23 Wend. 490.

[3] McClintock r. Graham, 3 McCord, 213; Rhodes v. Woods, 41 Barb. 471; Williams r. Herndon, 12 B. Mon. 484.

[4] Rhodes v. Woods, 41 Barb. 471.

[5] Ibid.

[6] McClure v. Sutton, 2 Bailey, 361.

[7] Arnold v. Fuller, 1 Ham. (Ohio) 458.

[8] Thompson r. Ford, 7 Ired, 418; 1 Ohio, 458; Cartney v. Reed, 5 Ohio, 221.

[9] Deposit Bank v. Berry, 2 Bush, (Ky.) 621.

[10] Weber v. Henry, 16 Mich. 399, 403.

V. When it will be Set Aside.

§ 1017.   A levy can only be removed by sale, or by an order of court, unless agreed to be displaced by the parties to the writ.[1]

§ 1018.   It will not be discharged by a release of the property made through mistake.[2]

§ 1019.   It will be set aside, if personal property be levied, without leave to the debtor to turn out realty, where he has a right so to do.[3]

§ 1020.   It will also be set aside if levied on property which is in the hands of a receiver under judicial authority,[4]

VI. Constructive Levy.

§ 1021.   Where a sheriff holds several executions in favor of different persons, but against the same judgment debtor, one of which being levied, the others come to his hands afterwards between the day of such levy and the day of sale, it is not necessary, so far as respects the property levied upon by the first writ, or the surplus proceeds of sale thereof, to make a formal levy of the subsequent writ or writs.   The levy on the first writ is valid in law as to all the writs subsequently received, so as to entitle them, each in their order, if more than one, to participate in and receive the surplus, if any, of the monies raised by the sale.[5]

[1] Smith v. Hughes, 24 Ill. 270.
[2] Walker v. The Commonwealth, 18 Gatt. 13.
[3] Pitt v. McGee, 24 Ill. 610.
[4] Robinson v. The Atlantic & Great Western R. R. Co. 66 Penn. St. 160.
[5] Slade v. Van Vechten, 11 Paige, Ch. 21.   In this case Chancellor Walworth lays down the rule as follows: "It is not material whether all the executions were levied or not, for if the sheriff had levied one execution and other executions were in his hands, or in the hands of his deputies, the levy would be valid as to all, so far as to entitle the others to the surplus, if any, raised at the sale under the execution upon which the levy was made, and the property advertised and sold."

CHAPTER XXIII.

THE SALE.

I. BY WHOM TO BE MADE.

§ 1022. The execution, though a judicial writ, commands the performance of a ministerial, and not a judicial act.[1] All such writs, when directed to the sheriff generally, by his style of office, may be executed as well by any one of his legally constituted general deputies as by the high sheriff himself.[2]

§ 1023. The rule in this respect is believed to be the same, whether the levy and sale is of real or of personal property. Therefore the reader is referred for a fuller discussion of the subject, to Chapters XVI and XVII of this work.

§ 1024. But we may add here, that neither the principal officer, nor his deputy, can execute the writ, or sell, when it is in favor of the officer as execution plaintiff, or when such officer has purchased, or otherwise become interested in the proceeds thereof, except for his fees.[3] Neither can the deputy, when in his favor or interest. In such cases the coroner must act.[4]

§ 1025. If the writ is not otherwise satisfied, and property subject thereto be found and levied, then a sale becomes an

---

[1] Bac. Abt. 8, 689, 690, 691; Wroe v. Harris, 2 Wash. (Va.) R. 126, 129.

[2] Wroe v. Harris, 2 Wash. (Va.) 126, 129, 130; Tillotson v. Cheetham, 2 Johns. 63; 8 Bac. Abt. 675, 676.

[3] Chambers v. Thomas, 3 A. K. Marshall, 536, 537; Riner v. Stacey, 8 Humph. 288, 467; May v. Walters, 2 McCord, 470.

[4] Singletary v. Carter, 1 Bailey, 467; Chambers v. Thomas, 1 Litt. 268; and Chambers v. Thomas, 3 A. K. Marsh. 536.

act necessarily involved in the execution of the writ; and it follows that whoever may execute the writ may sell. Therefore the principal sheriff, or any one of his legally constituted general deputies, may in ordinary cases sell.[1]

§ 1026. But whether the sale be made by the one or the other of them, a crier, or auctioneer may be employed to conduct the sale, provided his acts be done in the presence and under the direction of the officer.[2]

§ 1027. If, however, the writ be especially directed to the principal, or high sheriff himself, by his personal name, as well as style of office, then he only, and no one else, can execute it.[3]

§ 1028. In *Chambers v. Thomas*,[4] the Supreme Court of Kentucky say in reference to this subject: "The principal sheriff is never allowed to execute his own process; and so careful is the law in guarding the interest of the defendant in such cases that not even the deputy is permitted to execute the process; but it must go to the coroner, an officer not supposed to be under the influence of the sheriff." The identical point was previously adjudicated between the same parties and decided the same way in 3 A. K. Marshall, by the Supreme Court of Kentucky.[5]

§ 1029. An execution in the hands of an officer when he goes out of office, which is partly executed by him, may be completely executed afterwards. He continues sheriff for that purpose, and may carry out the work by him begun, by himself or by his deputy, as if he were still in office.[6]

§ 1030. In the case cited from 3 Cowen, the court, SAVAGE, Justice, lay down the rule in these words: "He is in office *quoad hoc*, and the acts of a deputy, in relation to such an execution are the acts of the sheriff himself."[7] Such, too, is the doctrine even on a *ca. sa.* where the defendant is holden in

---

[1] 8 Bac. Abt. 675, "Undersheriff," ib. 676.

[2] See Ante, Ch. xvii.

[3] 8 Bac. Abt. "Undersheriff," 676; Wroe v. Harris, 2 Wash. (Va.) 126, 129, 130.

[4] 1 Litt. 268.

[5] Chambers v. Thomas, 3 A. K. Marsh. 537.

[6] Jackson v. Collins, 3 Cow. 89.

[7] Jackson v. Collins, 3 Cow. 95.

custody by the old sheriff. He may retain the custody of the defendant and complete the work of executing the writ.[1]

II. How to be Made.

§ 1031. The sale must be made at the time and place appointed by the notice given thereof, unless it be adjourned; and if made before the hour appointed it will be void in case the property goes for less than its full value.[2]

§ 1032. The sale is to be made during the business hours of the day. An execution sale, made out of business hours, as for instance, after sun-set, is void, and the officer, by so making it, becomes a trespasser.[3] If made before the day appointed, it is, in Illinois, held to be void.[4]

§ 1033. In selling personal property, the property to be sold must be present, so that it may be seen, handled and estimated, and ready for delivery.[5]

§ 1034. In the case of *Herod v. Bartley*,[6] Chief Justice TREAT, of the Illinois Supreme Court, lays down the law of this subject in the following terms: "In the sale of personal property on execution, the property itself must be present. "Bidders should have an opportunity of inspecting the goods and forming an estimate of their value. This is the only way to secure fairness and competition at public sales. It is necessary to protect the rights of both debtor and creditor. It should also be in the power of the officer to deliver the property forthwith to the purchaser."

§ 1035. If a sale be made of personal property which is not present and capable of being inspected by the bidders, and of being delivered by the officer to the purchaser, the sale,

---

[1] Hemstead v. Read, 20 Johns. 64; Jackson v. Collins, 3 Cow. 95.

[2] Williams v. Jones, 1 Bush. (Ky.) 621.

[3] Carwick v. Myers, 14 Barb. (N. Y.) 9.

[4] King v. Cushman, 41 Ill. 31.

[5] Herod v. Bartley, 15 Ill. 58; Sheldon v. Sobe, 15 Ill. 352; Cresson v. Stout, 17 Ill. 116; Ainsworth v. Greenlee, 3 Murph. 470; Blanton v. Marrow, 7 Ired. 47.

[6] Herod v. Bartley, 15 Ill. 59.

according to the case of *Herod v. Bartley*, will be void.[1] Such, too, it is believed, is the weight of authority.

§ 1036. The sale must be at public auction, to the highest bidder, for the best price the property will bring,[2] and must be for money; cash in hand.[3] The officer may receive only gold and silver legal coin, or whatever else is by law a legal tender.[4] The rule in this respect is the same as on sales of real estate on execution.[5]

§ 1037. "As a matter of discretion,"[6] the officer may adjourn the sale to a different day, or place, or both; and if there be no fraud in it or abuse of discretion, the sale will be valid in that respect.[7]

§ 1038. Nor will a postponement by the plaintiff's order destroy his priority in favor of subsequent writs, if done in good faith and from fair motives, and to a day not beyond the return day of writ.[8] But otherwise, if to a day subsequent to the return day, it is said.[9]

§ 1039. A sale on execution has been holden valid as between the debtor, creditor, and officer when made without notice, being so made by consent of parties.[10]

§ 1040. But the mere silence of the debtor, in standing by and seeing his property illegally sold on execution will not render such sale valid, and will not estop such debtor from testing the validity thereof.[11]

[1] Herod v. Bartley, 15 Ill. 58.

[2] 1 Bouvier, 581; Swoitzell v. Martin, 16 Iowa, 519, 527.

[3] Noiz. Max. Ch. 42; Griffin v. Thompson, 2 How. 244; Saur v. Steinbauer, 14 Wis. 70; Mumford v. Armstrong, 4 Cow. 553; Swope v. Anderson, 5 Ind 213; Mitchell v. Hackett, 14 Cal. 661; Bigley v. Risher, 63 Penn. St. 152; Hilliard, Sales, 1230.

[4] Griffin v. Thompson. 2 How. 244.

[5] See Ante, Ch. XVII. No. 2.

[6] Tinkham v. Purdy, 5 Johns. 345; Russell v. Richards, 11 Maine 371.

[7] Tinkham v. Purdy, 5 Johns. 345; Russell v. Richards, 11 Maine 371; Swortzell v. Martin, 16 Iowa, 519; Phelps v. Conover, 25 Ill. 309; Payne v. Bellingham, 10 Iowa, 360.

[8] Lantz v. Worthington, 4 Barr. 153.

[9] Lantz v. Worthington, 4 Barr. 153.

[10] Burroughs v. Wright, 19 Vt. 510.

[11] Humphrey v. Browne, 19 La. Ann. 158.

§ 1041. The officer, in selling, is to exercise such wholesome discretion in regard to the manner of selling, as a prudent person ordinarily would in reference to his own affairs under like circumstances, with a view to obtaining the best possible price for the property at a fair and honest sale. He should, therefore, in selling various articles of property, sell them separately, if intended for separate use, and not *en masse*, unless some of them be more suited to go together.[1] In the latter cases, such articles should be sold together, if thereby it is inferable that they would bring the better price, or be more generally acceptable to bidders. By separation, some articles intended to go together, would be measurably destroyed in value, whilst, on the other hand, the uniting others together would tend to force bidders to either forego the purchase of those desired or else buy such as they may not want.

§ 1042. One buying at execution sale, under his own execution, will not ordinarily be compelled to pay over the money to the officer, further than the costs of others than himself; but may receipt the writ, if there be no other writ in the officer's hands claiming priority or contribution. "It would be unreasonable and injurious to debtors as well as creditors, to insist that the creditor in the execution, should advance money on his bid, when the sole object of the sale is to put money in his pocket by paying a debt due to him."[2]

§ 1043. But if there be a dispute about the application or distribution of the money, in case of more than one writ, then the officer may refuse to deliver the property to the plaintiff without payment, or may sell again.[3] The better course, however, would be to report the proceedings to the court, as we conceive, and have the priority settled.

§ 1044. In cases of execution sales made where there is a valuation law, the same principal prevails in sales of personal, as of real property.[4] That is, if the liability occurred within the same jurisdiction wherein the sale is being made, then the

[1] Bac. Abt. Vol. 3, 704; Cresson v. Stout. 17 Johns. 116.
[2] Nichols v. Ketchum, 19 Johns. 92; Russell v. Gibbs, 5 Cow. 390.
[3] Russell v. Gibbs, 5 Cow. 390; Swortzell v. Martin, 16 Iowa, 519, 526, 527.
[4] See Ante Ch. XVII., No. 6.

22

sale must be in conformity to the law, as it was when the liability occurred, provided the proper data to enable the officer to conform, in that respect, appears from the process.[1] If, however, the contract originate in one jurisdiction and the enforcement of it is in another, then the law of the state where and when it is being enforced is to govern the mode of sale.[2]

§ 1045. So, in like manner, if it do not appear where the liability occurred, then the enforcement is to be in accordance with the law as it exists at the place of sale at the time of rendition of the judgment.

§ 1046. Such are the general principles, as applicable to execution sales, of both personal and real property. But the result of a departure therefrom is not necessarily, in all cases, and in all the states, the same in one case as in the other.

§ 1047. In *Rosier v. Hale*,[3] the Supreme Court of Iowa, LOWE, Justice, held: "The doctrine laid down is, that the law in force when the contract is made is necessarily referred to and forms a part of the contract, and fixes the rights and obligations growing out of it, and that any substantial change in the law of the remedy which shall lessen its efficiency or burden it with new conditions and restrictions, comes within the constitutional prohibition.

III.   ITS EFFECT: WHAT PASSES BY IT.

§ 1048. The effect of an execution sale, realizing the amount of the execution, is a satisfaction of the judgment. Thereby it "ceases to exist." It loses its vitality. It can only be restored or revived by an order of court vacating satisfaction. The

---

[1] Bronson v. Kinzie, 1 How. 311; McCracken v. Hayward, 2 How. 608; Gantley's Lessee v. Ewing, 3 How. 707; Blair v. Williams, 4 Litt. 34; Lapsley v. Brashears, 4 Litt. 47; Pool v. Young, 7 B. Mon. 587; McKinney v. Carroll, 5 Mon. 98; Grayson v. Silly, 7 Mon. 6; Smith v. Morse, 2 Cal. 524; Hunt v. Gregg, 8 Blackf. 105; Coriel v. Ham, 4 G. Greene, 455; Burton v. Emerson, 4 G. Greene, 393; Shaffer v. Bolander, 4 G. Greene. 201; Willard v. Longstreet, 2 Doug. (Mich.) 172; Quackenbush v. Danks, 1 Denio, 128; Rosier v. Hale, 10 Iowa, 475.

[2] Hutchins v. Barrett, 19 Ind. 15; Doe v. Collins, 1 Carter (Ind.) 24; Shaffer v. Bolander, 4 G. Greene, 201; Story, Confl. of Laws, Sec. 556.

[3] 10 Iowa, 485.

making of this order requires a judicial power equal to that which originally entered the judgment. No less a power can impart new life to it, when satisfied by the acts, valid for the time being, of an officer having power so to do.[1]

§ 1049. Until such satisfaction be judicially vacated, and execution anew be ordered, no subsequent execution can legally issue on the judgment.[2] It is well said that "an execution executed is the end of the law."[3]

§ 1050. Payment of the money to the plaintiff satisfies the writ, by whomsoever the payment be made. The sheriff cannot, of his own funds, pay off the creditor for the execution in his hands, or otherwise satisfy him, and retain the writ and its vitality to enforce the same against the defendant as the means of indemnifying himself. If he thus pay off the creditor, both writ and judgment are thereby satisfied, and are *functus officio.*[4] This, too, irrespective of the inability of the officer to execute a writ for his own benefit. There remains, after such payment, no vital writ to be executed by any one. The vital force of both writ and judgment are, by the very act of payment, extinct.

§ 1051. The purchaser has a right to what he gets, and to nothing more. *Caveat emptor* is the rule. He takes only the interest of the defendant. If the defendant has no interest, then the buyer gets nothing; and he cannot avoid payment by showing that the goods belonged to some one else.[5] But if an innocent purchaser, he may have redress in equity against the execution debtor whose debt he has paid.[6]

§ 1052. By a sale of personal property on an execution against one of two common owners, the purchaser takes only the interest therein of the defendant in the writ. He becomes the tenant in common with the other owner. This, too,

---

[1] Hughes v. Streeter, 24 Ill. 647, 649.

[2] Ibid.

[3] 3 Bac. Abt. 687.

[4] Sherman v. Boyce, 15 Johns. 446; Reed v. Pruyn, 7 Johns. 426.

[5] Griffith v. Fowler, 18 Vt. 390; Popleston v. Skinner, 4 Dev. & Batt. 160; McGee v. Ellis, 4 Litt. 244; Austin v. Tilden, 14 Vt. 325.

[6] McGee v. Ellis, 4 Litt. 244.

although the officer assumes to sell the whole.[1] Therefore the common owner whose rights are not affected by the sale, cannot maintain an action in reference to the transaction against the purchaser or the officer who sells.[2]

§ 1053. But if after levy and before sale the execution defendant buys the interest of the other tenant in common in the property levied, then the officer, without further levy or notice, may sell the whole interest and entire property.[3]

§ 1054. If after levy on lands, they be sowed in grain by the debtor, before execution sale, and then another execution be levied on the growing grain, and the same be sold thereon, the latter writ will be entitled to preference in the proceeds of the grain.[4]

§ 1055. A distinction is taken between a sale of the property itself and of the mere interest of the debtor therein. In the former case the purchaser takes the property with its legal incidents, whilst in the latter he takes only the interest which the debtor, as such, has and may himself enforce.[5]

§ 1056. To a purchaser of growing grain, at execution sale, on execution against the owner, the right to enter and take away the grain, or to secure, harvest and preserve it, passes with the property to the purchaser; neither the purchaser nor officer will be liable to an action for acts necessary and proper to be done by them in regard to it.[6] But in an action therefor it is not sufficient that they justify under execution sale; but the plea must show the execution to have been against the owner of the property levied and sold. A mere allegation of purchase on execution sale, generally, will not amount to a defense.[7]

---

[1] Popleston v. Skinner, 4 Dev. & Batt. 160.

[2] Fiero v. Betts, 2 Barb. 633; Wilson v. Reed, 3 Johns. 175; White v. Osborn, 21 Wend. 75.

[3] Birdseye v. Ray, 4 Hill, 158.

[4] Stambaugh v. Yates, 2 Rawle, 161.

[5] True v. Congdon, 44 N. H. 48.

[6] Terrill v. Thompson, 3 Bibb, 273.

[7] Ibid.

IV. Void and Voidable Sales. ·

§ 1057. Execution sales of personal property, as is the case in similar sales of real property, made on executions that are satisfied, or that issued on satisfied judgments, are universally regarded as void when the purchaser buys or pays with knowledge of such satisfaction.[1]

§ 1058. And whether the purchaser has such knowledge or not, the better authority is that the sale being on a power that is exhausted, the sale is void. It is no better than a sale upon a void judgment. It cannot, under the usual circumstances, be sustained.[2] But if the execution debtor, with knowledge of such satisfaction, silently stand by and suffer others to purchase, or do acts calculated to mislead a buyer in making such purchase, it is a fraud on his part, and he is estopped to deny the validity of the sale.[3]

§ 1059. A sale fraudulent in itself, though made under color of execution, is of no validity, and, therefore, where the process of the court is prostituted to the fraudulent purpose of hindering and delaying other creditors, under semblance of a real sale, the transaction will be treated as fraudulent and void.[4]

§ 1060. In Louisiana, debts due to an execution debtor are subject to levy and sale, but are required to be appraised, before sale, at cash value, and to be sold for not less than two-thirds of such value. It is holden in that state, that a sale of such interest, on execution, without appraisement, though in other respects regular, is void.[5]

V. Who may not Buy.

§ 1061. The same person may not both buy and sell, by

[1] Jackson v. Anderson, 4 Wend. 474; Nielson v. Nielson, 5 Barb. 565.

[2] Nielson v. Neilson, 5 Barb. 565; Jackson v. Anderson, 4 Wend. 474, 479; Childs v. Bernard's Ex'rs, 3 Dana, 95, 96; Monchat v. Brown, 3 Rich. 117; Lavelle v. Rowley, 17 Ind. 36; State v. Salers, 19 Ind. 432; Sherman v. Boyce, 15 Johns. 443· Jackson v. Caldwell, 1 Cow. 622; Hammit v. Wyman, 9 Mass. 138; Lewis v. Palmer, 6 Wend. 368.

[3] Wood v. Colvin, 2 Hill, 556; Jackson v. Caldwell, 1 Cow. 622.

[4] Stephens v. Barnett, 7 Dana, 259; Corlies v. Standbridge, 5 Rawle, 286; Yoder v. Standiford, 7 Mon. 485.

[5] Collier v. Stanbrough, 6 How. 14.

mere force of. the process. Nor will his return thereof on the writ show such title in him as will be regarded even as against a trespasser.[1]

§ 1062. In the case here cited from Vermont, the title to certain cattle was involved. The sheriff claimed to own them by purchase at an execution sale made by himself. Though the levy vested a special property in the sheriff, yet the levy had become merged in the sale. So he had no longer a claim under it. Thus, the sole question, say the court, was "whether an officer acting under legal process can sell property to himself." They say that, "According to all the authorities, such an officer, in addition to his character as a minister of the law, is regarded as a sort of trustee and agent both of the creditor and debtor. The two characters place him on higher and more responsible ground than a mere private trustee or agent. And if the latter is not permitted to acquire a personal interest in the matter of his agency, much less should such indulgence be granted to the former." In the same case the court lay down the rule that even if the purchase be made by consent of plaintiff and defendant in the writ, that though it might then, as between the officer himself and the parties, be valid, yet it would amount to no more than a purchase from the defendant himself, yet it would in nowise partake of the sanctity of an execution sale.

§ 1063. But if the writ of execution be directed to his principal, and the sale be made by him, and the deputy be the execution creditor, then such deputy, it is believed, may rightfully purchase at the sale of his principal if it be fairly made.[2] And such, too, is believed to be the rule, whether the sale be of personalty or of realty. It is equally the interest of debtor and creditor that the execution creditor shall, in such case, be allowed to bid. It is very different from a case in which the principal sheriff is plaintiff and his deputy sells. In this case the court say, in reference to the act of assembly which pro-

[1] Woodbury v. Parker, 19 Vt. 353; see also Mills v. Goodsell, 5 Conn. 475; Pierce v. Benjamin, 14 Pick. 359; Perkins v. Thompson, 3 N. H. 144; Moorland v. Kimberlin, 6 B. Mon. 608.
[2] Jackson v. Collins, 3 Cow. 89.

hibits a sheriff from buying at execution sales: "It could never have been the intention of the legislature to have prevented a deputy sheriff, when plaintiff in an execution sale, from bidding, in order to secure his money. The object was to prevent abuse."[1]

§ 1065. In Massachusetts it is held that a sale made under an appraisement law, where a brother of the execution creditor was one of the appraisers, is illegal, and moreover, that thereby the officer selling becomes a trespasser.[2]

VI. WHEN THE OFFICER MAY RE-SELL.

§ 1066. If the terms of sale are not promptly complied with by the purchaser by payment of the purchase money, the officer may sell again without further notice, at the same time and place.[3] But not within the time allowed, if any, by terms of sale, for payment to be made.[4]

§ 1067. All such sales are for cash, and ought to be for cash in hand; if the purchaser do not comply, it is adjudged in some cases that he may be compelled to make good the deficiency in price, if any, on the re-sale of the property.[5]

---

[1] Ibid.

[2] McCough v. Wellington, 6 Allen (Mass.) 505.

[3] Illingworth v. Miltenberger, 11 Mo. 81; Winslow v. Loring, 7 Mass. 392; Haynes v. Breaux, 16 La. An. 142; Saur v. Stienbauer, 14 Wis. 7; Gaskill v. Morris, 7 Watts & Sergt. 32; Bigley v. Risher, 63 Penn. St. 152.

[4] Conway v. Noltee, 11 Mo. 74.

[5] Lamkin v. Crawford, 8 Ala. 153; Minter v. Dent, 2 Bailey, 291.

CHAPTER XXIV.

EXECUTION SALES OF CORPORATE FRANCHISES, PROPERTY AND STOCKS.

    I. AT COMMON LAW.
    II. BY STATUTE.
    III. EFFECT OF SALE.

I. AT COMMON LAW.

§ 1068. The Supreme Court of the United States, recognizing the rule that corporate franchises, being incorporeal hereditaments, cannot, upon the settled principles of the common law, be seized and sold on execution, declare that if they can be sold, in any of the states, "it must be under statutory provision." Such, too, is the current of authorities.[1]

§ 1069. Nor can the lands, easements, or works appurtenant to, or essential to the use and practical operation of the franchise be levied and sold on execution at law, separate from the franchise, so as to impair its value or impede its use.[2] Neither are the tolls or product of the franchise subject to such levy and sale, so as to prevent the company from demanding and receiving the same, or so as to divest it of its right of ownership and possession.[3]

---

[1] Gue v. Tide Water Canal Co. 24 How. 263; James v. Pontiac Plankroad Co. 8 Mich. 91; Coe v. Columbus & C. R. R. Co. 10 Ohio St. 372; Seymore v. Milf. & Chil. Turnpike Co. 10 Ohio, 476, 480; Stewart v. Jones, 40 Mo. 140; Youngman v. Elmira & W. R. R. Co. 65 Penn. St. 278; Western Penn. R. R. Co. v. Johnson, 59 Penn. St. 290; Atkinson v. M. & C. R. R. Co. 15 Ohio, 21; Canal Co. v. Bonham, 9 Watts & Serg. 27, 28; Wood v. Turnpike Co. 24 Cal. 474; Monroe v. Thomas, 5 Cal. 470; Thomas v. Armstrong, 7 Cal. 286.

[2] Gue v. Tide Water Canal Co. 24 How. 257; Amant v. New Alexandria & Pittsburg Turnpike Co. 13 S. & R. 212; Susquehanna Canal Co. v. Bonham, 9 Watts & Serg. 27; Plymouth R. R. Co. v. Caldwell, 39 Penn. St. 337; Coe v. Columbus R. R. Co. 10 Ohio St. 372; Young v. Alexandia & Western R. R. Co. 65 Penn. St. 278.

[3] Gue v. Tide Water Canal Co. 24 How. 263; Leedon v. Plymouth R. R. Co. 5 W. & S. 265; Seymore v. Milf. & Chil. Turnpike Co. 10 Ohio, 479. In

§ 1070. A railroad, if subject to execution sale at all, cannot be cut up into parcels and sold at different sales, in the different counties in which it is situate; it would defeat the purposes of the law in reference to the road.[1] Nor can the

the case cited from 24 How. a *fieri facias* issued to the U. S. Marshal for the district of Maryland, who "seized and advertised for sale a house and lot, sundry canal locks, a wharf, and sundry other lots," which belonged to the defendant, the Tide Water Canal Company, in fee. The company obtained an injunction against the sale, and the same was made perpetual in the Circuit Court of the United States for said Maryland district. From the decree perpetuating the injunction the case was appealed by Gue to the United States Supreme Court. There the decree was affirmed. We insert here the following extract from the opinion of the United States Supreme Court: "Now it is very clear that the franchise or right to take toll, on boats going through the canal, would not pass to the purchaser under this execution. The franchise, being an incorporeal hereditament, cannot, upon the settled principles of the common law, be seized under a *fieri facias*. If it can be done in any of the states, it must be under a statutory provision of the state; and there is no statute of Maryland changing the common law in this respect. Indeed, the marshal's return and the agreement of the parties show it was not seized, and consequently, if the sale had taken place, the result would have been to destroy utterly the value of the property owned by the company, while the creditor himself would, most probably, realize scarcely anything from the useless canal locks and lots adjoining them. The record and proceedings before us show that there were other creditors of the corporation to a large amount, some of whom loaned money to carry on the enterprise. And it would be against the principles of equity to allow a single creditor to destroy a fund to which other creditors had a right to look for payment, and equally against the principles of equity to permit him to destroy the value of the property of the stockholders by dissevering from the franchise property which was essential to its useful existence. In this view of the subject, the court do not deem it proper to express any opinion as to the right of this creditor in some other form of judicial proceeding to compel the sale of the whole property of the corporation, including the franchise, for the payment of his debt.   *   *   *   *   If the appellant has a right to enforce the sale of the whole property, including the franchise, his remedy is in a court of chancery, where the rights and priorities of all the creditors may be considered and protected, and the property of the corporation disposed of to the best advantage for the benefit of all concerned. A court of common law, from the nature of its jurisdiction and modes of proceeding, is incapable of accomplishing this object; and the court was right in granting the injunction, and its decree is therefore affirmed." Gue v. Tide Water Canal Co. 24 How. 263, 264.

[1] Macon & West. R. R. Co. v. Parker, 9 Geo. 377.

turn-tables of the road, or freight-cars found on the road or on
the side-tracks thereof, be levied and sold on execution at law
against a railroad company; they are a part of the realty, are
incident to the franchise, and cannot be thus severed and sold.[1]
So, likewise, stocks or shares in corporate companies may not,
except by statute, be taken on execution and sold at law.[2]   But
in New Hampshire it has been holden that locomotive engines,
passenger-cars and freight-cars of a railroad corporation are
liable to attachment and execution sale when not in actual use.[3]

§ 1071.   In Pennsylvania it is held that the right of way
and road bed of a railroad corporation, assessed to the company
" as a right of way or passage, with such occupancy as is necessary to give this right effect," being a mere easement, is not
the subject of execution sale.   The court say: "This being
the nature of the interest acquired by a railroad company in
land appropriated for the use of its railroad, a mere easement
or right of passage for a public purpose, it is a settled principle
in our law that this interest is not the subject of a lien or sale
under execution."[4]

§ 1072.   In California it is held that a sale of the road of a
corporate company on execution at law passes no title to the
franchise, or to the road.   In *Wood v. Turnpike Co.*,[5] the court
say, SHAFTER, Justice: "The plaintiff acquired nothing by the
purchase of the 'road' to which the action of ejectment has
any remedial relations."

[1] Titus *v.* Mabee, 25 Ill. 257; Seymore *v.* Milf. & Chil. Turnpike Co. 10
Ohio, 476, 480; Hunt *v.* Bullock, 23 Ill. 320; Palmer *v.* Forbs, 23 Ill. 302.
In Seymore *v.* The Milford and Chillicothe Turnpike Co. the Supreme
Court of Ohio hold the following language: "There can be no doubt that
the right of taking toll upon a turnpike road is a franchise, and is not at
common law, nor by our law regulating judgments and executions, the
proper subject upon which to levy an execution."

[2] James *v.* Plank-road Co. 8 Mich. 91; Titcomb *v.* Ins. Co. 8 Mass. 326;
Taylor *v.* Junkins, 6 Jones' Law (N. C.) 316.

[3] Boston, Concord & Montreal R. R. Co. *v.* Gilmore, 37 N. H. 410.

[4] Western Penn. R. R. Co. *v.* Johnson, 59 Penn. St. 290, 294; Armant *v.*
Turnpike R. Co. 13 S. & R. 210; Ridge Turnpike Co. *v.* Stover, 2 W. & S.
548; Leedom *v.* Plymouth R. R. Co. 5 ib. 265; Susquehanna Canal Co. *v.*
Bonham, 9 ib. 27.

[5] 24 Cal. 474, 478.

II. By Statute.

§ 1073. As authority to make such sales on executions at law can exist only by express statute, it follows that they can only be made in such manner as the statute prescribes.[1] There must be a substantial conformity to the statutory method of sale, otherwise no right will pass by the sale. Where the sale by the statute should have been to the one who for the shortest period of user would pay the debt and costs, and it was made for an absolute term, for part only of the debt and costs, the sale was holden to be void.[2] Nor will the mere acquiescence of the stockholders, or taking possession by the purchaser, give validity to the sale.[3]

§ 1074. In *Davis v. Maynard*, it is held that such conformity must be shown by the purchaser in case of litigation involving the validity of the sale; that such showing should be by the officer's return embodying the evidences of the required conformity; and that, therefore, without a return of the officer the purchaser takes nothing.[4]

§ 1075. Selling on different notice than that required by the statute, will (for instance) render the sale void.[5]

[1] Gue v. Tide Water Canal Co. 24 How. 257; James v. Plank-road Co. 8 Mich. 91; Titcomb v. Ins. Co. 8 Mass. 326; Taylor v. Jenkins, 6 Jones, Law (N. C.) 316; Seymore v. Milf. & Chil. Turnpike Co. 5 Ohio, 476; How v. Starkweather, 17 Mass. 240; Davis v. Maynard, 9 Mass. 242; Stanford Bank v. Ferries, 17 Conn. 259.

[2] James v. Plank-road Co. 8 Mich. 91; Taylor v. Jenkins, 6 Jones' Law, (N. C.) 316. There is this distinction in that respect between ordinary execution sales of personal property. There the levy is accompanied with tangible possession. It vest a special property in the officer, and the title passes to the purchaser, with delivery of the property by the officer, whether the sale be regular or not. But in sales of shares in an incorporated company, the interest being intangible and incapable of delivery, the title must pass by legal transfer, else not at all. Hence if the sale be not in accordance with the substantial requirements of the statute it will be inoperative and will not confer title on the purchaser. (Titcomb v. Union Ins. Co. 8 Mass. 326; How v. Starkweather, 17 Mass. 240.)

[3] James v. Plank-road Co. 8 Mich. 91.

[4] 9 Mass. 242; Hammitt v. Wyman, 9 Mass. 138; How v. Starkweather, 17 Mass. 240.

[5] How v. Starkweather, 17 Mass. 240; Titcomb v. Ins. Co. 8 Mass. 326.

§ 1076. A sale and transfer of bank stock to the bank by a stockholder, after imperfect levy of a writ of attachment thereon, and before levy of execution in the attachment proceedings, carries title to the stock as against an execution sale in the proceedings by attachment.[1]

§ 1077. The modern tendency is, in the absence of statutory declaration on the subject, to regard stocks or shares of incorporated companies as a personal interest, even where the tangible effects or property of the company is real property.[2]

§ 1078. They are not strictly chattels, but a mere interest of a personal nature, and the certificates are but the evidence of such interest, and are of no value in themselves other than as the best proof of ownership of the interest which they represent.[3]

§ 1079. The current authority is that such interest is not liable to levy and sale on execution at common law, as we have herein before seen;[4] but are only so by statute.[5]

§ 1080. When thus liable a sale thereof on execution at law emanating in attachment proceedings, fairly made to a *bona fide* purchaser, will override a sale and transfer of certificates

---

[1] Stamford Bank *v.* Ferries, 17 Conn. 259.

[2] Redfield, Railways, 38; Gilpin *v.* Howell, 5 Penn. St. 57; Angel & Ames, Corps. Secs. 557, 558, 559; Tippett *v.* Walker, 4 Mass. 595; Johns *v.* Johns, 1 Ohio St. 350; Arnold *v.* Ruggles, 1 R. I. 165; How *v.* Starkweather, 17 Mass. 243; Denton *v.* Livingston, 9 Johns. 100; Planters' Bank *v.* Merchants' Bank, 4 Ala. (N. S.) 753; The State *v.* The Franklin Bank, 10 Ohio, 91. But otherwise, if the property be land and is vested, not in the corporation, but in the individual shareholders. Angell & Ames, Corps. Sec. 559.

[3] Angell & Ames, Corps. Secs. 560, 561; Agricultural Bank *v.* Burr, 11 Shep. 256; The Same *v.* Wilson, 11 Shep. 273.

[4] Gue *v.* Tide Water Canal Co. 24 How. 257, and *ante* No. 1 of this chapter; Evans *v.* Monett, 4 Jones' Eq. (N. C.) 227; Ross *v.* Ross, 25 Geo. 297; Angell & Ames, Corps. 558, 559; James *v.* Pontiac Plank-road Co. 8 Mich. 91; Coe *v.* Columbus & C. R. R. Co. 10 Ohio (N. S.) 372; Western Penn. R. R. Co. *v.* Johnson, 59 Penn. St. 290; Stewart *v.* Jones, 40 Mo. 140.

[5] Angell *v.* Ames, Corps. Secs. 588, 589; Foster *v.* Potter, 37 Mo. 525; Gue *v.* Tide Water Canal Co. 4 How. 257; Weaver *v.* Huntingdon, etc., R. R. Co. 50 Penn. St. 314; How *v.* Starkweather, 17 Mass. 240; Denny *v.* Hamilton, 16 Mass. 402; Planters' Bank *v.* Leavens, 4 Ala. (N. S.) 753.

previously made in good faith, if no notice be given to the corporation of such sale.[1]

§ 1081. A state, or municipal government, or corporation, by becoming a stockholder in a business corporation descends to the level of individual stockholders of the same company; can claim no rights and no exemptions but those which private stockholders may claim.[2]

§ 1082. As a sequence from this it would seem to follow that if shares of ordinary or private stockholders are by law liable to execution sale, so are those of the state or municipal corporation, except that so far as relates to the shares of a sovereign state, it not being liable to suit there can be no writ of execution against it.

§ 1083. But what property or interests a municipal corporation may buy it may also sell, unless there be a restraining clause in the charter or the law to the contrary;[3] and it is well settled that what an owner may sell himself, may be sold on execution, if there be no law to the contrary.[4]

§ 1084. When shares of stock are levied on by more than one execution and sold under the senior levy, the surplus funds, if any, must be paid over on the junior levy.[5]

§ 1085. A requirement of the act of incorporation, where the incorporation is by act of assembly, defining the manner of executing and selling stocks or shares, supercedes in that respect the general law of anterior date as to execution sales, and must be conformed to.[6]

§ 1086. Where the officers of a turnpike company procured shares in the company sold on execution to be bought in for the company, and then appropriated a part thereof to them-

[1] Blanchard v. Dedham, 12 Gray (Mass.) 213; Naglee v. Pacific Wharf Co. 20 Cal. 529; Littell v. Scranton, 42 Penn. St. 500; Weaver v. Huntingdon, etc., R. R. Co. 50 Penn. St. 314.

[2] Bank U. S. v. Planters' Bank, 9 Wheat. 904.

[3] New Ark Town Council v. Elliott, 5 Ohio St. 113, 121.

[4] Combs v. Jordan, 3 Bland Ch. 39, 42; The Carpenter's Case, ib. 640.

[5] Denny v. Hamilton, 16 Mass. 402.

[6] Titcomb v. Union Ins. Co. 8 Mass. 326.

selves, it was holden that suit therefor lay against them by a shareholder for his damages.[1]

§ 1087. An execution purchaser of hypothecated stocks, knowing them to be such, takes subject to the right of the pledgee.[2] But the contrary is the ruling if bought in good faith and without notice.[3]

§ 1088. If a company, by its by-laws, have a lien on the stock of its stockholders, an execution purchaser with notice thereof will be postponed in favor of the company.[4]

§ 1089. A purchaser of mortgaged stocks at execution sale takes subject to the mortgage, but is entitled to the surplus proceeds of the mortgage sale, if any.[5]

§ 1090. The court lay down the rule in *Weaver v. The Huntingdon, etc., Railroad Company,* that railroad stocks, in Pennsylvania, standing on the books in the name of the real owner, are liable to levy and sale on execution against such owner; but bank stocks, in the same state, being ordinarily by law of the state subject to liens for any indebtedness of the stockholder to the bank, should be levied by attachment proceedings and garnishee, in which the precise interest of the debtor is necessarily ascertained, whereby useless expenses and litigation may be avoided in case the stock be so subject to prior lien that no interest would pass by sale.[6]

---

[1] Kimmel v. Stoves, 18 Penn. St. 155.

[2] Western v. Bear River & Auburn Co. 5 Cal. 186; Tuttle v. Walton, 1 Geo. 43; West Branch R. R. Co. v. Armstrong, 40 Penn. St. 278.

[3] New York & New Haven R. R. Co. v. Schuyler, 38 Barb. 534.

[4] Tuttle v. Walton. 1 Geo. 43; West Branch R. R. Co. v. Armstrong, 40 Penn. St. 278; Mechanics' Bank v. Merchants' Bank, 45 Mo. 513; Perpetual Ins. Co. v. Goodfellow, 9 Mo. 149.

[5] Foster v. Potter, 37 Mo. 525.

[6] Weaver v. Huntingdon, etc., R. R. & Canal Co. 50 Penn. St. 14. In this case the court say: "If the defendant, therefore, held the stock in his own name, the plaintiff may proceed by *fi. fa.* and sale under the act of 1819, or by an attachment under the act of 1836. There is a reason why the attachment is an appropriate proceeding under the act of 1836, not noticed by the judge whose opinion was adopted in Lex v. Patten. There are cases where the stock is held by the party in his own name, and where there is no owner to make claim, but where it is subject to a charge or lien upon the title. This is the case in all bank stocks under the laws of this state, the stocks being liable to a lien in favor of the bank for debts

§ 1091. A description of the shares, on execution sale, by their numbers, is sufficient, in connection with the owner's name,[1] and the actual possession, or surrender of the certificates, is not necessary as regards the validity of sale or transfer.[2] The certificates are but the evidence of title, as we have seen in the first part of the present chapter.

§ 1092. In Alabama stocks are subject to execution sale by attachment and proceedings in equity, under the statute.[3]

III. Effect of Sale.

§ 1093. Under the statute, in Massachusetts, the execution sale of a corporate franchise does not confer corporate capacity on the purchaser; it confers or passes "the franchise with all the rights and privileges thereof, so far as relates to the receiving of toll," and nothing more. The corporate capacity of the company still continues as if no sale were made.[4]

§ 1094. After such sale, proceedings for forfeiture of the charter, on the part of the state, are against the corporation and not against the purchaser; he is not even necessary as a party.[5]

§ 1095. Though ordinarily the sheriff's return of execution sale is not indispensable to the validity thereof, yet where a sale of stocks is made on execution for merely a nominal consideration, when compared with their real value, and there is no return of such sale showing advertisement or other particulars thereof, or of the sale itself, it will be set aside on motion of the party in interest. More especially so when other circumstances exist unfavorable to the fairness of the sale.[6]

due to it by the stockholder. In such cases it is important to the rights of the parties and to save litigation that the proceedings by attachment should be resorted to, and the precise extent and character of the claim of the corporation ascertained before final execution."

[1] Stamford Bank v. Ferries, 17 Conn. 259.
[2] New York & New Haven R. R. Co. v. Schuyler, 38 Barb. 534.
[3] Bank of St. Mary v. St. John, 25 Ala. 566
[4] Commonwealth v. Tenth Mass. Turnpike Co. 5 Cush. 509.
[5] Ibid.
[6] State Bank of Missouri v. Tutt, 44 Mo. 267.

§ 1096.   In the case cited from 44 Missouri the Supreme
Court of that state say: "The chief ground relied on is the
irregularity of the sale—that it was made without advertisement, or notice, according to law;" that there was evidence
"tending to show some management to get possession of the
bank stock at less than its value;" that stocks worth eighty
cents sold for twelve cents; and the only evidence of sale "is a
mere inference of a memorandum or calculation of what was
made by some sale."

PART SIXTH.

EXEMPTION FROM SALE.—APPLICATION OF PROCEEDS.

CHAPTER XXV.

EXEMPTION FROM SALE.

I. The Policy of the Law.
II. Its Legal Effect.
III. Waiver Thereof.

I. The Policy of the Law.

§ 1097. It is the humane policy of the law in most, if not all the states, to exempt certain property, real and personal, from execution sale.

§ 1098. This policy is the result of a duty due both to the citizen and to the state, as the prosperity of the latter is dependant on the security and prosperity of the people. Moreover, it is regarded as a protection due to the unfortunate and to the helpless.[1] It rests on those same principles of benevoledce which prohibit imprisonment for debt, and of selling one's self into slavery. The principles of humanity, and the welfare of the state.

§ 1099. The exemption is the same whether the liability be contracted in the state or out of the state where the judgment is taken. The law of the former, or tribunal where the judgment is rendered as it existed at the date of the contract or act of liability governs the case.[2]

---

[1] Woodward v. Murry, 18 Johns. 400; Kneetles v. Newcomb, 22 N. Y. 249; Meper v. Meyer, 22 Iowa, 359.

[2] Laing v. Cunningham, 17 Iowa, 510; Newell v. Hayden, 8 Iowa, 140; Helfenstien v. Cave, 3 Iowa, 287.

II. Its Legal Effect.

§ 1100.   The law in force at the date of the contract governs the rights of the parties in controversies arising under the homestead exemption.   And though the law be thereafter modified or repealed, still it remains as a constituent part of the contract, and such repeal will not repair the rights acquired whilst the law was in force.

§ 1101.   In *Brodgman v. Wilcut*,[1] Greene, Justice, the rule is laid down in the following language by the Supreme Court of Iowa: "The homestead law in force at the date of the contract, having been a part of it, the superceding of that law by the substitution of the new law in the code, cannot deprive the debtor and his family of the homestead rights; nor could the repeal of the homestead law weaken or impair the contracts made, or divest rights acquired while the law was in force. The debtor's right to the homestead was acquired under the law of 1849, and his homestead established while that law was in force, and his petition presents a *prima facie* case, showing his right to the premises as exempt from forced sale under the law."

§ 1102.   And so, upon repeal of a homestead law, or modification thereof, a saving clause in the repealing act, saves to debtors all rights of homestead which had accrued under the law thus repealed, irrespective of the question above referred to as to whether, without such saving clause, a repeal of the law may impair, or take away the rights of homestead, and the effect of contracts originating whilst the law was in force.[2]   In the case cited from 3 Iowa, the court hold that such saving clause as effectually protects the homestead from execution sale as would the law if no repealing act had passed.

§ 1103.   In the same case the court rule, substantially, that as the exemption right is purely statutory, the debtor, to avail himself thereof, must show the performance of all things on

[1] 4 G. Greene, 563, 566; Tillotson v. Millard, 7 Minn. 513; Bronson v. Kinzie, 1 How. 315.

[2] Helfenstien v. Cave, 3 Iowa, 287, 294; Clark v. Potter, 13 Gray, (Mass.) 21.

his part required thereby, if any, as necessary to confer or fix the right.[1]

§ 1104. Under the statute in Iowa, it is holden that to constitute a homestead so as to attach to the privilege of exemption from execution sale, there must be actual occupancy as the dwelling place of the owner, and that a mere intention to so occupy, will not impart to the property the legal attributes of an homestead. In the language of WRIGHT, Justice, in the leading case of *Charless v. Lamberson*, "To be the homestead, it must be 'used,' and used for the purpose designed by the law, to wit., as a home, a place to abide in, a place for the family."[2] "A mere intention to occupy, though subsequently carried out, is not sufficient."[3] And such, say the Iowa supreme court, is the unbroken series of decisions in that state.[4]

§ 1105. In Minnesota, prior to the act of April, 1860, judgments were held to be liens upon homesteads, and though the latter were exempt from sales, so long as occupied as such, it was at the same time holden, that if the debtor removed from or sold the same, the homestead thereby became liable to levy and sale, on execution.[5]

§ 1106. But by the act of April, 1860, "The owner of a homestead," under the laws of said state, "may remove therefrom, or sell and convey the same, and such removal, or sale and conveyance," will "not render such homestead liable or subject to forced sale on execution or other process." And it is further enacted that no judgment or decree of any court should thereafter be a lien on the homestead of the debtor for any purpose whatever.[6]

[1] Helfenstein *v.* Cave, 3 Iowa, 290, 291.

[2] Charless *v.* Lamberson, 1 Iowa, 435, 440; Hale *v.* Heaslip, 15 Iowa, 451; Holden *v.* Pinney, 6 Cal. 285; Benedict *v.* Burnel, 7 Cal. 245; Wisner *v.* Farnham, 2 Mich. 472; Prior *v.* Stone, 19 Texas, 371; Horn *v.* Tuft, 39 N. H. 478; True *v.* Morrill, 28 Vt. 672.

[3] Elston *v.* Robinson, 23 Iowa, 208, 211; Christy *v.* Dyer, 14 Iowa, 438; Pope *v.* Ewbank, 18 Iowa, 580; Cole *v.* Gill, 14 Iowa, 527; Williams *v.* Sweetland, 10 Iowa, 51; Hyatt *v.* Spearman, 20 Iowa, 510; Campbell *v.* Ayres, 18 Iowa, 252.

[4] Elston *v.* Robinson, 23 Iowa, 211.

[5] Tillotson *v.* Millard, 7 Minn. 513, 520; Folsom *v.* Carli, 5 Minn, 333.

[6] Tillotson *v.* Millard, 7 Minn. 513, 520.

§ 1107. In the case of *Folsom v. Carli*,[1] above referred to, the court say: "We hold that under the exemption law, as it existed at the time this judgment was rendered and docketed, and the property sold, the lien of the judgment attached to the homestead, as well as to any other real property of the judgment debtor. That the exemption of the homestead was only an exemption from sale on execution, while occupied by the debtor or his family, but did not affect the lien of the judgment. That when McKusick, the judgment debtor, abandoned the property as a residence, and conveyed it to another, the exemption ceased, and the judgment creditor had then the right to enforce his lien by a sale of the premises on execution and that the grantee, Carli, took the property subject to the lien of the judgment."

§ 1108. In Iowa the ruling is to the converse of this, and is there holden under the statute that the owner may change his homestead from time to time, at pleasure, and may sell and re-invest, without liability to execution.[2] And so, likewise, in regard to exempted personal property.[3]

§ 1109. In the case of *Lamb v. Shays*,[4] the court hold that although judgments are ordinarily liens against the real estate of a debtor, yet they are not so as against the homestead, and that the debtor may sell and convey the homestead at pleasure and the estate will vest in the grantee, if so sold and conveyed while occupied and used as an homestead. The court holds, substantially, that a judgment lien is only co-extensive with the power to enforce it by sale, and that if the sale is prohibited the lien is a dead-letter.[5] The court say, "the right of exemption continues until the sale and delivery of the deed to the vendee, and the lien cannot attach until the sale and delivery, nor until after it ceases to be occupied by the owner;" and that, "prior to this, the vendee's rights become absolute." In

[1] 5 Minn. 333, 338.

[2] Pearson v. Minturn, 18 Iowa, 36; Lamb v. Shays, 14 Iowa, 567.

[3] Bevan v. Hayden, 13 Iowa, 122.

[4] 14 Iowa, 567, 570; Cummings v. Long, 15 Iowa, 41.

[5] Such, too, is the ruling by Chief Justice MARSHALL in Scriba v. Dean, 1 Brock., 166; Bank U. S. v. Winston, 2 Brock., 252; and by Justice McLEAN in Shrew v. Jones, 2 McLean, 78.

Lamb v. Shays the court justly remark, that "If the lien of a judgment confessed by, or taken against, the husband alone, (and to which the wife never assented,) can attach to, and subject the homestead to the payment of his debts, it virtually destroys that peculiar interest of the wife in the homestead which the legislature seems to have been so strenuous to protect."[1]

§ 1110. It is a principle of law, that what a person cannot do directly he cannot be allowed to do indirectly. From this it results that, as the owner cannot, by prior contract in the creation of a debt, waive the exemption by direct agreement, he may not bring about a waiver by submitting to a judgment and thereby create a lien which will operate as such waiver.

§ 1111. But by the ruling in the same case, *Lamb v. Shays*, if the property ceases to be occupied and used as a homestead, the lien of the judgment then attaches thereto and it becomes liable to execution sale, as other realty. The language of the court is that "The moment it ceases to be used as such, the lien attaches, the same as it attaches against property acquired by the judgment debtor after the judgment is rendered, and the priority of liens can be determined in the same manner."[2]

§ 1112. However liable the homestead may be to execution sale for debts contracted prior to its occupancy as such, yet, ordinarily, the creditor will be compelled, if required at the time so to do, to exhaust all other property liable to execution before resorting to the homestead.[3]

§ 1113. In *Barker v. Rollins*,[4] it is held that the provision of the Revision section, 2281, that the homestead, when liable, shall not be "sold except to supply the deficiency remaining after exhausting the other property of the debtor which is liable to execution" applies only to the homestead while it remains the property of the debtor for whose debt it is sought to be sold, and not to the homestead property after it is transferred by conveyance to another party. The Supreme Court,

[1] 14 Iowa, 571.
[2] Lamb v. Shays, 14 Iowa, 570.
[3] Denegre v. Haun, 14 Iowa, 240.
[4] 30 Iowa, 412.

CoLE, Justice, after reciting the provision above referred to, say: "The difficulty with defendant Cogshill is, that he is not the debtor, and is not within the language or the spirit of the section quoted. His homestead was not within the contemplation of the parties to the contract sued on. The creditor will be held to have contracted with reference to all the phases of homestead claimed by his debtor; but not as to any such claim by parties who should voluntarily purchase the property with full knowledge of the incumbrance upon it." The case above cited was brought to foreclose a mortgage, to which the homestead was justly liable, in the hands of the mortgage debtor, but only so, under the statute, after the exhaustion of the debtor's other property subject to execution. The property was sold by the mortgage debtor to Cogshill, who was made a co-defendant in the foreclosure proceeding. He relied on the statutory privilege above referred to, as a protection and defense until the debtor's other property should be exhausted. Thus the question arose which elicited the decision that the privilege of exemption does not in such cases inure to the purchaser of the mortgaged premises. The homestead, that is, the homestead of the debtor, is not to be sold until his other property, subject to execution sale, is applied by sale to the discharge of the debt. Then only for the balance. But the court hold that, having been transferred and being no longer the debtor's homestead, it is no longer entitled to be exempted under the statute.

§ 1114. In *Tillotson v. Millard*,[1] it is held that the act of April 30th, 1860, though valid as to transactions occurring after it took effect, is unconstitutional and void as to contracts and judgments anterior thereto in date; that its operation is prospective only, and that it applies to such judgments and contracts as are subsequent thereto in date, and not those existing at the time of its enactment.

§ 1115. In the subsequent case of *Kelly v. Baker*,[2] the Supreme Court of Minnesota hold, that when the homestead is confined to the proper quantity or value required or limited

[1] 7 Minn. 513.
[2] 10 Minn. 154, 157.

by law, and is actually occupied by the dwelling-house and
residence of the party, he can subject such parts thereof as are
not covered by his dwelling-house "to any use which he" may
"choose," without rendering any part of it liable to execution
sale.

§ 1116.   In Iowa the ruling is so far the converse of this
that where the occupant of a three-story house and half lot,
used and holden as an homestead, underlet the lower story and
cellar to be used as a store, the Supreme Court held, (STOCKTON,
Justice, dissenting,) that the part so underlet was liable to execution sale.[1]   But we would not be understood as assenting to
the correctness of this decision; nor do we apprehend that it
will be approved of and followed by subsequent rulings, should
like cases hereafter occur.   We rather regard the dissenting
opinion of Justice STOCKTON as the more sound, though not
the more authoritative opinion.

§ 1117.   In Ohio, by the act of April, 1857, it is provided
that "no married man shall sell, dispose of, or in any manner
part with, any personal property, which is now or may hereafter be, exempt from sale on execution, without having first
obtained the consent of his wife thereto."   And that, "If any
married man shall violate the provisions of the foregoing section, his wife may, in her own name, commence and prosecute
to final judgment and execution a civil action for the recovery
of such property or its value in money."   It is held, by the
Supreme Court of that state, that under this statute, where the
husband, without the concurrence of the wife, mortgaged property otherwise exempt from execution, and the same was, after
breach of the mortgage, sold on execution emanating from a
judgment for the mortgage debt, the wife could maintain her
action for the property thus sold.   This, too, although the proceedings were not by foreclosure of the mortgage, but by an
action and judgment at law for the mortgage debt; for the
execution of the mortgage was holden to be a disposal of the
property which estopped the husband from claiming the benefit
of exemption.[2]

[1] Rhodes v. McCormack, 4 Iowa, 368.
[2] Colwell v. Carper, 15 Ohio St. 279.

§ 1118. In Iowa it is held that a threshing-machine, used by the farmer for threshing his own grain, and for threshing the grain of others for hire, does not come within the meaning of the statute which exempts from execution sale "the proper tools or implements of a farmer." The Supreme Court of that state say, DILLON, Justice: "We are of opinion that" it is "intended to exempt only the ordinary and usual tools of husbandry, and " does "not extend to a threshing-machine owned by a farmer, to thresh his own grain, and that of others for hire;" that the "law makes no extravagant exemptions. It is intended for the poor, rather than the rich. Its design is to enable the debtor and his family to live, by shielding from the creditor the ordinary and usual means of acquiring a livelihood."[1]

§ 1119. In Wisconsin, state exemption laws have been holden to apply to process of execution in the hands of the United States Marshal, issued on judgment in a court of the United States;[2] and that property exempt by law is not in legal custody when taken by a United States Marshal and held on execution issued from a Federal court; that, therefore, an action of replevin will lie in a state court, at the suit of the execution debtor, against such officer to recover the property so taken and held by him.[3] But however correct the former part of this decision is, on the supposition that the process and "proceedings thereon" of the state courts have been adopted by congress or by order of the United States court, yet the doctrine deduced therefrom, that an action of replevin will lie against the marshal on process from a state court, is unsound.[4]

§ 1120. As to the application of state exemption laws to process from a United States court in the hands of the marshal, that depends upon the adoption of the state laws, for the particular district, upon that subject. If by rule of court, or by act of congress, (as, for instance, was done by the act of

[1] Meyer v. Meyer, 23 Iowa, 359, 375.
[2] Gilman v. Williamson, 7 Wis. 329.
[3] Ibid.
[4] Freeman v. Howe, 24 How. 440, and cases there cited.

congress of May 19th, 1828,) such exemption laws have been adopted as rules of action governing processes from the United States court, then they are to be observed and conformed to in all their incidents of forthcoming bonds, appraisement and exemptions, by the United States Marshal, in the execution of process that may come to his hands. But if not so adopted, then he will be governed by the laws of the United States, and the exemption laws of the state will not be observed.[1]

§ 1121. If, however, such exemption laws are adopted, so as to become a rule of action to the marshal in executing the processes of the Federal courts, and he violate those laws by levying on and taking possession of property exempt from execution sale, or under any other circumstances make a wrongful seizure, yet no action will lie against him in a state court predicated on processes designed to wrest such property out of his possession; for his levy and possession places the property in the custody of the court, and no other court can disturb such possession.[2] To obtain possession from the marshal, a better claimant, if there be one, should apply by petition to the United States court from which emanated the process under which the property is holden.[3]

§ 1122. But this rule of law is no bar to a personal action for damages in money, in a different court, against the marshal for a wrongful levy of property not subject to execution; and, therefore, trespass or trover may be maintained in such cases.[4]

§ 1123. It is moreover held that when, by such acts of congress or order of court, the state process and forms are adopted in regard to final execution, that such adoption carries with it the attendant legal attributes, incidents and inhibitions, that under the state laws apply to like final process from the state

[1] Brightly's Digest, vol. i., 268, 269; United States v. Knight, 14 Pet. 301; Catheswood v. Gapete, 2 Curt. C. C. 94; Binns v. Williams, 4 McLean, 580; Ross v. Duvall, 13 Pet. 45; Amis v. Smith, 16 Pet. 303; United States Bank v. Halstead, 10 Wheat. 51; Beers v. Haughton, 9 Pet. 329, 362; McNutt v. Brand, 2 How. 9.

[2] Freeman v. How. 24 How. 440; Taylor v. Carryl, 20 How. 583; Hogan v. Lucas, 10 Pet. 400.

[3] Buck v. Colbath, 3 Wall. 334, 345; Freeman v. Howe, 20 How. 440.

[4] Buck v. Colbath, 3 Wall. 334.

court; and as a consequence, the state laws, so far as constitutional, in regard to exemptions from execution sale, and in reference to appraisement before execution sale, will then apply to the execution of like final process in the hands of the United States Marshal in like manner as if the process was from the state court and being executed by the sheriff, whether the same be expressly adopted or not;[1] with this difference, however, that if the appraisers summoned by the marshal fail to attend and discharge their duties, then the marshal may sell without appraisement, as hereinbefore stated.

§ 1124. Under the statute in Missouri, personal property to a certain amount in value is entitled to be exempt from execution sale, and the debtor, in case of levy, has a right to select the property. Under this statute it is the duty of the officer levying an execution on personal effects, to notify or inform the execution debtor of his right to make the selection. The omission of the officer so to do, and more especially refusal on his part to allow the debtor the privilege thus given by the law, is an oppression and wrong for which an action may be maintained.[2]

§ 1125. By the laws of Missouri, property and wages, which are otherwise exempt from liability for debt, become subject to attachment whenever the debtor " is about to remove out of" the state, " with intent to change his domicile." In such case " all that he possesses is liable to attachment."[3]

III. Waiver Thereof.

§ 1126. Whether a waiver of the benefit of the exemption law, embodied by a contracting party in the contract, will operate to render liable to execution sale, property exempt therefrom by law, is a point decided differently in different states.

§ 1127. In Iowa it is held that the contract of exemption is nugatory, and does not render exempted property liable to

---

[1] United States v. Knight, 14 Pet. 301; 3 Sumn. 358; Amis v. Smith, 16 Pet. 303.

[2] State v. Romer, 44 Mo. 99.

[3] The State v. Lais, 46 Mo. 108.

sale on execution. That the enactment is a matter of state policy, and not that which the citizen may disregard. That although the same property might be sold by subjecting it to a mortgage foreclosure, yet the mere assent of the debtor expressed in the contract of indebtedness, will not render the statute inoperative, and make the property liable to seizure on execution, and to sale thereon. That the functions of the writ or powers of the officer can not thus be enlarged. And this would seem to me the better view of the case. It is the interest of the state to protect the welfare of its people against improvidence and against oppression. The operation of the exemption law, in its beneficence, extends to the family, if there be one, of the contracting debtor, as well as to the debtor himself. If by his bare consent, the law be defeated, and that without consideration or benefit, the exigencies of the result falls not on the debtor alone, but on those whom he is bound by law to provide for and protect; on those whose hands are tied by infancy or coveture, and who therefore are unable to help themselves. There would be fully as much plausibility in contracting for personal imprisonment, as of old, for debt, and which the state has abolished. No process at law could in either case execute the contract. The office of the writ could not thus be enlarged. It is in either case a contract, if not expressly prohibited, at least against the policy of the law, and for the enforcement of which no process of execution exists at law. If its enforcement were attainable at all, it could only be by specified performance, which would operate unequally, as it is never awarded in personal matters; and if it were, could not be thought of for a moment to enforce an arrangement made against the policy and moral interest of the law.[1]

§ 1128. In Pennsylvania, and some others of the states, the ruling prevails to the contrary, and the waiver is allowed to render the property liable to execution sale, but to our mind the functions of the writ and powers of the officer cannot be

---

[1] Curtis v. O'Brien, 20 Iowa, 377; Troutman v. Gowing, 16 Iowa, 415; Warinbold v. Schlicting, 16 Iowa, 243; Woodward v. Murry, 18 Johns. 400; Maxwell v. Read, 7 Wis. 582; Kneetle v. Newcomb, 22 N. Y. 249; Crawford v. Lockwood, 9 How. Pr. N. Y. 547; Gilman v. Williams, 7 Wis. 329.

thus enlarged by agreement of parties. If the policy of the state was not in the way, the only force of such sale would be by estoppel, which may not be invoked to sustain acts done against the policy of the law, and therefore cannot be resorted to in favor of such sales where the policy of the law regards them with disfavor. Why not, by like agreement, restore imprisonment for debt, although by law it is abolished? We find, however, that by the ruling in several of the states, the exemption is holden to be removed when there is a waiver thereof in the original contract.[1]

§ 1131. But notwithstanding the ruling in Iowa, that by a cotemporaneous agreement, at the time of contracting the indebtedness, the debtor cannot so waive the benefit of the exemption law as to deprive him of the right to avail himself of it subsequently when there is a levy to satisfy the indebtedness, it is nevertheless holden by the same court that by surrendering to the officer property to be levied on, upon a writ of execution by the debtor, he thereby estops himself from reclaiming the same from being sold, and loses in that respect the benefit of the statute. That having voluntary rendered up property to be levied on and sold, as liable to such proceeding, he should not thereafter be allowed to say it is of a different character.[2]

§ 1132. In Indiana, where the ruling is in favor of a waiver of exemption, there is a constitutional provision that "the privilege of the debtor to enjoy the necessary comforts of life should be recognized by wholesome laws, exempting a reasonable amount of property from seizure for the payment of any debt or liability hereafter contracted; and there should be no imprisonment for debt, except in cases of fraud."

§ 1133. In Indiana, then, we see that both the exemption from sale and from imprisonment for debt rest upon the same

---

[1] Case v. Dunmore, 23 Penn. St. 93; Louck's Appeal, 24 Penn. St. 426; Line's Appeal, 2 Grant's Cas. 196; Johnson's Appeal, 1 Casey, 116; Browne v. Swiley, 31 Penn. St. 225; Smith's Appeal, 23 Penn. St. 310; The State ex rel. v. Melonge, 9 Ind. 196; Eltzroth v. Webster, 15 Ind. 21. Chamberlain v. Lyle, 3 Mich. 448.

[2] Richards v. Haines, 30 Iowa, 574

high ground of constitutional authority, subject simply to regulation by the legislature as to the amount of property to be exempted. The courts there hold that the debtor may waive the exemption.[1] Would not the same ruling apply with equal propriety to the imprisonment? And are the courts prepared to go thus far? We think the functions of the writ cannot be extended to either, by mere private will of the parties.

§ 1134. We conceive the correct doctrine to be holden in the case cited from 20 Iowa, and kindred cases. In the case from Iowa the court say: "We are agreed in the conclusion that a person contracting a debt, cannot, by a cotemporaneous and simple waiver of the benefit of the exemption laws, entitle the creditor, in case of failure to pay, to levy his execution, against defendant's objection, upon exempt property."

§ 1135. As the same law also exempts from liability to debt by garnishee, attachment, or execution, the money proceeds of daily labor, earned within a given time, in many of the states, it follows by a parity of reasoning, that wherever the doctrine of the Iowa court, above referred to, prevails, such earnings or wages, whether payable in money or property, are in like manner incapable of being subjected to the debt of a debtor, by waiver of the exemption at the time of and in the contract creating the debt. The cases are parallel. And by a like reasoning it would likewise follow that wherever the creditor may reach the one, he may also reach the other.

§ 1136. In *Kneetles v. Newcomb* and *Woodward v. Murry*,[2] it is held that the object of the law is "to promote the comfort of families and to protect them against the improvidence of their head." That "one object of municipal law is to promote the general welfare of society," and that "the exemption laws seek to accomplish this by taking from the head of the family the power to deprive it of certain property by contracting debts which shall enable the creditors to take such property on execution." In the case from 22 New York the whole subject is discussed with much ability. The court

[1] Eltzroth v. Webster, 15 Ind. 21; The State ex rel. v. Melonge, 9 Ind. 196.
[2] Woodward v. Murry, 18 Johns. 400; Kneetles v. Newcomb, 22 N. Y.

there say: "Could a person, when contracting a debt, agree, for instance, that the act abolishing imprisonment for debt should not apply to any judgment which should be recovered," on a certain contract, "or that on such judgment there should be no right in the debtor to redeem any land that might be sold under the execution, or that he should not be discharged under any insolvent act?" The court say, "Clearly this could not be done;" and that "upon the same principle," the debtor "could not, when contracting the debt, agree that exempt property might be taken on execution." That "the law does not permit its process to be used to accomplish ends which its policy forbids," though such use be agreed to. And so in the case of *Maxwell v. Reed*,[1] the court say, that "agreements to waive all right of exemption are null and void as against the policy of the law." The constitution of Wisconsin contains a provision requiring the Legislature to exempt a reasonable amount of property from sale on execution. This provision is substantially the same, if not in the identical words of the provision for the same subject above recited, as in the constitution of Indiana. In view of this, the Wisconsin Supreme Court aptly ask the question by way of illustration, "Can the contracting parties not only repeal a statute, but upset the constitution itself?" That court wisely assert that "the citizen is an essential elementary constituent of the state; that to preserve the state the citizen must be protected; and that to live he must have the means of living; to act and to be a citizen he must be free to act, and to have somewhat wherewith to act, and thus to be competent to the performance of his high functions." Hence the state policy, say the court, of exempting such interests from sale on execution as shall enable him to discharge such services and devotions as may be due from him to the commonwealth.

§ 1137. In Illinois a waiver of the homestead exemption is allowed by statute, "if the same shall be in writing, subscribed by the householder and his wife, if he have one, and acknowledged in the same manner as conveyances of real estate are by

[1] 7 Wis. 582, 594.

law required to be acknowledged." It is moreover declared to be the "object of the act to require in all cases the signature and acknowledgment of the wife as conditions to the alienation of the homestead." Now, under this state of the law in Illinois, where a homestead had been conveyed away by fraudulent conveyance, and was uncovered in chancery on a creditor's bill, and without such waiver in writing, was sold by decree of the court, it is holden that in an action of ejectment involving title under the decree and sale, the homestead could not be set up at law in such collateral proceeding; that the court having jurisdiction of the parties, the decree is final; that no claim of homestead having been interposed at the trial on the creditor's bill, it cannot now for the first time be made.[1]

§ 1138. The case of *Miller v. Sherry* does not involve the question of direct power to waive the exemption, but rests upon the unreversed decree of the court ordering the property to be sold in the ordinary course of judicial proceedings, made without any intervention at the time that the property was a homestead. Of course a regular and a fair sale, to a *bona fide* purchaser, made under such a decree, would carry the title and could not be questioned in a collateral proceeding upon the plea, or showing, that the property sold was the homestead. This being the only point relied on as against the validity of the sale, its validity was rightfully sustained in such collateral proceedings. Whether right or wrong the decree was binding until set aside or reversed, and so likewise the sale made in pursuance thereof. But where the power to waive the exemption, as in Illinois, is given by statute, by the same authority that confers the exemption, there could, of course, no question arise as to the ability of the debtor to contract for a waiver of the privilege. In the case of *Miller v. Sherry*,[2] the homestead seems to have been of greatly larger value than that allowed for exemption by the statute of Illinois. Hence the inducement, perhaps, to the fraudulent conveyance. The debtor still continued in possession notwithstanding the con-

[1] Miller v. Sherry, 2 Wall. 373, and so in Iowa on mortgage foreclosure; Haynes v. Meek, 14 Iowa, 320.
[2] 2 Wall. 251.

veyance, and occupied it as a homestead; but no such claim was interposed in defense of the chancery proceeding to subject it to sale for debt. On error in the United States Supreme Court, in the ejectment suit in which the claim of homestead exemption was interposed, the said Supreme Court lay no stress upon the excess of value, but say: "In regard to the homestead right claimed by the plaintiff in error, there is no difficulty. The decree under which the sale to Bushnell expressly divested the defendant of all right and interest in the premises. It cannot be collaterally questioned." Thus the United States Supreme Court hold that having jurisdiction, the decree of sale is final as well of the homestead as of other property, if the objection be not interposed before decree, or the decree be not, before sale, reversed.

§ 1139. A similar ruling is had in Iowa in the case of *Haynes v. Meek*,[1] where a mortgage debtor attempted to set up the homestead right as a defense against the title of a purchase at the mortgage sale, made judicially on decree of foreclosure. The court hold that the mortgagors having had their day in court as parties to the foreclosure proceeding, and having there omitted to make the alleged defense of fraud in obtaining the wife's signature to the mortgage deed, they could not set the defense up, collaterally, and thus go behind the mortgage decree. In this case the court say, that if the defense be true, "the plea is bad, for the reason that this homestead right, if it ever existed, was lost to him (defendant) by failing to set it up in the foreclosure proceeding; in other words, he has had his day in court upon this alleged homestead right.

§ 1140. But in Ohio it is held that a decree uncovering property from a fraudulent conveyance, made in behalf of an execution creditor, and subjecting such property to sale, is of no higher character than an execution would be, when issued on the same judgment, as against the operation of the homestead law, and that it is sufficient in point of time if the objection that the property is exempt from sale as an homestead is made at the time the decree is about to be executed.[2] In the

---

[1] 14 Iowa, 320, 321.

[2] Sears *v.* Hanks, 14 Ohio St. 298, 302.

case cited the court hold that, "though the final process on decrees in chancery for the sale of property was called 'an order of sale,' it was nevertheless 'a writ of execution on a decree' within the meaning of the statute;" that as the plaintiffs therein were only asserting the rights of judgment creditors, the "order of sale merely took the place of an ordinary execution upon their judgment;" and that the attempt to sell on such order is clearly within the statute by which the homestead is exempt. In the case cited,[1] the court go further, and hold that the execution of a conveyance of the homestead by a judgment debtor, which is fraudulent as against the judgment creditor, will not subject the property so fraudulently conveyed away to sale upon execution. Nor will the uncovering of it by a decree at the suit of the judgment creditor setting such conveyance aside; that such creditor's claim is not "under or through the fraudulent conveyance, but adverse to it;" and that when at their suit the deed is set aside, they, as creditors, "cannot set up such void conveyance to enlarge their rights or remedies against the debtor;" that "as between creditor and debtor the deed is simply void, and cannot, therefore, affect the rights of either;" that "if the debtor have no title or interest in the property levied on, there is nothing for the creditor to sell;" and that it is not competent for the debtor to deny the right of the debtor and at the same time sell the property as his; that "if he has an interest in the homestead property which the creditor can sell, he has interest enough to secure his homestead from sale;" that the homestead act is to be liberally construed as wise and humane, and as "intended to protect the family from the inhumanity which would deprive its dependent members of a home."

[1] Sears v. Hanks, 14 Ohio St. 300 301.

24

CHAPTER XXVI

APPLICATION OF THE PROCEEDS.

§ 1141. Whether the sale be a judicial one, or ministerial, as on ordinary execution, the officer should return the proceeds into court, for application or distribution. In executions, the command of the writ is to have the money in court. The court has power to control, by order, the application or distribution of the funds in cases of dispute.[1]

§ 1142. A motion at law is the remedy by which to obtain distribution or correct a distribution, and is to be made in the same court whence proceeded the authority to sell.[2]

§ 1143. The order, when made, is a protection to the officer, and if not appealed from is final.[3] But not against outsiders not parties to the proceedings.[4]

§ 1144. In *Howard's case*,[5] it was held, in Alabama, and again by the Supreme Court of the United States, that such adjudication, or order of distribution, will not affect the rights of outsiders not in some manner parties to the proceedings before the court. On the contrary, while the order of distribution, when made, is final, in like manner as other judgments or final findings, until set aside or reversed, as between the parties before the court, other parties in interest, if any, may assert their rights, by proper application to the courts, irrespective of such order, and may enforce the same against any or all of them who may wrongfully obtain such part of the

[1] Robinson's Appeal, 62 Penn. St. 217; Turner v. Fendall, 1 Cranch, 117; Wiley v. Budgman, 1 Head, 68.

[2] Chittenden v. Rogers, 42 Ill. 95.

[3] Noble v. Cope, 50 Penn. St. 17, 20.

[4] Matter of Howard, 9 Wall. 175.

[5] 9 Wall. 175; and see, as bearing on this, Butcher v. Drew, 39 Ill. 40, and Warren v. Icarian Community, 16 Ill. 114, involving wrongful distribution by the sheriff without intervention of the court. The injured party may sue those obtaining the advantage, but the sheriff cannot.

proceeds as would have inured to such outside party if in court at the making of the order of distribution.

§ 1145. The first levy, if there be no priority of either writ, withdraws the property from liability to be again levied while thus in the hands of the law, whether such first levy be on process from the state or from the United States courts, and gives such first levy priority of satisfaction.

§ 1146. But if there are two or more writs, from the same jurisdiction, in the hands of the same officer at one and the same time, and neither emanate from judgments that are liens, then, as before stated, they are to be paid ratably out of the proceeds.

§ 1147. This cannot be done, however, as between a United States Marshal and a sheriff. In the absence of liens, the first levy has precedence in distribution of the funds. A levy vests a special property in the officer. Such property cannot be thus vested at the same time in both.[1] If there is a lien contravened by the first levy the party injured should apply to the court issuing the writ on which such levy is made, for relief.

§ 1148. In *Noble v. Cope*,[2] the court say, in reference to the order of distribution, that " it was neither excepted to nor appealed from, but was acquiesced in by Noble and all other creditors of Klusmeyer. It concluded, of course, every issue that could have been properly litigated therein."

§ 1149. If there be several executions, and one or more of them emanated from judgments that are liens, then these are first to be satisfied. Their satisfaction is each in their order according to seniority.[3]

§ 1150. But the costs of the officer are not to be postponed to such seniority. He is entitled to his costs; and so, also, as to the costs generally of the writ on which the sale is made; whether it be senior or junior, the costs should be paid out of the proceeds.[4]

---

[1] Hagan *v.* Lucas, 10 Pet. 400.

[2] 50 Penn. St. 30.

[3] Steele *v.* Hannah, 8 Blackf. 326; State *v.* Salyers, 17 Ind. 432; Bagby *v.* Reeves, 20 Ala. 427; Lawson *v.* Jordan, 19 Ark. 297; Thompson *v.* McCord, 27 Geo. 273; Newton *v.* Nunnally, 4 Geo. 356.

[4] Shelly's Appeal, 38 Penn. St. 210; McNiel *v.* Bean, 32 Vt. 429.

§ 1151. If the senior judgment be against the defendant by a wrong name, or in a foreign language of his right name, then the writ emanating thereon loses its preference in the distribution; for the law requires proceedings in the English language.[1]

§ 1152. So, if the senior judgment be dormant, the writ issued thereon loses its priority.[2] And so between two writs where both have issued on separate judgments after the year and a day, the first levy gains priority.[3]

§ 1153. In case of several writs emanating alike from judgments that are not liens, neither will have preference, but they are to be satisfied ratably.[4] Though the leading case to the last point cited was a case of mortgages, yet the same rule applies to writs of execution generally, where there is no seniority of lien.[5]

§ 1154. In a question of priority of payment between executions issued from different courts, the court from which emanated the writ on which sale is made is the one to settle the priority.[6]

§ 1155. Though a plaintiff have the senior lien he cannot apply the proceeds of sale, if the debtor be insolvent, to the prejudice of a younger writ, for a debt for which he himself is security. The court will apply the funds to satisfy the junior writ.[7]

§ 1156. By omission to follow up an execution from term to term with an *alias, pluries*, etc., execution issued on a judg-

---

[1] Niel's Appeal, 40 Penn. St. 453.

[2] Lytle v. Cin. Manf. Co. 4 Ham. 459.

[3] Sellers v. Corwin, 5 Ham. 398.

[4] Birdenbecker v. Lowell, 32 Barb. (N. Y.) 9; Wilcox v. May, 19 Ohio, 408; Hagan v. Lucas, 10 Pet. 400.

[5] Wilcox v. May, 19 Ohio, 408; Stagg *ex parte*, 1 N. & M. 405; Hagan v. Lucas, 10 Pet. 400; Lawson v. Jordan, 19 Ark. 297; Matthews v. Warne, 6 Halst. 297.

[6] Woodruff v. Chapin, 3 Zabr. 566. The court issuing the senior execution, (if from different courts,) has the sole jurisdiction.

[7] Rowland v. Goldsmith, 2 Grant's Cas. 378; and as bearing upon the same subject, see, also, Collins' Appeal, 35 Penn. St. 83; Moss' Appeal 35 Penn. St. 162; The Matter of Corner, 12 Rich. Law (S. C.) 349.

ment rendered in the interim will gain precedence if the prior judgment be not a lien.[1]

§ 1157. But if the succession be kept up in a timely manner, the subsequent writs will relate back to the test of their original and carry its lien, as to the personalty, to that date.[2]

§ 1158. The safer course is a *venditio exponas*, with a clause of reference to the original writ and levy.[3]

§ 1159. If there are several writs, the one earliest in test takes preference for satisfaction out of the personalty.[4]

§ 1160. In proceedings against the heir of a deceased debtor the oldest judgment and execution take priority.[5]

§ 1161. Indulgence granted on the original writ does not destroy its lien as to the debtor and those claiming under him[6] by purchase from him.

§ 1162. In a conflict for satisfaction between a mechanic's lien and a prior mortgage, the rule in Illinois is to apportion the proceeds, when insufficient for both, in such manner between them as to give the mechanic's lien the relative portion of increased value caused by the improvements. That is, such sum as bears its just proportion to the proceeds of sale in reference to the mortgage debt.[7]

§ 1163. In Kansas an unrecorded mortgage of land is entitled to prior satisfaction over an execution and judgment junior in date to the mortgage. Though judgments are liens, they are not recognized as such as against lands to which others have an equitable priority for satisfaction of a debt.[8]

§ 1164. The rule in Louisiana is, that a mortgage creditor may follow the proceeds of an administrator's sale of the mortgaged lands and have them applied on satisfaction of the

[1] McBroom v. Rives, 1 Stew. 72; Carey v. Gregg, 3 Stew. 433; Darson v. Shepherd, 4 Dev. 797; Palmer v. Clarke, 2 Dev. 354.

[2] Starup v. Irvine, 2 Hawks, 232; Dilkey v. Dickenson, 2 Hawks, 341.

[3] Yarborough v. The State Bank, 2 Dev. 23.

[4] Green v. Johnson, 2 Hawks. 309.

[5] Irwin v. Sloan, 2 Dev. 349; Ricks v. Blount, 4 Dev. 128.

[6] Armstrong v. Sledge, 2 Dev. 359.

[7] Crosby v. N. W. Manf. Co. 48 Ill. 481; Howett v. Selby, 54 Ill. 151; Dingledine v. Hershman, 53 Ill. 280.

[8] Swartz v. Steers, 2 Kansas, 236.

mortgage debt. He is subrogated to the fund arising from the sale.[1]

§ 1165. In Alabama, as between writs of equal priority, the fund is equally divided between them, and if an excess over either one, the excess is equally distributed between the others.[2]

§ 1166. An execution for the purchase money of property sold on it, takes precedence over a mechanic's lien of subsequent origin to the original purchase of the property by the mechanic's lien debtor.[3]

§ 1167. In Illinois, in case of several mechanic's liens of equal priority, as to date of judgment, the proceeds of sale are equally distributed between them.[4] And so, in that state, in reference to satisfaction of several writs of attachment against the same defendant, the proceeds are to be applied *pro rata* on the judgments.[5] In distributing the proceeds of sales in admiralty cases brought to enforce claims for supplies, or material furnished the ships in foreign ports, the party commencing proceedings is entitled to priority of payment.[6]

§ 1168. An *alias fieri facias*, although issued subsequently to an original junior one, bears relation back to the date of the original writ, of which it is the *alias*, and will take precedence, in the same manner as would the original one which it follows; it will therefore overreach original executions of junior date to the original of the *alias* in the hands of the officer, in the application of the proceeds of sale.[7]

---

[1] Turcand *v.* Gex, 21 La. 253.

[2] Bizzle *v.* Hardaway, 42 Ala. 471.

[3] Stoner *v.* Neff, 50 Penn. St. 258; Occonner *v.* Warner, 4 W. & S. 223. The ruling to the contrary in Lyon *v.* McGuffey, 4 Barr. 126, was in a case where the vendor by his own laches, in not recording his judgment in time, lost his preference. See, also, Stoner *v.* Neff, 50 Penn. St. 258, 261, where the court, referring to the case from 4 Barr. say the vendor's lien was lost in that case "because the vendor let go his grasp upon the purchase money by omitting to file his judgment for ten days after parting with his title."

[4] Butcher *v.* Dew, 39 Ill. 40.

[5] Warner *v.* Icarian Community, 16 Ill. 114.

[6] The Globe, 2 Blatch. C. C. 427.

[7] Allen *v.* Plummer, 63 N. C. 307.

§ 1169. In admiralty sales, next after the satisfaction of privileged lien debts, for that which enters into the life or safety of the vessel, if there be of the proceeds of sale remnants remaining in court, mortgage debts will be entitled to satisfaction there out of, as against the owner or owners of the vessel. In 1 Olcott, by BETTS, Justice: "As the mortgage debts will absorbe the remnants in court, it is unnecessary to consider the point discussed at the hearing, whether an unprivileged debt, owing by the owner of a ship, in the American courts, can be satisfied by order of the court, out of remnants in court, from the sale belonging to the owner: that is, whether the court has an equitable authority to apply such moneys to a general creditor of the general owner, contrary to his desire and direction."[6]

[1] Remnants in Court, 1 Olcott, 382, 387.

INDEX OF CONTENTS.

DEED, THE — *Continued.*

    assignment if defective, 767.
    enforcement of right to deed in equity, 767.
    deed to tenants in common, 768.
  III. WHEN TO BE MADE, 265, 266.
    if no redemption by law, on payment of purchase money, 769.
    when there is redemption, 770.
        deed before expiration of term of, 771.
        in Tennessee, 772.
    after confirmation when required by law, 773.
    payment by plaintiff when purchaser, 774.
    delivery true date, 775.
    actual receipt of purchase money by officer, 776.
  IV. WHAT PASSES BY IT, 266–274.
    land and covenants running with it, 777.
    entire estate of execution debtor, 777.
        effect of redemption by, 777.
    growing crops, 778.
            in Indiana held to pass, 779.
            contra, in Ohio, 779.
            in Massachusetts pass when, 780.
    lien of subsequent installments of judgment debt, 781.
    Pennsylvania rule as to liens, 782, 784.
    on mortgage sale carries mortgagor's equity of redemption when 785, 789, 790.
    relates back to date of judgment when, 786.
    when purchaser is charged with notice, 787.
    sale on senior judgment and junior levy, 788.
    purchaser's remedy when debtor had no title, 791.
    imperfect description of, 792.
    as to fixtures on land with right of removal, 793.
    sale for balance of purchase money, 794.
    illustration, 795.
    estoppel of lien creditor by sale, 796.
    sale of equitable right of vendee by vendor holding legal title, 797
    Iowa rule as to enforcement of vendor's rights, 798.
    sale subject to vendor's lien, 799.
    sale of interest of one tenant of entirety, 800, 801.
        of easement, 802.
  V. RECITALS OF DEED, 275, 276.
    execution need not be recited, 803.
        must be referred to, 803.
    effect of in evidence, 804, 806, 807.
    as to proof of notice, 805.
    misrecital of name of party to judgment, 808.
  VI. ITS RELATION, 276, 277.
    if judgment is a lien, 809.

354 INDEX.

EXEMPTION FROM SALE— *Continued.*

rule as to, 1120–1124.

right of selection, in Missouri, 1125.

property and wages liable when debtor is about to remove, 1126.

III. WAIVER, 362–369.

different constructions as to, embodied in contract, 1126.

Iowa rule as to, 1127–1131.

Pennsylvania rule, 1128.

Indiana rule, 1132, 1133.

correct doctrine, 1134–1136.

Illinois rule, 1137.

construction of, 1138, 1139.

Ohio rule, 1140.

GUARDIAN'S SALES AND SALES IN PROCEEDINGS FOR PARTITION, Ch. vii, 124–133.

I. GUARDIAN'S SALES, 124–130.

in England sovereign is guardian of all infants, 313.

and this authority an attribute of judiciary, 313.

and transmitted to courts, 314.

and by courts delegated, 315.

origin of American authority in courts, 316.

authority regulated by statute, 317.

subjects to rights in equity, 317.

how to be exercised, 317.

general chancery jurisdiction to decree sale in some States, 318.

other rule, 318, 319.

probate courts have only statutory power, 320.

if jurisdiction attaches conformity to statutory power will be inferred, 321.

nature of proceedings, whether adversary or *in rem,* 322

proceedings *in rem,* 323.

cases illustrative, 324.

license to sell may be in alternative, 325.

guardian's deed, what title conveyed, 326.

warranty, effect of, 326.

requisites to sustain guardian's sale, 327.

sale of entire interest of several on application of one, effect of, 328.

guardian in *socage,* power of, 329.

sale made after termination of such guardianship void, 329.

affirmance of sale by ward, 330.

guardian cannot purchase at his own sale, 331.

report to next term of court, 332.

confirmation not necessary unless required by statute, 332.

failure of guardian to report, 332.

amount to be raised under order of sale includes costs, 333.

where amount raised is in excess of decree, 334.

REDEMPTION — *Continued.*

SALE, THE—*Continued.*

26

SALE, THE—*Continued.*

"head right certificates" in Texas, 223.

lands purchased in name of widow and heirs under pre-emption right, enured to decedent in his life-time, 224.

this rule discussed, 225.

Tennessee rule, 226.

Alabama rule, 227, 229, 230.

Massachusetts rule, 228.

power to subject decedent's lands to payment of debts, remedial, 231, 232.

but claims must be in conformity to statute, 233.

duty of executor or administrator, 234, 235.

II. WHAT DEBTS LANDS MAY BE SOLD TO PAY, 95–97.

debts owed at time of death, 236.

and legally, 236.

lands not liable for costs created by administrator, 237.

nor against administrator or estate, 238.

but such may be paid if there is a surplus, 238.

this principle illustrated, 239, 240.

"claimants must prove themselves creditors of decedent," 241.

"debt due from testator," 242.

individual lands liable for partnership debts when, 243, 244

III. WHO MAY CONDUCT THE SALE, 97, 98.

by executor or administrator, 246.

stranger or sheriff cannot, 246.

nor special administrator, 246, 247.

special administrator, powers of in Iowa, 247.

sale under legislative order, 248.

as to sale by one of several executors or administrators, 249.

IV. APPLICATION TO SELL; HOW, AND IN WHAT TIME TO BE MADE, 98–119.

application to sell; must be made by executor or administrator 250.

exception, in Texas, 251.

one or more of several may apply, 252.

statute of Iowa as to executors, 253.

application must be timely, 254.

one year a suitable time, 255.

circumstances of case determine, 255.

order of sale, if after unreasonable length of time void, 256.

three years in New York, 257.

application, what it must show, 258.

more than one order, if first insufficient, 259.

debts must first be allowed, 259.

allowance *nunc pro tunc,* 259.

must be by petition, 260.

allegations of, 260, 262, 279.

subject matter, conformity to, 261–284.

www.ingramcontent.com/pod-product-compliance
Lightning Source LLC
Chambersburg PA
CBHW032258280326
41932CB00009B/612